THE END OF ECONOMIC MAN

BY THE SAME AUTHOR

Economists Can Be Bad for Your Health
Political Deals That Saved Andrew Johnson

(with Lucile H. Brockway)
Greece: A Classical Tour with Extras

THE END OF ECONOMIC MAN

An Introduction to Humanistic Economics

George P. Brockway

Fourth Edition

W. W. NORTON & COMPANY
NEW YORK • LONDON

Printed in the United States of America

For information about permission to reproduce selections from this book, write to Permissions, W. W. Norton & Company, Inc., 500 Fifth Avenue, New York, NY 10110

The text of this book is composed in New Caledonia
Composition by Matrix Publishing Services, Inc.
Manufacturing by Maple-Vail Book Manufacturing Group
Book design by BTDnyc

Library of Congress Cataloging-in-Publication Data

Brockway, George P.
The end of economic man : an introduction to humanistic economics / George P. Brockway. — 4th ed.
p. cm.
Includes bibliographical references and index.
ISBN 0-393-05039-4
1. Economics. 2. Economic man. 3. Supply and demand
4. United States—Economic conditions. I. Title.

HB171 .B6499 2001
330—dc21 00-062464

W. W. Norton & Company, Inc., 500 Fifth Avenue, New York, N.Y. 10110
www.wwnorton.com

W. W. Norton & Company Ltd., 10 Coptic Street, London WC1A 1PU

1 2 3 4 5 6 7 8 9 0

To the absent members

CONTENTS

PART III

MODERNIST ECONOMICS AND ITS DISCONTENTS

PART IV

PROSPECT

PREFACE

economic man. *Econ.* A hypothetical man supposed to be free from altruistic sentiments and motives interfering with a purely selfish pursuit of wealth and its enjoyment.

—*Webster's New International Dictionary*, Second Edition

The purpose of this book is to offer an introduction to an economics in which all economic agents are literally agents, that is, autonomous doers of their own deeds, actors responsible for their own actions, free human beings. For convenience we may name this a humanistic economics—an effort to understand a fundamental aspect of the world as it is in the hope of contributing to what it ought to be.

In contrast, almost all other schools of economics, classical or contemporary, take as their agents profit or utility maximizers, or creatures of some psychological drive, or exemplars of a social class, or servants of a supernatural power. At least initially, a humanistic economics differs from these others mainly in respect to the agents. As it develops, it will differ from them in many other respects, but it will learn from them, too. As the philosopher John William Miller used to insist, "No one is all wrong."

To be fully human in the Renaissance, one had to participate in the rediscovery and rebirth of the ancient world. To be fully human today, one must be not only doctor, lawyer, or Indian chief but also a free, recognized, and responsible actor in the economic world.

Ironically, however, Economic man—the ideal economic agent—is not free and responsible. He is possessed by one idea: his own material gain. He is a fanatic. He is selfishness incarnate. He must be so, in order to perform his function. Whenever standard economics faces a problem, it looks to economic man for the answer. The monomaniacal monster reveals what he'd do in the circumstances. Most of the so-called laws of economics have been deduced from his consistently self-serving behavior. Or, as Arrow and Hahn put it more elegantly, "it is supposed, in the main, that . . . the choices of economic agents can be deduced from certain axioms of rationality."[1] These economic agents have been an organizing principle of standard economics, as mass and energy are organizing principles of physics, or as point and extension are organizing principles of geometry.

Monomaniacs reify their manias. Thus economics has concerned itself with things—resources, the gross domestic product, the bottom line—rather than with people. In any future economics this concern will be reversed. Human beings will be more important than things, and what Carlyle quite properly called the dismal science will take on a new and humane aspect.

The crucial chapter in the book is the fifth, which makes the point that in the actual world, prices—including wages and interest rates—are set and accepted by human beings, not by axioms of rationality, nor by Adam Smith's "invisible hand," nor by the law of supply and demand nor any other "law." This simple and obvious point makes it necessary to study economics as one of the "moral sciences," which consider the proper conduct of life. There is no point of view from which the solar system can be criticized; but if any economics system cannot be criticized, economics is an empty pastime.

Although far broader and more systematic, this book necessarily covers some of the same ground as my earlier book (*Economics: What*

---

1. Arrow and Hahn, *General Competitive Analysis*, p. v.

Went Wrong and Why and Some Things To Do about It) and, in order to stand alone, repeats some of that material.

As I have said on many other occasions, there is no idea presented here that is not directly or indirectly due to the teaching of the late Professor John William Miller of Williams College. Even turns of phrase and sentence rhythms are often his, as readers of the five volumes of his published essays will recognize. In addition, much of the material covered was discussed with him in person or by correspondence. I make no claim that he would have supported what I have written, but my indebtedness to him is impossible to overstate.

I am also greatly indebted to Myron Kolatch, executive editor of *The New Leader*, who has, for almost twenty years, given me access to an alert and responsive audience. Other editors who have kindly given me permission to use material I originally published in their pages are those of the *Journal of Post Keynesian Economics, Journal of Economic Issues, Challenge*, the *New York Times*, and *Washington Monthly*. Much of the material in Chapters 2 and 11 was included in a paper presented before a conference at Notre Dame University and published in Oliver F. Williams, Frank K. Reilly, and John W. Houck, eds., *Ethics and the Investment Industry* (Savage, Md.: Rowan and Littlefield, 1989). Much of Chapters 5, 15, and 16 was presented before a conference at Brigham Young University. And much of Chapters 21 and 25 was presented before a colloquium at the University of Tennessee. I am grateful to the universities for the invitations to participate in the conferences and for permission to reuse some of my material here.

In the best tradition of scholarship, many professionals in several fields have been generous with information, advice, caution, and encouragement, even on points with which they disagreed. In particular I thank E. Ray Canterbery, David C. Colander, Paul Davidson, Robert L. Heilbroner, Raymond L. Richman, L. Randall Wray, Gus Tyler, and the late Sidney Weintraub. I have tried to have the wit to benefit from their criticisms and, of course, absolve them of all responsibility for the result.

My old colleagues at W. W. Norton & Company—Donald S. Lamm, Candace Watt, Drake McFeely, Nancy Palmquist, Marjorie Flock, Andrew Marasia, Sarah Stewart, and Julia Druskin—were unfailingly helpful and good-humored. I salute them with old affection.

Unless otherwise noted, all the statistics herein either come from or are based on *Economic Report of the President, Statistical Abstracts of the United States*, or National Income and Product Accounts in *Survey of Current Business*. The footnotes throughout the text identify most works quoted or referred to. Full bibliographical information is given in the References section.

The index was prepared by Nancy Wolff and revised by the author.

THE END OF ECONOMIC MAN

PROLOGUE

Life Is Unfair. Why Should We Care?

Tonight as darkness flows across the face of the earth, eight hundred forty million men, women, and children will lie down hungry, some of them in beds. Twenty-four hours later, sixteen thousand of these people will have died of malnutrition or starvation, although other people of the world will have wasted enough food in that same twenty-four hours to have nourished those who lacked it. Life is unfair.

Today, in the two hundred twenty-fourth year of the independence of the United States of America, thirty-four million three hundred thousand American men, women, and children are living in poverty. Over thirteen million of these people are under eighteen years of age, their chance for a solidly based start in life rapidly slipping away. Almost four million are sixty-five years old or older, past the age at which they might have had a realistic prospect of improving the conditions in which they live. Life is unfair.

In this millennial year, widely acclaimed the most prosperous in our history, when the Federal Reserve Board feels obligated to slow the economy down, meaning thereby to throw a million or so people out of work, there are six million men and women who are counted as unemployed. A half million more aren't counted because they've become too discouraged to continue looking for a job. A couple of million more aren't counted because they're too turned off ever to have looked for lawful employment. Several million more are working part time, many at two jobs, because they can't find regular work, employers having learned to downsize their regular staff and make use of occasional workers, thus incidentally reducing their expenses for medical insurance and pensions. Estimates of the number of people unemployed or underemployed run as high as twenty million. For reasons that are easy to guess, Congress has budgeted too little for an accurate census. Life is unfair.

Why should we care?

Early in his career, Adam Smith thought it was natural to care. In the first sentence of his first book, *The Theory of Moral Sentiments*, he wrote: "How selfish soever man may be supposed, there are evidently some principles in his nature which interest him in the fortunes of others, and render their happiness necessary to him, though he derives nothing from it except the pleasure of seeing it."[1]

Later, in *The Wealth of Nations*, the study of economics had led him to a more sombre, not to say cynical, view: "I have never known much good done by those who affected to trade for the public good. It is an affectation, indeed, not very common among merchants, and very few words need be employed in dissuading them from it."[2]

Most economists today consider themselves practitioners of a science of the efficient allocation of scarce resources. When that is said and done, their most elegant mathematical models find the most efficient allocation to be accomplished by not regulating, by not interfering. By doing nothing. Laissez faire. That millions of people are now leading largely unregulated lives that, although hardly solitary,

---

1. Smith, *The Theory of Moral Sentiments*, p. 9.
2. Smith, *The Wealth of Nations*, p. 423.

are nevertheless poor, nasty, brutish, and short is not denied. Life is unfair.

Why should we care? It is not natural for us to care. Some animals care for others of their species. Some do not. Some are archetypically billing and cooing. Some are cannibalistic. We all have troubles, and so does everyone we know. Some of us believe that troubles are somehow sent to test us, and that to complain or to interfere is to fail the test. Some are emotionally so impoverished that, regardless of what Adam Smith believed, they are able to interest themselves only in the fortunes and misfortunes of duly celebrated celebrities.

Yet in the same year in which Smith published *The Wealth of Nations*, Thomas Jefferson declared, and the delegates of the thirteen colonies unanimously concurred, that all men are created equal. In the course of our history, we have subscribed to the Declaration, have clarified its meaning with the Thirteenth, Fifteenth, Nineteenth, and Twenty-sixth Amendments to the Constitution, and have reached an understanding that "all men" will include all human beings.

Obviously we are not equal in physical, or emotional, or mental, or moral strength or beauty. Obviously we are not equal in life expectancy or in progeny. Obviously we are not equal in worldly goods or worldly accomplishments. Despite what some of us claim, we obviously were not and are not equal in the opportunity to acquire worldly goods, to be recognized for worldly accomplishments, or to love and be loved. Not all of us have had that best good fortune to our friend a friend to be. How, then, can we say we are equal?

We can say we are equal because we *do* say so. We declare that we are. It is an act of self-identification. No object can do this. Objects are means to an end. We are not means to an end, but are all of us, each of us, ends ourselves.

This equality is not a matter of ranking. We cannot say that we're as good as anybody else is. Nor do we say that anybody else is as good as we are. What we say is that we are all equal—absolutely equal, and equally absolute. No object is absolute, but we are not objects.

This is the argument for ethical action—right conduct concerning other people, who are not objects but are ends in themselves. The rule is golden and categorical: What I do unto others I do to myself. When I am just to others, I am just to myself. If I am unjust to others, I diminish myself.

Most of what I do is of small consequence. Yet everything I do to others, or with others, or in the presence of others is a statement of who I am. My every action is a statement of the form, "I am the sort of person who does this sort of thing. It is my act, and I do it."

Every deed is a consequence of some prior deed. As a result of what was done yesterday, some further action is open (or perhaps is required) today. This is how we distinguish yesterday from today. The rare deeds that are world-historical are those that change the world in which we live and whose comprehension enables us to understand and to act responsibly in that world.

In our time and place, we are all personally responsible for our own deeds, our own thoughts, and our own sustenance. As we learn from anthropology, such responsibility is not characteristic of all societies, but our history has made it true of us. It is our idea, our rationale, our ideal, and to the extent that we embody it, we are ourselves members one of another.

PART I

WHY WE HAVE ECONOMICS

1

In the Beginning Is the Act

Economics is the study of the principles whereby individuals and corporations of individuals and nations of individuals exchange goods and services for money (and vice versa) in order to maintain and enhance the quality of human life. The primal action of economic life is a bargain and sale.

Like all definitions, the foregoing is only a starting point. It also implies limits; economics is not all of life. Some may object that the definition excludes many topics that recognized economists often discuss. Barter is an example. Adam Smith, in fact, placed a propensity to barter at the very *fons et origo* of the discipline. Yet there is no proposition in any system of economics—classical, neoclassical, or whatever—that is clarified by a consideration of barter, while there are many that are confused thereby. This is not to deny that almost everyone occasionally engages in barter, or that in some parts of the world or on some levels of society or at some times barter is or has been the dominant system; and it emphatically is not to imply that the lives lived in those places and times were or are unworthy of being lived or being studied. The point is merely that the modern world does not and could not run on barter, and no future economics will run on barter.

Of the words in the definition, "individuals" is obviously the most important. But Adam Smith took the wealth of nations for his subject, and modern schools concentrate on the gross national or domestic product or on a putative equilibrium or on the techniques of allocating resources to satisfy personal preferences.

In the early 1980s, when upwards of fourteen million men and women in the United States were unemployed, and there was much debate about whether we were in a recession or a depression and how to end whatever it was, public attention was lavished on statistics supposed to indicate when recovery was finally under way. Among the "indicators," the rate of unemployment was understandably included. But this rate was, curiously, a "lagging" indicator. That is to say, contemporary economics held that something entitled to be called a recovery could be achieved leaving 6 or 8 or even 12 percent of our work force unemployed. Furthermore, it was widely insisted that at least 6 percent must always be unemployed if inflation was to be controlled.

An economics that regards several million people as mere objects, of less importance than some level of prices, will clearly differ in substantial ways from an economics that holds that full and just employment of men and women is a central economic problem.

ORIGINATIONS

Like most of the social sciences, economics is a comparatively new discipline, a creation of the Enlightenment. Adam Smith is usually credited with being its father, and it was less than 250 years ago that he published *The Wealth of Nations*, the seminal book. Before that time, we find a few lines in Plato, a few paragraphs in Aristotle, a few admonitions in the Bible, some advice on farm management in Hesiod and later in Cato and Virgil, medieval sermons on usury and the just price, a flood of Renaissance pamphlets—several of them of considerable sophistication—together with some paragraphs in treatises on government. Until very late, the subject was what the Greeks said it was—*oikonomia*, household management. In the Renaissance, the nation was the king's household, and even by Adam Smith the nation is occasionally treated as an analogue of the private household. Indeed, we continue to find the same approach today.

When today's introductory textbooks tell students that they will learn about the efficient allocation of scarce resources, they are casting their subject as an aspect of man's struggle with nature. This was the problem for the Greek householder, for whom physical well-being, not to mention comfort, was precarious. This remained the problem for two millennia, but by Adam Smith's time its solution had become possible. It is a mark of Smith's genius that he recognized what had changed.

The steam-powered and water-powered machines of the Industrial Revolution concentrated production and brought forth the factory system, and the factory system made possible rapid progress in the division of labor. Plato had seen that the polis would be stronger if some men specialized in farming and some in soldiering, and it was common in quite primitive societies for the men to do the hunting and the women to do the gathering. These are instances of a division of labor of sorts, but they have nothing like the possibilities of the eighteen operations in the manufacture of pins that Smith described and immortalized in the opening pages of his book. Even a "small manufactory," employing only ten men poorly provided with machinery, "could make among them upwards of forty-eight thousand pins in a day. . . . But if they had all wrought separately and independently, and without any of them having been educated to this peculiar business, they certainly could not each of them have made twenty, perhaps not one pin in a day."[1]

---

1. Smith, *Wealth*, p. 5.

Such an explosive growth of production (aided, we may note, by a bit of machinery and a bit of education) immediately changed the terms of economic endeavor. Subsistence need no longer be an all-absorbing problem. From the Industrial Revolution on, it has been possible in principle to feed, clothe, shelter, and provide health care for all mankind. That this has not been accomplished in fact is due to a failure of will, not a lack of means. It is a moral problem. The economic problem, whose independence Smith declared, concerns human beings' relations with each other, not their struggle with nature.

THE INVISIBLE HAND

By the middle of the nineteenth century, the scientific method was carrying all before it. If every event has a cause and if the universe is uniform, miracles are no longer sought or feared. Scientific inquiry, once fairly begun, is interminable. If human illnesses are natural, the human body becomes a part of nature. And if the human body is natural, it would seem that the mind, if it is human, must be natural, too.

At this point, a curious reversal occurred. It appeared early in Karl Marx, in works written fifteen years before *The Origin of Species*, though published posthumously. Like Rousseau, Marx saw mankind in chains and searched for the means of liberation. He found it in history, which to him was comprehensible only as it was lawful, and lawful only as it was impersonal and inexorable. He considered himself a materialist, and understood history to be materialist in the same way that classical mechanics was materialist.

Developing his ideas, he wrote, "It is not a matter of what this or that proletarian or even the proletariat as a whole *pictures* at present as its goal. It is a matter of *what the proletariat is in actuality* and what in accordance with this *being*, it will historically be compelled to do."[2]

---

2. Marx, *Holy Family*, p. 159.

What was launched in search of freedom has paradoxically come aground on sociohistorical compulsion. Marx was not the last to sail these murky waters.

We find mankind liberated from spooks and spirits, from lords and priests, by becoming mechanized. Once the universe was running like a clock, there was nothing for it but to fit us to a wheel in the works—perhaps a greater thing than a cog, but mechanical nevertheless. For us to be fit for this function, psychology had to subject us to mechanical controls. Or, as the philosopher John William Miller said, we had first to lose our souls; then our minds; and finally, with the behaviorists, consciousness. Economic man is a prime example of this remarkable servomechanism.

Medieval ethical doctrine, which included medieval economics, concerned a static society in which the proper relations of individual to individual and of individuals to God were immutable. It was a world of six foreordained events, from the Creation to the Second Coming, to which St. Augustine had added a seventh, the Eternal Sabbath. Though these events followed one after the other, they described a sequence, not a history. The various events had been and would be reached and passed regardless of what anyone did or did not do; and what was virtuous or sinful had no relation to any period but was from everlasting to everlasting.

During the Renaissance, the medieval ban on usury spurred the first tentative steps in the direction of fractional-reserve banking, which made it possible to think of money as an idea that could be used and transmitted, and double-entry bookkeeping, which similarly idealized all debts and assets. These two liberal accounting procedures introduced a dynamism into business that was as fateful for the static medieval world view as was the cosmology of Copernicus. After Adam Smith, economic theory, following economic practice, abandoned religious dogma. It did not, however, reform its ethical base, but ultimately denied it.

In the second chapter of *The Wealth of Nations*, Smith announces that the "division of labor, from which so many advantages are derived, is not originally the effect of any human wisdom. It is the necessary, though very slow and gradual, consequence of a certain propensity in human nature which has in view no such extensive utility; the propensity to truck, barter, and exchange one thing for another."[3] This is clearly the theme of impersonality, but the definitive metaphor does not yet appear.

We hear of the invisible hand halfway through the book: "By preferring the support of domestic products to that of foreign industry, [every individual] intends only his own security; and by directing that industry in such a manner as its produce may be of the greatest value, he intends only his own gain, and he is in this, as in many other cases, led by an invisible hand to promote an end which was no part of his intention. Nor is it always the worse for society that it was no part of it. By pursuing his own interest he frequently promotes that of society more effectually than he really intends to promote it."[4]

Smith's less metaphorical, but perhaps as frequently cited, statement of the idea comes even further on, more than two-thirds through the book: "[T]he obvious and simple system of natural liberty establishes itself of its own accord. Every man, as long as he does not violate the laws of justice, is left perfectly free to pursue his own interest in his own way, and to bring both his industry and capital into competition with those of any other men or order of men." This passage comes at the end of an attack on the physiocrats. But now Smith goes on to state explicitly the factor of the idea that gave it its historical power: "The sovereign is completely discharged from a duty . . . for the proper performance of which no human wisdom or knowledge could ever be sufficient; the duty of superintending the industry of private people, and of directing it towards the employments most suitable to the interest of society."[5]

---

3. Smith, *Wealth*, p. 13.
4. Smith, *Wealth*, p. 423.
5. Smith, *Wealth*, p. 651.

Here Adam Smith made the wealth of nations seem an impersonal science on the model of Newtonian physics. Thus he changed irrevocably the conditions of our thoughts and lives. His words were so simple, so elegant, so appropriate to the spirit of the times that they carried instant conviction to all who heard them. Where only a few years earlier Rousseau had declared, "Man is born free, and everywhere he is in chains," the striking off of those chains now seemed an imminent possibility. And it would be done automatically, effortlessly, by the invisible hand, now that the heavy hand of sovereign lords was seen to be unnecessary. No one any longer needed to feel guilty in challenging the inherited authority of kings or the revealed morality of priests. The pursuit of self-interest would work, regardless of intention, for the benefit of all; and self-serving labor could achieve miracles of production, making use of the technical miracles of the natural sciences. The wealth of nations, which had previously been determined by military or dynastic maneuvering, could become the daily concern of commoners.

The free market, the free state, and free thought were thus intertwined in Smith's message. They did, in fact, grow up together—three robust children of the Enlightenment. As far as we know, all three depend on each other. Where one does not exist, the others have existed only in stunted form. In the ancient world, only personal wealth or patronage of the wealthy could liberate thinkers from the deadening requirements of subsistence grubbing. In the medieval world, the Church sponsored scholarship, but on its own terms; even the great St. Thomas spoke harshly of intellectual speculation. Only in the modern world of the West do we find the ideal of a free state formed of all adult citizens, all of whom are free and responsible as thinkers of their own thoughts, as providers of their own sustenance, and as definers of their own relations with their fellows.

Just as thought could not be free if liable to persecution by secular or ecclesiastical authority, so government could not be free as a function of feudal rights and duties.

More than control of the purse was involved. That struggle had gone on for more than half a millennium, starting at least as early as Magna Carta in 1215. As long as the issue was between the king and his barons, no economic question was implied. The English barons, like the First and Second Estates on the Continent, fought for the right to raise revenue in their own way, and that way did not differ, so far as the ultimate taxpayers were concerned, from the way followed by the king. In both cases it was a question of household management. The lord, like the king above him and the paterfamilias below him, did with his dependents and his property as he thought best. At every level, exchange between domains was minimal; and within each domain the problems concerned much agriculture, some engineering, and, too often, the tactics of small-unit engagements.

What matters for modern government and modern economy is that there is a purse, that is to say, that there is an undifferentiated fund to support unspecified and unanticipated needs of government. Such a fund makes actual the idea of the general welfare; without it, government has only ad hoc functions specifically authorized. If democratic, specific authorization is constitutionally narrow in scope and small in scale. The New England town meeting, much admired by Tocqueville, went about as far as one can go in this direction. Modern government would be impossible as an amalgam of the Social Security Trust Fund, the Highway Trust Fund, and so on. The ambitious projects of the ancient world, like the Athenian acropolis or the wars against Persia, called for some sort of dictatorship, benevolent and limited if possible. A strong and continuing government needs a strong and continuing economy.

As Alexander Hamilton wrote in *Report on Manufactures* (1791), "[T]he power to raise money is plenary and indefinite, and the objects to which it may be appropriated are no less comprehensive than the payment of the public debt, and the providing for the common defense and general welfare."

We have economics because it frees us to govern ourselves. And vice versa. The contemporary Russian economy founders because the Russian government is too disorganized to govern.

2

WHY ECONOMICS IS VALUE BOUND

Galileo, on the basis of a few almost-casual observations, proposed a mathematical formula for the velocity of any falling body, excluding all sorts of irrelevant data, and then devised measurable experiments that confirmed the formula. In the same way, Newton combined the astronomical findings and theories of Copernicus and Kepler with Galileo's formula to produce universal laws of motion. He then sought observations that would confirm these laws. At first he failed, and put his study aside. The story goes that a few years later, working with new figures, he became so excited as he saw confirmation looming that he had to call in a friend to finish the calculations.

In the social sciences an early, if not the first, work along these lines was done by John Graunt, a haberdasher and captain of militia, who studied the mortality records of the City of London and prepared what he called a "Table showing one hundred quick conceptions, how many die within six years, how many the next decade, and so for every decade till 76." His work appeared in 1661, twenty-six years before Newton's *Principia*. Graunt apparently prepared his table for fun, but it was quickly taken up by the nascent insurance business, and a general statement of the principles behind such work was made by Sir William Petty, a friend of Graunt's.

Because of this statement, Petty is credited as being one of the founders of modern statistics, which he called political arithmetic, and which he defined as "the art of reasoning by figures upon things relating to the government." Petty was a minor sort of Renaissance man, a professor of anatomy at Oxford, the organizer of the survey of Cromwell's grants of land in Ireland, a landlord himself of some fifty thousand acres in County Kerry, and an occasional essayist on economic subjects. A longish essay or short book, published posthumously because it contained references to France offensive to Petty's patron Charles II, was *Five Discourses on Political Arithmetick*. "The method I use," Petty wrote, "is not yet very usual; for, instead of using only comparative and superlative words, and intellectual arguments, I have taken the course . . . to express myself in terms of number, weight, and measure; to use only arguments of sense, and to consider only such causes as have visible foundations in nature."[1]

One would think that with Graunt and Petty and several others on the Continent, economics was well under way on a course parallel to that of astronomy and physics. It is therefore with something of a shock that we listen to Adam Smith pronouncing a full hundred years later, "I have no great faith in political arithmetic."[2]

What had gone wrong?

The biographical reason for Smith's rejection of political arithmetic no doubt turned in part on his vehement rejection of mercantilism, one of the principal themes of his book. Petty, like others of his time, was a mercantilist. Though it is most unlikely that Smith had not read Petty's work and it is certain that he was aware of the discipline Petty had named, yet Petty himself is not named in *The Wealth of Nations*.

1. Petty, *Economic Writings*, vol. 1, p. 244.
2. Smith, *Wealth*, p. 501.

This omission is surprising because, as Heilbroner notes, over a hundred authors are referred to by name in Smith's treatise.[3]

Personality aside, the episode would seem to suggest some reason to be wary of statistics in economics. Smith had what seemed to him sound reasons for opposing the Corn Laws. These reasons owed nothing to the figures that had been collected, even though they were in Smith's favor. "I mention them," he said, "only in order to show of how much less consequence, in the opinion of the most judicious and experienced persons, the foreign trade of corn is than the home trade."[4] He refused to bother himself about the accuracy of the figures and thought they proved nothing except the size of the problem. By the same token, the figures that persuaded others, including Petty, of the merits of mercantilism carried no conviction to Smith.

This sort of thing still goes on. In the past hundred years we have collected unbelievable quantities of statistics on everything one can imagine, especially on all aspects of economic life. The annual *Economic Report of the President* is thought to need 125 pages of statistics to support 285 pages of text, which are themselves heavily statistical. Yet that report is subject to debate within the establishment and to scorn from outside. It is commonplace—even expected—that economists will agree on figures and will dispute irreconcilably about their meaning.

A situation like this does not occur in the natural sciences. Once Simon Stevin showed that the velocities of falling bodies are not proportionate to their density, no student continued to hold Aristotle's side of the question. Newton was no doubt dismayed when his first calculations failed to demonstrate the inverse-square law. He may even have suspected that the number he had been given for the radius of the earth was wrong. But he did not pretend that the number didn't matter, that the law held regardless of the number.

---

3. Heilbroner, *Worldly Philosophers*, p. 49.
4. Smith, *Wealth*, p. 501.

Why should economists behave differently? The record suggests a fundamental difference between natural and social science. General acceptance of some difference is indicated by the usual division of the sciences into the two broad classifications, with physics always in one group and economics always in the other.

"Number, weight, and measure" will not actually take one very far in economics. One may no doubt count the bushels of wheat each farmer grows and then add the output of all the wheat farmers in the land to get the national output. And one can do the same for tons of coal and for almost anything produced by farming or mining. One can even classify and total the types and grades of steel produced by steel mills. Thereafter things get much more complicated. Some steel goes into stovepipes and some into cannons, some into bridge girders and some into snuffboxes. A pine forest may yield ships' spars, residential clapboarding, and paper products. Tables of the numbers, weights, and measures of these products may be of interest to individual producers, but they are too diverse for inferences of any generality. You cannot, as the saying goes, add apples and oranges.

It should, moreover, be noted that to divide fruit into apples and oranges, even to separate fruit from steel girders, is illicit on the premises of political arithmetic. An apple and a needle both have number, weight, and measure and therefore, on the premises, should be added together. Carry it a step further: It is illicit on the premises to distinguish a good apple from a rotten one or a potato from the dirt that is turned up when it is harvested. Newtonian mechanics works as well with a rotten apple as with a good one, but it would appear that economics may be somehow different.

WILLIAM STANLEY JEVONS

A strong statement in favor of mathematical thinking was made by William Stanley Jevons, who argued in 1871 that "*our science must be mathematical, simply because it deals with quantities*. Wherever the things treated are capable of being *greater or less*, there the laws and relations must be mathematical in nature."[5] His point, Jevons insists, is not merely that mathematical notation is used, because "[i]f we had no regard to trouble and prolixity, the most complicated mathematical problems might be stated in ordinary language." Rather, he holds that "[t]here can be but two classes of sciences—those which are *simply logical*, and *those which, besides being logical, are also mathematical.*" A logical science "determines whether a thing be or not be . . . but if the thing may be greater or less, or the event may happen sooner or later, nearer or farther, then quantitative notions enter."[6]

As so often happens in the history of thought, Jevons claims both too little and too much. The sort of question he assigns exclusively to logic—to be or not to be—is not merely characteristic of Hamlet but is also the basis of computer circuitry and so is the mathematics par excellence of our day. On the other hand, very little of logic is as restricted as Jevons suggests. The universal affirmative proposition of the form "All apples are fruits" certainly seems to meet his standard. But this proposition may be converted by immediate inference to the particular affirmative "Some fruits are apples," which is something else.

In any case, it by no means follows that all "sciences" that deal in quantities are merely mathematical. The obvious exceptions to Jevons's rule are legion, from penology to pharmacology. Criminals are sentenced to prison for a number of days or years or are required to pay a fine of a number of dollars; but no one supposes that judges do or should turn to mathematicians for advice in imposing sentence. Likewise, it is usual to prescribe 6.5 grains of aspirin for a headache, but the prescription does not appear in any mathematics text.

A task of algebra is to explore the relationship between dependent and independent variables. A decision as to which are dependent and which independent must be made to get the equation into usable form. One

5. Jevons, *Political Economy*, p. 3.
6. Ibid, p. 7.

may debate whether the interest rate depends on the rate of inflation, or vice versa; and not only the shape of the equation but the deduced policy recommendations will be at stake. And there is still a prior question: Do the given variables have a dependent-independent relationship at all? Or, if they sometimes have such a relationship, is it regular?

The answer to these questions is by no means obvious or automatic. We may, for example, brush aside as frivolous Jevons's proposed connections between sunspots and the stock market, but an astronomer as distinguished as Harlan Stetson took the matter seriously enough to write a book about it. The illustration is more sharply focused by the fact that shortly after he wrote his book Stetson joined in the furious attack on Immanuel Velikovsky's best-selling quasi-literal interpretation of biblical cosmology.

The point is that neither the sunspot question nor the biblical question is definitively answered by mathematics. One can, of course, make errors in any mathematical calculation, and such errors certainly vitiate the conclusion; but mathematical correctness is no guarantee of a meaningful answer. Stetson rejected Velikovsky not because of faulty mathematics but because if Velikovsky were right, the entire structure of modern science would crumble. More than astronomy was at risk, because astronomy is consistent with physics, and physics with chemistry, and chemistry with biology. In the same way, economics must be consistent with ethics in the broad sense and with all humanistic concerns, nor may humanism be inconsistent with natural science if our life is to be intelligible.

Contemporary economics leans heavily on analytic geometry. A curious fact about the rank jungle of multicolored curves choking the pages of the textbooks is that numbers rarely attach to them; and when numerical values are represented, they often turn out to be estimated or wholly imaginary—a schedule showing the supposed (or denied) price elasticity of wheat, the kinked oligopoly demand curve, and so on. In almost all cases, no one knows what the actual figures may be; the given figures are assumed in order to illustrate a theory.

The problem lies not in the fact that the actual numbers are truly difficult to come by or even, in some instances, impossible to come by. No one has been to the interior of the sun; yet astrophysicists talk confidently of what goes on there. This is possible because natural science is a unified structure. What the astrophysicists can observe about the sun can occur only if what they theorize about the interior is true. Hence it *is* true. Revisions occur every day, but the system stands. The textbooks talk as though a similar system works in economics, but actually it does not. Every business—especially every one selling by mail or Internet—has experimented with price changes and found instances where a price increase has increased sales. Nothing like this happens in natural science, where there never are exceptions supposed to prove the rule.

QUANTITY VS. QUALITY

In a 1925 article, Wesley Clair Mitchell, founder of the National Bureau of Economic Research, urged a shift from qualitative to quantitative work. "Our qualitative theory," he wrote, "has followed the logic of Newtonian mechanics. . . . In the hedonistic calculus which Jevons followed, man is placed under the governance of two sovereign masters, pain and pleasure, which play the same role in controlling human behavior that Newton's laws of motion play in controlling the behavior of the heavenly bodies. . . . The mechanical view involves the notions of sameness, of certainty, of invariant laws; the statistical view [introduced by Maxwell] involves the notions of variety, of probability, of approximations."[7]

This odd analogy invites a couple of comments. First, there is no qualitative-quantitative split between Newton and Maxwell; they are

---

7. Mitchell, "Quantitative Analysis," pp. 1–12.

both quantitative through and through. And, as we have seen, Jevons was an enthusiastic a supporter of quantitative methods in economics as anyone since; nor was he unaware of the fact that the numbers he worked with were imprecise. "Many persons," he observed, "entertain a prejudice against mathematical language, arising out of a confusion between the ideas of a mathematical science and an exact science . . . but in reality, there is no such thing as an exact science, except in a comparative sense. Astronomy is more exact than other sciences, because the position of a planet or star admits of close measurement; but, if we examine the methods of physical astronomy, we find that they are all approximate. . . . Had physicists waited until their data were perfectly precise before they brought in the aid of mathematics, we should have still been in the age of science which terminated in the time of Galileo."[8] This debater's point could serve Mitchell as well.

A second and more important comment on Mitchell is that the world of Maxwell, Einstein, and Heisenberg is not less subject to invariant laws than is the world of Newton. In physics, to be sure, the detailed precision of optics is confined to relatively gross phenomena, such as the refraction of a beam of light upon hitting a body of water. In a given experiment, the intensity of the beam and the angle of refraction never vary, regardless of the date of the experiment or the name of the experimenter. But whether a particular photon will be refracted or reflected cannot be said; the beam is the statistical result of a lot of photons. Yet nothing that can be said about a particular photon is in conflict with what can be said about gross phenomena. On the contrary, explanation of gross phenomena allows for, and must allow for, the diverse paths of determinate and regular proportions of photons. It does not happen that today 10 percent of the photons are reflected, although yesterday, under identical conditions, 20 percent were reflected, while the day before, the figure was 12. One would

8. Jevons, *Political Economy*, p. 6.

scarcely know how to grind and coat lenses in such an unreliable world, which would always be more or less out of focus.

A key phrase, of course, is "under identical conditions." The behavior that economists try to describe statistically is in fact in constant flux. Indeed, it is exactly this shifting of demand and supply from here to there, from high to low, from this to that, that is supposed to be measured by the market. The "market" of a beam of light is constant; the economic market is forever unstable. As Sir Thomas Browne said of the song the Sirens sang, the explanation of the market's rise and fall is not beyond all conjecture. But such explanation will not be of the same order as the explanations of optics.

SOCIAL SCIENCE VS. NATURAL SCIENCE

The attraction of mathematics for economists is no doubt enhanced (as Jevons suggests) by the hope that somewhere, somehow, they will discover something similar to Newton's inverse-square law. At first glance, Newton's problem and the econometricians' problem do seem similar. Both are confronted by a universe of infinite detail and variety, and both are sustained by the hope that, somewhere in that blooming, buzzing confusion, orderly and reliable laws may be discovered. In fact, Newton experienced the order and reliability every moment of his life and could not—literally—have taken a step otherwise. The notorious apple neither flew away erratically nor disintegrated in midair, but fell solidly, as anyone would expect.

The orderly reliability of nature not only is free of the invocations of priests but also is free of the hopes and fears of ordinary people, including the scientists who study it. Experiments will come out however they come out, naturally, regardless of the intentions of the experimenters.

The universe of physics is a universe discovered by human beings, but it does not depend on human beings for its operation. Distance and clock time are not values; it makes no sense to approve or disapprove of them; Margaret Fuller could not refuse to accept the universe. It is a fact that the chemical bond works in the way Linus Pauling discovered, and neither Linus Pauling nor anyone else can change it.

"The values of an objective science like physics," Max Planck said, "are wholly independent of the objects to which they relate."[9] No value appears in the physical description of an object. A physical description defines an object that obeys physical laws, not an economic object obeying economic laws, whatever they may be. A physical description of the piece of green-backed paper in my pocket does not reveal what makes it money or what money does. Any good that I buy with my money will obey physical law, but that fact is not what will make it a good. Every service that is performed must rely on physical law, but that fact does not explain what is economic about it. Every object is a physical object, and any object may come to be an economic object; but only some objects are actually economic objects. Whether or not a particular object becomes an economic object depends upon what human beings do with it.

Money, goods, and services are human values. Economic production and consumption are human activities. The consumption of food is essential to life, but that fact is in biology and says nothing about the price of apples. You may be convinced that apples are physiologically better for you than acorns, and your conviction may affect the price you are willing to pay; but it is only the price that is an economic concern.

As distance and clock time are fundamental physical concepts, money, goods, and services are fundamental economic concepts. Both lists can be extended, but one distinction will always separate them;

---

9. Planck, *Philosophy of Physics*, p. 113.

the former are value free, while the latter are value bound. If it made a difference to the laws of physics what Linus Pauling (or anyone) felt about electrons, physics would collapse. If it didn't make a difference how much money Linus Pauling (or someone) would pay for an electron microscope, either the microscope would not be an economic good or economics would collapse.

The vocabulary of physics is amoral—not antimoral, but amoral. Mass, force, and velocity have no moral implications because the laws describing them have no alternatives. The vocabulary of economics, in contrast, abounds in ethical terms. It is impossible to define "good," "service," or even "utility" without making ethical judgments. Every object has mass, but not every object has utility. Moreover, some people may consider a certain object a good while others do not, but there can be no disagreement about the equivalence and direction of action and reaction. There is no other or better way for a body to fall in a vacuum than $S = 1/2\ gt^2$; this is not because physicists don't happen to be interested in making this a better world. There is no unchanging price for a bushel of wheat; and this is not because economists don't happen to be interested in a stable universe. The price of wheat depends upon what people do, but bodies fall as they do regardless of what people do or think.

It is not the impartiality of experimenters or observers that distinguishes natural science from social science. If social scientists report what they wish they'd found rather than what they did find, they are as surely discredited as are natural scientists who falsify their data. It is in their different subject matters that the difference between natural science and social science lies. Physics is value free because electrons know no value. The events reported by social scientists are not value free because the human beings who act in these events have values. By acting this way rather than that, they declare that they judge this way to be better—that is, more valuable. Both natural scientists and social scientists may incidentally reveal their personal values in their writings, but a report of human action will always concern the values of the human actors.

Moreover, while physicists are certainly composed of electrons and have mass and generate energy, what makes them physicists is neither electron nor mass nor energy. Nothing physicists say about electrons or mass or energy validates or compromises their ability or authority to say it. It is different with the social sciences—economics in particular. Economists are, without exception, economic agents—producers or consumers, profit maximizers or utility optimizers—in most cases, all at once. Whatever economists say about economic agents as members of the class that is the object of their study, they necessarily say about themselves as also members of that class.

Being economic agents themselves, economists cannot reasonably say that the actions of economic agents are caused or determined as the motions of electrons are said to be caused or determined. If economists should claim (as sadly many have) determinism for economic agents, they would by the same token claim determinism for themselves. Claiming themselves to be determined, they would deny responsibility for their actions, including both the economic principles they teach and their claims of determinism.

Consequently, if there is such a discipline as economics, it must be a study of deeds of free and responsible men and women.

Economics is not value free, and no amount of abstraction can make it value free. The econometricians' search for equations that will explain the economy is forever doomed to frustration. It is often said that their models don't work, because, on the one hand, the variables are too many and, on the other, the statistical data are too sparse. But the physical universe is as various as the economic universe (they are, to repeat, both infinite), and Newton had fewer data and less powerful means of calculation than are at the disposal of Jan Tinbergen and his econometrician followers. The difference is fundamental, and the failure to understand it reduces much of modern economics to a game that unfortunately has serious consequences.

MATHEMATICS AND THE PRESENT TENSE

After a couple of pages of moderately abstruse mathematics, Keynes remarks, "I do not myself attach much value to manipulations of this kind; . . . they involve just as much tacit assumption as to what variables are taken as independent . . . as does ordinary discourse, whilst I doubt if they carry us any further than ordinary discourse can."[10] Alfred Marshall, Keynes's early mentor, wrote in the introduction to his influential textbook that "it seems doubtful whether any one spends his time well in reading lengthy translations of economic doctrines into mathematics."[11]

To these sentiments may be added the observation that mathematics derives power not only from the conciseness of its notation but also from its stability. Mathematics knows only the present tense and does not deal in particulars. Two plus three *equals* five. It is mathematically meaningless to say, "Two plus three used to equal five," or "will equal five next year," or "when you're counting white sheep but not black ones."

A mathematical relationship is reciprocal; it can go either way, and it can retrace its steps. If $2x - y = 4$, then $y = 2x - 4$, and $x = (y + 4)/2$, from either of which can be derived $2x - y = 4$, which is where we started. In economics, if you buy a shirt, you cannot sell it back for the same price, nor would there be any reason to do so unless something was wrong with it (in which case you didn't buy it but refused delivery). More important, economics operates in calendar or historical time, which is not reversible. Last spring I paid two men for two weeks' work painting my house. If I could somehow get the paint off the house, that wouldn't give the men back their labor or get the paint back in the cans, not to mention the money back in my pocket.

---

10. Keynes, *General Theory*, p. 305.
11. Marshall, *Principles*, p. IX.

3

Responsibility and Greed

At a crucial point in *The General Theory of Employment, Interest and Money*, John Maynard Keynes wrote, "The fundamental psychological law, upon which we are entitled to depend with great confidence both *a priori* from our knowledge of human nature and from the detailed facts of experience, is that men are disposed, as a rule and on the average, to increase their consumption as their income increases, but not by as much as the increase in their income."[1] The alleged law was intended to explain the fact that the wages and profits of industry are not immediately reinvested or spent on consumption. There is certainly no lack of evidence of that fact, and it can be explained by the simple economic (rather than psychological) observation that since the future is (as Keynes always insisted), unforeseeable, economic agents frequently conclude that the most satisfactory use for their money is not immediately before them. Hoarding then becomes a microeconomically sensible, but macroeconomically unfortunate, option.

1. Keynes, *General Theory*, p. 96.

The late Hyman Minsky proposed a psychological explanation of the fragility of the business cycle. At the low point, everyone is well aware of what happened in the previous cycle and proceeds conservatively, especially when undertaking new debt. Business improves. Entrepreneurs become more venturesome. The boom gathers strength. The bad times tend to be forgotten. What Minsky called "Ponzi finance"—borrowing to pay the interest on existing debt—becomes enthusiastically embraced. What, me worry? Sooner or later the fragile structure collapses.[2]

Again, there is an economic, rather than psychological, explanation. As an enterprise grows, it reaches a point where further expansion involves a fiercer fight for market share, or ventures into new fields, or both. In any case, a lot more money is needed. Moreover, if a firm starts to expand vigorously, its competitors have to defend themselves, and that costs money, too. It is a fact of business life, that it's very difficult to jog happily in one place; if you don't grow, you're in danger of being shrunk.

Note that the economic explanation doesn't require a business cycle or even an industry-wide struggle. There may be too many filling stations in a certain part of a village. Also, if a crash does come, the Ponzi-financed enterprise may have a better chance of surviving than does the mom 'n' pop store that didn't borrow a penny. Also, banks prefer to lend to big Ponzi operations rather than to the small ultraconservative borrowers. It is easier to charge high interest rates, and the cost of servicing the little guys is alleged to be too high.

The psychology invoked by economists has, it must be acknowledged, borne little relation to that studied by psychologists. This anomaly was noted as long ago as 1925 by Wesley Clair Mitchell, who made, in the article already referred to, what must be judged a preliminary

2. Minsky, *Stabilizing*, p. 206 ff.

and superficial attempt to tie his economics to the then-fashionable behaviorist psychology of John B. Watson.[3]

Economics has to come to ground somewhere. Almost universally, the ground chosen or assumed has been self-interest, an apparently simple, straightforward, and obvious concept. It is, nevertheless, easier to understand what is meant by the idea of self-interest or the pleasure-pain principle than to use the idea to further understanding. Every time Galileo released a brass ball at the top of an inclined plane, it rolled in the same way, accelerating in the same way. But regardless of Adam Smith's notion of a propensity to barter, sometimes a deal goes through, and sometimes it doesn't. One person will see self-interest in a swap and the next won't. This seems, so to say, perfectly natural. They're different people. Everyone is different. People are differently endowed and come from different backgrounds and have different needs, wants, hopes, expectations, fears, understandings, interests. Everyone is strange but me and thee.

In all honesty, human beings behave very strangely indeed. With the reports of thousands of cultural anthropologists before us, we know that there is scarcely a practice commonly seen in one part of the world that is not shunned in another. Even in Smith's day enough was known of the customs of the Chinese and the American Indians and, nearer at hand, some sadly disreputable Frenchmen, to understand that their behavior differed from that of a Scottish scholar who lived much of his life with his mother.

What, then, becomes of human nature? If people act differently because they *are* different, what is gained by claiming they are of the same nature because they act out of self-interest? Self-interest would appear to be as various as humanity. Is there such a thing as self-interest, after all?

---

3. Mitchell, "Quantitative Analysis," pp. 10–11.

The usual answer to this question says that it's *enlightened* self-interest that is really uniform. The form of the answer appears again and again in the history of Western thought and again and again as a proposed solution to economic problems.

The distinction between self-interest and enlightened self-interest is analogous to the familiar distinction between appearance and reality. We are used to mistrusting the appearance of things; it is prudent to look for the underlying or hidden reality. "Things are seldom what they seem," sings Little Buttercup in *Pinafore*, "Skim milk masquerades as cream." Nor is this search merely a question of prudence; it is also a mark of wisdom. It is a major theme of most, if not all, religions, which celebrate the superior reality of some world other than this, or the superior force of some supernatural power. It is a recurring concern of poets, who probe with Wordsworth "something far more deeply interfused," with Eliot "the world of perpetual solitude."

The notion of the underlying reality of enlightened self-interest (however defined) is the very model of an a priori judgment. It assumes what it pretends to prove. It claims that we should behave in a certain way if we knew what's good for us. If we don't behave in the prescribed way, it's because we don't know what's good for us. There is no way of attacking or even defending this form of argument. Enlightened self-interest is a dogma no more successful in subduing the riot of human behavior than is self-interest without the enlightenment.

MAXIMIZING PROFIT AND UTILITY

In the conventional story, economic suppliers (or producers) are profit (or income) maximizers; and economic demanders (or consumers) are utility (or satisfaction) maximizers. Economic man maximizes both profit and utility. Not surprisingly, there is a considerable literature questioning the realism of these propositions. Given the enormous range and variety of what people do, not to mention the comparative effectiveness of their doings, it is argued that these multitudinous doings cannot all be examples of profit maximization. In the same way, it is said that the different ways we spend our money—certainly idiosyncratic, frequently wasteful, occasionally counterproductive—suggest that utility maximization is also a protean idea without actual definition.

There is much merit in these objections; yet there is also force in the rejoinder that it would be strange not to try to maximize profit or utility, as the case may be. If you can get more of either, why shouldn't you? Indeed, since maximum profit arguably comes from the most efficient use of scarce resources, can it not be said that you have a duty to seek it? After all, this is the way Adam Smith's invisible hand seduces selfish behavior into producing public good.

Let us say that I am a profit-maximizing man. Not only am I clever, bold, and ruthless; not only do I stretch the law as far as it will go in my favor (but prudently no farther); not only do I push my employees to the limit and deal as sharply as I can with my suppliers and my customers; not only am I admired and feared as a keen and tough competitor—beyond these delightful qualities I am necessarily a workaholic. As long as there's another dollar—another penny—to be made, I am after it, not like a hawk (I have no time for soaring), perhaps the way a badger works. If I can't scratch more out of my regular employment, I'll go moonlighting; and when I finally fall into bed, if I lie awake, I am scheming ways to increase my profit tomorrow.

Unfortunately, I never get to enjoy my winnings. I'm too busy to. If I were to relax a moment, a main chance might pass me by. Literature is full of monsters like me. Dickens would have had to shut up shop if he hadn't had such people to write about.

Literature is also full of utility maximizers—charming wastrels who live a life of endless pleasure. Women were supposed to be enchanted by them. Until very recently, women were themselves supposed to live such lives. As Veblen saw it, it was only when women were successful in this utility-maximizing way that their profit-maximizing husbands enjoyed any utility—albeit a derived utility—from the profits they piled up.

So we have a conflict. A profit maximizer has to forgo utilities for lack of time. And unless a utility maximizer can manage to be supported by someone else, he (or she) will not have resources to pay for possible pleasures.

No producer is only a producer, and very few besides children, the senile, and the infirm are only consumers. Since producers are also consumers, they must simultaneously be both profit maximizers and utility maximizers, and that is impossible.

Can we narrow the situation down and say that economic man is a profit maximizer when he is producing and a utility maximizer when he is consuming? If so, we must then ask why he is producing at this moment instead of consuming. Why is he moonlighting instead of gazing at the moon? If he has a job, he has accepted the responsibility of maximizing profits at certain hours of the day, but why did he take the job? Why not emulate Henry Thoreau? (Of course, Thoreau was also an exemplary producer; goods he created still yield profits and utilities, all over the world, a century and a half after his death.)

An obvious modification of the scheme calls for utility maximizers to do their best, subject to the constraint of their wealth, while profit maximizers are clearly subject to the constraints of their abilities and their luck. But even an incompetent man may be a workaholic and so unable to enjoy even the few utilities available to one of his accomplishments, while a remittance man may steal enough time from his pleasures to make a little profit for himself, just for fun. Thus the proposed constraints are, if precise enough to support a calculation, limited to a single case. If they are vague enough to be general in application, they are also so general in implication that no useful inference may be drawn.

This conclusion is not merely a rhetorical flourish. If you translate your thoughts into mathematics, you will reach the same conclusion very quickly. Taking the problems of maximization literally (and how else should we take them?), we find that the decisive constraint in every case is that of time. There are only so many hours in the day. Hours devoted to profit maximization are not available for utility maximization, and vice versa. We can solemnly write this proposition in the form of an equation: P + U + W = 24 (profit-maximizing hours plus utility-maximizing hours plus wasted hours equals twenty-four hours in a day). Valid though this equation may be, it does not tell what values one should give to P or U or, for that matter, W.

The proper allocation of our time is a question each of us must decide. Our lives depend on our decisions. They are acts of will. They are mathematically indeterminate and without mathematical solution, as we have seen them to be illogical and without reasonable solution. These are no mere quibbles but go directly to the heart of conventional economic theory. Nor is appeal here being made to the realism or unrealism of the assumptions. Such empirical appeal is not without validity, but it is not being made here. Any theory that is illogical at the start will be illogical forever after. GIGO, as the computer people say.

PARTIAL ANALYSIS

In talking about self-interest and profit maximization and utility maximization, I have refrained from calling them by their common everyday name, which is greed. Economic man is greedy. Since everyone is some kind of economic man—a producer or a consumer or both—it would appear that everyone is greedy, which is manifestly untrue.

There are four possible resolutions of the difficulty. The first is to claim that whether people really are greedy or not, they act as if they were. But this claim gets us nowhere because it raises again a question of fact. Granted that Mother Teresa was not greedy, did she truly act as if she were?

A second way out is described by Amartya Sen: "The real issue is whether there is a plurality of motivations, or whether self-interest *alone* drives human beings."[4] Putting aside the question of whether it can be meaningful to speak of human beings as driven, and granting a plurality of motives (some of them doubtless contradictory), we see that one motive must be selected as ultimately efficient or the models economists construct will run only by unexpected fits and starts, like a Model T operated by Laurel and Hardy. If last Monday you were motivated by greed, Tuesday by altruism, Wednesday by snobbism, Thursday by bonhomie, and Friday by despair, who could build a model telling how you "really" behave? Whether greed is the single motivation or the efficient motivation is a distinction without a difference.

The third way is little more than a quibble over terminology. Shying away from vulgar "greed" and even from the relatively genteel "self-interest," some say that an economic system exists to provide people with all possible freedom to choose whatever they want whenever they want it. The popular press characterized a whole generation as so motivated—the "me generation." But these formulations are essentially identical; "greed" and "self-interest" and "me first" all come very close to the same thing.

The fourth way is what is known as partial analysis, which is signaled by the Latin ablative absolute *ceteris paribus*—other things being equal. This phrase is invoked so frequently by economists that they often drop in its abbreviation ritualistically, as a Tibetan monk spins a prayer wheel. "*Cet. par.*," they will say, and go about their business. What they are doing is holding unchanged all except one of the factors of a situation or equation and then varying that one to see how it affects the outcome or solution.

To nonprofessionals it often looks as though economists were merely spinning wheels, because other things generally are not equal; but partial analysis is a perfectly legitimate procedure and in many economic problems the only procedure. It is used all the time in busi-

---

4. Sen, *Ethics*, p. 19.

ness, in assigning costs to different parts of an operation, in deciding which advertising pitch pulls best, and so on.

What partial analysis does with the greed question is merely to say that, other things being equal, people want more of whatever it is they want. Moreover, *cet. par.*, people want more money, because, *cet. par.*, money is the best means of getting whatever people want. Thus Mother Teresa, who may have been perfectly altruistic and scornful of anything for herself, might, other things being equal, have been eager for more money to support her charitable causes. She wouldn't compromise her beliefs to get that money but, *cet. par.*—that is, when those beliefs were not affected—she'd go for it. And I, holier than thou though I may be, am the same. With a stroke of the pen, we're all made alike again; willy-nilly, we're all transmogrified into the classical economic man.

None of this is to say that Mother Teresa was greedy or that I am or that you are. We may sometimes act out of self-interest, just as the most depraved miser may sometimes act altruistically. Other things being equal—all contrary considerations aside—the miser would be willing to be a benefactor of his fellowmen, or some of them.

The same sort of reasoning applies to every honorable or dishonorable activity you can name. Aside from things I will not or cannot do, I'd rather be rich than poor (I hear that rich is better). I'd also like to be an internationally respected philosopher and a better bird watcher, have a better second serve, and be well and truly beloved. All of these motives are true under the partial-analysis rule, and they are just as true as my greediness.

We seem, however, to have proved too much. If greed can be established under the partial-analysis rule, every sort of motive or trait or predilection or interest whatever—together with its contrary—can be equally established. Greed is on no surer footing than altruism. Amusingly enough, conventional economics reaches the same conclusion. Competition between perfectly greedy producers is supposed to drive prices down to cost—but perfectly altruistic producers would set prices at cost out of the goodness of their hearts.

We have proved nothing at all. Partial analysis is valid in treating specific and limited problems; it is powerless before a universal problem, such as *all* economic action. Partial analysis can yield only partial results; it cannot yield general results. Whether antiseptically presented as self-interest or as profit maximization and utility maximization, or brazenly acknowledged as greed, the presumed psychological foundations of economics are fallacious.

Without the *ceteris paribus* disclaimer, the universality of economic man cannot be claimed; but with the rule, every sort of man or woman is universal.

THE ANTINOMIES OF GREED

Why should economists have singled out what nonprofessionals call greed as the basis of their study?

On the face of it, it is an astonishing choice, for greed or covetousness is one of the seven deadly sins. Not venial but mortal. This is no casual opinion, but the settled judgment of mankind. A fat anthology could be compiled of notable statements to this effect, and a bulky portfolio collected of artistic embodiments of the idea. From King Midas to Silas Marner, it has been well understood that greed shrivels the soul. St. Augustine wrote, "Every disorder of the soul is its own punishment,"[5] and secular humanists would join the religious in this formulation.

In persisting in talk about greed, economists are like the drunk in the old burlesque skit who searched at the street corner for a wallet he had lost in the middle of the block, because the light was better at the corner. Thus Sir James Steuart, nine years before *The Wealth of Nations*, wrote, "Were every one to act for the public, and neglect

5. St. Augustine, *Confessions*, bk. 1.

himself, the statesman would be bewildered."[6] Steuart's statesman prefers self-centered constituents because he thinks he knows how they'll behave in any situation. In the same way, economists assume they know what greedy economic man will do.

It is not enough, however, for economic man to be greedy; a greedy fool is an unpredictable as a sentimental altruist. Frank Hahn put the apparent solution in a convenient form of words: "I am rather convinced that the rational greedy economic agent will continue in a central role."[7] By "rational," Hahn means, "validly deducible from certain postulates." The chief of these postulates is that economic agents are greedy. Thus saying "rational greedy economic agent" amounts to saying "greedy greedy greedy."

A crucial question that is seldom asked is, What are the limits or controls that the rational greedy economic man must recognize? Can he lie, steal, cheat, terrorize, or kill in maximizing his objectives? Is his honesty merely the best policy, discardable when convenient? Is his morality no more than a prudent wariness of the policeman on the corner?

If these questions cannot be answered affirmatively, why not? A negative answer to any of them indicates that economics is not amoral, and that a rational economic man will be able to justify his actions, must be responsible for them, and cannot pretend to be driven to them by the law of supply and demand or any other economic "law."

There is another meaning of "rational"—as in Aristotle's, "Man is a rational animal." In that sense, rationality is the mark of humanity. It is the foundation of responsibility, as responsibility is the foundation of freedom. Rationality is not a tool usable toward some indifferent end; it is itself the end. It is achieved with struggle and is forever at risk. It is the method and the objective of all the arts and sciences. The alternative is nonsense—not an error or a mistake, but nonsense.

---

6. Steuart, "Inquiry," p. 49.
7. Hahn, *Equilibrium*, p. 68.

How, then, can it be possible to be both rational and greedy? It is not possible. The rational greedy economic man is a contradiction in terms. It is not rational to demean oneself. Our greedy economic man is a fool, after all.

These are what we may call the Three Antinomies of Greed: (1) Profit maximization and utility maximization cannot simultaneously rule us. (2) Other things being equal, greed and its contrary are equally universal. (3) Foolish greed is unpredictable, and rational greed is absurd.

Any one of these is conclusive. Together they overwhelm.

AUTONOMY

Neither self-interest nor utility maximization nor greed will do, and other psychological groundings are no better. Karl Marx hoped to release the creative and productive instincts of mankind by devising an economy in which it would be "possible for me to do one thing today and another tomorrow, to hunt in the morning, fish in the afternoon, rear cattle in the evening, criticise after dinner, just as I have a mind, without ever becoming hunter, fisherman, cowboy or critic."[8] Herbert Marcuse thought that this notorious passage from *The German Ideology*, written in 1846, was a joke, and others have thought it a young man's aberration. But the same notion appears thirty years later in *Critique of the Gotha Program*, where Marx announces that in the communist future, production will not be a problem, because it will have "increased with the all-round development of the individual."[9] Mao's China, during the Great Proletarian Cultural Revolution, made an attempt to reduce Marx's vision to practice. The result was chaos, satisfactory only to rampaging "youth."

---

8. Marx, *German Ideology*, p. 160.
9. Marx, *Gotha Program*, p. 531.

While it might consequently occur to a commonsensical person to question the premises of self-interest or greed or creativity on which these various programs are based, the point here is that motivation is the wrong idea, anyhow. It suggests what people do automatically, what they are programmed to do. In so far as psychology inquires into such doings, it is no longer a suitable foundation for political economy. It played a historical role in helping to free us from absolute kings. But the issue now is not freedom from, but freedom, that is, autonomy.

The way I define myself will dictate the outcome of my search for autonomy. If I start searching in a state of nature, whether nasty or benign, I shall, at every crucial point, find my norm to be an irresponsible existence. If I start in the Garden of Eden, I shall forever yearn for a similarly carefree Heaven.

But if, instead of starting elsewhere, in some erewhon-nowhere of the imagination, I start where I am, what then? If, instead of looking for impersonal laws, I start with myself, who am I? If, instead of directing my attention to others' self-interest, I consider my own self-assertion, what do I find? What does it mean to be a person?

The first requirement of being a person is being—existence. *Cogito ergo sum*; *dubito ergo sum*—there are many ways of saying it. But I do not think unless I have something to think about, nor can I doubt unless I have been credulous. There is, in short, no way of making a standing start; I am always in the midst of life.

Existence requires continuity. Continuity requires identity. I cannot continue in any meaningful sense except as I remain in some way the same. Continuity requires time, and time is not definable unless the present is in some way different from the past.

Self-assertion requires self-maintenance. I must maintain my identity through the time of my existence. I must; I am required to do so; I am compelled to do so. This is a special and curious compulsion. It does not come from outside, like a slave driver's whip. Nor does it come from inside, like a neurosis. This compulsion is the same as my existence. The alternative is nonexistence, nonentity, nothingness.

The self that I maintain—the life that I live—is always threatened with dissolution. Only I can forestall that dissolution. If my dissolution is forestalled, I am the one who does it; it is my doing. I can always let myself go—in indolence, drugs, or death: myriads of ways. If I do not let myself go, I hold myself to my life, to the situation in which I have my being—a situation that is extended in space and in time, in society and in history.

Yet of course I am continually letting go because I cannot hold on. The present is inexorably taken away from me. What makes the past past is change in my life. I am plainly in an impossible situation: I must hold on, I must let go, in the end I shall be defeated. This impossible situation is, nevertheless, the only one possible, the alternative being nothingness—an extinction so complete that it is not even *my* extinction. That same alternative, moreover, forces on me responsibility for my impossible situation. I am the one who must hold on here and let go there, for I do not exist except in this, my holding on and letting go. I do not exist except in my doing, in my willing and acting, and in my accepting the consequences of my acts.

There is no gainsaying the fact that this program is uncongenial to the prevailing temper. People today see themselves in the grip of forces beyond their control. Although C. P. Snow's two cultures fail to understand each other, they tend to agree on their basic irresponsibility. The one is a stranger and afraid, the other a sophisticated servomechanism. Both are in a world they never made. These are the fruits of analysis that starts outside of myself. If I am not I at the start of my search for myself, then there is no one searching, and no search and no discovery.

This much may be granted by the modernist outlook; but almost immediately a move is made to shift off the point, and I am asked to listen to stories of how my search is controlled by my id, or how my perceptions are limited by my genes, or how my judgment is affected by the appearance or nonappearance of certain trace elements in my brain cells. All of these stories may well be true, but they are not the point. The point is that these stories do not tell themselves; someone tells them. They do not sound in a silence. If they are meaningful, they are consistent; and if they are consistent, their consistency will include the teller, for without a teller—you, me, or someone—they cannot be told.

Many are tempted to say that consistency is a false or unnecessary or impossible demand. If so, they cannot tell you or me about it, for their telling depends on the physiological regularity of their voice production and our hearing, on the physical regularity of acoustics, on the historical and social usages of their words. Communication demands at least these consistencies; and as Tom Lehrer says, if you can't communicate, the very least you can do is to shut up.

You may tell stories about my id, genes, and trace elements and thus try to deny my autonomy—and even succeed in doing it. But *your* autonomy as a storyteller still remains and must remain. You may be able to prove that I am out of my mind, crazy, irresponsible; but you cannot at the same time prove your own irresponsibility, for if you are irresponsible, your proof is not worth attending to. At this point some have claimed that they may (willy-nilly) be telling the truth because they have been programmed to do so. Such alleged meaning can only be an external accident, as a watch with a dead battery or a broken mainspring is correct twice a day. The trouble is that there is no way of knowing when the correct accident occurs and so no way of identifying its correctness.

The foregoing may seem simple and too obvious to bother with. To emphasize its importance, let it be boldly said that it is the comprehensive theory of which Einstein's theories, both the general and the special, are instances. Einstein's initial problem was that of synchronizing two clocks. It turned out that the task of synchronization could not be performed except by identifying the specific coordinate system of a specific observer, who said that in his system, from his point of view, the clocks were synchronous. In the Newtonian world of absolute space and time—a coordinate system zeroed by Copernicus on the sun—the point of view of the observer was not considered. In effect, he did not exist. But in actuality he (you and I) does exist, and it was Einstein's great achievement to make his existence and his motion consistent with the existence of a physical world in motion.

In the same way, the consistency of every universe of discourse depends on the integral inclusion of the observer, the experimenter, the storyteller. His or her autonomy must be part of the system. If there is no autonomous observer—if you and I don't exist—there is no way of saying that the system exists. There is no saying at all.

The thrust of what must be postmodernist thought is that consistency demands autonomy. Put it the other way around: No system—no universe of discourse—that denies autonomy is consistent with its own existence. This is true of physics and psychology, the systems that many have tried to substitute for economics, and it is true of economics itself.

ECONOMICS AND PSYCHOLOGY

A consequence of economists' preoccupation with their special pseudo-psychology has been distraction from proper economic concerns. Keynes spent many pages of his great book analyzing the various motives for what he called liquidity preference, and his successors have spent many pages discussing his analysis. Yet in the end it does not matter whether money is withheld for the transactions motive or the precautionary motive or the speculative motive.[10] The economic consequence is the same either way; it is the withholding that matters. When the economic consequence is considered, it is seen that liquidity preference is effectively the same as speculation, although the motives may be quite different.

---

10. Keynes, *General Theory*, p. 195.

Economics and the law are both divisions of ethics. An important distinction between them is that motive or intention is central in the law but is insignificant in economics. A man is discovered with a smoking gun in his hand, standing over a bleeding corpse. It may be quickly proved that homicide has been committed by the man with the gun. But what did the man intend? If the killing was done with malice aforethought, it was murder. If it was done in a sudden rage, it was manslaughter. If the gun happened to go off when the man tripped, it was accidental death. If the killer shot to defend himself, the homicide is justifiable. And if the killer is unable to distinguish right from wrong, he is not a criminal, but may be, as they say, institutionalized. That a man has been killed is the beginning, not the end, of the law's concern.

With economics, it is the other way entirely. The intentions of economic agents matter only to them or to those entitled to pass judgment on them, but not to the economy—and not at all, as far as economic consequences are concerned, even to the agents themselves. Entrepreneurs may, with the best intention in the world, set the price for their products too high (or too low) and thus ruin their companies, their investors, their employees, and themselves. Their good intentions do not mitigate their companies' losses or the consequent diminishing of the GDP. Or, monetary authorities may raise the interest rate with the intention of keeping prices down; if the actual consequence is that prices are raised, that is what matters, not the intention. Or, three centuries ago mercantilist nations held that money was gold or some such commodity, which they therefore accumulated; they prospered not because they had gold but because, having lots of what for them was money, they kept the interest rate down.

Intentions, of course, matter in ethics and the law. They do not matter in economics proper. Thus all talk of profit *motive* or liquidity *preference* or *propensity* to consume is beside the point. Motive, preference, and propensity are psychological concepts. The economic questions are profit, liquidity, and consumption *tout court*.

Nothing in the foregoing denies (or affirms) the validity of any proposition in psychology or the virtue of the study of psychology. Every human action can be studied from the points of view of all the arts and most of the sciences. Nothing I do is without physical aspect; there is never a time when I do not obey the laws of motion, when I can step off a moving train without experiencing a rude, and equal and opposite, reaction. Nothing I ever do is without physiological aspect. If you prick me, I will bleed, and the blood will accelerate toward the ground at the rate of 32 feet per second per second. Nothing I do is without emotional content, and your assault will make me angry or sad. Nor is there much I do that is in principle noneconomic; if I stay home to nurse my wound, I'll also suffer a loss of income. But the acceleration of my falling blood is irrelevant to my loss of income.

Just as it would be a confusion of terms to say that the attraction of positive and negative charges for each other is an expression of love, or that the stars in their courses reveal the greatness of Beethoven, so it is a confusion of terms to search for psychological explanations of economic events.

THE ETHICAL SANCTION

The fathers of economics told us they were studying the implications of our self-interest. For our part, we concluded that our subject was rather our self-maintenance or self-assertion, and we have found that, even for the most abstract and recondite sciences, such assertion is an indispensable point of departure.

The assertive self is what is generally called the will. There are three aspects of the will that are especially important for our study of economics: it is embodied, it has a past, and it has limits.

To say that the will is embodied is merely to say that I am part of my world. Whatever the world is—matter or energy or spirit or what you will—that I am also. If it were not so, the consistency we have spoken of would be empty and our accounts of the world meaningless. On the most ordinary level, if I were not part of the world—and the world not part of me—I could simply let it go, forget about it, pay it no mind. Of course, my body would then melt, thaw, and resolve itself into a dew, but this disintegration of my body would not, on the premises, affect me. All who believe this are welcome to act upon it. Those of us who remain will conclude that the natural world is not a matter of indifference to us, because our body makes us a part of it and it a part of us. That we are embodied is constitutional, not accidental.

The limitation of my will follows from its existence. Whatever exists can be defined. Whatever is defined is this, not that. I am *not-you*. Because you are thus essential to my definition, you are, in the most fundamental sense, essential to me. If I destroy you, I destroy part of myself. My existence may require your destruction, as in war; but whenever and however I wrong you, I diminish myself. This is the ethical sanction; there is no other.

My autonomy requires this sanction. It is not imposed on me but is flesh of my flesh and bone of my bone. In detail, it may be concerned with my superego, with encapsulated love for or fear of my parents, or with what I learned before (or after) the age of seven. But in principle, and regardless of the details, it is an aspect of the compulsion that I maintain my existence.

As a consequence of the compulsion to maintain my existence, I must maintain yours; and on this requirement economics is grounded. Economics is not a question of an alleged propensity to barter or to seek profit, nor is it a question of the properties of numbers. Nor since the Commercial and Industrial Revolutions has anyone's comfort or physical existence been an insoluble concern. Household management is not now the problem—not even of the national household.

Economics is a question of the relations of human beings with one another. These relations are free; therefore they can be judged and controlled. Whatever is determined is beyond control.

Economic relations are special relations in that they are all concerned with money. Money is the distinguishing idea of economics. Without money, all the other economic ideas either do not appear (price) or fall back into general ethics (rights) or general psychology (demand) or general physiology (consumption) or agriculture and engineering (production).

To money, therefore, we now direct our attention.

PART II

PRINCIPLES OF ANY FUTURE ECONOMICS

4

Money: The Distinguishing Mark of Economics

Because we have money, we can be autonomous. However else it may be defined, money is a thing that enables us to move freely through space and time. Without money, we should have to consume our produce nearly where and when we produced it.

In a tribal society, in which all aspects of one's relationships and work and worship are foreordained, one has no need for money. Indeed, personal ownership of money weakens and generally dissolves tribal bonds. In medieval times, serfs were bound to the land not only by custom and force but by the need to sleep and feed. Without money, they could not survive far from the manor, and the same was true of the lord himself unless he could count on the hospitality of a neighbor. When money reappeared at the end of the Dark Ages, and the corvée and other duties could be (and eventually had to be) satisfied with money, the feudal system was doomed. Taxation is a mark of a free society.

According to tradition, money was invented in Lydia, a small kingdom in western Asia Minor, in the seventh century B.C. Before that time and place many of the functions of money were served in various ways, but money as we know it did not exist. It was unknown to the heroes of whom Homer sang. There is little mention of it in the Old Testament. Yet without money our present civilization could not exist, could not have come into existence. As we cannot escape history, we cannot escape money.

David Hume and many others have written that money is a convenience: "Tis the oil, which renders the motion of the wheels more smooth and easy." But it is more than that, and different from that. It is not a convenience or a tool. A hammer is a tool; it is useful—arguably necessary—in building a building, but the finished structure—even the partially finished structure—can be, and is, described and defined without reference to hammers or saws or wrenches used in construction. A yardstick, however, is different. Measuring is essential not only in the construction of the building but in the specification of the size of the whole and of the parts, and of the relation of part to part. Without measuring, the structure is formless, and a description of it is merely a list of building materials and their sense qualities. Measuring is similarly necessary and creative in economic affairs, and economic measuring is done with money.

In general, measuring is a comparing of something with some standard. By laying a ruler across this book, we determine that the page is about 5 3/4— inches wide. But how long is an inch? Well, an inch is 1/36 of a yard, and since 1893 a yard has been 3600/3973 of a meter. Originally, as one of the reforms of the French Revolution, a meter was defined as 1/1000 of a kilometer, which in turn was 1/10000 of the surface distance from the equator to either pole. Of course, that distance could not be measured directly, especially not by laying a meter stick along the route ten million times (that would be a literally circular fallacy). Instead, reliance was put on geometry, which gave the circumference of the earth as $2\pi r$, and the distance from the pole to the equator as $2\pi r/4$. The radius of the earth is stated in terms of some unit of measurement. When it was first calculated with reasonable accuracy, by Eratosthenes in the third century B.C., the unit was the stadium, which may have been equal to 600 of some king's feet. In Newton's time, and in the time of the French Revolution, the unit was the yard, which may have been the circumference of some king's belly or the length of some king's stride. So we have come full circle after all: A yard is defined in terms of a meter, and a meter is defined in terms of a yard.

In the meantime, frequent refinements in calculating the radius of the earth led to unsettling changes in the length of a meter. Consequently it was agreed that a meter was the distance between two scratches on a certain platinum-iridium bar. This bar, which was deposited in Sèvres, outside Paris, was obviously more precise than the meter stick incised on a slab of marble that in 1848 was built into the wall of the Chancellery (now the Ministry of Justice) in the Place Vendôme in Paris, where it can still be seen. Both meter sticks—the marble one and the platinum-iridium one—were artificial. We do not find meters in nature, as we find sticks and stones. The present standard, in use since 1984, which is equal to the distance light travels through a vacuum in 1/299792458 second, is presumably more convenient and more precise, at least for some scientific purposes, but it is no less artificial. In the end, as it was in the beginning, we stand up and declare that *this* is a meter, and no fooling. Our declaration is artificial, but it is not arbitrary. We can and must make it because of the history of our struggle to make our world our own. It is an act of will.

There are two further points to be made about measuring. First, the relationship between the measuring standard and the thing measured is not reciprocal. This book is about 5 3/4 inches wide; but an inch is not defined as 4/23 of the width of this book. The standard defines the thing, not vice versa; the alternative is circular reasoning of the sort that threatened us at the start of the metric system.

Second, the meter standard, although perfectly artificial and, moreover, consciously agreed upon, is not a convention in the sense that a red light means danger or stop or the port side of a ship, or that a tennis set, which used to have to be won by two games, can now be settled by a tiebreak. The nautical rules of the road, which are conventional, require ships meeting head-on to pass red to red, that is, left side to left side; and everyone, with the exception of the British, the Japanese, and some others, has adopted the same system for highways and airways. It is convenient to have an agreed-on system; but it would not be impossible for drivers of automobiles meeting each other to get out and debate the right of way, as I have seen happen on a narrow road in Greece. Without the rules of the road, no one has the right of way, but the right of way implies nothing beyond itself. Using a yardstick, on the other hand, defines spatial relations, and hence space. Space is an inevitability, not a convenience. A game, of course, is not even a convenience. The introduction of the tiebreak changed the strategy of tennis, but this matters only to tennis players, and no one has to be a tennis player. One can't help being spatially oriented, and the orientation had better be measurable. If not, the physical universe is beyond comprehension and ordinary life chancy as a squirrel's.

MEASURING AND MEASUREMENT

The ancients were casual about weights and measures. The cubit was the distance from one's elbow to the tip of one's middle finger. Obviously this changed from person to person, and in the same person from time to time. Limited attempts at standardization were made then (or have been made by scholars), so that it is said that the ancient Egyptian cubit was 52.5 cm, while the Greek was 46.29 cm, the Hebrew 44.65 cm, and the Roman 44.36 cm. Measurement of time was even more vagrant, since everywhere except in Egypt the time from sunrise to sunset was divided into twelve hours, and likewise the time from sunset to sunrise, the length of an hour thus varying from day to night, from season to season, and from latitude to latitude. The Western world consequently had no reliable clock until the fourteenth century, and even two hundred years later so much ingenuity was invested in making clocks that showed the phases of the moon and the like that fine measurement was disregarded and Galileo had trouble timing his first experiments with a jury-rigged water clock.

In any event, there was little need for universal systems of measurement until the rise of experimental science. As long as the world was a parade of miracles and portents, measurement played a small role in understanding, and replication of awesome events was unthinkable. Precision was, to be sure, required in building, and it was readily attained: foundations were level, the proportion of part to part was meticulously observed, and stones were fitted one to another so closely that a knife blade could not be slipped between them. Such precision, however, did not need to be universal; it merely needed to be consistent within the bounds of each separate building. Whatever the cubit used in the construction of the Parthenon, it was strictly followed, but a different unit could have been used for the Odeon of Herodes Atticus, a stone's throw away. In the same way it was, within the memory of men now living, not unusual for New England farmers to erect barns using not a yardstick but a "story pole," various multiples of which yielded the desired proportions. I myself have used a story pole and found it handy in building a trued and squared playroom in a roughly finished cellar.

Local systems of measurement are satisfactory for local purposes. Among many examples, medieval Vienna required its bakers to measure their loaves against standard sizes carved on the wall to the left of the main portal of St. Stephen's; in Renaissance Ragusa (Dubrovnik), the standard cubit was that of a statue of Roland or Orlando that still stands in the town square. Specific large projects, such as those of Eratosthenes and Newton, could make do with some local system; and in any case, astronomy had long had one important universal system—the Babylonian invention of degrees, minutes, and seconds for measuring angles.

Although the scientific revolution had started in the sixteenth century, it was not until after the invention of the metric system that the remarkable burgeoning of physical science began. In the same way, trade requires reasonably stable measuring units, and the spread of such units calls trade into existence. The Lydian invention, which was quickly and widely embraced in the Mediterranean world, made possible the slow, halting, and still-continuing shift away from a world of plunder and rapine.

The facts that trade grew so slowly, that almost every jurisdiction boasted its own currency, based on its own weight measure, that statistical information was almost nonexistent, and that for two and a half millennia the only money that men were conscious of was coined metal—these facts for a long time hid the further fact that although both a yardstick and a dollar are measuring units, they measure in fundamentally different ways.

THE AMBIGUITY OF MONEY

When my wife and I were buying our present house, I made some measurements, using a steel tape I've since lost, and determined that the room I'm now writing in was eleven feet two inches by sixteen feet seven inches. That was twenty-five years ago. This morning I measured the room again, using a wood (presumably birch) yardstick given me by the local hardware store. The answer this morning was the same as that a quarter century ago: eleven two by sixteen seven.

Now, when we bought the house all those years ago, we paid a certain number of dollars for it. Of course, we gave the seller a certified check, but we could have legally tendered him a stack of dollar bills. If I were to sell the house today, I'd receive from the buyer a certified check, but the number of dollars represented by the check would (I trust) be considerably greater than what we paid. If the buyer tendered me a stack of dollar bills, they'd look almost the same as those of twenty-five years ago, but it would take many more of them to accomplish the same purpose. The house would be substantially the same, but the price would be different. On the record it's hard to avoid concluding that the measuring unit has changed.

Nothing like this happens with physical measuring units. The steel tape I lost expanded or contracted a bit as the weather was warmer or cooler, but this change could, if necessary, be allowed for, or the temperature controlled. If a thermometer is calibrated so that the freezing point for distilled water at sea level is 32 degrees and the boiling point 212 degrees, then the normal temperature of the human body will be 98.6 degrees today, as it was yesterday or last century. If the boiling point is taken as 100 degrees and the freezing point 0 degrees, it is easy to make the appropriate conversions from Fahrenheit to Celsius. Without this uniformity, chemistry would be impossible or infinitely reduced in power. A talented cook can achieve brilliant results by seasoning to taste; but if you want to get water from hydrogen and oxygen, your proportions have to be precise, and precise proportions will always give you the same result.

It is clear that a dollar does not measure physical properties of objects, nor does a yardstick measure economic properties. Nowhere is there a standard for the franc or the dollar similar to the platinum-iridium bar at Sèvres. Even when the dollar was said to be redeemable for 15 5/21 grains of gold 9/10 fine, there was no need for—indeed no possibility of—comparing a dollar bill with a lump (very small) of such gold. Furthermore, a mason can lay his meter stick against a stone he wants to measure and immediately have his answer, but there is no point to laying a dollar bill alongside something one wants to buy. A physical measurement is direct and absolute, but a monetary measurement is somehow different.

Unlike shoes and sealing wax, money is ambiguous in its meaning. The dollar bill I have in my pocket is an asset to me, but represents a debt of the nation. The balance in my checking account is also an asset to me, but it is a liability to the bank. On the other hand, the check I put in the mail to my creditor will be an asset to him but a debit to me. In contrast, goods are goods to whoever holds them and are nothing to anybody else, except as they enter into and so swell the national commerce.

Another ambiguity of money was revealed by Keynes's analysis of liquidity preference, which is partly a function of the convenience of keeping money at hand for the transaction of ordinary business, partly a preparation for investment or speculation, and partly a function of holding money as a store of wealth because of uncertainty about the trend of the economy (and that, too, is a form of speculation). A strong preference for liquidity thus indicates grave doubts about future business and, at the same time, great faith in the continuing strength of the money-issuing institution, which strength must in turn be partly based on the state of business.

INDEXING

We should not be surprised to have discovered that economics and Newtonian physics, which are fundamentally different, should have fundamentally different ways of measuring. It is nevertheless disturbing to find money floating, as it were, between goods, instead of setting an unequivocal value to each one; and this idea has been resisted, and is resisted to this day.

Historians as well as economists feel a recurring need for some sort of constant that will permit comparisons of income and costs from year to year or century to century and from place to place. Hence the Bureau of Labor Statistics publishes the Consumer Price Index and the Producer Price Index, while the Federal Reserve Board publishes the Industrial Production Index. There are many other indexes, both official and unofficial, at this level of sophistication.

Lay citizens speak of the purchasing power of money and call attention to the declining value of the dollar. This way of speaking seems to assume that money has value, like any good or service, and that this value can be measured. Measuring the value of the dollar would mean comparing it with something else, either the "market basket" of the Consumer Price Index or something similar. Although the contents of the market basket can be changed by legislative or executive or merely bureaucratic fiat, the basket seems real, while money seems only nominal or, as Karl Marx called it, a "purely ideal or mental"[1] form of value. But measurement, as we have seen, is not reciprocal; so if the "value" of money is stated in terms of a market basket, the basket becomes the standard of measurement, and money becomes a curious commodity with a curious price.

There is no objection in principle to making this market basket, or any part of it, or anything else our monetary unit. As everyone who has had a little Latin or Anglo-Saxon knows, many ancient peoples counted their wealth in terms of cattle, as the Masai do today. This is clumsy and imprecise, but not impossible. But if we did something like this, we should not delude ourselves into thinking we had established a "constant dollar."

No market basket is the same to different people at any given time. My wife and I set up housekeeping many years ago; so we became relatively unconcerned with the price of furniture. Nor is that basket the same in different historical situations. Of all the things in the basket, the price of bread is sometimes urged as basic, and it was indeed a central issue in the French Revolution. But today food is so small a part of the family budget, and bread so indifferent a part of the diet, that all the bakeries in the land could shut down tomorrow without causing much inconvenience, let alone starvation. It is the same with indexes of industrial prices; the price of steel is of less importance to a book publisher than it is to a builder of office buildings, and it is more to a builder today than it was before the inventions of the elevator and the electric light made skyscrapers feasible.

---

1. Marx, *Capital*, p. 107.

The constructors of indexes are of course not unaware of such shifts of demand, and they try to keep up with them by shifting and refining the contents of their market baskets. Such shifting obviously compromises the constancy of the index, which thus becomes a historical standard, like any other form of money.

Although the attempt to devise a constant dollar is often launched in the hope that the economic world can thereby be placed beyond the reach of human judgment and the errors and vices to which it is prone, it is not so easy to escape the necessity for judgment. Indexing, in fact, depends on judgment from the very beginning, for someone (or a committee of someones) must decide which items are to be included and how the various items are to be weighted. And someone must decide how the weighting is to be changed from time to time.

In the extreme case, indexing is far from harmless. The reason is appropriately given in a 1923 lament of Hans von Raumer, minister of economics in the Weimar Republic then awash in one of the notorious hyperinflations of all time. "The root of the evil," Raumer complained, "is the depreciation adjustment [that is, the index]. Inflation goes on unchecked because one must add enormous increments onto wages and prices alike, and these in their turn work in such a manner that the depreciation provided for actually occurs through the inflation thus caused."[2]

CREDIT

Starting, very likely, with the first coinage in Lydia, there has also been a search—or a longing—for some rare and durable commodity (usually gold or silver) to act in the same way as an unchanging yardstick. The trouble with this notion is that money has never been merely a

---

2. von Raumer, p. 126.

rare and durable commodity. Even when such a commodity has been the money of account, the work of money has also been done in other ways. A society in which the only acknowledged money is gold, and in which fractional-reserve banking is unknown or prohibited, will still do much—perhaps most—of its business on credit. Small retail transactions may be carried out with cash on the barrelhead, but any work done for hire—to take the simplest case—involves credit. Either the work is paid for in advance, in which case the hirer is extending credit to the hired, or, in the more usual case, the hired extends credit by doing the work first and being paid weekly or monthly or when the job is done. There is, in fact, no other way of doing such business; if the pay were measured out as the work proceeded, both the hired and the hirer would be too preoccupied to get the job itself done.

This credit relationship does not, of course, increase the number of gold coins circulating in the economy. If in my business the application of a hundred dollars' worth of labor to a hundred dollars' worth of raw materials will produce something I can sell for three hundred dollars, I need only a hundred dollars to get things rolling. I use my money—all hard coin carefully counted out—to buy the raw materials. When my employees have done their work, I take the finished product and sell it for the three hundred dollars, again hard coin, a hundred dollars of which I pay to my employees, leaving me with my original hundred dollars plus a hundred dollars' profit. Putting the profit aside for consideration in another chapter, we see that my implicit credit arrangement with my employees, together with my skill or luck in selling the product quickly (or in advance), made it possible for my hundred dollars to underwrite the work of several hundred dollars. Everything was paid for in hard coin. No substitute was offered or accepted. Credit made work for my employees, a profit for me, and goods for the purchaser.

There are four important lessons to be learned from this little scenario. The first is that money is not merely a method of measuring a static situation but is essential for planning and contracting ahead. The employees and I could agree on the work and the pay because money enabled us to compare the value to each of us of their present work and their future pay. As a yardstick measures and thus defines a static situation, money measures and thus defines a dynamic situation, one in which people reach present agreement for future action. Without money, the employment relationship is at best sharecropping and at worst slavery.

The second lesson is a corollary of the first. Money functions in planning ahead; it is commonly called a store of value but is more precisely called a store of buying power. My employees can agree to work today for money next week because money next week will be useful. Money next week can be useful because it is not consumed in trade. Goods and services are ultimately consumed, but money is not.[3] Money may be lost in speculation, as we shall see in Chapter 14, but it is not consumed. The work for which I pay my employees will be over and done with, but the money I pay them will perform its function again and again. Indeed, if it could not do so, it could not function at all. My employees would not accept my money for their services if they could not subsequently use it to buy goods or services themselves.

The third lesson is the implicit one that money is not an isolated phenomenon. Even in our relatively primitive scenario, it is an element—a necessary element—in a financial system that in turn is a necessary element in an economic system and a society. That the gold

---

3. Understanding trade as barter, St. Thomas wrote, "Now money, according to the Philosopher [Aristotle], . . . was invented chiefly for the purpose of exchange [*Nichomachean Ethics*, 1133a]: and consequently the proper and principal use of money is in its consumption or alienation whereby it is sunk in exchange." ("Whether It Is a Sin to Take Usury for Money Lent," in *Summa Theologica*.) The story seems to be that I sell you so much beef for a dollar and you sell me so much bread for a dollar; I eat my roll and you eat your hamburger and you have your dollar back. The dollar was merely a convenience or, as Say put it much later, a veil; hence St. Thomas could argue the money was not necessary and did not deserve to earn interest.

coins I paid my workmen were minted by the system is obvious. The rules for acceptance and circulation of the coins were developed by the system and are part of the system. And so on. In the modern capitalist economy the financial system is articulated and complex and constantly developing (not always in directions devoutly to be wished). As Alex J. Pollock points out, it is primarily the lack of such a system (and the difficulty of its creation out of the void) that impedes the advance of Russia into a free economy.

The fourth lesson is that money is what John William Miller called a functioning object. The functioning of a yardstick—measuring—defines space. The functioning of money—buying and selling—defines commerce, creates commerce, calls enterprise into existence. Physics is what you do when you measure with yardsticks, clocks, voltmeters. Economics is what you do when you exchange or contract for money.

COUNTING MONEY

If you want to know how much money you have, how do you set about counting it? You can count your spoons and arrive at a precise number that will satisfy even an analytical philosopher. Bertrand Russell writes, "If a set of numbers can be used as names of a set of objects, each number occurring only once, the number of numbers used as names is the same as the number of objects."[4] This may seem like an odd procedure, but you can follow it with your spoons and will then know how many people (presumably counting them the same way) you can invite to dinner.

When you seem to do that with the cash in your pocket, it would appear that the folding money is a different sort of object from the coin. The number of greenbacks you have is less significant than the

---

4. Russell, *External World*, p. 147.

figures engraved on each one. Still more esoteric and insubstantial is the money you have in a checking account, which can nevertheless be added to and subtracted from and thus counted. But there's more to it than that. You may have some stocks and bonds, perhaps all of them listed on the New York Stock Exchange and so sufficiently liquid for you to sell them at a moment's notice; the money you can get for them nevertheless varies from moment to moment. Others of your holdings are probably less liquid. If you have a house for sale, it will almost certainly take you weeks, and may take you months, to find a buyer willing to pay you almost what you hope it's worth. What you might get for your books and furniture is even more dubious.

Your stocks and bonds and house and chattels are counted as part of your wealth but not part of your money. This seems a distinction without a difference, because your credit depends in part on your wealth. For most of us, with comparatively little net wealth, credit depends on income. In either case, we can spend our credit like ordinary money—and more easily than ordinary money, a credit card being more convenient to handle than a pocketful of change. The total credit we have is not fixed, and it depends upon our continuing sources of income, that is, upon us as going concerns.

Because I don't throw away all my junk mail, I now have three bank credit cards, not to mention a couple put out by department stores—each stating a different line of credit. Almost every mail brings me another that I can have merely for answering a few not remarkably searching questions. In addition, my bank tells me I can overdraw my account for what they pretend to believe is a trifling fee, and four other banks offer to refinance my mortgage at a bargain rate more than double what we paid when we bought the house.

All of this is credit. But it is not money. It is not even potential money (whatever that might be), for at least some of these eager purveyors of credit are likely to exchange information and begin to wonder whether I'm such a good risk after all.

To become money, my credit or pseudo-credit must become actual. I must draw it down—that is, borrow on it. It then becomes actual and determinate. Credit becomes money by becoming debt. Money looks both ways, like a contract. It is an acknowledgment of indebtedness. Federal Reserve notes, which are, as they say on their face, "legal tender for all debts, public and private," were issued by the government in payment for some good or service, and the government will take them back in payment for some fee or tax. Until the government does take the notes back, it is in debt to whoever holds them.

FIAT MONEY

Money has no price (it would make no sense to pay $100 for $100); but the fee for the use of money, which is interest, does have a price. In the United States, the basis for this price is established by the Federal Reserve Board. The federal funds rate is the lowest rate at which banks can be sure of getting money; hence, it is the implied or explicit starting point for negotiations. Without such a starting point, borrowers and lenders would be as unsure of what to offer as were the Pilgrims and Massasoit in setting the price of corn.

As the Reserve, an official arm of the government, sets the rate, it determines a vital aspect of the sort of society we will have. It is a willful act of the Reserve, which itself was established by a willful act of the people. In technical jargon, our money is fiat money. To this extent, the gold standard was no different. The "value" of a gold dollar was said to be determined by the cost of mining and refining gold bullion, and of course that cost was denominated in gold dollars.

Only in a command society is money legal tender merely because the state promulgates a law to that effect. In a free society, the economic reason for accepting money is that it can certainly be exchanged for goods and services; and as the adage has it, taxes are the one certain thing in one's lifetime. The state buys goods and services and pays its money for them. That money, which is nothing but the state's IOUs, then circulates freely, not because of its design or physical specifications, not because of its "backing" or convertibility into something else, but because of its acceptability by the tax collector. The Continental Congress had authority to issue money, but it did not have power to tax; so its notes were "not worth a Continental."

Money is a tradeable claim on the economy. The claim can take many and various forms. The actuality of the claim is what matters. In a primitive society the claim comes into existence through saving. In a somewhat more advanced society (such as the one of our employment scenario of a few pages back), there is also the factor of income anticipation in the employees' lending of their labor power. In a capitalist economy, profit anticipation is the major organizer of economic activity.

Both income anticipation and profit anticipation require contracting or planning ahead; so neither is possible (sharecropping and slavery aside) without money. Trade between households or firms that are widely separated in space or time is impossible as a routine activity without money of account. Besides facilitating commerce and industry, money is *ipso facto* a store of wealth; it is always equal to itself, and it does not grow on trees. Because money is a store of wealth, it can be withheld from both investment and consumption by economic agents puzzled by uncertain opportunities. (As John William Miller said, "There is no science of what to do next.")[5]

As conventional economics imagines the world, profits are immediately spent, preferably reinvested. There is then no need for borrowing or lending except to help someone in an emergency. (The absence of necessary borrowing partly explains the inability of equilibrium economics to find a place for money in its system.) Production then creates its own demand, and economic progress is serene and steady. There are no failures, there is no waste, and there are no unused resources or unemployed workers.

Because the future is unforeseeable, we do have failures and waste. Our profits are consequently too small to employ all the resources and

5. Miller, *Paradox of Cause*, p. 96. See Davidson, *Post Keynesian*, chap. 6, for the implications of uncertainty in economics.

workers. But they could be employed if we could anticipate the results. Entrepreneurs cannot guarantee results, but they can try to anticipate them. They borrow to achieve them, thus creating money.

THE MONEY SUPPLY

Since money takes such various forms, determination of the money supply becomes a question for monetary theory. It is more a scholarly conundrum than an actual problem for the world we live in. The Federal Reserve releases four different estimates of the supply every Friday, but the business press pays little or no attention. *Barron's*, *Business Week*, *The Economist*, and *Forbes* don't bother to print the figures, although they regularly report various interest rates.

One may regard with some bewilderment the lists of objects that make up the Reserve's definitions of M1, M2, M3, and "Monetary Base (St. Louis)." M1 consists of currency, traveler's checks, and checking deposits. M2 adds ordinary savings and time deposits, money-market funds, and overnight Eurodollar deposits, but it does not count time deposits of $100,000 or more. M3 has no $100,000 limitation and also counts repurchase agreements (REPOS). On August 14, 2000, the seasonally adjusted totals were M1, $1,090.8 billion; M2, $4,806.6 billion; M3, $6,831.9 billion. The "Monetary Base (St. Louis)," which satisfies a monetary theory that has its orgins in the St. Louis branch of the Federal Reserve, was $590.3 billion. For many years another estimate, "L," was published; it included in addition nonbank public holdings of U.S. savings bonds, short-term Treasury securities, commercial paper, and banker's acceptances, net of money-market mutual-fund holdings of these securities.

The range of the estimates is extraordinary. M1, which is the one the Federal Reserve tried to control for several years following 1979, is double St. Louis's "Monetary Base" but a quarter of M2, which the Reserve still claims to try to target, but no longer uses, as it once did, as an indicator of future inflation. And M3 is six times M1.

It also should be noted that while the Bank of England, the European Central Bank, and other central banks also talk about M1 and M2, they don't always mean what the Federal Reserve means. The variety of the estimates suggests that there is no "realistic" way of counting our national money—at least no way that would satisfy a Bertrand Russell. The reason, of course, is that our money is not real in the sense that our spoons are real.

Money is not a commodity, not even a commodity of a special sort. It is certainly an object. It may be metal or paper, stone or beads, an entry in a ledger or a byte in a computer hard drive; its physical specifications are not what make it money. It is money because it is used as money—because it functions as money.

The recognition that money is not a commodity is a historical turning that is still not complete. It marks the transition from mercantilism to capitalism. Mercantilism was not altogether unlike a barter system. Merchant adventurers traded commodities for gold and silver, and both they and their sovereign hoarded gold and silver, which they could do because gold and silver were commodities.

Business practice today has generally made the turn. Enterprise is ongoing. The actual market is open; it is not "cleared." But theory, especially monetary theory, is still quasi-mercantilist. As we scan the hodgepodge of items the Reserve lists under its Ms and L, we are struck by the fact that all of them, except for a few in L, are static. They are sitting in bank vaults or on computer disks. They may be ready for work, but they're mostly not working, and there's no assurance that they'll ever be called to work. They are in effect hoards, finite and physical, like the treasure heaped up by the mercantilists.

THE MONEY SUPPLY AND PRICE LEVEL

Although a person can become rich by accumulating money, a nation must accumulate and distribute commodities, and it must have a system for continuing to do so. A nation cannot become rich merely by multiplying the amount of its money in circulation. Running the presses at the Bureau of Engraving and Printing faster, or printing hundred-dollar bills where only one-dollar bills were printed before, will not affect the national wealth. Likewise, raising the prices of all goods and services will at most make work for those who change the price tags.

These facts have suggested to some that the quantity of money in circulation has a determinate effect on the price level—on inflation or deflation. In brief, the theory holds that the greater the money supply, the higher the price level. More money will be chasing fewer—or the same—goods; so prices will rise. It seems obvious.

Let us assume that half the citizens of your village have a supply of some one good, and that the other half have a supply of some conveniently coined money. Say 100 goods and $100. If goods are exchanged for dollars, the price will be a dollar apiece. But suppose the president or the chairman of the Federal Reserve Board or the Tooth Fairy decrees that when the sun rises over Passamaquoddy Bay tomorrow morning, everyone who went to bed with $100 will wake up with $200. When the exchange is made now, the price has jumped to two dollars apiece. Now generalize the situation. Introduce as many goods as you need or want, and you will be tempted to conclude that doubling—or merely increasing—the money supply is a sure prescription for inflation.

The silent—and illicit—assumption is that all the many and various commodities—from safety pins to bulldozers, from hairstyling to heart surgery—that are brought to market in your village are sold, that the villagers spend all their money in buying them, and that the market is cleared. It has been an exhausting day, and one not likely to be repeated, although the theory would seem to require that the new holders of the money get rid of it as soon as it crosses their palms.

David Hume, a progenitor of the quantity theory of money, was also one of the first to observe (but perhaps not appreciate) the error. "If the coin be lockt up in chests," he wrote, " 'tis the same thing with regard to prices as if it were annihilated: If the commodities be hoarded in granaries, a like effect follows. As the money and commodities, in these cases, never meet, they cannot affect each other."[6]

The only money that matters is functioning money. The money in the chests will stay there until someone lowers the price at the granaries, or, conversely, the commodities in the granaries will remain until someone offers a higher price for them. In both cases, it is an offered and accepted price that governs the exchange, not the quantity of money or the quantity of goods.

THE INTEREST RATE

According to the quantity theory of money, the price level is a function of the quantity of commodities and the quantity of money. The Federal Reserve Board has only the most tenuous influence on the first quantity and can't make up its mind about the other; so the theory would seem to be estopped before it starts. In any case, the curious fact is that what is actually done by the Federal Reserve Board has no direct effect on any of the items listed under the various Ms and the L. The Federal Reserve doesn't issue traveler's checks, and it doesn't create commercial paper or banker's acceptances. It doesn't even print additional banknotes, except to the order of the Treasury. What it does do is make it more or less expensive, or more or less difficult, for banks to lend money.

If it wants to contract the money supply, the Reserve generally does one or both of two things: (1) By raising the federal funds rate or the discount rate (interest rates that banks pay for short-term loans from member banks or from the Reserve) the Reserve increases the banks' cost of funds and hence the rates the banks charge their customers. (2) By selling government securities at low prices (that is, bearing high

6. David Hume, "Of Money," in *Political Discourses*.

interest rates), it leads banks to commit their reserves to government securities, rather than to business loans, and increases the interest that banks can earn in perfect safety, consequently inducing them to raise the rates they charge their commercial customers. Thus the immediate effect of the Board's operations is to raise the general interest rate. The Reserve also has the power to increase banks' reserve requirements, thus reducing their capacity to lend, but has used it sparingly in recent years.

Although the Reserve has, from its beginning, had control of the money supply among its objectives, the immediate effects of its actions are on the interest rate. The Reserve's theory says that the money supply is an independent variable, but the practice treats the money supply as a dependent variable. (As we shall see in a later chapter, supply in general is a dependent variable.)

Of course, the interest rate has an effect on the price level, for it is a cost of doing business. Books written only a few years ago tended to make light of this cost, for the rate was then low.[7] At the present time, however, interest costs are more than 20 percent of GDP.[8]

The cream of the jest is that a high interest rate, introduced to contract the money supply, usually with the intention of lowering prices, has actually increased costs and so has forced increases in prices. Moreover, should the Board use its currently disused power and increase

---

7. A frequently cited report of the role the interest rate played in 13,119 cases collected at the Harvard Business School through 1938 shows only 10 cases in which interest was a substantial factor and only 30 in which it was even mentioned. See J. F. Ebersole, "The Influence of Interest Rates upon Entrepreneurial Decisions in Business," *Harvard Business Review* 17 (Jan.–Feb. 1939): 35–39.

8. A warning: Giving interest costs, the money supply, and other statistics as percentages of GDP does not imply that these percentages can be summed to 100 percent (they can't). But since GDP varies from year to year with the size of the economy and the rate of inflation, as do these statistics, the percentages of one year can be compared with the percentages of another with reasonably small distortion.

banks' reserve requirements, the consequences would be similar, at least in the short run. For the demand for money is a demand that must be constantly met by every business. It is difficult or impossible to change plans rapidly on short notice, because business is an ongoing affair. Thus a sudden reduction in the availability of borrowable funds would force businesses to pay higher interest rates and charge higher prices (or absorb losses), at least until their plans could be modified (reduced, actually) to meet the new conditions.

In times of recession or depression, the Reserve may try to increase the money supply. It turns out, however, that while a contraction of the supply is said to have an effect after a two-year lag,[9] an attempted expansion may have no effect at all, as the recent experience of Japan demonstrates. Economic agents will respond as seems reasonable to them. Some will no doubt be expansive but certainly not all. Making it easier to lend does not necessarily increase borrowing.

The textbooks say that bankers create money by lending it,[10] but actually bankers produce nothing except some useful services. The active partners in the creation of money are borrowers. If no entrepreneur plans a better mousetrap, if no consumer longs for a bigger and better big-ticket item, if no speculator schemes for a big killing, the banker sits idle. The banker can refuse to support plans, longings, and schemes and can thus single-handedly *not* create money; but the first and essential step in creating money is taken by borrowers. If no one borrows, no money is created, regardless of the intentions of bureaucrats and the complaisance of bankers.

No one borrows money for the fun of it. It would be an expensive pastime, especially when interest rates are usurious. Borrowers want

9. Friedman, "Burns," p. 111.

10. Although James Tobin argues that bankers do not create money at all, his argument holds only if the sole consequence of borrowing is the speculative shuffling of portfolios. But entrepreneurs do create value as they establish or expand businesses. Borrowing (and lending) for these purposes thus creates (or loses) money. See Tobin, *Essays in Economics*, vol. I. *Macroeconomics*, pp. 272–82.

borrowed funds for one of four purposes: to spend on consumption, to invest in productive enterprise, to refinance existing indebtedness, or to speculate. Only the first two purposes contemplate the buying and selling of goods and services, and only the first is certain to have such an effect.

If you buy something for your own use, you have unequivocally been a factor in aggregate demand. But if you hire workers, build a factory, stock a warehouse, you do not necessarily add to aggregate supply. Enterprise is systematically uncertain.[11] What's to come is still unsure. Actual output is not necessarily economic production. Things may be manufactured and services made available but there is no guarantee that anyone will buy all or any of them. The price may be too high, the quantity offered too great, the specifications unattractive, the timing wrong, the advertising misdirected. Or the entrepreneur may merely have bad luck. As demand must be effective, supply must be effective too. Wanting something you can't afford is no part of demand, and offering something nobody wants is no part of supply. Or, as Augustin Cournot, one of the forefathers of mathematical economics, wrote, "[W]e do not see for what reason theory need take account of any demand which does not result in a sale. . . ."[12]

THE TRANSACTIONS EQUATION

One of the most publicized equations in economics is what is called the transactions form of the quantity of money equation. It was put into its present form some ninety years ago by Irving Fisher, and is

11. Davidson, *Money*, chap. 6; Knight, *Risk, Uncertainty*, chaps. 7 and 9; Shackle, *Time and Thought*, chap. 7.
12. Cournot, *Mathematical Principles*, p. 46.

regarded by some authorities (though not by others) as the essence of monetarism.[13]

The equation, written all in capitals, looks formidable ($MV = PQ$). It merely means that the quantity of money, multiplied by the velocity of its circulation, is equal to the general price level, multiplied by the goods and services produced.

Difficulties occur with each term, starting of course with *M*, for there is no agreement on the definition of the money supply, and hence none on its size. Next, it turns out that velocity (*V*) cannot be determined except by means of this equation. Fanciers of the quantity theory contend that over the past several years, the velocity of M2 has been fairly constant; so M2 is the now favored quantity, and *MV* becomes a simple term, meaning the total money spent for goods and services.

The right-hand side of the equation presents different problems. *Q* represents the total of the goods and services produced, that is, the real (stated in things), as opposed to the nominal (stated in money), gross domestic product. I'll express doubts about the GDP, whether real or nominal, but for the moment we may accept it at its face value. We are immediately struck by the fact that its face value is expressed in money, that is, nominally. Moreover, it cannot be expressed in any other way, for money is the only unit of economic measurement applicable to apples and pears and tons of steel and all the rest. The paradoxical fact is that "real" GDP can only be quantified nominally.

What, then, is the price level (*P*)? It is an index derived by combining the prices of a great variety of goods and services, each one weighted to allow it its proper importance in the economy. But, of course, the

13. Fisher wrote that "under the conditions assumed [by the equation of exchange], the price level varies . . . directly as the quantity of money in circulation. . . . [This relation] constitutes the 'quantity theory of money.' " Fisher, *Purchasing Power*, p. 29. Friedman, however, disagrees. See Friedman, "Quantitative Theory of Money," p. 3.

actual prices of the goods and services are already and necessarily included in the GDP, which cannot otherwise be added up, while the price level is necessarily derived from those prices. So the only way that multiplying the price level by the GDP could make any sense would be for the GDP to be expressed somehow other than in money. And that we have seen to be impossible. For this reason, PQ becomes a simple term, meaning the total money charged for goods and services. Translating this equation back into English, we learn that the total money spent for goods and services equals the total prices of those goods and services, which is a tautology and sterile as a guide to policy.[14]

The only way to tease policy recommendations out of the equation is to restore it to its original form and forget about the ambiguities and imprecisions and contradictions. Then one can solve it for P, like this: $P = MV/Q$. From this equation, it would appear that the way to keep the price level down is either to restrict the money supply or to increase real output. Since the Federal Reserve Board's direct powers run to the money supply, that's what the Reserve worries about, regardless of the effects on every other aspect of the economy.

But still taking the equation in its original form ($MV = PQ$), reducing the money supply must reduce either the price level or real output, and there is nothing in the equation to tell us which will be the result. Monetarists hope it will be the price level that falls; but if prices are at all sticky (and there are enough contracts of various sorts in force to ensure that at least a great many are sticky), then output must be the factor to fall. And if output falls, the money supply must be further reduced to compensate—and so on and on, until total collapse.

---

14. Schumpeter, *History*, p. 1096, held that "this equation is *not* an identity but an equilibrium condition. . . . [G]iven values of M, V, [Q] tend to *bring about* a determined value of P, but they do not simply *spell* a certain P." This seems a meaningless distinction, since the value of V is determined only by the equation.

LIMITS ON MONEY

Since money exists, it is necessarily limited. Ultimately, the limit is set by functioning, and the possible functioning is set by the state. Marx thought the state would wither away, and both monetarist and neoclassical economists tend to agree with him that all public questions are economic questions. But willy-nilly, for good or ill, directly or indirectly, the state is responsible for the uses to which money may be put and for the fees that may be charged for these uses. To take a simple example, money may not be used to buy stolen goods or to suborn perjury, and these prohibitions have at least some effect on the demand for money.

In the United States, the Federal Reserve Board controls the lending capability of the banking system, thus limiting the functions money can serve and who can use it. Not everyone who wants to borrow can do so. In effect a sort of triage is imposed. Ideally the triage is based on the economic viability of the proposed uses of the money. One inescapable test of that viability is the availability of labor. As long as citizens are looking for work, the banking system should be looking for projects which, if properly financed, could employ them. It is conceivable that some projects have such specialized requirements that a suitable labor force could not be culled even from our present unemployment and underemployment pool of several million men and women. Such projects should not be financed in the United States today, at least not without powerful national-interest reasons, because they can proceed only by hampering or destroying existing projects. This sort of triage, which applies to a specific industry or specific firm, is quite different from the present practice of the Federal Reserve Board, which, as we shall see in Chapter 20, uses the interest rate to transfer income and wealth from one sector of the economy to another.

In the years when Regulation Q limited the interest banks could pay on deposits, and state usury laws limited the interest banks could charge on loans, the triage tended to be guided by bankers' judgments of the security of the loans; but in the years of deregulation, bankers have been forced by their higher cost of funds to favor aggressive borrowers willing to pay high interest rates.

Overnight every sort of company was put into play, taken over, bought out, merged, broken up. Wall Street apologists pretend that the result is the triumph of efficiency and vision over stodginess and lethargy, and it is true that considerable fortunes are made for many lucky stockholders and investment bankers. Yet industrial efficiency should increase production of goods and services, while the general result of all the speculative activity was stagnating production, falling wages, and rising prices.

The rising prices alarmed the financial community, especially the Federal Reserve Board, which adopted policies that narrowed the triage and ensured that speculation, rather than efficiency and vision, would rule the American economy. Any general control the Board now attempts hurts the producing economy more than it does the speculating economy. Until the government is again willing to take responsibility for the uses to which our money is put and to regulate and tax accordingly, no other outcome is to be looked for.

FAITH IN MONEY

As a practical matter, it has always been understood that money depends on credit or faith, that it passes from hand to hand because people have faith that it is what it purports to be. When the king of Lydia put his stamp on a lump of electrum, traders all over the Mediterranean had faith that the lump weighed what the stamp said. It was no longer necessary for traders to carry scales and weights with them at all times—as was done until recently on the Gold Coast—and make an elaborate ritual of the simplest transaction. Buying and selling could be accomplished in the few minutes it took to count out and examine the necessary coins.

Clipping and counterfeiting, to be sure, became worrisome, and various ways of combating them were developed. One of the most remarkable was devised by thirteenth-century Florence, where it became customary to circulate brand-new florins in small leather bags sealed by the mint.[15] It is noticeable that acceptance of these purses was still an act of faith; it was assumed that they contained genuine and sound florins because one had faith in the inviolability of the purse and the legitimacy of the seal.

Faith in money neither starts nor ends with the currency itself. Obviously something more than appreciation of the design or printing is at work in the acceptance of inconvertible paper money. It is made legal tender by law and acceptable by the tax collector. It, too, can be counterfeited and so circulates only on faith in its genuineness; to this extent it is like coin. In the same way, checks can be forged or kited, balances can be overdrawn, and banks can fail.

The more fundamental and fruitful faith is in the society as a going concern. What is at stake is not the purity or genuineness of the money per se but confidence in the continuity of a society in which money can be spent. The South will not rise again; so Confederate money is of value only to collectors, and Confederate war debts (and thus war credits) were wiped out by the Fourteenth Amendment.

An unstated reason for the persisting interest in gold—in "hard money" generally—is an aloofness from the present polity. As John William Miller wrote, in a personal letter, "Gold is the economic dropout. Within an economy no object or service has an intrinsic value. It has only exchange value at a place, time, and for personal desire. Gold is an attempt to make the market incidental, to evade it. Gold has no economic discipline." Gold expresses a willingness to opt out of the present society and an expectation of maintaining one's position in a

15. de Roover, *Medici Bank*, p. 32.

successor commonwealth. This, too, is an act of faith, and one not infrequently belied by the event. Hoards invite plunder or confiscation. The Inca's treasure did him no good.

Nor does faith in money stop with faith in a society in which money may be spent. What matters at least as much is that the society will be such that what is bought with money may be peaceably used and enjoyed. Society is a going concern. Thus the acceptance and circulation of money are possible when we have faith in our fellows and in the society created with them.

FUNCTIONING MONEY

Money functions or serves as it is used in buying, selling, and contracting for goods and services, in settling debts, and in storing wealth, and only as it is so used. Money declares or publishes or makes possible comparative prices, both present or spot prices and future or forward prices, and only money does this. To engage in economic activity, one must put money in one's purse. Just as war is too important to leave the generals, money is too important to leave to the bankers.

The services money performs command a fee, which is interest, just as workers are paid wages for their labor and landowners exact rent for the use of their property. In all these cases, whatever performs the service is eventually returned to its owner, unless it is destroyed or damaged (whereupon the owner has a claim on the person responsible). Interest, wages, and rent are paid for the service, not for what performs the service. With ordinary commodities, it is the other way around.

Interest, wages, and rent are all contractual payments, whether explicit or implicit. An agreement is reached on a service to be performed and on the payment that will be made for it. When a loan is discounted, the interest is paid before the service is performed, and similar arrangements can be made with wages and rent. In either case, the services of money, labor, and land are all continuing services, and the contracts governing them necessarily look to the future.

Most economists have tried to validate interest (or in the case of St. Thomas, to invalidate it) on some special ground, usually psychological. Nassau Senior established his reputation with the notion that interest rewards abstinence; Alfred Marshall, observing that rich lenders are not necessarily abstainers, defined it as the reward for waiting; Keynes called it liquidity preference, or the reward for not hoarding; and Irving Fisher gave it a base in impatience.[16]

These theories approach interest from the point of view of the lender, although the borrower is, as we have seen, the active partner in the transaction. In any case, it is not important for economic theory, even when true, that borrowers are impatient and lenders patient. The same distinction can be made between employers and employees, between renters and landlords, and between buyers and sellers of any commodity. I hire someone to mow my lawn, partly because I am lazy and partly because I am impatient to get it done and claim to have other things to do. I rent a house because I'd have to wait too long if I first tried to build one or to accumulate enough to buy one. I buy a hat because I don't know how to make one.

ANIMAL SPIRITS AND WILL

One borrows money to make money, not for the fun of it, just as one lends money to make money, not because one can't think of a motive or reason not to. Borrowing and lending are almost-ordinary business transactions. In the days of the gold standard, when money was thought to be a commodity, they were perfectly ordinary. They are not quite

16. Senior, *Industrial Efficiency*, pp. 197–202; Marshall, *Principles*, p. 193; Keynes, *General Theory*, p. 174; Fisher, *Theory of Interest*, p. 66ff.

ordinary now because the fundamental interest rate is set not by the parties to the transaction but by the monetary authority.

It is here that what Keynes called animal spirits (and I call will) most clearly reveals itself. An open, generous, and optimistic society will set the fundamental interest rate low and will set a low value on all forms of liquidity preference. Both borrowers and lenders will be eager to invest in production.

This is not psychology. It is not a response to a stimulus. It is will. It is one way we declare in economics and show in action the sort of people we are.

What matters economically is that someone sees a way to make a profit by borrowing some money, and someone else sees a way to make a profit by lending it. If two "someones" have these modest complementary visions, they are in a position to reach an agreement upon a mutually acceptable fee for the use of the money.

They do not start with a *tabula rasa*. They have before them the fundamental interest rate set by the monetary authorities and the customary or historical variants from that rate to cover the type and duration of the loan they have in mind, together with estimates of risk, of transaction costs, of the likelihood of inflation, and so on. On this basis they separately judge the value of the services (the use of some money) that one proposes to buy and the other to sell. As in any other economic exchange, one party (either one) makes an offer, and the other accepts it, or makes a counteroffer, which may itself be countered. Whether through groping or not, eventually they come to an agreement; if they don't, there has been no economic event and, as Cournot said, there is nothing to explain.

One retains the services of a moneylender for the same sort of reason one retains the services of a laborer or a landlord—because one needs them or wants them. Turgot put the economic situation clearly: "Lending at interest is simply a kind of trading, in which the Lender is a man who sells the *use* of his money, and the Borrower a man who buys it, just as the Proprietor of an estate and his Farmer sell and buy respectively the *use* of leased property."[17]

What is done in the labor, money, and real estate markets is more significant of the sort of people we are than are the doings in the various markets for goods, because labor, capital, and land are involved in every economic transaction, while one rarely must have a new hat. The money market, however, is in principle different from the labor market or the real estate market; it is a condition of their operation, as it is a condition of the operation of all markets, that is, of the price system.

As we have noted, an economy with comparatively high interest and low wages (consequences of high planned profit) is one marked by cynicism and greed. A cynical and greedy society will make inadequate use of its labor and inappropriate use of its money and so will be less productive than it might have been. Its speculating economy will outweigh its producing economy.

17. Turgot, *Riches*, p. 65. For somewhat similar views, see Menger, *Principles*, p. 156; Keynes, *Writings*, vol. 14, pp. 221–22.

5

The Primacy of Price in Economics

Since we now have money, we have economics. We are surrounded by prices. Economic analysis starts with a given system of prices. Adam Smith wrote, "There is in every society or neighborhood an ordinary or average rate of both wages and profit. . . . This rate is naturally regulated . . . by the general circumstances of the society, their riches or poverty, their advancing, stationary, or declining condition. . . ."[1] Ricardo agreed: "[T]he natural price of labour . . . essentially depends on the habits and customs of the people."[2] We shall have occasion to cite Walras and Debreu to the same effect, and it would not be hard to find similar statements from practically every economist.

How could the price system not be given? Only by not being a system. Once upon a time as we read in Homer, when alien cultures met without fighting, one side would lay out its wares or "gifts" on the strand, and the other would lay out what it would give in exchange. There was no history and no system.

1. Smith, *Wealth*, p. 55.
2. Ricardo, *Principles*, pp. 54–55.

When we say that the price system is given, we recognize that we do not start with a *tabula rasa*. We are necessarily in the midst of life. If our tablet is not scraped clean, the marks on it were placed there in the past, either by mechanism or by history. If by mechanism, the story stops there, for there is no one to tell it. So the price system is historical.

If the price system is given to us by history, it will be given to our successors by history, which then will include the story of our doings. Because our predecessors were free agents, creators of our past, we are responsible, too, creators of the future. We cannot escape history.

At least since Adam Smith, price has been the resolution of a tension between supply and demand. If the supply is small and the demand is great, the price will be high, while a large supply and a weak demand will result in a low price. We seem to have known this always, to have learned it at our mother's knee, and never to have had occasion to doubt it. It is one of the Enlightenment's self-evident truths.

Yet the law of supply and demand was not revealed to the Greeks, the Jews, the Romans, the Ostrogoths, or the schoolmen of medieval Europe. In the ancient world justice was a reciprocal relationship between individuals, and so was trade. Aristotle cites the Pythagoreans as recommending literal reciprocity, a theory that with the Jews was the Mosaic talion law—an eye for an eye and a tooth for a tooth. After giving reasons for preferring proportionate reciprocity, Aristotle writes, "It is by exchange that men hold together. That is why they give a prominent place to the temple of the Graces—to promote the requital of services; for this is characteristic of grace—we should serve in return one who has shown grace to us, and should another time take the initiative in showing it."[3]

Aristotle evidently understood grace to be more than prudence or calculation. In *The Republic* Plato had shown, as Adam Smith was to

---

3. Aristotle, *Nichomachean Ethics*, 1133a.

show two millennia later, that the division of labor increases output, and that as a practical matter it makes a just society necessary.[4] But Aristotle had his eye out for what holds the polis together, and what he glimpsed was a system of mutual obligations freely entered into and objectified in exchanges of goods and services.

The Church Fathers, whose precepts were based on the equality of all men before the Lord's throne, developed the idea of the just price. "Therefore," St. Thomas argued, "if either the price exceed the quantity of the thing's worth, or, conversely, the thing exceed the price, there is no longer the equality of justice; and consequently to sell a thing for more than its worth, or to buy it for less than its worth, is in itself unjust and unlawful." He saw, however, as his mentor Aristotle had seen before him on the question of justice in general, that this admirable rule was not altogether easy to apply. Among exceptions, he cited "for instance, when a man has great need of a certain thing, while another will suffer if he be without it. In such a case the just price will depend not only on the thing sold, but on the loss which the sale brings on the seller. And thus it will be lawful to sell a thing for more than it is worth in itself, though the price paid be not more than it is worth to the owners."[5]

The Church's rules, exceptions and all, became meaningless when Venetian merchants traded glassware in Beirut for spices to sell at home. The Venetians certainly got much more for their Murano goblets than they could have done at home, while the Levantines are likely to have held up their end.

Society has an interest in price that may be different from that of either of the traders. Are the services of any corporation executive worth $5 million a year? Did comparatively high wages paid to steelworkers ruin the industry and damage the economy? On the other

4. Plato, *Republic*, 2.370–76.
5. St. Thomas Aquinas, "Of Cheating," in *Summa Theologica*.

hand, are the wages paid to teachers so low that educational standards suffer?

Thus the idea of the just price has persisted. Advocates of any form of price fixing have acted in the name of justice. This was true of the medieval and Renaissance guilds; it is true today of marginal utility analysts, of labor unions, and of proponents of agricultural price supports, metropolitan rent controls, and prohibition of international "dumping." Utility regulation seeks prices that will be fair both to those who have invested in the utilities and to the public.

THE IDEAL MARKET

The idea of justice was not foreign to the free market. The invisible hand was supposed to achieve a result compatible with "moral sentiments" and so to attain a natural as opposed to a theological justice, a natural price as opposed to a just price. Adam Smith wrote, "When the price of any commodity is neither more nor less than what is sufficient to pay the rent of the land, the wages of the labour, and the profits of the stock employed in raising, preparing, and bringing it to market, according to their natural rates, the commodity is then sold for what may be called its natural price."

Smith is careless here. There is no "natural" rate in economics. $S = {}^1/_2\, gt^2$ expresses a natural rate, but there is no natural rate of wages or profits in bringing a commodity to market. There are often customary rates and legal rates, but such rates can be changed, as $S = {}^1/_2\, gt^2$ cannot.

We may, however, forgive this slip because Smith recognized that once goods were brought to market, the "natural" price had nothing to do with the price actually paid. What then controlled was what he called effectual demand, which "is different from the absolute demand. A very poor man may be said in some sense to have a demand for a coach and six; he might like to have it; but his demand is not an effectual demand, as the commodity can never be brought to market in order to satisfy it."[6]

The effectual demand may be so great that "a competition will immediately begin" among those who want and can afford a certain commodity, and this will push the market price above the natural price. And if the effectual demand is weak, competition among sellers will force the market price below the natural price. A high market price will attract new producers to the field; the resulting increased availability of the product will deflate the competition among the buyers; and the price will fall. A low market price will have the opposite effect. So the market is supposed to tend toward the natural price, at which point price will be in equilibrium.

This ideal market is served by many competitors producing many interchangeable goods. There are usually substitutes available for any scarce commodity; while a stone won't serve the purposes of bread, cake may. To forestall cartels, producers must be able to enter or leave the market easily. There must be many consumers, too, for a monopsonist can control a market as readily as a monopolist; a manufacturer who has only one buyer for its product is at the mercy of that buyer.

When many producers can supply easily substitutable goods, all have to take the price the market will bear. Even the giant oligopolies of the *Fortune* 500 are too small in relation to the total market to set their prices as they please. They are price takers. On the other hand, if I want to buy a certain kind of car, I haven't much choice in what I have to pay. The president of General Motors doesn't care whether I buy one of his cars or not. There are too many like me. I am a price taker.

In a freely competitive world, every buyer and every seller—that is, everyone—is a price taker. Prices come from the reconciliation of supply and demand or the tension between them. The market sets the prices. But if the market sets the prices, all economic agents—both

---

6. Smith, *Wealth*, pp. 55–56.

buyers and sellers—are price takers. They are passive agents—a contradiction in terms. The market is presented as an impersonal process, an automatic process, one that no person controls and hence all persons can enjoy. It seems a Cartesian paradise.

But it is a pathetic fallacy. A market can't do anything. It is a place, a condition—not an agent, a doer. Of course, it is a figure of speech. No one pretends that the market literally sets prices. How could it? It can't speak or read or write or make gestures. Yet prices are somehow set.

SUPPLY CURVE/DEMAND CURVE

The textbooks reduce the market to two curves, a supply curve, showing that more goods are supplied as the price is raised, and a demand curve, showing that more goods are demanded as the price is lowered. Where the two curves cross is the equilibrium price that the market is supposed to set. It is said, moreover, that at this price the market is cleared; all that is brought to market is sold, and there is no incentive to bring more.

The textbooks still show the supply curve sweeping gracefully upward to the right, but in every production run and every supply contract the actual curve is a straight horizontal line, because the unit costs of a production run are uniform, and so are the unit prices of a supply contract. Even where there are economies of scale or when suppliers offer quantity discounts, the supply curves of actual transactions are parallel to the x axis. Successive production runs or supply contracts may show curves at different levels. They need not be continuous, but they will be horizontal.

A preliminary demand curve is often derived from market research, which is notoriously imprecise and not infrequently catastrophically mistaken. A market research curve may look like a classical demand curve, dipping gracefully to the right. In actuality, however, the demand curve, like the supply curve, is a horizontal line parallel to the

x axis. The length of the line is determined by the extent and effectiveness of the merchandizing campaign in selling the given commodity at a given selling price. Different campaigns may show curves at different levels, as do different supply contracts. As before, each "curve" is straight and horizontal.

Obviously, a chart like the foregoing, which is essentially an assemblage of disconnected lines, is useless. Unlike the classical charts, it does not show the equilibrium demand or the equilibrium supply or the equilibrium price or any equilibrium at all, nor should it be expected to. No such equilibria exist in the actual world, where the independent variable is price, and supply and demand are dependent on it.

It is, even in the classical case, an objective of business management to see that the supply and demand curves do not cross, because profitable business stops at the point of contact. In pursuit of that objective, prices are actually set in all sorts of ways at all levels—manufacturing, wholesaling, and retailing. At each level the price setter (or offeror) may be either seller or buyer. The price taker (or acceptor), without whose complementary action there is no sale, may likewise be either buyer or seller. In modern economies, retail prices are almost universally set by the seller, and the buyer's choice is to take it or leave it. The balance is more even at the other levels, but there is no essential difference in the importance of the roles: every sale must have both a price maker and a price taker—an offeror and an acceptor.

COMPETITION PUSHING PRICES UP

The invisible hand was supposed to drive prices down and quality up. Galbraith has taught us not to expect the market to work that way in the world of big business, which he calls the planning system.[7] But it

7. Galbraith, *Economics and the Public Purpose*, chap. 9.

doesn't work as it is famed to do even in what he calls the market system.

In the textbook business, which is minutely fragmented and fiercely competitive, competition frequently has the effect of pushing prices up rather than down. As an apposite example, we may consider one of the biggest submarkets of the textbook market—the freshman principles of economics course. Sixty years ago the texts for this course looked like ordinary books; you could hold them in one hand while you read them; and you could carry them to class without backache. Then one of the publishers got the idea of dressing up its entry with a second color and a larger paper size, which would sometimes make the graphs a bit easier to understand and might make the whole thing look livelier—more like a magazine. The innovations would have approximately doubled the printing costs if the publisher had not dramatically increased its market share. The increased attractiveness increased sales, which permitted longer press runs, which helped hold the price down. But, of course, the other publishers quickly copied the innovations, with the result that each publisher soon had roughly the same market share as before. Press runs were necessarily reduced to those of precolor days; so unit costs went up. As costs went up, so did prices. It cannot be pretended that students' understanding of economics has improved proportionately.

Such a competitive dance is performed in many another industry, forcing prices up rather than down, reducing the variety of goods offered for sale, and generally (as a book of business advice once had it) selling the sizzle rather than the steak. This outcome is a puzzle to classical economists, but it can be readily explained. The explanation does not, I hasten to add, turn on the slyness of the competitors, who are no worse and no better than anyone else.

The explanation does turn on one or two facts about the industries involved. In the textbook business, for example, demand is restricted. There are only so many students taking freshman economics in any given year; so there is nothing any publisher can do to make much difference in the size of the market, aside from publishing supplementary readings and study guides, and preparing and even grading tests. Students who have one textbook have no use for another at any price. The students, moreover, themselves have restricted options. Assuming that they're going to study at all, they can buy a new copy of the textbook, or they can buy a secondhand copy, or they can borrow their roommate's copy. They do not have the option of substituting something else. If the assigned text is Mansfield's, they can hardly make do with Samuelson's, and they certainly can't substitute *The Norton Anthology of English Literature*, no matter how great a bargain it is.

Faced with this restricted market, publishers have correspondingly restricted options. If they want a larger share of the market, they can seek it by lowering their price or "upgrading" their product, or both. A little business experience will convince them that price lowering, by itself, is seldom the solution of choice. Henry Ford almost ruined his company by sticking doggedly with his Model T long after Chevrolet had come out with a somewhat more practical, more comfortable, and more stylish competitor at a higher price. At the other end of the business scale, restaurants find it profitable to serve extra-large portions at extra-large prices. The gourmands among their customers will happily eat what's put before them, and the gourmets will be delighted to take home a doggy bag full of expensive morsels for their pets (or for their own next day's supper). In all these instances, producers have found again and again that while price may be a factor, it is by no means the most significant factor in the competition for market share.

A restricted supply will similarly upset the classical theory that competition invariably benefits consumers. Competition forces retailers to bid the price of special Beanie Babies up in order to get something to draw customers into their stores; consequently a little shortage becomes, as a result of competition, a temporarily big one. Something like this happens almost every Christmas without hurting anyone very much. (There is one case in which almost everyone is hurt, and seriously, and that is the case of banking.)

The failure of competition to perform as theory says it does is no surprise to anyone, not even to classical economists. Examples of the failure are too many and too obvious, but they are blandly countered by the proposition that the public gets what it demands. No one really believes that, and the proposition cannot be proved or disproved on its own terms. The theory says that competition gives the public what it demands; therefore what the public gets is what it demanded. This form of reasoning is known as *petitio principii*, or begging the question, or assuming what you pretend to prove.

CAVEAT VENDITOR

If the invisible hand actually did turn unregulated competition to beneficent ends, the ancient rule of caveat emptor should perhaps be resuscitated. The late Professor Herbert Stein, formerly chairman of the Council of Economic Advisers, once made a widely retailed mot to the effect that people of liberal mind trust anyone over eighteen to vote for president of the United States but don't think the common man or woman capable of buying a bicycle without do-gooding governmental intervention.

But a purchase is not a one-way transaction; I don't get a bicycle for nothing. When I, the emptor, bought one from Herbert (both Professor Stein and I had five years of Latin and could call each other by our first names) for $199.99, I gave him two hundred-dollar bills, and he gave me a penny and the bike. Herbert said that I should make myself a self-reliant expert on bicycles before I traded in his shop and that if what he sold me proved dangerous or shoddy, it was my fault, not his.

If so, why shouldn't caveat emptor be balanced by caveat venditor? If Herbert could (unintentionally or maybe not) sell me a dangerous or shoddy bicycle at my peril, why couldn't I pay him with counterfeit hundred-dollar bills, at his peril? Or a rubber check? Why shouldn't he have been required to make himself a self-reliant expert on these matters, and not go running to the sheriff for help?

Obviously it's no answer to say that counterfeiting is against the law. That law could be repealed, just as the Federal Trade Commission can be hamstrung. Nor is it any answer to say that check bouncing is cheating and so immoral and bad for the soul; the same can be said for selling dangerous bicycles. Nor is it any answer to say that government regulations impose an intolerable burden of paperwork on the bicycle business. The legal requirement that I have enough money in my account to cover my checks means that I must balance my checkbook, and that's an intolerable burden of paperwork, if you ask me.

Paper money, personal checks, and credit cards have been good for business. They make business easier to transact. Seller and buyer don't need to wear out their teeth biting coins. Within broad limits, they can trust what is proffered. They can trust, because this is in general a trustworthy society. And it is a trustworthy society in part because the sanctions of the criminal law enforce the trust.

If recipients of rubber checks had to rely on the civil law, they'd be faced with endless delays and absurd costs. They would spend hundreds or thousands of dollars, not to mention hours of court appearances, to get a judgment that they'd still have difficulty collecting. They couldn't afford such costs, so they couldn't afford to accept checks, so they'd have to restrict themselves to much slower and smaller cash-only business. The threat of criminal penalties, enforced by the state, deters check cheats and makes it possible for merchants to trust the rest of us, to the merchants' benefit and ours.

What's sauce for the goose is sauce for the gander. I'd have been readier to buy Herbert's bicycle if I knew it was safe and I'd have been surer it was safe if I knew the law would crack down on him if it weren't. I couldn't afford to sue him for damages unless I'd been catastrophically hurt, which neither of us wanted to happen. Since he actually did not intend to cheat me, and I actually did not intend to cheat him, we both would have been better off if we knew the law would call those who do cheat to account; we'd have been better able to trust each other.

Perhaps more important, if the law made it possible for me to trust what is offered for sale, I'd no longer have to make dubious reliance on brand names as guarantees of product quality. Then Lewis Mumford's vision of the efficiency of parochial production might become a reality, and so might E. F. Schumacher's vision of the beauty of smallness. Then, too, Ralph Nader would at last be recognized as the great champion of the free market.

PRICE IS THE INDEPENDENT VARIABLE

The law of supply and demand may do as a reasonably accurate description of the operation of the market of an eighteenth-century shire town. But in the third quarter of that century, Adam Smith noted the expansion of the ancient idea of the division of labor into the Industrial Revolution's idea of a factory. Almost a hundred years later, Karl Marx was fearful (or scornful) of what he called the commodity fetishism of bourgeois production for sale in the market instead of for use. These two interrelated innovations—factory labor and production for sale—revolutionized the actuality of the market and rendered the law of supply and demand irrelevant.

Smith's "small manufactory" capable of turning out 48,000 pins in a day was obviously too productive for anyone to have a detailed idea of what was to become of those pins, where and how they were to be used, and who was to use them. The pins were produced for the market. The factory organization of labor made production for the market inevitable, and wondrously inexpensive. Production for the market made selling, merchandising, and advertising inevitable, and wondrously expensive. Only grudgingly have economists accepted the universe; one can still find some willing to argue that advertising is economic waste. It is probable that even now most pay unconsidered allegiance to the law of supply and demand.

Yet it is a matter of common observation that in developed economies today supplies of manufactured goods—both producers' goods and consumers' goods—are indefinitely reproducible. Shortages certainly occur, but even managed shortages of natural resources, such as OPEC's embargoes, are short-lived. Supply is no longer an independent variable. It is no longer (if it ever actually was, except on a parochial scale) one of the two determinants of price.

It is only slightly different with demand, which likewise is no longer an independent variable. Demand is managed. That is what advertising and salesmanship are accused of doing, and what they actually do. There is no doubt that much such activity promotes tawdry and corrupt commodities and ways of life. There is also no doubt that much of it is ineffective. There is equally no doubt that, by and large, it does manage. Smith's pin manufacturer could not have sold 48,000 pins in a day or a decade if seamstresses and tailors had not known at least where to buy them and how to use them.

In the market, supply and demand are determined by price, not the other way around. What is objective is price. Demand is not what I'd like to have, or what I desperately need, or what I might buy. All that is formless and indeterminate. Demand is what I actually buy at a price either the seller or I quoted. Supply, too, is indeterminate. A novel nobody wants to read is not, as a book, a factor in supply (it may, however, be a supply of scrap paper and be sold as such). In short, supply and demand are dependent variables; the independent variable is price.

A FREE MARKET IS NOT CLEARED

Neither supply nor demand is satisfied all at once. The market is not a one-time thing, like the auctioning off of a bankrupt farm. Not only does it take time for supplies to be produced; it also takes time for demand to develop. Sixty years ago the demand for a dishwasher or a TV set or an automobile with automatic shift was weak. Of course, these products were not so efficient or so inexpensive then as they are now; but also people didn't know they wanted them, and initially they didn't know such things existed—because they didn't.

Since both demand and supply take time, the market must stay open. And if it is correct to consider a free market in some way necessary to a free society, it is a mistake for some economists to think of a market being cleared in a succession of essentially unconnected and irresponsible happenings. Indeed, a defining characteristic of freedom is openness to the future. Free men and women are responsible for the consequences of their actions. Free speech is openness to definition and criticism. A free market is openness to new commodities and new prices.

The whole idea of market clearing is foreign to the idea of business enterprise. I want the market to be cleared if I am auctioning off my goods and chattels; but if I am in business, I want to stay in business. If I am a book publisher, I do not close up shop when I sell an edition of a textbook. I order a new printing and look around for another book to publish. Like my academic authors, I must publish or perish, and I set my prices accordingly. In the same way, even fishmongers, whose wares must be sold today, set prices with an eye to tomorrow's business.

Cost is a factor, not in determining price, but in setting a floor under price. In setting prices for a continuing business, I must consider what it will cost me to reproduce or replenish my supply. Yesterday's costs are sunk, but tomorrow's must be met. Everyone's business has the same problem; hence it seems to some reasonable to say that price is determined by cost.

But there is no royal road to price setting (or price taking). The relationship between cost and price is not axiomatic. The most that can be said is that if a business or the economy as a whole is to continue, its accepted prices must in the aggregate equal or exceed its aggregate costs. There is no requirement that the price of each product exceed its cost, that each sale or purchase be profitable, or that the total income of a week, a month, a year, or any period exceed the costs of that period as long as financing is available. Well-organized businesses can survive years of deficit.

The setting of a particular price, therefore, is not determined by impersonal forces of society or nature. My costs are not "natural"; they are my suppliers' prices, and my suppliers' costs are their suppliers' prices, and so on, ad infinitum. No cost is original. No supplier is without costs, which are somebody else's prices.

Ricardo thought that the regress was stopped by the fact that the ultimate cost is labor, and that the laborers have certain bare necessities—the simplest food, the cheapest clothing, the minimum housing. The cost of labor cannot fall below the cost of these necessities, and so their cost seemed to him to be the irreducible cost upon which the price system is based.[8] Yet these so-called wage goods, too, are produced, and produced in the same ways as other goods. A firm producing such goods can reduce its prices by controlling its costs in the same ways other firms do. There is thus no final or natural price for wage goods; hence no natural price for labor; hence no mathematically determinate system of original costs or prices or values. The regress is infinite.

The only way to stop an infinite regress is not to let it get started, and of course this one does not get started in the world we live in. What actually happens is that some person—some willful human being or corporation of human beings—for some reason that is personally satisfactory (regardless of how it may appear to anyone else) names a price for some commodity, and some other willful human being accepts it.

Wages (the price of employing labor), interest rates (the price of borrowing money), and rents (the price of using land) are arrived at in essentially the same way as the prices of commodities. As with commodities, some willful human being or corporation of human beings makes a price and some other willful human being or corporation takes it; and as with commodities, the price maker may be either party to the bargain, and so of course may the price taker. "Willful" is perhaps too strong, but "willing" is too weak. What I am naming are free, responsible, and decisive acts.

---

8. Ricardo, *Principles*, p. 52.

THE SETTING OF PRICES

Trade starts with a price, whether quoted by producer, middleman, or consumer, but the quotation is not made in a vacuum. It does not appear de novo, a complete surprise to all concerned. It is not the first offer made on earth. The person quoting the price is not the first ever to have bought or sold. What Keynes called the stickiness of wages and other prices is a consequence of history, of the irreversibility of time. Prices are set in a negotiation that starts with where prices were yesterday or this morning and moves, if it moves at all, slowly, because today's agents are in competition with yesterday's agents.

Wheat was sold at a certain price yesterday. If today I make a bid much lower than that, I shall buy no wheat. If my price is much higher, I shall place myself at a disadvantage with my competitors, who will have bought at yesterday's lower price and so can undersell me in the bread market. Or they may make an effortless profit by selling me what they bought. As the price I offer was not the beginning of the history of wheat prices, so it is not the end. It will have an effect on subsequent offers and acceptances.

A pricing decision may come out of a computer, or it may be a gut feeling or the result of tossing a coin, but it is a decision. Even the computer's answer depends on someone's decisions about the relevant data and the proper program. A price may be set to achieve a certain markup over costs, to maintain or expand market share (perhaps to the extent of monopoly), to establish a reputation for a certain sort of excellence, to outwit the competition in one way or another, even to use the product as a loss leader; and the action may be taken on the basis of market research or experience or hunch or whim, because of a computer analysis or a gut feeling or the toss of a coin, or just for the fun of it. The list is obviously far from complete; in fact it cannot be completed.

None of the methods of price setting guarantees business success to the seller or personal satisfaction to the buyer. It may be that on the average businesses operate at a fairly constant markup over unit cost; but many a business that has used the usual rule of thumb has gone down in defeat, while many another that has broken all the rules has been triumphant. Likewise many a careful shopper has been disappointed, and many an imprudent purchase has given great pleasure.

Pricing the fundamental factors of the economy is not an essentially different problem. The fees for the use of labor, of land, and of money are all arrived at in much the same way as the prices of ordinary commodities. Moneylenders may systematically weigh the transactions, precautionary, speculative, and finance motives of liquidity preference in deciding on an acceptable interest rate. Or they may not. Certainly borrowers (who are the active parties to the proceeding) do not, for liquidity is precisely what they do not prefer. In the end, an interest rate is agreed on, if the borrower can see a way to make a satisfactory profit in the deal, and if the lender can see how to make an acceptable profit. What is satisfactory or acceptable is as idiosyncratic as the pricing policies of a grocery store and the shopping practices of its patrons.

Recognizing that all prices are idiosyncratic is not suggesting that they have no urgency. Some are close to being matters of life and death. All, even the most casual or trivial, are evidence of the character of buyer and seller. All are also modes of self-definition and self-understanding.

PRICING IS AN ACT OF WILL

A pricing decision is an act of will. It is a free act. It is determining, not determined. Like all acts, it is limited. It is an event in an ongoing world, not an imaginary world. Furthermore, I am limited to the prices I actually set. I set these prices, not some others. I do this, not that. A something is limited. The alternative to limitation is nothingness.

Price determination is not the only willful act in business. Anyone proposing to sell a certain product in the market may, and usually does, embark on the enterprise before the product exists. An automobile manufacturer sees an opportunity for a new mid-range car. In the beginning, all that exists of the new car are its target price and target date, a menu of special features, and a schedule of standard specifications. If the design and engineering departments can put it all together to the satisfaction of the financial and sales departments, the car is built.

The decision to be a haberdasher rather than an automobile manufacturer is similarly willful. Determining the prices of shirts and ties is secondary and subordinate to deciding to be a haberdasher and also to deciding what clientele one intends to attract, what kind of haberdasher one intends to be. All these acts are rational in the sense that one can give reasons for them. None is rational in the mathematical sense that it is the determinate answer to an equation.

With the willful act we arrest the infinite regress that has plagued us hitherto. When we say, "I'll sell this at that price," "I'll buy this at that price," we launch ourselves into the future; we progress, not regress. Accepting—seeking, rather—the consequences of our action, we declare our membership in, and responsibility to, an ongoing world.

PRICES AND CONTRACTS

However else a price may be defined or determined, it is a consequence of an offer and an acceptance. At common law, an offer and an acceptance constitute a contract. Contracts are enforced by the will of traders to continue trading, hence by the will to form civil society, hence by the state. Thus every price presumes the state and is dependent upon it, and the same is, of course, true of any price system. If the state should be privatized or wither away, so would trade, which could not advance beyond barter.

It is important to be clear on this point because there is a perhaps pardonable tendency among economists, from the most extreme Marxists to the most absolute believers in laissez-faire, to consider all questions to be, in the end, economic questions. While R. H. Coase, for example, is willing to say in a famous essay[9] that "problems of welfare economics must ultimately dissolve into a study of aesthetics and morals," the "theorem" for which he is famous holds (*inter alia*), "The aim of such regulation should not be to eliminate smoke pollution but rather to secure the optimum amount of smoke pollution, this being the amount that will maximise the value of production."

But elimination of smoke pollution may be a legitimate aim of the state, regardless of "the value of production." In the case of asbestos, whose leukemia-causing properties may not show up for twenty years, the optimum amount of pollution would, according to Coase's theorem, be the largest amount that could be "secured" without, say, immediate damage to machinery. An "externality" two decades in the future could hardly affect the value of current production.

Since the essential economic concept of price is both a manifestation of personal will and dependent on the state, all economic questions are systematically questions of ethics and law.

THE LAW OF SUPPLY AND DEMAND WORKS BACKWARDS

The traditional law of supply and demand has been the indispensable cornerstone of all economics since Adam Smith. The theory of the self-regulating market depends on it, and self-regulating markets are supposed to determine all prices—not merely the prices of ordinary commodities, but also wages and interest rates.

In Chapter 3, we confronted the traditional theory with the Three

9. Coase, "Social Cost," 1–44.

Antinomies of Greed. In Chapter 4, we noted the turn from mercantilism to capitalism—from money as a special sort of commodity to debt. In this chapter, we have marked another turning point to any future economics.

In short, the law of supply and demand works backward. It has long been noted that the law does not work at all unless supply is limited. Air is free because the supply is not limited. Penny stocks are cheap because they can, in effect, be made to order. The stock market rises when speculators try to increase their portfolios because the number of acceptable shares is limited.

The point we are now making—and it is the most important point in the book—is that *price is a primary economic fact*. It is not a fact to be explained. It is an original fact that explains others. It is a fact without which economics does not exist. A price precedes a bargain, and a bargain precedes a sale. Without a sale there is no economic event.

By restating the law of supply and demand, making price the independent variable on which supply and demand depend, we have opened up consequences both powerful and liberating.

First, the infinite regress in which economics has been entangled is stopped before it gets started. Previously, when price was a variable determined by the intersection of supply and demand curves, the regress on both sides was infinite. The quantity of anything supplied varied with its cost or price, likewise the quantity demanded. If price must be explained, these prices must be explained; so each factor cost was said to be determined at the intersection of its own supply and demand curves, both of which had price as a dependent variable and so on, ad infinitum.

On the demand side, the regression tended to take leave of economics altogether. Demand was said to be determined not in terms of price or money but in terms of psychological satisfaction, which could in turn be explained in terms of physiology, physiology in terms of chemistry, chemistry in terms of physics, atoms in terms of electrons, electrons in terms of quarks—and still there is no end, as the newest, more powerful atom smasher will demonstrate.

Second, while the classical regress led steadily away from human beings, the restated law of supply and demand, by defining price as determining rather than determined, places price setting and price taking at the start of economic activity, thereby recognizing that economic goods are human goods, and establishing price setters and price takers—human beings—in positions of responsibility and freedom. It will no longer be necessary to make heroic—which is to say, contrary to fact—assumptions about the "nature" of humanity. Greed need no longer be the engine driving economics.

6

The Primacy of Labor in Life

Until modern times, society was based on a division of function rather than a division of labor. The nobility of all degrees were responsible for protecting the domain and keeping the peace. The commoners of all degrees were responsible for producing the goods and performing the services that supplied the society. Both nobility and commoners owned the tools of their trade. The higher nobility owned castles and the petty nobility owned a horse and a sword. Commoner professionals owned books and writing materials; commoner villeins owned a span of oxen; commoner serfs owned a spade and an axe. In this society, the various functioners were often in conflict with each other, and every functioner might come to loathe the tools of his trade; but there was little conflict between labor and capital, because every kind of laborer was a capitalist after his kind.

THE CORPORATION AND ITS LABORERS

Today most men and women spend their working lives as employees of one corporation or another, which decides what they, as economic persons, can do and how they will do it. By determining the conditions of their economic lives, the corporation largely determines the extent to which they will live lives of freedom and responsibility.

The modern corporation provides a sadly narrow and restricted definition of freedom for many, if not most, of those who participate in it. It sometimes seems that only a fragile veneer distinguishes the life of a worker today from that described by Adam Smith more than two centuries ago and by Karl Marx a century and a half ago.

Smith wrote, in the course of an argument for public education: "The man whose whole life is spent in performing a few simple operations, of which the effects too are, perhaps, always the same, or very nearly the same, has no occasion to exert his understanding, or to exercise his invention in finding out expedients for removing difficulties which never recur. He naturally loses, therefore, the habit of such exertion, and generally becomes as stupid and ignorant as it is possible for a human creature to become. The torpor of his mind renders him, not only incapable of relishing or bearing a part in any rational conversation, but of conceiving any generous, noble, or tender sentiment, and consequently of forming any just judgment concerning many even of the ordinary duties of private life."[1] And so on.

Marx wrote: "Labor is not the satisfaction of a need; it is merely a *means* to satisfy needs external to it. Its alien character emerges clearly in the fact that as soon as no physical or other compulsion exists, labor is shunned like the plague. . . . Lastly, the external character of labor for the worker appears in the fact that it is not his own, but someone else's, that it does not belong to him, that in it he belongs, not to himself, but to another. . . . As a result the worker no longer feels himself to be freely active in any but his animal functions—eating, drinking, procreating, or at most in his dwelling and in dressing up, etc. . . ."[2]

---

1. Smith, *Wealth*, pp. 734–35.
2. Marx, *Estranged Labor*, p. 74.

The devoted work of thousands of reformers, social workers, industrial psychologists, engineers, efficiency experts, labor leaders, and businessmen and women of good will has enormously improved the conditions of our lives since Smith's and Marx's times. And whatever one can say in criticism of our TV-Inspired, Internet, shopping-mall consumerism, it must be granted to be at least a pleasanter life than that led by the contemporaries of Oliver Twist.

CONTROL OF CORPORATIONS

A contrasting sketch may be made of capitalists. As owners of capital, they toil not, neither do they spin; how can they justify their raiment?

Ownership—ownership of anything, a bank account, a factory, a house, a toothbrush—means control, not absolute control, for there is no such thing, but effective control. Some person or some organization of persons must be somehow in charge. A machine that is not under someone's control is so much scrap metal: it is not even that, for it does not become scrap until a junk dealer takes control of it.

Nevertheless, some kinds of control are often tenuous. Frank Knight argued that stockholders actually control corporations because their purchase or sale of shares implies approval or disapproval of management, which is tantamount to selection of management.[3] Thus they register approval or disapproval of management policies even though they personally may not have the slightest knowledge of who the managers are or what they do. Depositors in commercial banks have no idea at all of what is done with their money. They couldn't find out if they wanted to, and similar systematic ignorance is the general lot of corporation shareholders or bondholders.

In the modern economy, control of capital reduces, as Robert Heil-

---

3. Knight, *Risk*, p. 297.

broner puts it, to the power to withhold.[4] This is a very great power. A company that can't get the use of capital must go out of business. Far more than the power to tax, the power to withhold is the power to destroy. Such power should not lightly be given to anyone.

In our society, this power is legally allocated to people who work hard and save, to people who are lucky, to people who marry people who have money, and to people who inherit it. Inheritance is justified on the ground that testators (or the testators of testators) worked hard and saved and so earned the right to do what they wanted with their money. Sometimes this right is presented as a necessary incentive for the original hard work. The marriage contract, express or implied, has a similar base. As for the lucky, they are always with us. In sports, a spectacular play is often greeted with the comment that it's better to be lucky than good. Obviously it's best to be both, and the same rule applies in business. Luck is assumed and is in principle uncontrollable. It all comes down to working hard and saving.

This is the work ethic, and we learned about it at our mother's knee. Yet the theory is flawed. For the purposes of argument (and only for such purposes), we might grant that John D. Rockefeller, Sr., was entitled to the wealth he amassed, and that a leading reason for his amassing it was his hope of establishing a living for John D., Jr., who thereby had a right to that wealth. But surely John D. Jr.'s right was somewhat attenuated. His hard work and saving were not involved. All he could have claimed was that he did not squander his patrimony (which would have been pretty hard to do). What gave him the right to leave it to Nelson and David, and what gave them the right to it? Well, they were good citizens, or at least tried to be; but there were some (one may guess) who shared in the patrimony of whom this cannot so confidently be said. Moreover, the world is happily full of people trying to be good citizens, and no one proposes that they be similarly rewarded. Good citizenship is a sine qua non.

---

4. Heilbroner, *Nature and Logic*, p. 38.

Thus we come to the not surprising conclusion that the modern corporation is legally controlled by people who can claim neither knowledge enough to control it, nor any other personal qualification for ownership. Everyone knows that this is the case. It is an open secret.

For in the modern corporation it is not only the worker who is, as Marx said, "alienated." The stockholders, too, do not "affirm" themselves in the corporation they legally own. Here the shallowness of Marx's materialist analysis has been exposed by the invention of the limited liability corporation and the development of efficient stock exchanges. What distinguishes a capitalist today is not possession of material things but possession of liquid assets. A liquid asset is a bundle of rights without balancing duties. In the modern world, possession is not commitment. Prudent investors diversify their holdings and constantly shift their "positions." The enterprises underlying these positions have only an incidental and transitory interest for them.

The other side of this coin is that the investors, as human beings, have only an incidental and transitory interest for the enterprises. They are not people but capital. Moreover, the liquidity of capital is, so to say, vaporized by mutual funds, stock options, puts and calls, and gambling on market index futures. Those whom the law holds to be the owners of a modern corporation are, as human beings, of less consequence to it than the proverbial office boy.

When capital and labor confront each other, the ultimate power of capital is the power to withhold, and so is the ultimate power of labor. Abstractly, they are equal in necessity and equal in power. We have here another theoretical equilibrium—and, as we all know, another actual disequilibrium. Whether theoretical equilibrium or actual disequilibrium, the fulcrum is at the division between capital and labor, between owners and workers. Changing the metaphor, this is the fault line of the economic problems of our time. If the free enterprise system collapses, it will be because of unresolved conflict along that line.

LABOR THEORY

The great economists have all been essentially decent men. The meaning of the myth of Midas has not been lost on them, nor have they been able to stomach the proposition that a miser fingering his hoard is the pinnacle toward which civilization has been building. On the other side, they are all children of the Reformation, they are all celebrants of the work ethic, and they all earned the acclaim accorded to achievers.

With this background, it is not surprising that they have almost all been at least half persuaded that the true, the real, the fundamental, the everlasting standard of value is labor. The theme is announced by Adam Smith: "Labour alone, therefore, never varying in its own value, is alone the ultimate and real standard by which the value of all commodities can at all times and places be estimated and compared. It is their real price; money is their nominal price only."[5] (The words "real" and "nominal" aren't the same as those of medieval philosophy, but they do give rise to similar difficulties.)

Smith's successors made the point in terms somewhat different from his. Ricardo argued that the issue was the commodities "necessary to enable the labourers, one with another, to subsist and to perpetuate their race." Keynes held that "the unit of labour" was "the sole physical unit which we require in our economic system."[6]

Yet it is a matter of common observation that the amount of labor required to produce a commodity has almost nothing to do with either its use value or its exchange value. Useless artifacts, shoddy artifacts, defective artifacts, illegal artifacts, unhealthful artifacts, dangerous artifacts, all require labor, many of them much more labor than articles of good repute. It is not the amount of labor embodied in them

---

5. Smith, *Wealth*, p. 33.
6. Ricardo, *Principles*, p. 52; Keynes, *General Theory*, p. 214.

that makes them useless, shoddy, defective, illegal, unhealthful, or dangerous, nor would more labor necessarily correct their failings. Again: A house in a depressed suburb, which was worth a quarter of a million dollars a few years ago, can be had for half that price today. It is the same house, and the amount of labor it embodies is the same, if not actually more. Again: It took much labor to install asbestos ceilings in classrooms; but the asbestos was worse than valueless; it was harmful and had to be removed—with the expenditure of more labor.

Karl Marx sought to get around such difficulties by insisting on "socially necessary" labor.[7] Socially necessary labor is labor that produces a socially useful product. Marx said, "[N]othing can have value, without being an object of utility. If the thing is useless, so is the labour contained in it; the labour does not count as labour, and therefore creates no value."[8] Thus it is not labor that is the test of value; it is value that is the test of labor. A corrupt tree bringeth forth evil fruit, but the evil fruit proves the tree to be corrupt, not the other way around.

It is not always easy to say exactly what labor is. The army sometimes taught rambunctious soldiers to mind their manners by having them dig a hole six feet wide, six feet long, and six feet deep and then fill it up again. There was plenty of labor involved in the exercise, but not much economic consequence. Yet the labor was, at least in theory and perhaps even in intention, socially useful, because the result was supposed to be a better-disciplined soldier. Similar problems arise in trying to find a common measure of skilled labor and unskilled labor, efficient labor and inefficient labor, mental labor and menial labor, labor paid and unpaid, earnest labor and timeserving.

Consider the CEO of a *Fortune*-500 company, who has six or eight division presidents "reporting" to him, but really running the company, as much as anybody does. From sheer boredom he may throw himself into politicking somewhere, or he may throw the company into

---

7. Marx, *Capital*, p. 46.
8. Ibid., p. 48.

a frenzy of mergers and takeovers and spin-offs. Either way, the net consequence is not much greater than the soldier's six-by-six-by-six hole in the ground. In what sense is the soldier or the CEO laboring? How can their disparate laboring be a universal standard of value?

There are two ways of reducing what they do to a common denominator. The first is to accept their pay as the yardstick, or perhaps some ingenious accounting of the value they add in production; but such a solution equates money values with "real" values, and it was precisely to avoid this equation that the notion of a labor standard was introduced. The other possible measuring unit is time; the unit of labor is an hour of laboring.

THE ENTREPRENEUR

The Clayton Antitrust Act declares that "the labor of a human being is not a commodity or article of commerce." Labor is certainly not an ordinary commodity. It cannot be alienated more than once. An ordinary commodity can be sold and resold until it wears out, but free laborers sell their time only once. They work from sun to sun, and tomorrow is another day. Speaking more strictly, employers do not buy laborers' time or labor power; rather, they pay a fee (wages) for the temporary use of it, as a borrower pays a fee (interest) for the temporary use of money. The employer who "buys" today's labor power cannot sell it to someone else, who might in turn resell it. There are of course exceptions: slavery and peonage (which are different modes and so don't count), possibly certain sports and entertainment contracts, and some hiring practices, especially of farmhands, longshoremen, and part-time workers. All of these are limited in their incidence.

If labor is not a commodity, and if it is not a standard either, what is it? It is, what no one will ordinarily question, essential. It is fundamental, primary, irreducible, original, basic, ontological. It is, moreover, human. We do with it what we will; we will what we do with it.

How we labor is one of the principal ways in which we assert ourselves. We define ourselves by what we do and how we do it and how we treat the doings of others.

Labor may not be a commodity; yet we expect to be paid for our work. The program of "From each according to his abilities, to each according to his needs," first enunciated by Louis Blanc, then publicized by Marx in his *Critique of the Gotha Program*, and embalmed in the Soviet constitution, has not had broad appeal, at least among those with the abilities to make themselves heard. Even the towering prestige of Mao Zedong could not advance the idea much beyond sloganeering. We must assert ourselves in the world and must likewise look there for recognition.

The laborer who makes the most insistent—and usually richly rewarded—claim to recognition is the entrepreneur. Historically, the entrepreneur was both capitalist and executive. Adam Smith and John Stuart Mill, if they made the distinction at all, thought of the executive as a sort of overseer or foreman or clerk of the works or supercargo. He represented the owners, was an extension of their will, followed their orders. Occasionally he was able to accumulate funds of his own, whereupon he became a capitalist in his own right and abandoned his subservient position.

This structure, which was comfortably suited to individual proprietorships, partnerships, and even joint stock companies, was carried over, in the latter half of the nineteenth century, to the new limited-liability company. Arguing from one analogy or another, legislatures and courts developed a theory of the corporation whereby each share of stock, like each citizen of a democracy, had a vote in the election of the directors, who acted as a sort of legislature, established company policy, and hired the managers to execute that policy.

Even as this theory was being developed, it was recognized as a legal fiction. Subsequent critics, like R. H. Tawney, emphasized the corporate divorce between ownership and work. A. A. Berle and Gardiner C. Means documented the passing of control of the typical corporation from stockholders and directors to management. The shift of control to management tended, as John Kenneth Galbraith argued, to change corporate objectives from profit maximization to the protection of what he called the planning system and its technicians.[9] Today all public corporations are at risk of seizure and dismemberment by raiders interested neither in control nor in work but in capital gains.

Joseph A. Schumpeter was probably mistaken in seeing these changes as the result of "technological progress." Business may indeed, as he said, be increasingly conducted by "teams of trained specialists who turn out what is required and make it work in predictable ways." There is also much evidence that "[b]ureau and committee work tends to replace individual action." But it is not true that "the leading man . . . is becoming just another office worker—and one who is not always difficult to replace."[10]

The leading man has not in fact sunk into gray anonymity, as he would have done if his role had actually been reduced by technological progress. He is as colorful and as active as ever—and generally much better paid. His activities have been redirected, as Keynes understood, not by technology but by the development of the stock and futures exchanges, the voracious appetite of "institutions" for securities, and the consequent opportunities for arbitragers and raiders to make enormous fortunes out of takeovers and spin-offs. Keynes observed that "there is no sense in building up a new enterprise at a cost greater than that at which a similar existing enterprise can be purchased; whilst there is an inducement to spend on a new project what may seem an extravagant sum, if it can be floated off on the Stock Exchange at an immediate profit. Thus certain classes of investment [a footnote explained that these classes include practically all investment] are governed by the average expectation of those who deal on the

---

9. Tawney, *The Acquisitive Society*, p. 56ff.; Berle and Means, *Modern Corporation*, passim; Galbraith, *Economics and the Public Purpose*, chap. 10.
10. Schumpeter, *Capitalism, Socialism and Democracy*, p. 133.

Stock Exchange as revealed in the price of shares, rather than by the genuine expectations of the professional entrepreneur."[11]

The triumph of speculation over enterprise does not, of course, eliminate the human element. The leading man (in Schumpeter's phrase), no matter what kind of activity he leads, still needs animal spirits (in Keynes's). Someone must undertake to do whatever is done. It is convenient to continue to call him (or, it may be, her) the entrepreneur, though some of his or her activities would not be recognized by Smith or Mill or by Schumpeter or Keynes.

The entrepreneurial function, Schumpeter wrote, "does not necessarily consist in either inventing anything or otherwise creating the conditions which the enterprise exploits. It consists in getting things done."[12] The person with the special and comparatively rare talent that satisfies this function was earlier characterized by Frank H. Knight as an economic surd—that is, irrational. No perfectly prudent person is an entrepreneur; the risks of failure are too obvious and too great. As Keynes said, "If human nature felt no temptation to take a chance, no satisfaction (profit apart) in constructing a factory, a railway, a mine or a farm, there might not be much investment merely as a result of cold calculation."[13]

All of this is true; yet it is not impossible that the case for the entrepreneur has been overstated. There may be no industry without him, but industry depends also on those who toil in the vineyard, and it has occurred to many to wonder whether all that toil is necessary or desirable. Hesiod's *Works and Days*, which might be said to be the first economics text, as well as one of the oldest of literary works to come down to us, announces a theme that still teases mankind. After an invocation to Zeus, Hesiod laments:

---

11. Keynes, *General Theory*, p. 151.
12. Schumpeter, *Capitalism, Socialism and Democracy*, p. 132.
13. Keynes, *General Theory*, p. 150.

From men the source of life is hidden well.
Else you would lightly work enough today
To keep you a year while you lounged at play.

More recently, the same idea inspired Thoreau to retreat to Walden Pond, and more recently still, so-called alternate lifestyles have been celebrated.

Against these seductive notions, it has been argued that Thoreau's experiment depended not only on Emerson's support but also on the industries that originally produced the shanty boards and used windows and one thousand old bricks that he bought secondhand. Somebody worked at those industries, even though Thoreau didn't. Even Marx advanced a similar argument, contending that the historical role of capitalism was the rationalization of production necessary to make decent work and leisure generally available in the communist future. It is unquestionable that grinding poverty was the common lot in the Western world until very recently.

It is, however, equally unquestionable that hunters and gatherers, where they still exist, live comparatively toil-free lives, and that an appropriate ordering of priorities would enable even a New Yorker to work a stress-free thirty-five hours a week and have twice that time free for libraries and museums and botanical gardens and such. It would therefore seem necessary to recognize that the common laborer is as much an economic surd as is the entrepreneur. They are both essential for the work of the world; but there is no reason why either should work so hard at it—no reason, that is, except that work is one of the ways in which we define ourselves.

MANAGERS' PAY

In the meantime, entrepreneurs and managers are paid very richly, and common laborers are paid very poorly. When justification is sought for the interstellar differences, attention is usually called to the responsibilities accepted by the corporation CEO. If a workman on the assembly line makes a mistake, it is likely to be caught by someone else; and if it isn't, the possible damage is limited. But if the CEO makes a wrong decision, he may bankrupt the company. Furthermore, the workman cannot make a *correct* decision that is more than routine, while the CEO may, with a clever move, multiply the company's earnings many times.

The importance and difficulty of all this decision making are certainly overrated. As Galbraith has somewhere pointed out, difficult decisions usually are difficult because they are close, and close decisions tend to be close because there is not much to choose among the alternative possibilities. In such situations, it doesn't make much difference which way the ball bounces. Really important decisions, on the other hand, decisions that do make a difference, are often blindingly obvious.

That this analysis is in general correct is indicated by customary corporate practice. Apologists for big business—especially those inimical to government—are fond of contrasting the risky career of the business executive with the life tenure of the civil servant (in such discussions, the volatile life of the elected official is not mentioned). As a matter of fact, however, it is rare for a CEO to be dismissed for malfeasance, let alone for misfeasance or nonfeasance. In most companies it would be lèse-majesté to suggest that the old man had made a mistake. The life of a CEO is so stable that it caused some fluttering when Robert Townsend suggested in *Up the Organization* that the term of a corporation president ought to be no more than five years. If decision making were all that difficult, a CEO's life would not be such a happy one.

Although the difficulty of decision making may be exaggerated, it is true that most people are willing to let someone else do it. Successful business executives do display a willingness to make decisions, however easy or difficult, and are rewarded for that. In addition, they are said to have valuable experience to call on. Again there is something to the argument, but again perhaps less than is claimed for it. For it is reasonable to inquire how they came by all that experience. They were, as the saying goes, lucky enough to be in the right place at the right time, and not uncommonly they inherited the right place.

In any case, as people climb the corporate ladder, several important things are being tested beyond their ability to do sums in their heads and their cheerful willingness to anticipate what their boss wants. Perhaps most important of all, they are exhibiting their ability to learn, and especially their ability to understand at a glance how things work. If they're going to get ahead, they've got to have a quick ear and a sharp eye.

It must be acknowledged that the quick ear and the sharp eye are far from common. At the same time, it is possible that we may have here another of those nature versus nurture problems, like the debate over whether women are naturally slow at mathematics or merely are brought up that way. One's genetic composition (whatever that may mean), home environment, and formal education may be of the most promising, but a few years in the lower reaches of a large organization that happens to be riddled with office politics can be devastating. The winners in such contests prove themselves adept at politics; and if they're good at their jobs too, that's a plus. The losers' talents never have a chance to develop.

The winners, in fair contests as well as in foul, gain something more than pay raises. They gain experience. They have increased opportunities to practice the use of their eyes and ears. They learn by doing. Perhaps more important, they join C. Wright Mills's "power elite" and gradually expand their business connections so that they are eventually on familiar terms with the most "useful" people among their firm's customers, suppliers, and competitors, not to mention lawyers, bankers, and regulators. All of this makes them—or seems to make them—many times more valuable to their firms than the inexperienced, dispirited, though almost equally talented, losers. And this is said to justify the enormous difference in their salaries.

There is also, in the minds of the directors who formally set the high CEO salaries, another justification. They believe that they must pay their CEO well, or he (it's almost always "he") will decamp for some competitor that does pay well (after all, he knows them all), thus subtracting his skills from their company and adding them to the competition. It is not impossible that this reasoning is sound, especially since paying him an extra million, say, to hold him, is just a drop in a *Fortune*-500 bucket. Moreover, if he really and truly can increase his firm's profit by a million and one dollars (and who's to say he can't?), he will have proved, as standard economists say, the marginal utility of his raise.

This reasoning may remind us of the free-agent auction in baseball. And indeed the same principles operate, with the same results: astronomical salaries for a few stars, who are expected to attract the crowds, whopping raises to keep the most important and most powerful of the rest in line, and higher prices for the paying customers. This is a curious situation in which one individual, or a very small group, can have what Galbraith calls countervailing power[14] against a large corporation or even against the economy as a whole.

THE MANAGERIAL LADDER

At this point it may repay us to look a little more closely at the compensation of one of these fortunate few. Let us suppose a bright and well-educated young man of twenty-one, who does not inherit his position but is thought to be of "management potential." In the present state of the business world, it would not be quite realistic to suppose

---

14. Galbraith, *American Capitalism*, chap. 9.

a young woman in the same situation. So a young man. He starts work for a *Fortune*-500 company, not as an apprentice sweeping the factory floor, or even as a clerk running errands in accounts receivable, but as a management trainee. He is by no means at the bottom of the ladder, but it's still a long way to the top, and at every rung he's in head-to-head competition with others like himself, many from outside his company (and he may shift companies himself). If he gets to be CEO at age fifty-one, he will have prevailed in perhaps ten such contests—a competition rather like a tennis-club ladder, in which one periodically challenges the player above or is challenged by the player below.

At any rate, our man finally makes it to the top. The question is, How much better was he than his competitors? The difference may be thinner than a double-edge razor blade. Jimmy Connors was undisputed 1982 Wimbledon champion, but he and John McEnroe won the same number of games in the final match and even scored the same number of points. Beyond that, it is, as the announcers say, a game of inches.

Let's give our man all the credit we can. Let's suppose that, at each rung of the ladder, he shows himself 10 percent better than his competition. That is, one must admit, a pretty big margin if he runs into any competition at all. So if we give our hero a 10 percent superiority at every stage, we're not understating his attainments.

On this assumption it is reasonable to claim that when he finally pulls himself to the top, he has proved himself ten powers of 1.1 (1.1^{10}), or 2.59 times, better than the losers in the first contest. Thus it would seem reasonable for his pay to be 2.59 times theirs. If the permanent losers, with modest seniority raises, got themselves up to $60,000 at age fifty-one, the winning CEO should be earning 2.59 times that, or $155,400.

This is of course ridiculous. There is no *Fortune*-500 CEO who doesn't make many times $155,400, without even thinking of fringe benefits, options, and other perquisites. A $5-million-a-year man gets 32 times the amount we've calculated for a more run-of-the-mill CEO.

And consider: $5 million is 83 times the pay of the losers in the race, who were no fools to begin with, or about 250 times the poverty level for a family of four.

It is doubtful that anyone really believes that these fantastic differentials can be justified on any basis of amount of work or difficulty of work or contribution to the general welfare. It is sometimes contended, not without a show of reasonableness, that if a foreman (or forewoman) supervising six or eight workers receives a paycheck one or two thousand dollars higher than the workers', the CEO supervising sixty or eighty thousand workers is entitled to a proportionately higher reward. Or if the CEO of a firm with annual profits of a million dollars takes home a hundred thousand a year (and probably much more), the CEO of a company earning a billion dollars would be entitled to take home a hundred million. Of course, few *Fortune*-500 CEOs do (the really large salaries are paid by financial companies). The typical *Fortune*-500 CEO is actually supervising not sixty or eighty thousand people but six or eight subsidiary presidents, who in turn supervise six or eight vice presidents, who in turn supervise six or eight division heads, and so on down the line. This is, moreover, the chain of command; the CEO has an extensive staff to assist him and so do all his subordinates, except those at the end of the chain.

In the end, the argument is that in a free country with a free market, one is entitled to get whatever the market will bear. If the demand is great, it is right to reap the benefit of that demand. If there is strong demand for computer programmers and if few are available, competition will push their wages up. The same is true of common laborers, though they tend to get pushed in the other direction. It is all a question of supply and demand.

So it is said. One would have to be a fool not to be aware that given the way a modern corporation is set up, the CEO and those at the top can pretty much write their own tickets or, to change the figure, design their own golden parachutes. It is difficult to contemplate some recent performances of this sort without disgust. But this is not the present point. For the moment it is enough to observe that when you rely on the market to justify your salary, you are reducing your labor—and yourself—to a commodity, a mere thing.

THE EMPLOYER OF LAST RESORT

The aims of a human life are, as Freud said, loving and working. These are two of the ways in which we declare our membership in society and acknowledge our obligations. These declarations and acknowledgments are not passive; they must be actively pursued, and in this some are more fortunate than others.

On the other side, one has no obligation that is not confirmed by rights. Society can do little about loving—except to refrain from admitting impediments—but working is at the very heart of it. A political economy that fails to allow its citizens to contribute to the commonweal fails fundamentally.

This is not a matter of prudence or of benefit-cost analysis. The citizen's right to make a contribution is equal to society's right to hold him or her to obedience to the laws. No one has a right to a particular job with a particular firm, but everyone has a right to make a contribution. As a consequence, the state must be, as used to be said, the employer of last resort. The last resort is not the citizen's but the state's. It is the state's obligation to enable its citizens to advance the state's purposes. The problem is not, as the nineteenth century conceived it, one of forcing people to work by threatening starvation. Nor is it one of enticing people to work by promising rewards. Galbraith showed in *The Affluent Society* that while the economy can proceed very prosperously with large numbers of potential workers on the dole, the good society cannot proceed in that way.

Some emphasize the hurt to society when people, whether willfully or not, live without working. Others emphasize the hurt to individuals who are not permitted to make a contribution to—or to enjoy the privileges of—society. Both hurts are severe and unquestioned.

DIRECT ACTION

During the expansion of the 1990s, over 12 million men and women found jobs, but scarcely a million of these had not had at least some college education. It is safe to say that the ratio will be much less promising among the millions now counted as unemployed and the millions more too discouraged or too turned off to look for work. It must therefore be reluctantly concluded that the private sector is unable to do more to solve the unemployment problem, especially since the Federal Reserve Board seems determined to choke off any further expansion of the economy.

Aside from the dole (which of course does not affect employment), there are two principal programs available to the government. Both of them were adopted by the New Deal, and both were partially successful, although the Great Depression was a far more dreadful time than the present, and the New Deal did not—could not—summon the nation to go far enough. Yet a great deal was done by, and much can be learned from, the Works Progress Administration and the Public Works Administration.

PWA was a "pump priming" endeavor. The idea was to start large government projects—schools, hospitals, highways, dams, atom-colliders—with the expectation that the people employed on such projects would spend their earnings, which would stimulate retailers to re-stock their inventories, and pretty soon the economy would be humming. The trouble, of course, was that business was so slow that most stores and their suppliers could meet the increased demand without hiring many more workers. So while much good and valuable work was done, and those who had the jobs benefited, the "pump" did not get going on its own until World War II.

WPA was more like an ordinary relief organization, although it employed the unemployed in all sorts of original and exciting ways, but, again, the funds were too spare. Nevertheless, between the two programs, thousands of schools, libraries, hospitals, post offices, dams, and other public buildings were built. Electricity was brought to the farms. A start was made on public housing. Thousands of miles of highways were constructed. Thousands of square miles of public lands were improved by the CCC. Hundreds of pictures were painted; scores of plays were produced; uncounted amounts of literary and historical material were collected, preserved, and made available for study; fifty or more guidebooks were published, many of which have not been superseded more than a half century later. And millions of men and women were enabled to make a contribution to society. The extent of these contributions is obscured by the statistical quirk whereby those who worked for the WPA, CCC, NYA, and the rest of the so-called alphabet soup are counted as unemployed.[15]

The cost of the program was not substantially greater than the cost of inaction.[16] The deficit in 1933, the last Hoover budget, was $2.6 billion, whereas in 1939, the last prewar year, it was $2.8 billion.

Of course there was waste. There is waste in private industry, waste in private homes; life is wasteful. It is safe to say that the Pentagon now wastes more in a week than Dr. New Deal did in the entire eight years before being replaced by Dr. Win-the-War. But that is not the point. Nor is it relevant that most of the nongovernment art of that period, like most of the WPA art, no longer satisfies our aesthetic taste. The point is that millions of people were enabled to preserve their self-respect.

---

15. Michael R. Darby, "Three-and-a-Half Million U.S. Employees Have Been Mislaid," *Journal of Political Ecomony* 84, no. 1 (1976): 1–16.
16. See Gus Tyler, "Those New Deal Years," *The New Leader* LXIV, no. 24 (Dec. 28, 1981): 8ff.

How the government does or does not provide for the general welfare is crucial for the prosperity and the morale of the people—not just those involuntarily unemployed, but all the people. The government may fail at its task, leaving the rejected citizens with nothing to turn to and the government with nothing to show. It may succeed in ways that, for various reasons, foreclose development. Egyptian necropolises, Greek acropolises, Roman circuses, medieval cathedrals, all were magnificent public efforts, inevitably flawed. As for us, it is an open question whether we shall be remembered for e-mail or space stations.

There is no denying the probability that full employment would allow many people to make wage demands and improve their position. Nor can it be denied that the position of many people should be improved. The present price system would be upset; and even for those with increased money wages, the "real" wages might prove less than expected, because a measure of price inflation might ensue. The major shift, however, should come against the interest rate. This would be merely the inverse of what has been happening for fifty years.

In contrast with the cost of money, the cost of labor has been a remarkably steady factor in our economy. It is not, however, incised in granite that labor's share should be 60 percent, rather than much more or much less. A further caveat should be entered: When we talk of compensation of employees we lump together the multimillion-dollar salary of the *Fortune*-500 CEO with the fringe-free hourly wage of the part-time handyman setting out geraniums at the corporation's suburban headquarters. Especially in the past fifteen years, the salaries and "perks" at the top of the pay scale have grown astronomically (and after-tax income has grown faster yet), while hourly wages at the bottom have actually fallen, in so-called constant dollars, by 10 percent.[17]

---

17. For sordid details, see Crystal, *In Search of Excess*; Mishel and Frankel, *State of Working America*; McIntyre, *Inequality and the Federal Budget Deficit*.

WAGE SCALES

Self-justification—not market justification—is crucial if self-definition is the ground of labor. It would be absurd to find one's meaning in one's work and at the same time to declare the work unworthy. Such absurdity does, however, abound, whence the banal apology of businesspeople caught in sharp or mean practice, that they're not in it for their health.

Searching for the legitimation of private property, John Locke wrote, "As much land as a man tills, plants, improves, cultivates, and can use the product of, so much is his property."[18] He felt that a man's legitimate possessions were limited to what he could produce and use before it spoiled, but he granted that money as a store of value allowed one to pile up as much as one had a mind to. This piling up, it may be noted, was to be strictly in money, not in producers' goods. As early as Aristotle, however, it had been seen that the "so-called art of money-making" had no limit. This, of course, was a fatal defect to the Greek mind. Those who practiced this art were, Aristotle said, "intent on living only, and not upon living well; and as their desires are unlimited, they also desire that the means of gratifying them should be without limit."[19] Such people are still with us. The other day the son of a Texas oil multimillionaire dropped out of college, went to work for his father, and in short order had made some millions of his own. The father was asked why the son needed to do this. "What else is there to do?" was the rejoinder.

In all candor, it must be admitted that this sort of thinking is perfectly congruent with the introductory paragraphs of many (if not most) of today's economics-principles textbooks. In terms of desires or wants or material gain, there is no limit to moneymaking or to the bottom

---

18. Locke, *Second Treatise of Government*, chap. 5, secs. 32 and 50.
19. Aristotle, *Politics*, 1258a.

line or, for that matter, to the GDP. No invisible hand guides them. The compensation of labor—executive labor as well as common labor—has no "natural" standard; it is not a "scientific" question. It is an expression of the standards, the ideals, the will of society and its members. It is an ethical question.

Wage scales are, from top to bottom, a social creation, and they are an indicator of the sort of people we are. We demand to see expert tennis and so pay the top players in excess of a million dollars a year. We don't demand to see expert croquet and so pay croquet masters little or nothing. I myself share the preference for tennis; nevertheless, I recognize that there is nothing in the relative difficulty of the sports or the relative rarity of the requisite skills to justify the million-to-zero differential. The same is true of the relative contributions of the CEO and the unskilled laborer whose job he has just eliminated. The CEO and his company would be valueless in the Amazon rain forest or on the Antarctic icecap; their value is a social value. There are certainly differences in the social contributions of the CEO and the laborer, and even of the tennis star and the croquet shark. But the ranking of these differences and the prices that are put on them are not natural phenomena; they embody social judgments in which we all share.

That we Americans allot the richest rewards of our economy to speculators is a question of mores; that we allow one-sixth of our fellow citizens still to be ill housed, ill clad, and ill nourished is a question of morals; that we shrink from our problems instead of attacking them with eagerness, generosity, and hope is a question of morale. The questions are obviously interrelated.

It would be brash to expect much change in our ethics. Studies like Amartya Sen's recent book of lectures, with its awesome parade of scholarship (some 600 items in the bibliography for a book of 89 pages) are so bloodless that they may even be an impediment to change. He concludes: "I have argued that the rewards [of 'bringing economics closer to ethics'] can be expected to be rather large."[20] Who can be rallied to passionate endeavor by so diffident a call?

In the meantime, we should do well to remember that ethics in economics or business is not a special problem. There has been doubt about the relevance (that memorable word) of ethics in economics; but once this doubt is resolved, the remaining problems, though knotty, are well understood. Distinguishing right from wrong in economics (if it is to be done at all) is no harder than it is in marriage or public service or even sports. Nor is it any different. Ethics concerns all action. It inheres in everything we do. We perform ethical acts all the time, just as we ordinarily talk in prose.

Conventional economics is a world-historical idea. It is not trivial. It did not spring up casually. Economics was not split off from ethics by accident. The split would not have occurred if it had not satisfied an urgent need strongly felt by intelligent and vital and sincerely troubled men and women. The need, then as now, was for a revolution in ethics. Dogmatic moralism was no longer tolerable, but it was so domineering that the only escape from it seemed to be the denial of ethics altogether.

THE ETHICAL RULE

The ethical rule can be simply stated: Any full-time job that any employer finds necessary, desirable, or convenient is entitled to compensation sufficient to support a life of decency and dignity. If the job is not worth at least that much, it is not worth being done except as a favor or a hobby or a punishment.

It is obvious that "full-time" and "a life of decency and dignity" require definition. Furthermore, it is obvious that the definitions are

---

20. Sen, *Ethics*, p. 68.

social and historical. The 40-hour week is a comparatively recent standard in the United States; and the New Deal's first public housing had to omit interior plumbing because most neighboring private housing lacked it. Finally, it is obvious that to be truly effective the definitions will be codified and enforced by the state. It is then that we show the world and ourselves the sort of people we are.

7

The Corporation and the Entitlement of Labor

The idea of a corporation has its origins in eleventh- and twelfth-century problems in France concerning ownership of manorial parish churches, in fourteenth- and fifteenth-century problems in Italy concerning banking, and in sixteenth- and seventeenth-century problems in England concerning royal prerogatives, especially grants of monopolies. Though lines can be traced from these beginnings to the present, this history is now very dim, like the lines from medieval alchemy and astrology to modern chemistry and astrophysics.

The crucial concepts on which the modern corporation is built are limited liability, virtually unlimited powers, quasi-immortality, and readily alienable ownership. The last was facilitated by the extraordinary development of the stock exchanges, which would not have been possible without the first. All of them were facilitated in the United States by the remarkable persistence of the doctrine of states' rights, which allowed the states, particularly Delaware and New Jersey, to experiment with favors for new corporations.

From earliest times, partnerships had united the assets and skills of several individuals in enterprises larger than could have been undertaken by any of them separately. From the Renaissance, joint stock companies became a convenient way of organizing "adventures"—originally quite specific adventures, such as a single trading voyage of a single ship. The joint stock company differed significantly from the partnership in that it combined its holders' assets, but not necessarily their skills.

Shares in joint stock companies were attractive to people who, quite literally, had more money than they knew what to do with. The shares were also a convenient and business-like (that is to say, business seemed to be involved) vehicle for speculation. Their transaction costs, compared with those of, say, tulip bulbs, were minimal. The age-old bourses and money exchanges handled them readily and avidly. But they had a drawback. If the company issuing the shares failed, the shareholders were liable for its debts, so that they stood to lose not only what they had paid for the shares, but everything they owned besides. This provision had, as we might say, a chilling effect.

The chill was not serious until the Industrial Revolution supplanted the Commercial Revolution. Despite occasional embarrassments, there was little difficulty in assembling the necessary finance for even the most elaborate mercantile operations. "Bubbles" were caused not by a lack of finance but by an excess. Some people had, as aforesaid, more money than they knew what to do with.

With the Industrial Revolution, the financing required was of a different order of magnitude. Steam engines were large and expensive; they required large factories to contain them; in each factory, many expensive machines had to be powered by each engine, if efficient use was to be made of it. Large supplies of coal and inventories of raw materials had to be constantly on hand to keep things running smoothly. Because the production process was rationalized into many divisions, the inventory of partially finished goods was also great; and since at the end of the process there were more goods, which had to be distributed more widely, the costs of distribution were also large. Last but not least, many "hands" had to be employed. All of this took money. A few families, like the Lowells and Wedgwoods, could make a stab at family-owned factories, but there weren't enough such families to supply the opportunities. There was plenty of money around; the problem was to get it invested in fledgling industry rather than in country manors and stately homes. Such investment was resisted, partly out of snobbery, but partly also because of the risks of failure.

The solution was the limited liability corporation, formally created in Britain by the Acts of 1855, 1856, and 1862. Stockholders still stood to lose what they had paid for their shares, but they accepted no further risk. As W. S. Gilbert put it in *Utopia, Limited*:

> *You can't embark on trading too tremendous—*
> *It's strictly fair and based on common sense—*
> *If you succeed, your profits are stupendous—*
> *And if you fail, pop goes your eighteen pence.*

Corporate shares became less worrisome to buy and so easier to sell.

As the stockholders' liability became limited by statute, the corporation's powers became unlimited through judicial desuetude. Originally, a corporation was formed for a specific purpose, which was spelled out in the agreement or charter that set it up. Any activity not in conformity with the founding purpose was an *ultra vires* act, beyond the authorized powers of the corporation, and so not enforceable at law and sometimes subject to criminal sanctions. Founding purposes often displayed a lively imagination. R. R. Palmer tells of early eighteenth-century English schemes for "a company to bring live fish to market in tanks, an insurance company to insure female chastity, a company 'for an undertaking which shall in due time be revealed.' "[1]

For two hundred years sporadic attempts were made to control such fancies, but ultimately it became simply too difficult to define an *ultra vires* act. A company formed to trade in Asia could reasonably build

---

1. Palmer, *Modern Europe*, 6th ed., p. 260.

and man ships and protect its fleets on the high seas; it could produce the goods, of whatever description, it proposed to sell abroad; it could also maintain and defend warehouses (or "factories") in foreign lands and, where locally permitted, produce the goods it proposed to sell at home. There was little a state could do that such a company could not do; the British East India Company eventually ruled a subcontinent.

In the United States there was never much litigation under the *ultra vires* doctrine. Today a corporation's purpose is generally assumed to be just to make money; and the corporation is, as a juridicial person, protected in its pursuit of that purpose by the Bill of Rights and the Fourteenth Amendment.

With limited liability and unlimited powers came immortality. And with corporate immortality came the steady erosion of the role of the individual entrepreneur. An individual may be the catalyst to get a corporation going or to keep it on track. But nobody lives forever, and the most vigorous captain of industry has but a little while upon the stage. The corporation lives after him or her and itself performs all the functions formerly performed by personal entrepreneurs.

PROFIT

Profit is the economic reward of enterprise, as wages are the reward of labor, interest the reward of lending money, rent the reward of lending land or utilities in the broadest sense. Profit, whether personal or corporate, is what is left after expenses have been paid.

Profit is something other than wages, interest, or rent. It does not have any analyzable cause or any assignable amount. It is merely the remainder, at any given point, of the income from the sale of the enterprise's products, or, mayhap, assets, less their costs of production.

Profit is systematically different from interest, though the two are often confused. Interest is a fee paid according to contract for the use of money. Profit is the uncertain return of enterprise—that is, of making or doing something. When an entrepreneur provides his own money (or when a firm finances this year's expansion out of last year's profits), a tightly run firm will charge itself an opportunity cost for the use of these funds, which might have been invested, say in the money market, and thus have earned a relatively carefree profit. Opportunity cost is of course not recognized by the taxing authority, but it is essential for measuring the comparative profitability of different projects or divisions of a firm or different private investment opportunities.

Enterprise always has something left over—it may be loss or it may be gain—because the future is unknown and unknowable. No matter how carefully we plan, we must, in the end, be more or less surprised. This is not merely a statistical result, as is the fact that half of the parties to a bet must be disappointed. Nor is it merely an empirical observation of the outcomes of the best-laid plans of mice and men. More important than statistics or empiricism, the systematic uncertainty of the future is a requirement of responsible action. If Pandora's box had not kept the future hidden, the present, too, would have been foreordained; life would have been a walking shadow; and there would not even have been a meaningful way of claiming that it was meaningless.

The definition posits no specific source for profit. In some cases profit may be the result of chance or of a risk well run; in others the chance falls the other way. Sometimes it is the consequence (which for some enterprises may be favorable) of war or pestilence. Sometimes innovation is richly rewarded, and sometimes it is cruelly punished. Sometimes vigor achieves wonders; at other times what was hoped to be vigorous action proves to have been the rushing in of fools. Whatever we may decide, after the fact, to have been the source of a particular profit, an enterprise has no way of systematizing all sources of future profits and losses. Whatever is systematically accounted for is thereupon allocated and charged to wages, interest, or rent. Profit or loss will still be left over.

PLANNED PROFIT

"Planned profit" is an informal concept regularly used in business. Though informal, the concept has a great effect on the price level and on the state of the economy in general. It is not a determinate figure; statistics do not explain it. Rather, it is a determining figure; it sets a goal, a target, a standard by which prospective enterprises are judged.[2] It is not an absolute standard like, say, the amount of radiation a human body can tolerate at a certain point. It is, instead, a rate, a percentage—which is understandable because its opportunity cost usually is a rate, the interest rate.

Though related to interest, planned profit is not, as the interest rate is, a contractual rate, but is a hoped-for rate, based on experience and subject to great fluctuations depending on the prevailing morale of society. A society or a firm marked by creative energy and good will will set the rate low, while one racked by pessimism and financial greed will set it high.

A high planned profit tends to impede enterprise because fewer enterprises will be judged likely to earn so much. Not only will fewer new businesses be started, but many existing businesses will reduce their operations, shutting down those "profit centers" that seem unlikely to earn that planned profit.

If you expect it to be difficult to make a profit, you will make your task harder by demanding a higher rate before you undertake the job. A higher planned profit will require higher prices, which will tend to reduce sales, which may cause diseconomies of scale, which will adversely affect total profits and, probably, the achieved rate of profit, too.

Adam Smith argued that increased profits have what he called a geometric effect on prices, as opposed to an arithmetic effect of in-

---

2. Planned profit is, in Myrdal's terminology, *ex ante*, and actual profit is *ex post*. See Myrdal, *Monetary Equilibrium*, pp. 45–47.

creased wages. But actual profits are merely what's left over after bills are paid and receivables collected; so they are affected by, but cannot affect, actual prices. Planned profits, on the other hand, being calculations made before the project begins, do have an effect similar to the one Smith described, since the usual business practice, now as then, is to calculate planned profit and prices as percentages of costs. (Actual profit is usually reported as a percentage of sales or of invested capital.)

Consider a firm with a wage bill (which, for our present purposes, may be taken as its only expense) of $1 million, and a planned profit of 10 percent, or $100,000. If the firm decides to increase both wages and planned profit by 5 percent, it will calculate the new wage bill to be $1,050,000, and the new planned profit to be 0.105 times $1,050,000, or $110,250.

Originally the firm priced its product to achieve a gross income of $1,100,000. Now it must achieve $1,160,250—a price increase of 5.48 percent, rather than the 5 percent that the increase in wages and planned profit might seem to require. The wage increase is truly 5 percent, but the planned profit is increased 10.25 percent.

If the firm decides on a similar 5 percent increase in a second year, the results will be: wages, $1,102,500; planned profit, $115,763; and gross income, $1,218,263. Over the two years the apparent increase of 10 percent has instead become: wages, 10.25 percent; planned profit, 15.76 percent; and gross income (or prices), 10.98 percent. In short, prices go up considerably faster than wages, and planned profit goes up the fastest of all. Further increases will only amplify these results.

There is, of course, no natural law that requires planned profit to be calculated in the foregoing way, and certainly no law that requires all firms to do it in the same way. This is, however, the normal way in our society. Indeed, what I am calling planned profit is commonly referred to as normal profit. The rates of the examples are likewise not "natural" but are set by each individual firm under the influence of the interest rate set by the monetary authorities. So the most we have here is a trend or influence.[3] The influence, nevertheless, is powerful, because interest is a necessary cost of all business and therefore affects the planned profit of every firm in the chain of production, from raw materials to final sale, and the increased planned profit of every firm lower in the chain is included in the base of higher firms. "The rise of profit," Smith concluded, "operates like compound interest. Our merchants and master-manufacturers complain much of the bad effects of high wages in raising the price, and thereby lessening the sale of their goods both at home and abroad. . . . They are silent with regard to the pernicious effects of their own gains."[4]

THE CORPORATION AS ENTREPRENEUR

Since profits result from enterprise, it would be reasonable for profits to go to enterprise. As all modern economies have developed, however, profits accrue to capital, which is merely one of the factors of enterprise. This is obviously true of capitalism, and it was true of communism as well, where the means of production, which was another name for capital, were the property of the state, not of the enterprises that do the producing.

It is easy to understand how these arrangements came about. Until recently, all enterprises were conducted by individuals or small groups of individuals who had, in one way or another, amassed the wealth used in their businesses. Whatever land they used was also owned by them. And they themselves directed the enterprises and in

---

3. Nicholas Kaldor, in his Arthur M. Okun Memorial Lectures at Yale, was satisfied to put it this way: "[E]very increase in wages will raise profits, since for each unit of output, much the same percentage is added to value-added as is added to wages." Kaldor, *Economics without Equilibrium*, p. 39.
4. Smith, *Wealth*, pp. 97–98.

many cases performed all the work involved. Consequently it was reasonable for the profits to go exclusively to them; and when it was a question of selling the business, the decision was theirs and the rewards were theirs. Today, however, though individual enterprises in the classic manner are large in number, they do a small proportion of the business of the country, reap a minuscule share of the profits, employ a tiny minority of the workers, are typically not in manufacturing, and generally have short and erratic lives.

The modern corporation is itself the entrepreneur. It may have started as a one-man or one-woman show, and it may continue under the dominance of one man or woman. But he or she does not own it, and the profits go to those who do. The owners, moreover, and only they, have the right to sell the corporation or any part of it and to take for themselves the entire net proceeds of the sale. This is an unreasonable state of affairs, because, as everyone knows, the legal owners of a modern corporation have practically nothing to do with it. The legal fiction has it that the stockholders elect the directors, and that the directors appoint and oversee the officers who conduct the daily business of the corporation. In practice, unless a hostile takeover is in progress, officers generally select and dominate the directors, who are routinely elected by those stockholders who bother to return their proxies.

Not only do most stockholders have practically nothing to do with the corporation, they never wanted to have anything to do with it. They merely wanted to make an investment or to speculate on a takeover or merger. They had somehow come into some money, and they wanted to place it where it would be reasonably liquid and also have a chance of returning something more than bank interest. The invention of the limited liability company was a blessing for such people, and the blessing was magnified by the creation of comparatively efficient securities markets. Since, with few exceptions, shares are "fully paid and nonassessable," those who hold them need not worry about the company's debts, nor need they fear the loss, even in the extreme case, of more than they paid for the stock. And since they can sell out at any time, they need not fuss about providing alternatives to company policies they find unsatisfactory. Instead of trying to organize opposing points of view, they can sell out and register their disapproval in that way.

No matter what careless or even deliberate horror is perpetrated by their company, the owners accept no responsibility. They would not, they insist, have become owners if responsibility had been expected of them. How could they have known that the gasoline tank of the Pinto was unsafely designed? How could they have known that DES might cause cancer? How could they have known that exposure to asbestos could lead to leukemia twenty years later? And if there had been some way in which such knowledge could have been available to them, what could they as individuals, each with a few shares or even a few thousand shares, have done about it? There was no way in which they could effectively participate in the daily operations of Ford or Lilly or Johns Manville; and on the other side, the managements of those companies would claim that they could not operate with such participation. Aside from the confusion that would result, what could then be done to protect trade secrets (whatever they may be)?

What we have said so far is neutral as to persons. The personal ownership of consumers' goods presents no great problem; whoever consumes them thereby owns them. You can't possess the bread that I eat, and you have no desire to possess my toothbrush. I may be indebted to you for the cost of the bread or the toothbrush, but the bread and the toothbrush, themselves, are mine.

In general, there is no doubt that at least some consumers' goods can be personal property, although the rights they consist of may be limited or modified in various ways (for no right is absolute), and the limitations and modifications may change as the world changes. The great problems concern the ownership of producers' goods, because that ownership includes the right to control production. Those who own producers' goods have control of their fellows in a vital way.

USE VALUE AND EXCHANGE VALUE

Property is not a thing but a bundle of enforceable rights. In the beginning, rights are enforced by one's strong right arm, and property is accordingly what a person can physically take possession of. "An Englishman's home is his castle" expresses the idea, which was, over the centuries, elaborated by the common law. Adam Smith called this right "value in use," which he distinguished from another right, "value in exchange."

The recognition of exchange value is indeed a characteristic of modern capitalism. In the United States it is scarcely a hundred years old and is not yet fully understood. In *Legal Foundations of Capitalism*, one of the neglected great books, John R. Commons wrote, "Finally, in the first Minnesota Rate Case, in 1890 the Supreme Court itself made the transition and changed the definition of property from physical things having use-value to the exchange-value of anything."[5] Prior to that decision the courts would enforce only one's right to hold property. The question did not come before the Supreme Court until the Thirteenth Amendment ended property in people and the Fourteenth Amendment extended responsibility for civil rights to the states. In the Slaughterhouse Cases of 1872, the Court, in a split decision, held that, under the law, property was merely use value. The contrary view was presented powerfully in dissent but did not finally prevail until eighteen years later.

Exchange value makes property an idea, not a datum. It is what people think they can do with it that determines it. Its setting is historical. It looks to the future. It is an opportunity for doing. It is also a problem, the consequence of a past doing. Less abstractly, if I have worked to build up a bookstore, I can work to continue to or expand

---

5. Commons, *Legal Foundations of Capitalism*, p. 14. See also Heilbroner, *The Nature and Logic of Capitalism*, esp. pp. 34–37.

it or even sell it, but I can scarcely turn it into a filling station. Past doing makes present and future doing possible; it establishes opportunity but not formless or unrestricted opportunity.

Exchange value is the capitalization of expected profits, not of realized profits. Past profits are spent, just as past costs are sunk; future costs and future profits are what rule. As property becomes idealized in this way, it comes to include what Commons called good will, which is not merely reputation based on past performance but a system of continuing relationships. Commentators attempting to explain the Asian debacle of 1997 made much of "cronyism," as though friendship were necessarily corrupt and business could or should be inhumanely impersonal. A business is a going concern or it is nothing. If I auction off my goods and chattels, I do not establish a continuing relationship with the buyers or even with the auctioneer; my auction is not a business.

The organization of a business counts for more than its physical assets. Tools and machinery, factories and warehouses, can be bought outright, or their services can be rented. It is not different with good will, which is frequently the real object of takeover and buyout contests. Without the brand names, RJR Nabisco's factories and warehouses would scarcely have been worth what was paid for the company in 1989. Good will can be rented as well as bought, as when large sums are paid to advertising agencies for discovering and dramatizing the secret built-in goodnesses that identify products, when enormous sums are paid to electronic and print media for access to audiences they have built up, and when further sums are paid to athletes and other celebrities for endorsements. Even good organization can be rented, as witness the burgeoning business of consulting.

"Owning capital," Joan Robinson said, "is not a productive activity."[6] Extending her remark, we can say that neither ownership of cap-

---

6. Robinson, *Essay on Marxian Economics*, p. 18.

ital, nor ownership of land, nor ownership of labor power, nor ownership of money is a productive activity. Ownership of assets, goods, or services is not the enterprise and so is not entitled to the profits of the enterprise, but only to the profits of assets, goods, or services themselves, that is, to sales prices or fees for service. It may happen that any of these various owners participates in a given enterprise, but only workers necessarily do so. From the point of view of the enterprise, managers (who are paid salaries and bonuses) and even directors (who collect fees for service) are employees, grander perhaps but not essentially different from laborers on the factory floor.

THE ENTITLEMENT OF LABOR

Because labor, whether current labor or past labor, is the source of economic goods, many have attempted to find in labor the source of value. These attempts have failed, but the impulse behind them was sound. It is by labor and only by labor that we produce goods and come to possess them. No goods exist except in conjunction with human activity. Whatever is made is made by the hand of man or woman, and whatever services are performed are performed by men and women. Labor is primary, though not the source of value. Instead, as Locke said, labor "gave *a Right of Property*,"[7] which we may call the Labor Theory of Entitlement.

Even conventional theory is ultimately based on the Labor Theory of Entitlement. Whatever one owns came into existence—not as a mere object but as an economic good—as a result of labor. Its production entailed the use of producers' goods, but they in their turn are the result of labor, and they came into one's possession as a result of labor, whether one's own or someone else's. Land and natural re-

7. Locke, *Second Treatise*, sec. 45.

sources remain natural objects unless cultivated or collected. Thus the entitlement of land and capital to participate in profit depends, even as understood by apologists for the present system, on the fact that they are the embodiment of past labor. The entitlement of current labor is immediate; the workers are present, and the sweat glistens on their brows. But the entitlement of the owners of capital is secondary; it depends on the fact that their capital was itself once a direct entitlement of labor. Thus their entitlement cannot rise higher than that of labor, which is its source. What is past, what is even dead and gone, cannot take precedence over what is now and is continuing.

Abstinence, the classical basis for the rights of capital, is not the exclusive province of stockholders and bondholders. The workers' abstinence is no less severe; they stay on the job instead of going fishing or lying in the sun. Some workers may not absent themselves from felicity to the satisfaction of some observers. The same can be said of some holders of portfolios.

Nor is risk taking an exclusive function of capital. Life is risky, and no life more risky than that of propertyless working men and women. The stockholders' risk is obvious; they may lose their shirts and have to work to get others. The laborers' risk is not less actual for being possibly less dramatic; they devote time and sometimes money to learning a skill that may become worthless if the enterprise fails. They are also more closely committed to the enterprise (even when they hate it) than are the stockholders or bondholders. It is more difficult for them to pull out at the first sign of faltering, for jobs are hardly ever easy to find, and they cannot handily move from town to town in search of work. The stockholders or bondholders have only to call their brokers. Finally, the workers may be ruined by the company's decision to move from one locality to another, while the stockholders may gain from such a shift.

The right of labor to participate in profit is bolstered by the implications of any employment contract. As we saw in the little hiring scenario in Chapter 4, it is in the nature of things necessary either for employers to pay their employees in advance or for employees to do a job before they are paid for it. The latter option being the custom in our system, the employees of any business have their earnings for half a pay period on perpetually revolving interest-free loan to the business. As a result, the business can make a corresponding expansion of plant or inventory or marketing services. In short, its capital is increased by this contribution of labor as effectively as it is by the cash contributions of capitalists.

Thus there is no right that capitalists can claim that laborers do not have a claim to. If capitalists have a right to control enterprise, so do laborers. If capitalists have a right to receive profits—or suffer losses—so do laborers. So far, the right of one is not stronger than the right of the other. A good society, however, will recognize the wisdom and justice of Jefferson's dictum: "The earth belongs to the living and not to the dead."

OWNERSHIP RIGHTS AND DUTIES

Rights exist only as they are asserted. No right exists merely because it is asserted, but no right exists unless it is asserted. The assertion of a right is an act of will, and the recognition of a right, as by law, is an act of will in which everyone participates as a member of society. The failure to assert a right is also an act of will, as is the failure to accept responsibility; and the failure of the law to assign a responsibility is a failure of the will of the society.

Il gran rifiuto of today's economic life is the stockholders' assertion, supported by the law, of ownership rights and their simultaneous refusal, also supported by the law, of all ownership duties whatever. Classical entrepreneurs were proud of their enterprises. They were textile manufacturers, dry-goods merchants, railroaders. No one claims that such commitment was or can be a certain preventive of abuses of all kinds—abuses of workers, of investors, of the public—

but it does clear a ground of responsible action for those with the will to occupy it. To be a conglomerate person is to be nobody in particular, with no commitment to anything in particular except the bottom line, the bottom line or a speculative killing being in fact the only excuse for the conglomerate.

To be a portfolio holder is to be even less significant, especially since so much of today's typical middle-class portfolio is made of stock funds, money-market funds, insurance policies, and the like. Although the funds' shareholders regularly receive reports of the securities their funds own, it is safe to say that they could not name many of them and are unlikely to know more about any of them than may be compressed into a couple of sentences of a broker's newsletter. They have nothing to do with the success or failure of their funds and far less to do with the companies they partially and indirectly own than the proverbial office boy.

The attenuation of ownership has reached a point where between one-third and one-half the shares of most of our large corporations are owned by "institutions"—not only mutual funds, but insurance and pension funds, charitable endowments, churches, colleges and universities, public service foundations, and private trust funds generally. At first glance one might think that the vesting of ownership in such responsible hands would make for stability. Quite the contrary. The managers of the funds are indeed responsible, but theirs is a fiduciary responsibility, which constrains them to accept whatever offer promises the highest immediate gain for their beneficiaries. If they do not, they may find themselves defendants in a suit for damages. Thus it can happen that the trustees of a corporate pension fund that owns some of the corporation's stock will vote those shares in favor of a takeover, and the takeover will result in the beneficiaries' loss of their jobs and possibly of the pension rights that presumably were being protected. Nor are the managers of mutual funds less likely to jump for the quick buck, for their performance will be judged by what they have done this day or this quarter. Neither trustees nor managers can afford to be bothered by what may happen to the companies they have temporarily invested in. And individual stockholders, too preoccupied with their own affairs to take an intelligent interest in their companies, are no different.

This triumph of finance over enterprise is inexorable so long as ownership carries no responsibilities. Irresponsible owners are classical economic men par excellence, and they will go where they can get the most of what they are interested in, which is money. They will consequently put pressure on brokers to find for them companies that will slake their thirst; brokers will pressure investment bankers to float the issues of such companies; investment bankers will pressure commercial bankers to give priority to such companies; and all pressure will be brought to bear on the management of every public company to do whatever needs to be done to thicken the bottom line.

That frequently the easiest way to increase the bottom line is to go, as they say, the merger-and-acquisition-and-diversification route is only the most visible outcome. Such maneuvers generally can increase the bottom line only by "rationalizing" the merged companies—which means downsizing, or closing plants and firing people. In such circumstances, loyalty is comprehensively destroyed. No one is or can afford to be loyal to the enterprise—not the owners, not the fiduciaries, not the financiers, not the suppliers, not the management, not the work force, not the customers. Nor are owners, fiduciaries, financiers, suppliers, managers, workers, or customers encouraged to be loyal to each other.[8] This atomization of concern is doubtless a major cause of the widely deplored decline in standards of workmanship. It certainly is a major consequence of increased speculation on Wall Street.

---

8. Royce, *Philosophy of Loyalty*, p. 139.

CAPITAL VS. LABOR

Marx had an apocalyptic vision of a final battle between capital and labor, but it didn't come to pass on any of the several occasions when he expected it in his lifetime, nor is there reason to expect that the struggle will end of itself. To be sure, there is no lack of peacemakers ready to demonstrate that capitalists and workers need each other, nor is there a lack of more or less grudging acceptance of that mutual need. Otherwise the economy would not work at all. But there are times when the mutuality disappears. There are, typically, times of change, when a business is faltering or, contrariwise, when a technological leap forward seems possible or desirable.

In depressions or recessions some capitalists lose some money, but many workers lose their jobs. This outcome is so commonplace that no one even thinks to defend it. I doubt that it can be defended. If both capital and labor are essential to production, by what right are things more worthy of protection or conservation than people?[9]

As for technological advances, they have always been resisted by workers. Yet Britain could not have achieved its first breakthrough if landowners had not enclosed the commons and driven tenants off the land to make way for sheep. Later, if the Luddites had had their way, the Industrial Revolution would have been aborted; and if the followers of Captain Swing had prevailed, the denizens of the cities could not have been fed even as well as they were.

Economists scold when automobile workers resist giving up their jobs to robots. Labor-saving machines are opposed as labor-eliminating devices. Editorialists ask, Why can't these people see that new robotic industries will make new jobs, just as automobile making turned out to employ many times as many people as harness making? Why should

---

9. "When output [of a United States corporation] falls $1, the income of workers tends to decline 48 cents and profits 52 cents. In Japan, by contrast, virtually 100 percent of output fluctuations [is] borne by stockholders." Frank R. Lichtenberg, in *New York Times*, February 16, 1992, p. F13.

anyone in his right mind fight to preserve mind-deadening work on the old-fashioned production line? What is so great about conditions in Southern textile mills that leads people to want to keep them going in the face of cheap imports from Asia?

Society is certainly better off with more mechanization, more robotization. Taylor management increased the productivity of shovelers and bricklayers, and it also made the work itself less exhausting. It is a blessing that the bulldozer and the earthmover have supplanted those who used to push-a, push-a, push on the Delaware-Lackawan'." It is a blessing that the backhoe has made "ditchdigger" an obsolete term of opprobium. It is a blessing that the dishwasher has replaced the scullery maid. Not only is such progress irresistible, it is largely beneficial.

But there is trouble in paradise. The trouble is systemic. The individuals who are displaced by progress are systematically denied the benefits of progress. The working class or the worker as function may be better off in the famous long run, but the individual workers will often lose not only money but job, career, independent livelihood, sometimes forever.

There is no reason for those who are displaced by robots to be consoled by the prosperity of those who build robots. Nor is there reason for the owners of a factory to invest in and so become owners of robots unless they reap the reward of that investment in a better return, which means reducing costs, which means firing people. It is this allocation of ownership and its rewards that turns labor-saving machinery into labor-displacing machinery. None of this is necessary. It is a result of the faulty design of the modern corporation.

STOCKHOLDERS' IRRESPONSIBILITY

The irresponsibility of stockholders has been widely noted, and much ingenuity has been lavished on proposals to correct the situation. Some of these notions try in one way or another to make it easier for dissidents to be elected to the boards of directors, thus presumably encouraging stockholders to pay attention. Others would mandate representatives of "the public" on the boards, thus trying to make the boards responsible to somebody, regardless of the fact that the stockholders are responsible to no one but themselves.

Such schemes are doomed to failure, not because they are necessarily wrong-headed, but because no one actually wants them. A few enthusiasts now busy themselves in attending and speaking up at stockholders' meetings, but investors with prudently diversified portfolios could not possibly master the intricacies of the businesses they partly own. They realize they could not; so they sensibly find better things to do with their time. Public board members would not be in much better case. They could not expect to make a career attending board meetings, nor could they reasonably expect to learn enough about any company to be useful. The most likely outcome is that they would be co-opted by their genial colleagues; and if they should entertain ideas at variance with those of the rest of the board, they would find it difficult to overcome the pressures of small-group psychology, especially as the public to whom they were supposed to be responsible not only would be largely indifferent but would have no way of supporting or rejecting or learning about the board members' ideas.

More important, the public's interest in any particular company is abstract and can be satisfied by general laws. The public is reasonably concerned that the corporation pay its taxes, abjure fraud, respect its workers, not harm the environment, and refrain from skittering hither and thither in search of weak regulation and lower taxes. These ends could and should be served otherwise. There is, however, no rational possibility of framing a law requiring stockholders to assume any responsibility that they could not in practice discharge—one, moreover, that neither they nor the corporations they invest in want them to have.

Why, then, should stockholders, who refuse the duties of ownership, be protected in the rights of ownership? There is actually only one reason: They now enjoy those rights. Abstinence and risk taking they share with bondholders and employees; management they leave to a special kind of employee. What is left is possession, and that is nine points of the law. The tenth point, however, is rationality, and one would like to see movement in that direction.

CORPORATIONS' IRRESPONSIBILITY

More fateful than the stockholders' irresponsibility toward the corporation is the corporation's irresponsibility toward the people who do its work. Corporations (and individual employers as well) assume the right to hire at will, to set wages, to assign any work not forbidden by law, and to fire at will. There is now, to be sure, a considerable body of law that restricts these rights in one way or another, but basically they are unquestioned. The corporation is said to require these rights if it is to enforce the discipline necessary in the modern workplace.

Discipline is not actually the issue. The business press used to blame the decline of British trade on labor laws passed by the postwar Labor governments. That Conservative relaxation of these laws did not improve trade has gone unnoticed. Workers everywhere—even in Germany, where they are notoriously self-disciplined—can be fired for reasons that have nothing to do with the quantity or quality of their work. Indeed, a truly work-related firing is everywhere the most difficult to achieve. But a corporation or part of one can be sold or abandoned, and people who have spent a lifetime diligently doing what they were told can forthwith lose their jobs. There is some talk about protecting people caught up in such catastrophes, but no thought at all is given to a more fundamental situation—the universal practice of hiring people when business is good, and letting them go when it is bad.

The curious thing is that no one wonders whether it might be otherwise. A business finds itself, for whatever reason, troubled or merely disappointed. Profits are vanishing or merely down, occasionally the company's continued existence is at stake. What does it do? It cuts costs, and the costs of labor are, as previously noted, the largest, most visible, and most convenient component. Wages are cut where possible; and even where wage cuts are deemed impossible, people are fired. Belts are said to be tightened. All of this seems perfectly natural and necessary. How could the system work otherwise? This is the way of the world.

Yet this way of the world is a modern development. Nothing like this went on in ancient Greece or in the medieval world. The way of the world changed with the liberation of the serfs. As the serfs achieved the right to leave their lords' domains, the lords achieved the right to force them out. If anyone thought about the matter, it might have been argued that these new rights balanced each other. But no one thought about it; it went without saying that the owners of property could do what they wanted with it. The rights of ownership were paramount. More than that: they were necessary to power and hence to independence and hence to freedom. This line of argument was congenial to the Enlightenment and is congenial to this day.

An apparent corollary is that people who own no property enjoy a certain license but not freedom in the full sense. They not only have severely restricted rights but ought to have severely restricted rights. Thomas Jefferson would have lifted the restrictions by giving every man fifty acres, as ninety years later Thaddeus Stevens would have given every freedman forty acres and a mule. Without such a patrimony, the common man could not be expected to be a free and responsible citizen. And what did responsibility mean? Then as now responsibility was first and foremost respect for property. A recurring fear of political scientists is that the rabble of the propertyless will be roused to seize or destroy the property of the rich and well born. As Adam Smith was among the first to observe, it is indeed a wonder that such arousal has not generally occurred.

The rights that constituted physical property—land you can dig in, things you can touch—have been extended to the new form of property, which is a share in a corporation. In effect, they have been extended to the corporation itself. Hence the corporation has the right to recruit people to work with its property and also the right to discharge the recruits at its convenience. These rights of property are sacrosanct. "Employment is generally considered to be property of the employer rather than the employee."[10] The rights to life, liberty, and the pursuit of happiness are subsidiary to the rights of property, even though the latter are not mentioned in the Declaration. Property, which is not and never has been alive, is more important in the eyes of the law than living men and women.

WORKERS' IRRESPONSIBILITY

The great refusal of the stockholders has an apparent parallel in the reluctance of the generality of workers to participate in management. The parallel is only apparent. The stockholders refuse to play a role that is now legally theirs, while the workers are slow to fight for a role that is rightfully theirs.

There are many reasons for this. In the history of American labor relations, workers have been able to improve their lot primarily through tradewide and industrywide unionization. Given what must be reckoned a persistent bias of the courts, the workers have been at the scarcely restricted mercy of the bosses. Their survival has depended on their solidarity with one another, rather than on the prosperity of the firms they work for. Even profit sharing has been looked at askance and usually rejected as a disguised form of the speedup.

Employee ownership is not without its supporters. In the 1920s Edward A. Filene, searching for a way out of the misery of early-twentieth-century industrialism, became a strong advocate. Accordingly he tried to establish a form of employee ownership in his Boston department

---

10. Areeda, *Antitrust*, p. 73.

store, but was disappointed to discover that most of the employees were not interested or were overawed by a few of their more energetic fellows.

In spite of many such experiences, enthusiasts for employee ownership claim that self-interest will make the employees work harder, and that employee-owned firms will therefore outperform conventional corporations, if not drive them out of business.[11] Nothing like this has happened. Self-interest remains undefined; and some employee-owned firms are efficient; some are not. Efficiency is not the issue; justice is. It is desirable to be efficient, it is vital to be just.

In his book *Beauty Looks After Herself*, Eric Gill wrote that a slave does what he has to do when he is at work and what he wants to do on his own time, while a free man does what he wants to do when he is at work and what he has to do on his own time. On this basis, most men and women are slaves, though in bondage only to themselves. The reasons for this are various, and they are by no means all economic.

The economic reasons flow largely from the authoritarian and megalomaniac structure of most contemporary business enterprises. Small is indeed beautiful. This is not because small is more efficient than giantism. Sometimes it is, and sometimes it isn't. The beauty of smallness is in the eye of the producer, not necessarily of the consumer. A small company can be a better place to work than a large one. Small institutions can allow more scope for individual assertiveness and creativity and responsibility of all kinds than large ones do. But there is no necessity about this. Her people and her institutions made Athens the school of Hellas, as Pericles said. The less distinguished neighboring city-states were less remarkable but not because they were larger or smaller.

The beauty of smallness is that it diffuses power, not that it expands

---

11. Pigou, *Economics of Welfare*, p. 200.

competition. Neither competition nor its mirror image, cooperation, is an end in itself.

THE REFORM OF CORPORATIONS

Although it is impossible to imagine the easy success of any movement to reform the modern corporation, it is not difficult to suggest points that such reform might encompass. Starting with the understanding that the corporation is the entrepreneur and so entitled to the profits and the capital gains, one would ask, Who are the *people* of the corporation? And the answer would be that they are first and foremost those who do the work of the corporation, namely, the management and the other workers, and secondarily the stockholders, under the present system, and that they should all be able to share in both rewards and control.

As a first approximation of how these shares should be allocated, one might assume that there is some rationality behind the present distribution. At present, management and other workers get wages and bonuses and fringe benefits, and stockholders get dividends, and these are the more or less satisfactory result of explicit or implicit negotiations. Each individual's proper share might then be determined by taking the individual's income from the corporation, whether wages or dividends or both, and dividing it by the total of all individual incomes from the corporation (not counting interest, which is a cost of doing business). Cash dividends would be paid in accordance with such shares, which would be recalculated annually. In addition to cash dividends—and it is a crucial addition—new stock equal in value to the corporation's increase in net worth would be issued in the same proportions as cash dividends (or stock would be canceled if net worth fell). This stock—and sooner or later all stock in the corporation—would be inalienable. It could not be sold or bequeathed or pledged as security for a loan or given away; but it could at any time be exchanged with the corporation for a negotiable note or bond, or, at the corporation's option, cash. And such an exchange would *have* to be made when the owner of the stock left the corporation, retired, was fired, or died. Over the years—within a generation at the outside—most of the present stockholders would be converted into bondholders. They would have their reward. The remaining stockholders would all be active in the business. They could, of course, like their predecessors, run it well or ill; could sell it or merge it or abandon it; but whatever happened, it would be their doing, and they would be the ones to benefit or suffer from it.

Let me state most emphatically that what I call the Labor Theory of Entitlement leads to employee ownership, not to profit sharing. Profit is, as we have repeatedly noted, a residual. It is systematically unpredictable. It is, nevertheless, affected by decisions regarding everything from product development to marketing. During World War II, an excess profits tax reached 85 percent, and profitable companies ploughed as much as they could into upgrading their plant, institutional advertising, and the like. Book publishers loaded the book reviews with Christmas advertising. Airplane manufacturers boasted of their successful military planes. And so on. Such business expenditures made business sense because they cost only fifteen cents on the dollar. Regardless of the cost, the benefits—good will or whatever they were—accrued to the corporate owners, not to the workers.

The interests of laborers and owners in such decisions are rarely identical; sometimes they are diametrically opposed. In profit sharing, conflicts are resolved in favor of owners. When laborers and owners are the same people, decisions can turn on the interests of the enterprise rather than on class advantage. Decisions may still turn out to be right or wrong, but they will be so for everyone. There will be neither scapegoats nor isolated windfall profiteers.

It is very likely that reform of corporate internal structure would have to be complemented by reform of external structure. Certainly all corporations, regardless of internal reform, should be nationally chartered and subject only to national taxation and regulation. Only in this way can one hope to overcome the states' temptations to play beggar my neighbor by luring companies away from each other with tax breaks and permissive regulation.

Friedrich Hayek makes a more important point: "Once we extend the power to make contracts from natural persons to corporations and the like, it no longer can be the contract but it must be the law which decides who is liable and how the property is to be determined and safeguarded which limits the liability of the corporation."[12] In particular, corporations, which are chartered by the state, should not be permitted to take the Fifth Amendment, which after all, was adopted to protect the rights of natural persons.

Sooner or later, too, it will probably become apparent that antitrust laws should turn on size, not on "competition"—partly because competition is by no means always efficient, and partly because small is beautiful.[13]

A LIMITIST PROPOSAL

In an essay entitled "The Ethics of Competition," Frank H. Knight examined in careful detail what we know in our hearts, namely, that the competitive race is seldom fair, and that the effort it stimulates is as likely to result in chicanery as in beneficial innovation.[14] On the other side, Milovan Djilas and now all of Eastern Europe and Russia are witness that cooperative societies, with the best will in the world, tend to degenerate into stultifying dictatorships.[15]

---

12. Hayek, *Individualism and Economic Order*, p. 115.
13. von Wieser, *Social Economics* pp. 209–10.
14. Knight, *Ethics of Competition*, pp. 41–75.
15. Djilas, *The New Class*, passim.

Having experienced the courts' inability to define competition, much less enforce it, Fred I. Raymond put forward what he called a limitist law.[16] The speed limit is such a law. If you go over fifty-five miles an hour, you are in violation, no matter what arguments you can make about safety or efficiency or the similar behavior of others. Observing the way business works, Raymond concluded that seeming economies of scale are often (if not generally) fruit not of technology but of the favored access great size can command to financing and to special markets. Raymond therefore proposed that a business organization could be as large and as spread out, horizontally and vertically, as it wished, provided that it had only one place of business with its customers. If a business had more than one point of delivery, like a chain of stores, it would be limited to a certain number of employees. Raymond suggested one thousand as the maximum.

The beauty of Raymond's scheme is that it does not interfere with the advertised virtues of the free-enterprise system, or with the necessity for large-scale planning in major industries. Any limitation based on profits or sales would interfere, for once a business reached those limits, it would have no incentive to improve its performance. Raymond's proposal, however, leaves every honorable incentive in place.

---

16. Raymond, *The Limitist*, passim.

8

Competition and Diminishing Returns

As we noted in the first chapter, the free state, the free market, and free thought grew up together in the Enlightenment, little more than two centuries ago. This was not an accident. Without a free market, technological change has no opportunity, except by grace or command of dictatorial rulers. Without a free market, technology is, as it was in the Dark Ages, an "art" or a "mystery," or as it was in premodern China, a toy with which to titillate the emperor.

At the same time, a free market requires technological change. Without constant improvements— or at least variety—in the goods offered for sale, a market quickly becomes competitive only on price, as it is in classical theory.[1] When price is thus forced down to cost, profit must be sought in cartelization. And variety, even of style, scarcely appears, as one finds today when one shops the competing supermarkets and discount-store chains.

1. Hayek, *Individualism and Economic Order*, p. 96; "Perfect competition means the absence of all competitive activities," because advertising, undercutting, improving, or otherwise differentiating the goods and services produced are all excluded by definition.

Technology depends on free thought, on freely circulating ideas, on free speech. All thought grows out of existing thought. All inventions are dependent on existing inventions. There is no point to a better fuel pump if there isn't a motor that can use it. In a similar way, there is little point to an electrically controlled rear-view mirror unless such a feature becomes a selling point in a free competition. Even safety devices, such as airbags, are installed more quickly in a free market than in a command economy. A danger in today's merger fad in American industry is that a giant corporation, whose purpose is to eliminate competition, tends to become, within itself, a command economy.

The usual theory emphasizes that competition spurs workers to greater productivity and entrepreneurs to cheaper and more plentiful products. Without this spur, it is said, the world would stumble, while with the spur the economy leaps from triumph to triumph—and not just the economy, because statesmen and artists and scholars compete for power and fame, as workers and entrepreneurs compete for money.

This is a pretty story, often told, and there is much truth in it, but it has an ugly side. As early as Ricardo, it was argued that competition drives wages down to the subsistence level and keeps them there. The competition of entrepreneur against entrepreneur prevents even the tenderhearted from paying more, while the competition of worker against worker prevents even the stouthearted from holding out for more. This is the Iron Law of Wages, which prompted Carlyle to call economics the dismal science.

Not only does competition have an ugly side; it also turns out to be diffuse and shapeless. One can, for example, read only so many suspense novels in a year; so a given suspense novel obviously competes with all the other suspense novels in print. But it also competes with true spy stories, with movies, with a TV on the installment plan, with other forms of entertainment, with forms of quasi-entertainment (like a new gadget for an automobile), and ultimately with everything on the market. At any given moment, whatever a consumer spends on one thing cannot be spent on something else. This fact emboldens apologists for big business to argue that even oligopolies must operate in the market as if so-called perfect competition obtained. If automobile manufacturers tried to gouge consumers, it is explained, the latter would run their old cars a while longer and spend their money on something else.

There is some truth in this tale, too. But if everything competes with everything, there is no need to worry (as some, like Friedrich Hayek, did) about an end to the "competitive system."[2] What exists anyhow, regardless of what anyone does, needs no defense and indeed admits of none. Consequently it is understandable that the courts have been unable to settle on a clear approach to antitrust law.[3] A prime example of the absurdity of trying to use competition as a touchstone for the organization of business is the provision of the Clayton Act that a company may engage in certain business practices otherwise defined as unfair if it can show it does so to meet competition.

THE FOLKLORE OF COMPETITION

The idea of competition is embedded in current American ideology and folklore. There is scarcely an aspect of private or public life that is not touched by it. We expect males to compete for the favors of females and vice versa; and we expect the resulting pairs to compete within themselves for dominance. Consequently, we are not surprised to hear that siblings compete with each other for their parents' atten-

---

2. Hayek, *Serfdom*, p. 38.

3. Antitrust cases are, as George L. Stigler said, "an almost impudent exercise in economic gerrymandering. The plaintiff sets the market, at a maximum, as one state in area and including only aperture-priority SLR cameras selling between $200 and $250. . . . The defendant will in turn insist that the market is worldwide, and includes not only cameras, but also portrait artists and possibly transportation media because a visit is a substitute for a picture." Stigler, *Economist as Preacher*, p. 51.

tion, and that the Oedipus complex is a form of intergenerational competition. We expect very young children to compete to get on the fast track at school, and we expect all children to compete in sports, which are said to be character builders and essential preparation for the great game of life. Competitive examinations open—or close—the way to college and to graduate school. Civil service careers depend on competitive examinations, and much prayerful thought as well as vociferous debate is devoted to their formulation. Politicians compete for our votes, and artists and scholars for our acclaim. Our legal system is adversarial, making justice the result of a competition between plaintiff and defendant, or, more realistically, between their lawyers.

That ours is a competitive society is a flattering notion to those on top. If you're on top of a competitive society, you must have got there by being better than others. Your success being merited, the rewards must be deserved. Not only that, but the failures of the others must likewise be deserved. No guilt attaches to the fabulous wealth that goes with winning, and losing is shameful.

It is doubtful that anyone really believes the system works this way. Everyone has had personal experience of incompetents who got ahead because of inherited wealth. Everyone knows that the poets needed no license to speak of the spurns that patient merit of the unworthy takes or of those whom chill penury repressed.

Since the glorification of competition persists despite these things everyone knows, it may reasonably be concluded that the notion at least contributes to the satisfaction of an urgent need. The need is not merely physiological, like that for vitamin C to prevent scurvy; nor is it merely psychological, like that for a stimulating environment to prevent intellectual and emotional stagnation. It is, rather, a moral need. It is a need to see ourselves as agents, doers, masters of our fate, responsible for our actions, free.

In the history of the West, competition is a relatively recent idea. It does not appear as we know it in Plato. Even when using sports as an analogy, Aristotle is interested in personal excellence rather than competition. "As at the Olympic Games," he writes, "it is not the finest and strongest men who are crowned but they who enter the lists, . . . so too in life, of the honorable and good, it is they who act rightly who win the prize." St. Paul, too, speaks of sports in a personal sense. "Well," he writes the Corinthians, "I do not run aimlessly, I do not box as one beating the air; but I pommel my body and subdue it, lest preaching to others I should be disqualified."

Until the end of the Renaissance, men were more concerned about their relation with the universe than about their relations with each other. The shift was gradual and appears in many contexts. Trial by ordeal and trial by combat (in both of which the innocent are upheld by God) are displaced by trial by one's peers. Machiavelli advises men, especially princes, to "be prudent enough to avoid getting a bad name." Hamlet asks Horatio to tell his story in this harsh world. Piero della Francesca's Madonna del Parto imperiously demands that we others acknowledge her importance.

An early theory of competition was advanced by Thomas Hobbes in the seventeenth century. Inspired by Galileo to look for a motive force common to all men, he concluded that the fear of death leads to "a perpetual and restless desire of power after power. And the cause of this is not always that a man hopes for a more intensive delight than he has already attained to, but because he cannot assure the power and means to live well . . . without the acquisition of more."[4]

The Hobbesian war of all against all is explicitly brutalized by the not uncommon assumption that social life recapitulates Malthusian demography and Darwinian evolution. Let competition be unrestrained, it is enthusiastically urged, and the best will survive and the incompetent be eliminated. In the nineteenth century this notion enjoyed considerable popularity under the slanderous rubric of Social Dar-

---

4. Hobbes, *Laviathan*, p. 161.

winism. Ironically, it is embraced today by the far Right, which at the same time rejects evolution in favor of creationism.

COOPERATION AND GAMES

The foil to competition is cooperation. It, too, is embedded in our ideology and folklore. In kindergarten we learned how two donkeys could both have their fill of hay if they shared the piles instead of each trying to get a pile all for himself. Later we understood why the colonies had to hang together if they did not want to hang separately, and why the Constitution formed a more perfect Union than the Articles of Confederation. We mourned the failure of the League of Nations and greeted the United Nations with resurgent hope. On the playing field, we celebrated the team effort, cheered the team player, emphasized the teamwork in sports from tennis doubles to soccer.

On the world stage, cooperation has had a longer run than competition. Describing the vast effort that produced the fifth-century Athenian Acropolis, Alfred Zimmern writes, "There is no competition here to keep the rival builder out of a job, and no rivalry for big winnings."[5] And the Romans taught the virtues of working together by the symbolism of the fasces, whose rods when bound together were far stronger than the sum of them taken separately.

Anthropological studies have described many tribal societies based on cooperation, among them the Maori and the Ojibwa. The latter, Ruth Landes tells us, "phrase an objectively cooperative economy in the most individualistic terms. The man hunts alone on his isolated trails; the wife works alone in the wigwam, with the occasional assistance of her children or elderly mother; and they exchange the products of their work." The ostensible individualism is dependent on

5. Zimmern, *Green Commonwealth*, p. 262.

observation of rigid rules—"the cooperation of unequal individuals."[6] The rigidity of the Maori is even more marked. Margaret Mead writes that they "obtained cooperation on the basis of virtually inalienable and unalterable status, by which the rank of an individual and the form of his obligations were fixed at birth."[7]

These observations call to mind another by Alfred Zimmern. The Greek commonwealth was, he says, "a sequestered and stable world where competition and unemployment are unknown, where hardly anyone is working precariously for wages or a salary, where life goes on without visible change or desire of change from generation to generation and century to century."[8] In a word, a society without competition tends to be based on status.

A society based on status can last for centuries or millennia and can develop a highly sophisticated civilization. In comparison with such civilizations, competition is an explosively liberating force. Released from the restraints of status, spurred by the need for self-maintenance, enticed by the possibility of achieving renown, men and women can perform miracles in the arts and the sciences and government and add to the enrichment of everyday life.

There is a close connection between competition and competence, and indeed the two words are from the same root, which means something like "to seek together." If there is a difference in the ideas, it lies in the fact that competition always involves some sort of rivalry, while competence may be judged merely by reference to a standard. Yet standards, unless mad, are not altogether private. They are social and historical. A man's reach cannot exceed his grasp unless he already has some understanding of what he is reaching for, and what he is reaching for bears some relation to what others like him have pre-

---

6. Landes, in Mead, *Cooperation and Competition*, p. 91.
7. Mead, *Cooperation and Competition*, p. 478.
8. Zimmern, *Green Commonwealth*, p. 224.

viously grasped. Without the example of Rafael's achievement, Andrea del Sarto could scarcely have been aware of his own failure, which was not absolute but relative.

Competence implies standards, and competition implies rules. The competitors in any sport obey the rules of that sport. Without the rules, there is no sport, and no competition. As the rules define the game, they also define the ways in which players can demonstrate competence. Competence is not an abstraction; it is a creation. Apart from the rules, there is no competence.

For this reason, mathematical game theory, which, like any analogy, is at best merely suggestive, often brings forth results that prove irrelevant or downright misleading. One of the most widely played games (it lends itself to computerization) is called the Prisoners' Dilemma. Two prisoners are separately questioned by their captors, who promise each one freedom if he implicates the other in the alleged crime. What are the poor prisoners to do? If both steadfastly refuse the offer, they will be punished, but not harshly. If only one gives evidence, he will be freed and the other severely punished. But if they implicate each other, they will both be in for it.

There are thus four possible outcomes: both lightly punished; the first freed and the second heavily punished; the second freed and the first punished; and both condemned. Games theorists assign scores to these outcomes (say 3–3 for the first, 5–1 for the second, 1–5 for the third, and 1–1 for the last). They then use the game as a model for social or economic competition, with refusal to implicate representing cooperation, and mutual incrimination representing destructive competition.

The game is played many times, each player trying to achieve the higher total score, no matter what the other player does. Many patterns of play are possible, and it is said that this particular game is almost always won by a player who initially makes a cooperative move and thereafter mimics what the other player does. This is called, in capitals, TIT-FOR-TAT.

It will be quickly seen, however, that TIT-FOR-TAT is, appropriately enough, a case of GIGO, or garbage in, garbage out. If, instead of 5, 3, 1, scores of 100, 2, 1 were assigned to the moves (and why not?), the outcome of the game would be quite different. The outcome would be altogether unpredictable if different scores were assigned each time the game went into the computer (which would surely be more "realistic"). Since there is nothing immutable or even plausible about the scoring, there is nothing enlightening about the outcome. The Prisoners' Dilemma is a game, like contract bridge or field hockey; its scoring system dictates the way the game is played; and the winners win merely a game.

The rules of a good sport will establish some sort of equality between teams and even between styles of play.

Similar considerations govern all games, not just sports. A friend and I once invented a variant of checkers, which we played for several months with great enthusiasm. Then one of us stumbled on a series of moves whereby the first player would always win, no matter what the other tried to do. Naturally, the game lost its interest, and we gave it up. The unbeatable strategy made the game no game at all.

Meaningful competition seems not to exist unless there is rough (and shifting) equality among players and teams. If such equality does not exist, rules must be devised to create it. If such equality does exist, rules must be devised to enforce and reinforce it.

Rules of course imply agreement on ends and means, acceptance of authority—in a word, cooperation. Members of teams obviously have to cooperate for the team to compete successfully, and competing teams have to cooperate in defining the competition. The analogy with sports thus suggests that, as we move into the world of economics, we shall find the ideas of competition, competence, and cooperation perpetually interrelated. The ideas and their interrelations, moreover, will be constantly changing. We shall be dealing with history, that is, with the actual deeds of men and women.

Competition is the mode of our individuality; cooperation is the mode of our humanity. The two modes are dialectical. They imply each other, and they are both necessary. Their necessity is not abstract or esoteric but appears at the very start of every discourse, including this one. Like it or not, this discourse is the work of an individual, and it is separate from other works. At the same time, it depends on social and historical—that is to say, cooperative—creations, the chief of which is language. Competition and cooperation appear everywhere in relations of men and women with each other, and not least in their economic activities.

Of the many differences between games and the actual world, perhaps the most important is that the progress of a game does not affect the rules of an ongoing or subsequent game. But, as Richard Levins observes, "In nature, unlike game theory, the plays of the game are not permanently distinct from a change in the rules."[9] That is to say, the rules of a game are imposed, while in nature they are organic and are continually changing. A mutation may produce a biological form more successful in a given ecological niche than the previous form. Not only is the previous form pushed aside, but also the new form changes the niche.

In fact, something like this happens in business. The mass-market paperback book business was created in the 1930s by the invention of a new set of publishing "rules," which included certain manufacturing processes, a new method of distribution, new (and very low) royalty rates, and a new low price. After the Second World War, increased printing and shipping costs forced paperback publishers to raise their cover prices. The increased cover prices yielded higher dollar royalties even at the existing royalty rates (when you stop and think of it, 35 cents is a 40 percent jump from 25 cents), whereupon it was seen that a further increase in cover prices would so increase gross profits that the royalty rates could be increased, thus exponentially increas-

---

9. Levins, *Evolution in Changing Environments*, p. 99. The same point is made from the other direction by Erik Erikson: "The sunlight playing on the waves qualifies for the attribute 'playful' because it faithfully remains within the rules of the game." Erikson, *Childhood and Society*, p. 212.

ing dollar royalties, and stimulating increased demands from authors. Step by step, prices and royalty rates were increased until it became possible for publishers to bid in the millions for expected bestsellers, and it became necessary to make such bids to maintain their place in the market. In this way, the plays in the paperback "game" changed the rules and, of course, the game, which continues to change. In the world we actually live in, the rules are always changing. Our universe is not absolute but historical.

PERFECT COMPETITION

Nevertheless, for a century after Adam Smith, one might have rested fairly comfortably in the belief that perfect competition was not only possible but actually existent; that it was in fact the normal state of affairs; and that exceptions, when they appeared, were always, or almost always, the result of the sovereign's interference with the market. The articulated, elaborate, and imposing structure of classical economics was erected on this belief, and so was the mathematically elegant supporting theory of marginal analysis.

It took the Great Depression to shock experts into seeing what the naive (and the ruthless) had always seen—that perfect competition did not exist. Yet no sooner were the economic crisis and World War II ended than the old belief reasserted itself.

It was claimed, first, that the world really operated *as if* there were perfect competition, and that predictions made on the assumption of perfect competition were generally correct, while predictions made on the assumption of imperfect or monopolistic competition were indeterminate.

Second, it was claimed that the assumption of perfect competition was an axiom, like the axioms of Euclid, which assumed points without dimension, and so on, that everyone knew did not really exist in the world.

Third, it was claimed that physics made similar assumptions, for example, the assumption of a perfect vacuum, without which the formula $S = {}^1/_2\, gt^2$ wouldn't work.

On the first claim, we may consider the analogous case of the Brownian movements in a Wilson cloud chamber, where the tracks of droplets look as if whatever caused them were alive. If these movements were actually living, the distinction between biology and physics would ultimately collapse. Either all things would be living, or all things would be inanimate. Similarly, if the economy were actually ruled by perfect competition, oligopoly and monopoly could not exist, and the *Fortune* 500 would be a mirage. In both cases, the *as if* argument is the ancient logical fallacy of affirming the consequent. If the earth is flat, then we won't fall off. The consequent (we won't fall off) is true, but that doesn't prove that the earth is flat, nor would the fact (if it is a fact) that people act as if there were perfect competition prove that there actually is perfect competition. More important, it would not prove (what libertarians go on to assert) that there should be untrammeled competition, and that all government regulation should therefore be repealed.

The second claim betrays misapprehension of what Euclid is about. A straight line, says Euclid, is the shortest distance between two points. Yet if you try to draw a straight line, your result will have breadth and height as well as extension and will, moreover, display various irregularities, especially under a magnifying glass. Euclid's line is claimed to be an abstraction from the real world, and the notion of perfect competition is said also to be an abstraction from the real world.

But Euclid is not an abstraction. Euclidean diagrams are a convenience but are no part of the proofs. Euclid is not describing forms he finds in the world; he is defining space. In order to do this, he must, for one thing, be able to say that one object is farther away than another; and to say that, he must be able to say that the distance to one is greater than to the other. He must, in short, establish rules for comparing distances; hence the straight-line axiom.

Geometry has practical uses, and these expand our world. A little elementary trigonometry was used by Thales in the sixth century B.C. to make a fortune by determining which grain ship was likely to reach Miletus first, and he could not have done this if distance were indeterminate.

The 3, 4, 5 triangle was early used to lay out fields with square corners (and I have done the same with the lines of a tennis court). The Pythagorean theorem is not an abstraction; it is a consequence of the definitions of triangle and right angle. The Pythagorean Brotherhood did not make a collection of objects and abstract from them the idea of a right triangle. Without the definition they could not have known which objects to collect.

Euclid is about space. Space is not an abstraction; it is a necessity. Perfect competition may be an abstraction, but it obviously is not a necessity.

The formula $S = {}^1/_2\, gt^2$ is different because it clearly has an inductive origin. Galileo may not have disproved Aristotle by dropping stones of different weights from the Leaning Tower (a similar experiment had anyway been performed by Simon Stevin in Holland a half century earlier). But Galileo did make "a brazen ball, very hard, round, and smooth"; he did roll it down an inclined plane; he did time its fall with a water clock "with such exactness that the trials being many and many times repeated, they never differed any considerable matter."[10] And on the basis of the statistics so compiled he did develop his version of what became this formula.

Here we have a true case of abstraction. Galileo considered only distance and clock time. He disregarded the color, taste, sound, and odor of his brass ball. He disregarded especially its weight. And he came up with a formula that applied to all falling objects. The slow

---

10. Galileo, *Two New Sciences*.

and erratic fall of a feather was not an exception, because he allowed for the atmosphere.

Libertarians claim that Galileo thereby assumed a perfect vacuum, and that a perfect vacuum is no more possible in the actual world than is perfect competition. But physics does not assume a vacuum, and the feather is not an exception. The brass ball, too, was affected in its fall by the atmosphere. Science proceeds by isolating and studying such effects, not by assuming them away. In contrast, advocates of perfect competition assume its existence, fallaciously affirm its validity by assuming its alleged consequences, and proceed to lobby for policies supposed to be in harmony with their original assumption.

ECONOMIC COMPETITION

Economic competition may be defined as what happens when two or more firms or individuals seek to buy the same scarce commodity or seek to sell the same commodity in a limited market. Competition among buyers tends to push prices up, and competition among sellers tends to push them down, at least sometimes. These tendencies, however, can be assumed only if we also assume that the competitors are substantially equal. If one competitor is very much stronger or better informed than the others, he will be able to skew prices in his favor. A further skewing will result when a buyer is stronger or better informed than a seller, allowing the buyer to set the price that the seller must take or leave. It is possible for a given firm to be strong as a buyer but weak as a seller, and vice versa, as a retailer may dominate a local market but be of small account to its suppliers.

The buyers and sellers in each industry are, with few exceptions, supposed to be roughly equal in strength and information, and to be small in relation to the size of the market, as a result of which none is in a position to set prices. All are price takers. Prices are set, impersonally, by the market.

Several corollaries follow from this basic proposition. Most important, prices will tend to fall to the minimum, which will be just enough higher than the cost of production to encourage producers to produce. No firm or industry will be able to maintain prices much higher than this minimum, because higher prices, and the consequent profits, would attract additional firms to the industry, and the added competition would push the prices down. On the other side, no firm or industry would be able to maintain prices lower than the minimum and stay in business. Firms leaving the business would reduce competition, allowing prices to rise to the practical minimum. In either case, prices hover around an equilibrium point, which is cost; and no firm is able to monopolize the market.

THE LAW OF DIMINISHING RETURNS

In the eighteeth century, monopolies were creatures of the sovereign—the king or the state—and were exclusive licenses or franchises to conduct or control certain forms of trade in certain places or under certain conditions or at certain times. They were granted to favorites of the crown or to those able to pay handsomely for them. Needless to say, they were popular only with those who held them. "Laissez faire, laissez passer" became the universal slogan of the opposition.

With this background, it was important for classical economists to demonstrate conclusively that monopoly—except for certain public utilities—would not recur in the new free economy. The law of diminishing returns seemed to be the answer.

As first promulgated by Turgot in the eighteenth century, the law of diminishing returns was obvious and simplistic. When increasing quantities of a variable factor (such as capital or labor) are added to unchanging quantities of all other factors, the average output attributable to the variable factor will, after a certain point, decline. Or, after a certain point, scattering more seed on a given plot of land is wasteful.

Although the pure law is not much more than a reminder not to be foolish, a modification of the law became a cornerstone of laissez-faire theory. Just as Ricardo's theory of rent argued that since not all land was of equal fertility or convenience or proximity to market, the best land would be cultivated first, so it could be argued that, after its initial successes, a business would have to employ progressively less skilled workers and less suitable or more expensive resources as it tried to expand. At some point new or "sunrise" producers would be able to underprice the original or "sunset" producer. Thus the law of diminishing returns would support the invisible hand and enforce free competition.

But of course, the new competitor would be equally in need of skilled workers and suitable resources and so would be faced by expenses at least as great as those of the original producer, who would not, at least for that reason, be underpriced.

The debate took a different turn in 1933 with the almost simultaneous publication of two books attacking the traditional school from new and closely similar angles. In England, Joan Robinson published *The Economics of Imperfect Competition.*[11] In the United States, Edward H. Chamberlin published *The Theory of Monopolistic Competition.*[12] In a subsequent article (included as a chapter in later editions of his book), Chamberlin argued that his theory of monopolistic competition concerned the individual firm, while Robinson's theory concerned the separate industry, and that any classification of industries was "exceedingly arbitrary." Nevertheless, in spite of important technical differences, both writers were agreed that perfect competition not only did not exist but never had existed and never could exist.

In the actual world in which we do our doing, every firm's product has its aspect of monopoly. If nothing else, it is offered for sale here, where the buyer is, rather than next door, which is, to that extent, in-

---

11. Robinson, *Imperfect Competition*, p. 5.
12. Chamberlin, *Monopolistic Competition*, 9th ed., p. 201.

convenient to the first buyer, though it may be handier for another. Beyond such simple differences of location, there are endless and inevitable differences, not only in the product itself but in how it is sold and who sells it, and all this quite apart from the strict monopolies of franchises, patents, copyrights, and trademarks. That this is so is a matter of common observation. Following this line of thought, we are, as Robinson said, "reduced to regarding the output of each producer as a separate commodity."

The separateness of each commodity, however, is offset by the interchangeability of most commodities. If I find that my favorite supermarket's spinach is wilted, I am likely to settle for broccoli rather than go to the trouble of seeking spinach elsewhere. There are of course limits to the substitutability for any particular product. But very few goods are free from the competition of many plausible substitutes.

Substitutability—"a great law," Léon Walras called it—prevails in producers' goods as well as in consumers' goods. It is applicable even to the valuation of land rent. The traffic on Main Street may be greater than that on Spring Street, but at some point it is advantageous for a retailer to settle for less traffic at lower cost.

The law of diminishing returns is irrelevant where the unit of analysis is not an industry or a commodity but a business enterprise. It hardly ever happens that an enterprise, of whatever size, deals only in a single homogeneous commodity. If one product seems to fall under the law of diminishing returns, it may be continued as a sideline or a loss leader or dropped altogether, while other products or lines may be upgraded or added.

ECONOMIES OF SCALE

In addition, the law of diminishing returns runs head on into economies of scale—the rock on which modern mass production is founded. Production can be expanded much faster than fixed costs rise so that overall costs will fall, even in the few cases where variable costs tend to rise. Moreover, in modern industry, expanded production generally makes possible the utilization of more—not less—efficient machines and processes; and large enterprises, by exploiting possibilities for the division of labor, make possible the employment of more specialized and more productive laborers. Consequently, the firm's supply curve falls, and marginal cost (the cost of producing one more item) is always below average cost (which determines the profitability of the enterprise as a whole over a given period of time).

When this happens, there is no longer an automatic limit to the expansion of the firm. More precisely, there is nothing to prevent any given firm from expanding so vigorously and cutting costs and prices so aggressively that all other firms are driven from the market. There may be a moment of cutthroat competition as a few expanded firms battle for survival. Bankruptcies may proliferate, and even the ultimate winner may be grievously wounded. Not only is this struggle wasteful and inefficient, but in the end, instead of an equilibrium of interchangeable competitors constrained to take the market price, we have a monopolist able thereafter to set the price.

It is difficult to overstate how devastating this analysis is. The strength of the traditional view lay in the fact that it was automatic. Adam Smith's metaphor of the invisible hand was a world-historical idea of profound and pervasive implications. It appealed to the practical world of the Industrial Revolution, because its acceptance ended the state's control of or even interference in business affairs. It appealed to the intellectual world of the scientific revolution, because it offered an impersonal, quasi-mechanical explanation of one aspect of human behavior. It even appealed to the religious, because the invisible hand, which could be thought of as the hand of God, was an inexorable force for good. All of this depended upon the economic world as a self-regulating equilibrium that, no matter how disturbed, always (and rather quickly) returned to the best possible position in this the best of possible worlds. And the equilibrium depended on the law of diminishing returns.

There are, to be sure, many arguments against monopoly—and some in favor—that are extraneous to the traditional theory. There is a continuing debate as to whether monopolies are more or less efficient than freely competing enterprises, whether they are more or less innovative, whether they stabilize or destabilize the economy, whether or not they are better employers, better citizens of the community, better standard bearers in the world market. These are not insignificant questions, but they are all secondary to the traditional argument. Answers that appear favorable to that argument are a sort of bonus granted by a beneficent providence, a series of debater's points that may help enlist supporters. But the traditional argument stands or falls without them.

And what has happened, strictly within the terms of the traditional theory itself, is that, with the fall of the law of diminishing returns, the traditional argument as a whole has fallen. It was "The Deacon's Masterpiece: or The Wonderful 'One-Hoss Shay' " all over again. "It went to pieces all at once." There is no natural bar to monopoly; there is no natural equilibrium; there is no natural price set by the market.

9

Goods and Services

Natural resources are valuable because of their importance in a particular economy, at a particular time and place. A thousand years ago the Maya treasured and traded for obsidian, or volcanic glass, from which they made knives, scrapers, projectile points, and jewelry. The Mayan artifacts are now sought after by museums and collectors. The stuff itself is practically valueless. On the other hand, for us today, petroleum seems essential, and it is for our economy. But it was insignificant in Adam Smith's time (when coal was only coming into its own), and the world will not come to an end when the Arabian sands run dry. The world will be different, but it will not end. No resource is absolute.[1] Physical resources are of course limiting in particular situations, but an ideal society values ideas, and there is no fore-

1. "It is only after the institutional framework has been constructed that the 'rationality' of consumers' behavior in the market has any meaning in economic theory. . . ." Simon, *Models of Bounded Rationality*, p. 75. See also Larson et al., "Beyond the Age of Materials," p. 34ff.

seeable physical limit to the production and enjoyment of poetry or history or mathematics or even economic theory.

For this reason, the familiar definition of economics as determining the optimal allocation of resources begs the question. It assumes that resources are absolute, whereas a resource is recognized as a resource precisely and only because of the way it is allocated in the present economy. An optimum is such only in relation to a given standard or given constraints. One can speak of the best economics textbook or the best red wine, but not of the best thing or the best good. Whatever allocations a given price system achieves are optimal only in relation to that price system. The allocation argument is circular. It is, moreover, notorious that, left to himself, economic man will destroy the ecosystem, wasting topsoil, polluting air and water, and spreading poisons with profit-maximizing abandon.

When we talk of economic goods, we have more than subsistence in mind. Subsistence, as we have remarked, is a physiological problem. Even for Ricardo, the subsisting laborers were producing something more than their own and their employers' sustenance. What made that something a good?

Let us begin by inquiring how a service becomes an economic good. That nothing intrinsic to the service makes it an economic good a few examples will show. Home cooking of the highest quality is not an economic good, but hash slinging of junk food is an economic good. Home handiwork is not an economic good, but hired plumbing is. Whether you pray standing on the corner of the street or in your closet with the door closed, what you do is not an economic good, but when a priest or parson prays for you, that is. It is even possible to argue that our hapless soldier digging that hole in the ground is performing an economic service, since he does it in the line of duty, for which he is paid.

Economics is a necessary part of modern life, but it is not all of life. An economic service is work done for pay, regardless of what else may be said about it. The service may be good, bad, or indifferent—

performed shoddily or with grace. It may be one of general usefulness, as maintaining telephone communications. It may be one of special usefulness, as praying for the faithful. It may be one of nil or negative usefulness, as offering a teetotaler a drink in a restaurant. All that matters is that it be done for pay. Since it certainly is not uncommon for people to be so delighted with their work that they do it for pleasure, it is more precise to say that an economic service is paid service.

This insistence on pay is not arbitrary. The alternative is to consider everything anyone does—at least everything that involves two or more people—as economic. Such analyses quickly reduce to such absurdities as Marx's theory that slavery is latent in the family[2] or the variation of this theory that sees marriage as an exchange of sexual favors for security. That some marriages may seem like that, even to the partners, says nothing about most marriages, and certainly nothing about any humanistic view of marriage. Furthermore, if such an exchange were truly economic, one would have to look for the resulting income, which could be stated only in money. Without an actual monetary exchange, the statement would be arbitrary, and the taxing authorities would be dragged into foolish calculations. If the husband leapt from the marriage bed to prepare breakfast, would his wife's income be greater than if he turned over and went back to sleep? If so, by how much?

Insistence on a monetary transaction makes an economic service an ephemeral good. The service doesn't exist unless it is done and paid for, and once it is done, that is the end of it. They also serve who only stand and wait—provided they are paid for it. An unemployed waiter produces no economic value. Nor can services be stockpiled. In slack times, or in anticipation of a strike, I cannot take extra rides up and down in the office elevator and so be prepared for crowded or nonexistent service to come. We have already noted that labor power—the power to perform a service—generally cannot be resold.

---

2. Marx, *German Ideology*, p. 159.

In all this, services seem different from material goods. But all material goods are also more or less ephemeral. Not only do moths and rust corrupt and thieves break in and steal, but material things may lose their marketability, which, in fact, many material things never had.

Prompted by personal enthusiasm, by the acclaim of respected critics—by any number of things—a book publisher may produce more copies of a novel than can be sold at any price. There may be several thousand left after the regular sale at the full price and even after the remainder sale at the lowest price that repays the cost of handling. In the end, to make room in the warehouse, the rest are shredded if there is a sufficient need for waste paper or dumped in a "sanitary" landfill otherwise.

This is not an esoteric scenario in the book business, and it has myriad parallels in other lines, even under communism. In the heyday of the Gang of Four that followed Mao, several streets of Shanghai were lined with hundreds or thousands of good-size boilers quietly rusting under the plane trees. Somebody had no doubt been praised for exceeding a quota, but what was turned out (if not still there) has had to be reduced to scrap. These things happen, whether as a result of American know-how or in accordance with Mao Zedong Thought, because no one can foretell the future.

The novel was an economic good (we are not commenting on its literary merit), not because of the labor (that did the writing and tended the machines that made the paper and printed the books), the land (whose trees were made into paper), the capital (that provided the paper mill, the printing press, and the warehouse for the publisher's inventory), or whatever other factors of production you care to name. All these were necessary, but they were not sufficient to create a good. The factors of production resulted in an artifact, not an economic good.

The artifact became an economic good as it passed from hand to hand through the economic system. The passing did not have to be constant, but it did have to be constantly offered. Once the possibility of movement was foreclosed or abandoned or ended, the economic character of the artifact vanished.

At every stage, the product depends on the system, and the system is prior. While today's product may modify tomorrow's system, it could have been produced only because today's system was already a going concern. The system includes the market but is not confined to that. There is scarcely an aspect of the society and its government that does not bear on it. Seen in its most obvious terms, an automobile is worthless without roads and gasoline and people who know how to drive. The Inca's hoard, as we have remarked, was worth nothing to him in the face of the destruction of his society; with distribution facilities destroyed, a stock of corn would have done him no better. Goods and services have no economic value unless they are available to an effective demand. The author of our landfilled novel has friends and relatives unable to find the book in a convenient bookstore. The sales are lost; rather, they never existed, and so more books go to the shredder or dump. Many things for which there is a brisk demand in one society are unsalable at any price in another. Few refrigerators are sold to Eskimos living on ice floes, or so we are given to understand.

The wealth of a nation consists not in its mass of material things but in its system. The natural resources of South America are not greatly inferior to those of the United States, but the wealth of the two regions is vastly different. The distinction was not understood by bankers who made large loans on the basis of the resources. The land of India is far richer than that of Japan, but the comparative wealth of the two nations is reversed.

Nor is accumulated capital crucial. As John Stuart Mill pointed out, capital is constantly being consumed and reproduced, and this fact explains "what has so often excited wonder, the great rapidity with which countries recover from a state of devastation; the disappearance, in a short time, of all traces of the mischiefs done by earthquakes, floods, hurricanes, and the ravages of war."[3] In 1871 the fledgling German Empire imposed a five-billion-franc war indemnity on France, intending to impoverish her for a generation, but in spite of the loss of Alsace and Lorraine, and in spite of the disorders following the Paris Commune, the entire debt was paid off in two years. At the end of World War II, Germany was in ruins, but in short order it became again one of the most prosperous nations of the world—and this without the eastern provinces.

What is true of national wealth is true of goods. What counts is system, a going concern.

CONSUMPTION

"Consumption is the sole end and purpose of all production," wrote Adam Smith, "and the interest of the producer ought to be attended to, only so far as it may be necessary for promoting that of the consumer. The maxim is so perfectly self-evident, that it would be absurd to attempt to prove it." The maxim certainly does seem self-evident. Why bother to produce something that's not going to be used? Yet in the history of economics, the maxim has been remarkably little attended to. Smith himself noted that "in the mercantile system, the interest of the consumer is almost constantly sacrificed to that of the producer."[4] The same was true of medieval guilds; it was true of Karl Marx, who insisted that distribution was not the issue;[5] it was true of Andrew Carnegie, who amassed wealth in order to give it away, and of Thorstein Veblen, who satirized the conspicuous consumption of

---

3. Mill, *Principles of Political Economy*, bk. 1, chap. 5, sec. 7.
4. Smith, *Wealth*, p. 625.
5. Marx, *Critique of the Gotha Program*, p. 531.

Carnegie's contemporaries; it is true today of Marx's followers, who inveigh against consumerism, and also of the supply-siders, who think of themselves as exemplary anti-Marxists.

These views, as R. H. Tawney suggested, were no doubt focused by the Church's doctrines of the sins of avarice and gluttony.[6] The rival teachings of Calvinism had a similar effect. Salvation was solely a question of divine election, and mundane triumph was a possible forecast of election; therefore it was only prudent to work hard to give the forecast a chance to show itself. At the same time, it was imprudent to enjoy the fruits of the triumphant labor, because anyone who did so obviously valued this world more than the next and therefore could scarcely be one of the elect. Thus predestination led to vigorous emphasis on production and to studied indifference to consumption. As is the case with success in every line of endeavor, the example of Calvinist businessmen had a widening influence on others of other faiths or of no faith. We have already met the Texas oil multimillionaire whose son left college to make his own millions. "What else is there to do?"

In spite of the self-evident priority of consumption, Adam Smith placed his emphasis, like the others, on production. He titled his book *An Inquiry into the Nature and Causes of the Wealth of Nations*; he did not promise a discussion of the uses of wealth, nor did he supply any. Given the state of the world then—given the state of the world now—the overwhelming problem has been to produce enough to feed, clothe, and shelter the huddled masses of the earth. Until that political problem is solved, it seems frivolous to fuss about the purposes of wealth. But the fact remains that most economic activity is neither directly nor indirectly concerned with the subsistence problem. Economic theory likewise has its mind on higher things; and when it thinks of consumption at all, as Ricardo and Malthus did, it concludes that

---

6. Tawney, *Religion and the Rise of Capitalism*, pp. 35–36.

the mass of mankind is forever condemned to abject poverty, like it or not, while the work of producing the pleasures of the rich and well-born provides employment for the poor. There is no suggestion that these pleasures, whether dainty or coarse, serve otherwise than as a goad to envy, ambition, and emulation.

CONSUMPTION AS AN ACT OF WILL

The most enthusiastic advocates of production *à outrance* will hesitate over agricultural practices that maximize this year's crop but deplete the topsoil. They understand that overcutting the forests of the Himalayas will result in crop failures in India and floods in Bangladesh. The amount of production, in short, cannot be stated except with a time frame, and there is nothing sacrosanct about the calendar. Indeed, it is now fashionable to argue that American industry has faltered because executives have been maximizing short-term gains. On the other hand, who is eager for pie in the sky by and by?

Even if the time question were satisfactorily solved, there would still remain the problem of counting. How do we know that production is being increased? The problem looks simple enough for a book publisher or a boilermaker; just compare the number of books or boilers manufactured this year with the number manufactured last year. But we have seen some of the books shredded and some of the boilers scrapped. Very well, one can count what's left. Counting will work well enough provided what is counted is homogeneous, as would be the case with a small foundry making only one style and size of boiler. But even a very small publisher will publish many different sizes and kinds of books, and it appears that they are not thought of in terms of size or weight or number of pages or number of words or number of anything. A think piece on economics will cost more, word for word, than a popular novel, regardless of intrinsic merit.

We have drifted from adding up numbers of things to adding up prices of things; there is no other way to solve our problem. But is this a rational solution? If prices are what matter, it is no trick to increase them. Anyone could do it in a trice, simply by debasing the currency. This has been done more than once in the history of the world. It has even been done in reverse; when in 1969 France exchanged one new franc for ten old francs, did that cut French production by 90 percent?

Now, this is all obvious enough, and economists have long since solved the problem to their satisfaction by the construction of indexes. But we have noted that such constructions all depend on judgment. There is no shirking the responsibility of judging. Even when responsibility is refused at the start of analysis, it presents itself again and again. The persistence of the problem is a reliable indication that the initial refusal to accept responsibility was illicit, and that wants are not absolute but are liable to judgment.

I cannot be judged—nor can I judge myself—except by what I do. Consumption, to the extent that it is not merely physiological, is an activity. It is as much an activity as is production. The consumer is, like the entrepreneur or laborer, an economic surd, a human being. No one is driven by necessity to work as hard as producers do. No one is driven by necessity to consume as much as consumers do. Production and consumption are acts of will, not of necessity.

What, then, is it that consumers do? How can these doings be judged?

WHAT CONSUMERS DO

Thorstein Veblen judged the behavior of consumers, especially those with a great deal to consume, very severely. His position was that the economic "struggle is substantially a race for reputability on the basis of an invidious comparison." What he called "the habit of pecuniary emulation" was not the only motive for economic activity, but all other motives were "greatly affected" by it. In order to demonstrate one's reputability, one supported conspicuous consumption, which was as lavish as one could make it, but not formless. In fact, the prescribed pecuniary canons of taste and dress, which required the conservation of archaic rituals and observances, were so difficult to master that they were specially assigned to the leisure class, which was made up mostly of women. Under a veneer of quasi-scientific objectivity, Veblen plainly despised what he analyzed, and contrasted pecuniary emulation with the instinct of workmanship. "[T]he end of vicarious consumption," he wrote, "is to enhance, not the fulness of life of the consumer, but the pecuniary repute of the master for whose behoof the consumption takes place."[7]

That much of the world runs as Veblen described—though perhaps less now than a century ago—and that what he described was deserving of his scorn there is no doubt. Nevertheless, his analysis left consumption essentially outside the economic process. It was the end—in the sense of terminus—of economic activity, but it was an unworthy end of unworthy activity. The contrasting instinct of workmanship perhaps led, in some not clearly explained way, to fullness of life, but the enjoyment of this presumed fullness was a private affair.

Consequently, it remains that "the very idea of consumption itself has to be set back into the social process," as Mary Douglas and Baron Isherwood say in their book *The World of Goods*.[8] These writers are concerned with "an anthropology of consumption," but their analysis opens the way for economic theory. They point out that in the history of anthropology "enlightenment has followed a decision to ignore the physiological levels of existence which sustain the behavior in question." Accordingly they see consumption not as sustaining life but as "the joint production, with fellow consumers, of a universe of values. Consumption uses goods to make firm and visible a particular set of

---

7. Veblen, *Leisure Class*, p. 121.
8. Douglas and Isherwood, *World of Goods*, p. 4.

judgments in the fluid process of classifying persons and events."[9] Darwin made a similar observation regarding taxonomy. "With plants," he exclaims in *The Origin of Species*, "how remarkable it is that the organs of vegetation, on which their nutrition and life depend, are of little significance!"[10]

The universe of values does not exist except in the process of becoming firm and visible. By what I spend my money on—the clothes I wear, the food I eat, the furniture, books, music, and pictures with which I surround myself—I discover and refine the standards to which I repair and thereby demonstrate to others the sort of person I am, the sort of people with whom I associate and whose good opinion and good fellowship I value.

The problem of judging consumption is not different from the problem of judging production. In neither case does one face the problem as a newborn babe or from behind a Rawlsian veil or blindfolded. One is in the midst of one's life, of one's society, of one's times, of one's history, and one does not exist otherwise. No solution will be valid that disregards the situation in which one finds oneself or forgets what the past has left unsolved.

I am the judge of my purposes, but I am not the only judge. If my actions are unworthy, it is my soul that is shriveled. I pay that price and have my reward. But society also has an interest in what I do and is my judge because I am literally nothing if not social. All of this works both ways. Individual and society are symbiotic, reciprocal, mutually necessary, ontological. Society is literally nothing except as a membership of individuals, and this fact lays upon me the right and requirement to judge society. If a society's actions are unworthy, all the citizens suffer. All Americans were diminished by the Vietnam War; all are diminished by economic policies that condemn fellow citizens

---

9. Ibid., p. 61.
10. Darwin, *Origin of Species*, chap. 14.

to lives of desperate poverty; all are diminished by the persistence of unjust laws.

The point is simply this: I define myself, even to myself, by what I do. There is no other way. What I do includes what I, as an economic agent, consume—what I do with my money. I must confess that I am not strong enough or wise enough or good enough to be proud of everything I do. Yet I insist on my responsibility because only the responsible are free. In classical economics, consumers are said to be sovereign. What does this mean, except that consumers are responsible for the values of the economic world? Whatever consumers do—what they actually do—defines and enlarges or diminishes their humanity, and the humanity of all of us.

Consumption is no less a human activity than is production.

Consumption has consequences not only for the consumer but for the economy. What is consumed today must in some way be replaced so that we can live to consume another day. Economic consumption and production do not end, any more than the market is cleared. Failure to consume the quantity of goods produced will, of course, discourage further production. A drop in production will cause roughly proportionate drops in employment and investment, and these will affect subsequent consumption. And so on.

In the modern economy of mass production, while it may not make much difference who does the saving or the investing or the producing, it makes all the difference in the world who does the consuming. Affairs might be so badly skewed that one person did all the saving and all the investing and (effectively) all the producing, and the system might creak along reasonably well. But the system would not work at all if one person did all the consuming (a manifest absurdity); and it does not work very well when 20 percent of the people do only 4.3 percent of the consuming (which is the way we try to run things in the United States today).

In a mass-production economy, consuming is a chore that cannot be delegated. A feudal economy can do everything it has to do when one-tenth of one percent of the people dine on paté of reindeer tongue, while ninety-nine and nine-tenths make do with carrot soup. A modern economy falters whenever a sizable percentage of the population is denied access to the economy's output. If the output isn't substantially consumed, there's no point in producing so much; and if there's no point in producing so much, there's no point in employing so many people, whereupon things start to unravel—rather, many things are not knitted up in the first place.

The relation of production to consumption is historical. The drop in production that follows a drop in consumption is not a correction that restores a previous equilibrium; it is a determinant of a new situation, which will have consequences yet to be discovered.

10

Marginal Utility

Thirteen years after the invisible hand had its epiphany in *The Wealth of Nations*, another world-historical idea was launched—Jeremy Bentham's utilitarianism. It sought some impersonal factor of personality, and it aimed from the start at being mathematical. Bentham developed what he called the "felicific calculus," which assigned utility values to commodities in accordance with their contribution to pleasure or to the avoidance of pain. Bentham thought his calculus objective in the same way Newton's laws of motion were objective.

What is astonishing is that the idea has hung on for so long. Even today, power company lawyers talk solemnly about the "utils" of satisfaction their services afford their customers. Bentham himself pointed to a fatal weakness. "Quantity of pleasure being the same," he said aphoristically, "pushpin is as good as poetry."[1] In other words, one man's pleasure is another man's pain, and both are private. What is useful is what provides pleasure or enables the avoidance of pain, but pleasure and pain are exquisitely subjective. As the old wheeze has it,

1. *Encyclopedia of Philosophy*, vol. 1, p. 283.

a sadist is one who enjoys giving pleasure to masochists. It would be arbitrary for you to insist that I really derive pleasure from something I say pains me. How could you know? Pierre Dumont, who translated Bentham into French, put it baldly: "Everyone will constitute himself judge of his own utility."[2]

In spite of its inescapable subjectivism, utilitarianism tantalized the nineteenth-century mind. Independently and almost simultaneously, three writers—Léon Walras in Switzerland, Carl Menger in Austria, and W. Stanley Jevons in England—hit upon the idea of marginal utility, which seemed to them and still seems to most economists today to purge the theory of its subjective taint. It was done by means of the differential calculus.

Walras defined the role of the calculus as follows: "We may say in ordinary language: 'The desire that we have of things or the utility that things have for us, diminishes in proportion to the consumption. The more a man eats, the less hungry he is; the more he drinks, the less thirsty; at least in general and saving certain regrettable exceptions. . . .' But in mathematical terms we say: 'The intensity of the last desire satisfied, is a decreasing function of the quantity of commodity consumed'. . . . It is not an appreciable quantity, but it is only necessary to conceive it in order to found upon the fact of its diminution the demonstration of the great laws of pure political economy."[3]

Because of this conceivable but nonappreciable quantity, it is possible for each of us to rank our utilities and to make mathematically reasonable choices. Economists tend to talk of equally (or "indifferently") desirable commodities, but if trade is to occur at all, some commodity seems to someone at the moment of trading more desirable than all other possibilities.

In the same way, infinitesimal differences will recommend one investment over another and over all others. In each industry one firm will become strongest in resources and most successful in trading. The

2. Dumont, quoted in Newman et al., eds., *Source Readings*, p. 169.
3. Walras, "Determination of Prices," 47–48.

outcome is described by Walras: "If, in short, at a given point, a certain quantity of manufactured products corresponds to the absence of gain and loss [that is, if price equals cost], the parties in the transaction who manufactured less take the losses, restrain their production and finish by liquidating, those who manufactured more take the gains, develop their production and attract to themselves the business of others; thus, . . . production in free competition, after being engaged in a great number of small enterprises, tends to distribute itself among a number less great of medium enterprises, then among a small number of great enterprises, to end finally, first in a *monopoly at cost price*, then in a *monopoly at the price of maximum gain*."[4] Walras comments, "This statement is corroborated by the facts."

From this unexceptionable analysis, we must infer that on the assumptions of marginal utility, free competition is impossible except perhaps as a transient initial point. Since free competition is itself an assumption of marginal utility, we might expect the theory to have been abandoned at this point. Instead, the contradiction was swept under the rug, just as Adam Smith blithely continued to rely on competition and the invisible hand even though fully aware that "[t]o widen the market and to narrow the competition, is always the interest of the dealers . . . an order of men, whose interest is never exactly the same with that of the public, and who accordingly have, upon many occasions, both deceived and oppressed it."[5]

THE FINAL DEGREE OF UTILITY

The last desire satisfied, which Walras called *rareté*, and which earlier English writers had called the final degree of utility, is now generally called marginal utility. To this point, Walras is saying scarcely more than Bentham had said, but he has got his ideas in shape for for-

---

4. Ibid., p. 57.
5. Smith, *Wealth*, p. 250.

mulation in a series of simultaneous equations that are in principle solvable because there are as many equations as there are unknowns. Not only may the marginal utility of orange juice for me be related to my marginal utility of graham crackers, but these utilities may be related to yours for a sports car and even to the nation's for a new fighter plane, and these utilities may be summed to determine aggregate demand. Or so it is said.

In actuality, of course, nothing approaching this is done. Quite apart from the practical impossibility of collecting the data necessary for even a substantial number of the equations, it must be objected that the best and in fact the only way of measuring the marginal utility of orange juice for me is by discovering what I pay for it. Any other value assigned to that utility is arrogant guesswork. Market research—what I might pay for it in a different situation—is pretty iffy, as President Franklin Roosevelt would have said. More to the point, what I do pay for orange juice, and what I might pay for orange juice, are both quantified in terms of money—the price of orange juice at certain times, in certain situations. But the whole point and purpose of marginal utility theory is to explain price. By using price to explain price, we are chasing our tail.

Walras, to be sure, considers the case of Robinson Crusoe, or of a colony of Crusoes, with goods to exchange, but no money. "If," he writes, "all these individuals held a market on the shore in order to exchange their commodities with each other, these would have current prices perfectly determined and entirely independent of the cost of production. This is the problem of exchange and shows how the prices depend only on the *rareté*, that is the utility and quantity possessed of these commodities."[6]

The little scenario may go to show that price sometimes doesn't depend on cost of production (which may be granted), but it shows lit-

6. Walras, "Geometrical Theory," p. 60.

tle else. The problem, again, is that utility is quantifiable only as price. Crusoe and his friends may get along without money as a store of wealth, but they are still making use of what Walras calls a *numéraire*, or money of account, if their exchanges are at all general; and utility is expressed in terms of that *numéraire*, and in no other way.

It is pointless to pretend that some force or entity or whatnot lies behind a price if the price is the only evidence for that force or entity or whatnot. If I pay a lot of money for an object, you know that it's worth that amount of money to me, and that's all that you, as an economist, do know or need to know.

As often happens in the history of economics, Walras enunciated with great and unreflective assurance a psychological truism that as a matter of fact is not true. It simply is not so that the intensity of the last desire satisfied is always a decreasing function of the quantity of commodity consumed. Seekers after knowledge are insatiable; collectors, even of match folders, commonly become more eager as their collections grow; someone assembling a tract of land will willingly pay more for the available parcels as the tract approaches its goal. Even among appetites there are many that increase by what they feed on. If we really had nothing but decreasing functions on our hands, we should expect consumption in general to taper off, with a consequent steady fall in prices.

Hobbes's insight into the motive for accumulating goods is closer to the way of the world than Walras's decreasing function. Goods convey power, and the most vital power is control over the conditions of one's life. In this respect, money is pure power, making all goods available. One can never have too much money, as one might have more food than one could eat. There are always many reasons—moral, prudential, even whimsical—because of which one is not willing to go beyond a certain point in the pursuit of money, but rich is always better.

It may also be observed that Walras did not pursue the calculus as far as it will go. Infinitesimal differences will enforce preference of one industry over all others, just as one firm is preferred within each industry. The really final end will be one firm making one product; and complete analysis might well determine that the single firm had a single owner, a single employee, and a single customer for its single product, whose sale is a single apocalyptic event.

Such a conclusion is obviously absurd, but this outcome is perfectly congruent with the traditional theory of free competition, which contemplates the reduction of price to cost, the survival of the fittest enterprise, the cost-minimizing settling of each industry on its "best" product, and the flocking of investors to the most profitable industry. In the world we live and move in, it is a historical fact that this absurd conclusion has so far been avoided. The white radiance of pure political economy is necessarily stained by the willful actions of us poor mortals, whose last desires satisfied are not imaginary utils but historical or biographical facts—which is fortunate, since whatever the ultimate single product proved to be, the final single consumer would either starve to death or choke to death on it, provided that he (or she) didn't sooner die of boredom.

MEASURING SATISFACTION

Walras's notion of a decreasing function has suggested a somewhat different attempt, made by economists as various as Abba Lerner and Milton Friedman, to establish an "objective" basis for motivation.[7] A rich man, it is said, suffers less pain from the loss of a dollar than a poor man gains in pleasure from the acquisition of a dollar. This is certainly not universally true, for there are misers among us and also blithe spirits aware that the best things in life are free. Bob Cratchit was a happier man than Ebenezer Scrooge. Experienced money rais-

---

7. Friedman, "Lerner on the Economics of Control," pp. 310–19.

ers know that in general the rich are less likely to tithe than the poor. And experienced politicians know that it is harder to increase the top income tax brackets than to boost a sales tax, regardless of the relative numbers of people involved and the relative worth to each of them of a dollar more or less.

Despite much common observations, it is argued that if people gain satisfaction (or experience satisfaction), some kind of comparison can be made among satisfactions; some are greater than others. The intensity or amount of satisfactions will bear some relation to each individual's situation. Someone who has much will be dissatisfied less by the loss of a unit than someone who has little will be satisfied by the gain of a unit.

This conclusion has been adduced to justify taxing the rich to feed the starving, as though there were no better justification than the (remote) possibility that the rich won't mind. Perhaps the rich ought to be made richer; then they'd mind it less. And the poor ought to be made poorer; then they'd appreciate a crust more.

However all that may be, we still don't know how to measure satisfaction. What is the unit that may be added here and subtracted there? Keynes enjoyed collecting rare books, and I enjoy rereading *The General Theory*. How are these enjoyments to be compared? Since he had more of rare books than I have of *The General Theory*, would he have suffered less at not getting a book than I would gain by reading a chapter? Perhaps so, but how are the gains and losses to be measured? Walras's notion that "it is only necessary to conceive" of the intensity of the last desire doesn't fit the case when desires are to be compared. To compare, one must measure; and to measure, one must have a unit of measurement.

Temporary escape from this morass may be sought by measuring with the special unit that can be exchanged for satisfaction of any (well, almost any) sort: money. If I enjoy reading Keynes (which I can do for little) and he, a richer man, enjoyed collecting rare books (which cost a lot), money meant more to him than it does to me. But this example, which is by no means unusual, turns the theory's conclusion on its head. This unit—or any unit—can mean more to someone who has much than to someone who has little. Or the contrary. There is no stable or reliable relationship between the satisfactions of the rich and those of the poor.

Friedman nevertheless presses ahead. He advocates "an exact, operationally defined, reasoning" that first divides the population into classes, then within each class takes the members two by two to evaluate relative satisfactions, continuing the comparisons until a unit of satisfaction for each class is determined. Then the classes are compared, again two by two, finally determining a universal unit.[8]

More important, the procedure assumes that what can be described has been performed. But this rigamarole would take time. By the time the analysis completes the circle linking the first pair to the last, their schedules of satisfactions are certainly changed (unless death has intervened). The theory requires an impossible simultaneity, which is not at all like the simultaneity where the values within each frame of reference do not change. Here the first equation, which is based on undefined units, is meaningless, and the transformations are strictly imaginary.

Looking back now at the special unit used to measure and compare satisfactions, we note that the unit is money, that is, price. Marginalism, which was developed in hopes of explaining price, winds up trying to use price to explain price.

Marginalism fails when comparisons turn on questions of money,

---

8. This procedure is reminiscent of the use of comparative scores to rank football teams. A college friend once amused himself by proving in this way that our winless small-college team could beat the undefeated national champions. We lost to B, 7–0; but C lost to B, 14–0. This made us 7 points better than C. C beat D, 45–30. D beat E, 27–21. E beat F, 14–13. Thus we were 29 points better than F. F lost to the national champions, 28–0; so we were one point better than the champions. Q. E. D.

for the purpose of marginalism is to establish a base for value, and its need follows from the feeling that price needs explanation. Price, of course, does not exist without money, and vice versa. Thus arguments about the psychology of rich men and poor men seek to find objective values to explain prices—but they must use prices to do so. It cannot even be said who is rich and who is poor without appeal to the prices of the goods the rich and the poor possess as wealth or income. An appeal to satisfaction rather than to price makes Cratchit a richer man than Scrooge. The theory would then have to explain why the loss of a sentimental satisfaction would be less important to Bob than a sentimental gain would be to his employer. But no such game is played; and if it were, it would make a shambles of the allegedly predictable or "rational" behavior of economic man.

PRICE IS THE EXPLANATION OF PRICE

Even when not reduced to absurdity, the calculus of marginal utility did not claim to do more than rank utilities for a given individual, and that at a given moment. Your pleasures and mine cannot be compared, nor can the utilities we exchange be explained mathematically. It turns out that on the assumptions of profit maximization and free competition, nothing happens. No exchange takes place, and so no exchange value appears.

Authority for this judgment is Léon Walras himself, who writes, "What reason is there to exchange net income against net income, to sell, for example, a house yielding 2,500 francs in rentals for 100,000 francs, only to buy a piece of land for 100,000 francs yielding 2,500 francs in rent? Such an exchange of one capital good for another makes no more sense than the exchange of a commodity for itself." Then he adds, "To understand why purchases and sales take place in the market for capital goods we have to fall back upon certain crucial facts of experience in the world of reality."[9] Quite so. As Pogo might say, we have met these crucial facts, and they are us.

Walras conceived of the market place as a series of auctions in which, through groping ("*tâtonnement*"), economic agents arrive at definite prices. The groping cannot be assumed; it has to be actually performed, and there is no way of telling how it will come out. Nor is it certain that it will come out at all. There is no axiom that says that the series of bids and the series of asks must converge, or that they must exhibit any regularity at all. In fact, they are pretty erratic in the securities exchanges, the real-life auctions that most resemble the one imagined by Walras.

The price appears only in the actual sale. There need be no groping from sale to sale, nor must the next offer, leading to the next sale (if any), be the same; it may be higher or lower. The prices actually agreed to are therefore the only determinate values in Walras's equations. Walras himself made the same point on another occasion: "*Rareté* is *personal* or *subjective*; value in exchange is *real* or *objective*."[10]

Walras talks only of production goods, but Carl Menger, the second of the independent developers of marginal utility, made a more general observation: "Commodities that can be exchanged against each other in certain definite quantities (a sum of money and a quantity of some other economic good, for example), that can be exchanged for each other at will by a *sale* or a *purchase*, in short, commodities that are *equivalents in the objective sense of the term*, do not exist—even on given markets and at a given point in time. And what is more important, deeper understanding of the causes that lead to the exchange of goods and to human trade in general teaches us that equivalents of this sort are utterly impossible in the very nature of the case and cannot exist in reality at all."[11]

---

9. Walras, *Elements*, p. 310.
10. Walras, *Elements*, p. 146.
11. Menger, *Principles*, p. 193.

If every good had, as Bentham imagined, a determinate objective value, there would be no point in trading (unless one cheated). For trade to proceed, traders must put personal valuations on the goods to be bought or sold. I may want to sell my cow because I'm tired of feeding her, or because her milk makes me sick, or because I lust after more gold to fondle, or because I want to do you a favor. You may want to buy her for reasons equally subjective and idiosyncratic. All this is indeterminate. Our subjective valuations are made objective and determinate in the money that changes hands in the act of buying or selling, and only thus.

Or put the issue this way: If every good has a determinate objective value, how do we know what it is? If utility explains price, the question then becomes, How do we know what has utility, what affords pleasure or suppresses pain? W. Stanley Jevons, the third of our triumvirate (though actually the first in time) has the answer. In his classic exposition of marginal utility, he calls for increased efforts to collect statistics. "The price of a commodity," he writes, "is the only test we have of the utility of the commodity to the purchaser. . . .[12] And, he might have added, to the seller, too. The theory says that price is explained by utility, but unhappily all we know of utility is price. The theory of utility tells us nothing we did not already know. We are back where we started.

The same point had, indeed, been made sixty-eight years earlier by Jean-Baptiste Say. He wrote, "[P]rice is the measure of the value of things, and their value is the measure of their utility."[13] Logically, therefore, price is the measure of utility. In a note on his next page, Say wrote, "For the present it is enough to know that, whatever be the state of society, current prices approximate to the real value of things, in proportion to the liberty of production and mutual dealing." It is then not clear how one detects the alleged distinction between current prices and the

---

12. Jevons, *Theory*, p. 146.
13. Say, *Treatise*, p. 62.

"real" value of things, let alone how such a distinction could be maintained if "[P]rice is the measure of the value of things. . . ."

Although Say's observation destroyed the foundations of marginal utility almost before Bentham finished pouring the footings, and although Jevons destroyed the framing even as he erected it, this dizzily circular argument is today a leading doctrine taught in American universities.

Cournot had a surer grasp of the problem than did his marginalist contemporaries. He wrote: "The abstract idea of *wealth* or *value in exchange*, a definite idea, and consequently susceptible of rigorous treatment in combinations [i.e., mathematically] must be carefully distinguished from the accessory ideas of utility, scarcity, and suitability to the needs and enjoyments of mankind, which the word *wealth* still suggests in common speech. These ideas are variable, and by nature indeterminate. . . . [T]here is no fixed standard for the utility of things."[14]

No matter how we try to explain price, all we know is price. The impulse behind an offer to buy or sell may be physiological or psychological or sociological—or chemical or physical. It doesn't matter. The "cry" in the market is certainly physical; so how many ergs of energy result in a dollar bid for wheat? Or if, as has been assumed since Bentham, the impulse is merely psychological, how many "utils" of satisfaction, depending on how severe a course of toilet training, result in a dollar bid? All that is nonsense. Everyone knows it is nonsense. There is no way of starting with ergs or utils or the Oedipus complex and getting to dollars. A connection might be shown in a particular case after the event, but it has to be after, and it has to be shown. It cannot be assumed to be regular, nor can it be assumed to have been proved. As there is no way of starting with ergs and getting to utils, so there is no way of starting with utils and getting to price.

---

14. Cournot, *Mathematical Principles*, pp. 10–11.

THE IDEA OF THE MARGIN

The idea of a margin was proposed as an answer to the indeterminateness of the satisfactions encountered in utility analysis. The margin is the point at which utility changes to disutility or the point at which profit changes to loss. On one side of the point or line, values are positive; on the other, they are negative. Marginal analysis studies the last item consumed or the last item produced before the line is crossed, and that last item seems clear and determinate.

From the point of view of the producer, wherever supply and income curves cross, business stops because each additional sale would represent a loss. This can occur in short periods or long periods—or never. In the typical business enterprise, the curves do not cross, because short periods are irrelevant. Just as a year's supply of butter is not sold in a day, so a year's supply is not churned in a day. The supply cost may be subject to seasonal variations, but sales and production plans (and consumer purchasing) include at least a cycle of seasons.

In an ongoing enterprise there is, strictly speaking, no margin.[15] There are various pseudo-margins. The most commonly used are the end of a production run and the point at which sunk costs are recovered, and these may serve to direct management's attention to questions that should be answered before an enterprise is undertaken or expanded. They do not provide the answers.

The costs of each production run are given, and prices are what the market will bear. Obviously the enterprise will be more profitable if costs can be shaved and prices raised; you don't need an economist to tell you that. In the typical enterprise, the first production run will probably be a loser. What you have to decide is whether you'll be able to sell enough product at a high enough price to get a satisfactory re-

---

15. Wicksteed, *Alphabet*, p. 102.

turn on your investment in a reasonable time. All of these points call for judgment, and for what I've elsewhere called will, and marginal analysis has nothing definitive to say on any of them.

It is ordinarily useful to separate overhead costs and start-up costs from run-on costs, and in such a classification run-on costs seem something like marginal costs. But you'd be a fool, and soon bankrupt, to start a project with only run-on costs in mind.

Something like marginal analysis is also done in respect to elective costs. The advertising manager, for example, may produce charts showing that an extra $100,000 for space will pull in at least an extra $100,001 in business. He may persuade you. But then the sales manager may have charts showing that putting a couple of extra reps on the road will also bring in $100,001. You'd better not believe them both unless you also believe your market is infinitely expandable, for there will be plenty of other claimants with plausible proposals; the production manager may advocate a state-of-the-art plant, and the art director may advocate a more attractive design. It may even occur to you to wonder whether you'd not work a lot harder if your own pay were bumped up another $100,000. Somebody has to think of these things.

Every business cost is more or less elective. Unimaginative types may doubt the relevance of a modernistic sculpture garden to the soft-drink business, but Pepsi Cola management evidently feels that their headquarters in Purchase, New York, helps attract good staff and helps impress customers and licensees.

Fritz Machlup brushed aside studies purporting to show that most businesspeople do not consciously use marginal analysis in their work. He argued that they use it intuitively in the same way an automobile driver intuitively gauges the chances of passing a trailer truck before a bend in the road.[16] He was no doubt right, but the whole point of marginal analysis is precision. Machlup's answer merely says that suc-

16. Machlup, "Marginal Analysis," p. 535.

cessful businesspeople are successful, and that successful automobile drivers live to pass another truck. True enough.

In the allocating of costs to the various factors (especially labor) it is claimed that the costs at the margin are the "real" ones, which should be guidelines for future costs, if not reasons for renegotiating previous contracts. If, however, the factors producing the marginal item are proportional to those producing the total output, there is no change. On the other hand, if the factors are not proportional, the change is uninformative unless total output can be produced with the new mix of inputs; it is a technological, not an economic, question. In either case, the pseudo-margin (or genuine one) is a function of costs already incurred and prices already charged. The factors of the marginal item are functions of the original factors, whatever they may have been, for if the original factors had been different, the margin would have been different. The marginal factors are therefore no more authoritative or "objective" than the original factors.

Vilfredo Pareto proposed to use marginal analysis to determine the proper "scientific" wage for labor. What he actually proved, as Wicksell said, was "simply that under free competition the worker receives the greatest possible wage *compatible with the state of rents and interest*."[17] Pareto assumed the price system. Since the wage scale is part of the price system, he assumed what he pretended to discover.

In short, marginal analysis is irrelevant in practical affairs and theoretically indeterminate.

---

17. Wicksell, *Selected Papers*, p. 144.

11

Saving and Investing

The goods we have been discussing are consumers' goods—things and services to be used and enjoyed. Their role in the economy is systematically different from that of producers' goods—things and services to make consumers' goods or other producers' goods. Producers' goods exist in every system, no matter how primitive or advanced. The first producers' goods were no doubt clubs to attack game or stones to crack shells. Puny humans would barely survive without such goods, but with them they perform miracles.

The discovery of the sixteenth century was, as Keynes put it, the discovery (or perhaps rediscovery) of compound interest. He once calculated that every £1 that Sir Francis Drake plundered from Spain and brought home to the queen in 1580 had become £100,000 by 1930, and that the total was equivalent to the entire overseas wealth of the British Empire at its height. Looking ahead, he indulged the hope that the same process would solve "the economic problem" in another hundred years or so (more than sixty of which have already gone by) and that economists would then be "thought of as humble competent people, on a level with dentists."[1]

Keynes was speaking of producers' goods bought with Drake's gold and silver, and of the progressive investment and reinvestment of a part of the proceeds of those goods in further producers' goods, and so on, for 350 years. The reinvestments were small, averaging about $3^1/_4$ percent a year; but the results were stupendous. Spain, in contrast, although her plunder from the Americas was vastly greater than Drake's plunder from her, used practically all her gold and silver to pay for consumers' goods, from castles in Iberia to armies in Italy and the Low Countries, with results that left her far in the British wake.

PRODUCERS' GOODS VS. CONSUMERS' GOODS

Just as there is nothing inherent in an object that makes it a good, there is nothing inherent in a good that makes it a producers' good. A hammer may be used in producing something for sale, in which case it is a producers' good. Or it may be used about the house or even become an object for collectors, in which cases it is a consumers' good. Or another time, a harried collector may grab a handsome specimen to drive a nail into something he intends to sell; then it becomes a producers' good again. A hen is a producers' good if her eggs are sold, but she herself may be literally consumed and so lay no more eggs. Even a steel mill may become a consumers' good; one near Völklingen, in the Saar, sheltered displaced persons for a time after World War II.

These classifications seem to reduce the real world to one of shifting and contradictory appearances. A hammer would seem to be both a consumers' good and not a consumers' good, which is logically impossible. But the object in question is not even a hammer in its sense qualities or in its shape (it might be a gavel) but in its use. The ham-

1. Keynes, *Persuasion*, p. 373.

mer is neither a producers' good nor a consumers' good—nor a good at all—except in the way it is used.

In the National Income and Product Accounts, a new single-family dwelling counts as a capital investment, no matter who pays for it or how anyone uses it. Some writers justify this sort of classification on the ground of the size or the durability of the house. But durability is an uncertain test: I have many books that are older than any house I have ever owned or lived in. Some go still further afield and classify consumer durables and even clothing as "savings." It is true that my dinner jacket is older than most houses on my street and, given the amount of wear it gets, may well outlast them. It is also true that it cost me less when I bought it than a replacement would cost me today, but this difference is savings only in the huckster's sense of "Sale! Up to 50% Savings!" I did not buy it for any productive purpose. Nor did I buy it for a speculative purpose, and I'd have been disappointed if I had, for in the absence of an established market for secondhand clothes, the cost of selling it would have eaten up the putative "profit." On the other hand, if I were a headwaiter, the dinner jacket might be a necessary uniform and so productive.

The danger in all nonfunctional classifications quickly appears when we look again at the question of compound interest. Castles in Spain were big-ticket items and durable, and the grandees who built them saved or borrowed money for the purpose. But the castles were consumers' goods; they were not used to produce anything except plunder and extortionate rents, both of which are, literally, counterproductive. In contrast, the British steadily plowed 3 1/4 percent of their earnings back into the shops for which Napoleon scorned them, and into mines and railways and factories and ships, all of which, in turn, produced further goods. The Spanish investments satisfied the durability definition; the British investments satisfied functional definitions. There is a practical difference.

We must not conclude, however, that there is a standard percentage of income that an economy should invest, year in and year out.

Here again, it proves impossible to avoid passing judgment. The 3 1/4 percent rate of British imperialism may for some purposes have been too high, for others too low, though we can be pretty sure that it was more suitable than the near-zero Spanish rate.

In studies of the distribution of wealth, the faulty classification is misleading. As Lester Thurow points out, "Standard economics . . . assumes that people accumulate wealth solely to provide future consumption privileges," but great wealth results in economic power, "which entails the ability to order others about." Most Americans have little or no net wealth, and even the middle class have most of their wealth in the form of their homes. Since late-twentieth-century inflation increased the price of residential housing, the distribution of wealth seemed more equitable than formerly. But home ownership conveys little economic power, and Thurow shows that about 40 percent of all fixed nonresidential capital is controlled by only 482 families and individuals. Thus very few can order very many about.[2]

PRODUCTION IS PRIOR TO SAVING

Producers' goods are things that have been saved. Agriculture is impossible unless seeds are set aside, reducing current consumption to ensure future consumption. In addition, labor must be devoted to making tools, building fences, turning pots for storage; and all these activities reduce the time available for idleness, recreation, and other forms of current consumption.

Saving is a consequence of production. Nothing can be saved until it exists. No artifact exists until it has been manufactured. Production is inescapably prior to saving. Even the standard agricultural model fails; seed corn cannot be saved unless it has already been harvested.

---

2. Thurow, in *New York Times*, October 11, 1984, op-ed page.

In a modern economy, the priority of production is even more striking. When a corporation plans a new product, contracts are entered into with a construction company to build a factory, with tool manufacturers for the necessary machines, perhaps with an advertising agency for marketing plans, and so on. The corporation also assures itself of a line of credit to meet payments on these contracts as they come due. The bank that grants the line of credit gets its affairs in order so that it can do what it has agreed to do. The various contractors and subcontractors and their banks all go through similar motions. Aside from a down payment here and there, no money is paid over until quite a lot of time has passed and quite a lot of work has been done. In short, a great expansion of debt takes place, including the credit extended by the workers (who customarily wait a week or a month for their pay), that extended by merchants satisfying the demands of the newly employed workers, that extended by wholesalers restocking the merchants and manufacturers restocking the wholesalers, and so on.

The expansion comes about not as a result of savings but as a result of production put in process by the corporation. No amount of saving by bankers and potential workers and suppliers would, in itself, have called the new production into existence. Nothing would have been produced if the enterprising corporation had not decided it could make a profit on it and if the people and firms it dealt with had not had faith in its ability to do so.

NOT-CONSUMING

Saving means not-consuming, but not-consuming does not mean investing. You can save or not-consume until you starve or freeze to death, but your not-consuming will not cause investment. Investment is a separate and deliberate action. Investment is making use of things that have been processed but have not been consumed: machines and tools that have been fashioned, resources that have been mined or harvested and perhaps partially processed but not sold, ideas that have not been developed or realized. Such things have been produced and saved.

Money is used to buy and operate and develop such things; but until it is so used, it is not invested, any more than it is spent on sober consumption or riotous living until it is so spent. Money spent on securities is speculative, not productive.

It is common to find politicians, pundits, and even economists making remarks like, "If the United States only put more of its income into savings, it would have more money to invest in education, factories, and new technologies, and this would make the nation's economy grow faster and richer."

In everyday speech, it seems perfectly clear that if people invest more they will have to consume less; must forgo better food, clothing, shelter, entertainment, or health care; and so have money left over to save. What then?

They will take their saved money to a banker or, more likely, to a manager of one of the several thousand extant mutual funds. In the present state of the economy, the banker, who pays depositors something like 0.4 percent interest, will probably lend the new funds to credit-card spendthrifts at 18.9 percent, or perhaps buy some Treasury securities paying 6 or 7 percent. The mutual-fund manager will buy stocks on one of the domestic exchanges or, in accordance with contemporary fashion, on one of the foreign exchanges.

Since the present exercise was begun with the idea of reducing consumption, the banker's financing of credit cards must be judged counterproductive, while investing in Treasuries instead of in struggling small businesses is not the kind of investment that readers of pleas to decrease consumption rationally expect. As for the mutual funds, the principal effect of their playing the stock market may be a run-up of stock prices. If enough money has been "saved" (and the recent multimillion-dollar-a-day growth of mutual funds and the even faster growth of "derivatives" show that such saving is really not our desperate need), the consequence can be more like a firestorm than a running of the bulls. In that case, all the smart money in the economy may be sucked into the market. Funds that otherwise would have been available to underwrite productive enterprise will be thrown into speculation. A bull market can cause a credit crunch.

In the meantime, the not-consuming has necessarily reduced demand. Fewer goods and services are bought or hired; consequently fewer are produced or provided, and fewer people are employed producing or providing them. With fewer people employed, demand inevitably falls further. In the abstract, there's no reason why the fall should not become a free-fall.

In our time, however, the size and viscosity of the federal budget (and of state and local budgets, too) have apparently fixed something like a buffer under the economy so that no more than 8 or 9 percent of the labor force will be unemployed—unless the Federal Reserve Board decides that more people must be denied work in order to try to control inflation, or the president and Congress make the same decision in order to continue balancing the budget.

ORGANIZATION AND CAPITAL

The modern mode of production differs from previous modes not in that it uses or exploits producers' goods (for all modes do that), nor in that it uses or exploits labor (for all modes also do that), but in that it is organized as a system of continuous and interrelated flows. Such retail trade as existed in Aristotle's time was frowned on by him because he could not see how a retailer produced anything. In the ancient and medieval worlds, enterprises were relatively discrete and ad hoc affairs, as the construction industry is largely organized to this day. If one wanted a pair of shoes, one went to a cordwainer and had a pair custom made; there was no store in which one could buy what one wanted off the shelf.

The cordwainer, to be sure, was a specialist in leather working, and the apprentices he employed were, so to say, subspecialists, one perhaps being more skilled at preparing the leather, another at sewing.

What was true of small transactions was true of large. The merchants of Venice organized each commercial voyage as a separate affair. Their personal experience taught them the sorts of goods most likely to be wanted on the Golden Horn, and they stocked their outward-bound galleys accordingly. Likewise they brought home the sorts of things they could sell quickly and profitably at the quayside. The system was a series of speculative ventures, making the most of expected and unexpected opportunities to buy and sell. Those involved were, as they called themselves, merchant adventurers.

The first modern business was probably the wool trade, a trade that peculiarly lent itself to such organization. In the first place, the wool itself was, comparatively, not perishable. At all stages—as raw wool, as yarn, as cloth—it could be fairly safely stockpiled; working capital was born. Each stage, moreover, required a special machine—a spinning wheel, a loom: fixed capital. Entrepreneurs bought wool from the farmers, put it out for spinning and weaving, generally on their own looms, gathered the finished cloth, and held it for sale to merchant adventurers, or sometimes handled the distribution themselves in an early form of vertical organization. The flow could be steady because the end product—clothing—was in universal and perpetual demand.

Yet no one knew, when the sheep were sheared, what would ultimately become of the wool, nor could the entrepreneurs be perfectly sure they would find a ready market, at a price to cover their costs, when they collected the finished cloth from their weavers. The rationale of their enterprises required them to keep going. With flowing enterprise came increased uncertainty and possibility of profit. The medieval or Renaissance guild master manufactured products to order, reducing uncertainty and possible profit to a minimum.

Every new enterprise must accumulate producers' goods in the forms of fixed capital and working capital. To buy them, it needs liquid capital—money. Every continuing enterprise has similar needs; machinery wears out and raw materials are used up. Investment in producers' goods is never ending. All these goods are necessarily saved in the sense that they are withheld from consumption. As fast as they are used up (or dissaved) in the production of consumers' goods, they must be replaced. If the enterprise continues, the saving does, too.

Investments are bought with money, which is either borrowed, supplied from funds on hand, or derived from the sale of assets or equity. If finance is borrowed, the interest rate is the explicit fee for its use. If finance is supplied from funds on hand or derived from the sale of assets or equity, the opportunity cost of using those funds is implicitly related to the prevailing interest rate.

THE "WORTH" OF MONEY

Money has no price; it has a fee for its use, which is interest. (Similarly there is no price for laborers; they are not for sale; wages are fees for their employment.) Although money has no price, it has what we may call its "worth," which is not merely its purchasing power but its borrowing power. In a modern economy, borrowing power leads to something vastly larger and more important, namely, investing power.

The Federal Reserve Board, in its diurnal wrestle with inflation, seems to have its eye fixed almost exclusively on increasing the fee for the use of money in order to hold down demand for "interest-sensitive" commodities (housing and automobiles and other big ticket items). There are two (presumably unintended) results. The first is that (to rephrase "Engine Charlie" Wilson) what is bad for General Motors is bad for the economy. In other words, you can't slow down the building trades and the automobile business and their many auxiliaries without risking a recession. Second, raising the interest rate inevitably reduces the investing power of money.

Assuming that a projected investment is sound, the size of the investment will depend on the interest rate and the credit and resources of the investing company. The interest rate determines the amount of investing that can be financed with a given amount of money. The range of possibilities is enormous, as four historical examples will show. Before the 1951 "accord" that freed the Federal Reserve Board from its wartime commitment to maintain the prices (and, of course, the interest rates) of Treasury securities, the prime rate was 1.5 percent. In the Volcker years (1979–87), the prime averaged above 12 percent. In 1993, it stood at 6 percent, and at present writing it is 9.5 percent. Thus a corporation that can afford an annual interest expense of $150,000 and can borrow at prime, could in the first example have borrowed and invested $10 million, but only $1.25 million in the second example, $2.5 million in 1996, and about $1.50 million at midyear 2000. Corresponding amounts, with appropriate adjustments for risk and the like, will apply to every enterprise in the economy, and to the economy in aggregate.

In short, the "worth" of money moves inversely to the interest rate, and is like the price of government bonds, which, as the *New York Times* never fails to remind its business readers, moves inversely to the interest rate. Money and government bonds are IOUs of the government; they differ in that money may always be tendered, while bonds only at a time certain, and only bonds pay interest. But they are alike in their response to the general interest rate. The price of bonds falls as the interest rate rises, and so does the "worth" of money. This is another way of saying that a rise in the interest rate causes a fall in investment and a rise in the price level. In short, raising the interest rate causes both stagnation and inflation. Corresponding amounts, with appropriate adjustments because of risk and the like, will apply to every enterprise in the economy and to the economy as an aggregate. Thus we are discussing no small matter.

Two subsidiary points should be noted: First, it is often said that while a rising rate of interest may have adverse effects on the economy, a high rate does not. But given each firm's credit rating and its budgeted interest expense, its amount of possible borrowing, and hence of investment, is specific for each rate of interest, whether rising or falling or stationary. It is greater when interest is low and smaller when interest is high and, a fortiori, falling when interest is rising. Second, the differences among the examples are due entirely to the differences in the interest rate. The possible effect of inflation on the actual quantity of producers' goods purchased is an altogether separate question. Needless to say, "real" investments are likely to be greater when prices are low.

Now, it might well happen that the corporation we've been talking about couldn't find suitable investments for all the money that a low prime would allow it to borrow with the $150,000 it has budgeted for interest. The unexpended balance would not, however, be wasted but would go toward a price cut (which would obviously be counterinflationary), a wage increase (which would not affect already budgeted unit costs and so would not push up prices), or a stronger bottom line (which would enable the corporation to borrow at a still lower interest rate). Whatever the mix of outcomes, a low interest rate allows low or nonexistent inflation.

THE EQUALITY OF SAVING AND INVESTING

With a few notable exceptions, producers' goods, as well as consumers' goods, are now produced for the market, and the market is not cleared. A colonial ranch house, a jetliner, a specialized machine tool, an evening gown, may be custom made; yet most of the materials of which they are made have been produced to meet an anticipated general demand, not a special-ordering particular demand. No scavenger of aluminum cans scours another roadside because Boeing gets a new order for a 727. No farmer plants another row of beans because I get a job. No automobile manufacturer builds an extra convertible because I now can afford one, nor does a steel mill open an extra furnace to supply the auto company's sudden need. The aluminum, beans, car, and steel are being produced anyhow. The resources they embody are being saved anyhow, as is all work in progress.

Money—the liquid capital—is likewise being saved anyhow. An enterprise needs money to buy materials, to pay rent and interest and taxes and wages. That is what cash flow is all about. The enterprise manages to save or borrow the necessary money, or it goes out of business.

We come here to an important distinction. While almost all production requires saving in the form of liquid capital, not all liquid capital is spent on production. In the course of defining "income" and "saving," Keynes constructs and solves a pair of simultaneous equations as follows:

Income = value of output = consumption + investment.
Saving = income − consumption.
Therefore saving = investment.[3]

---

3. Keynes, *General Theory*, p. 63.

The Polish economist Michal Kalecki reaches the same conclusion via a quite different proof. First, he divides all economic activity into two divisions. Division 1 consists of the incomes earned by the producers of production goods, which are defined as all goods that have not yet achieved final sales to consumers. Division 2 consists of incomes earned by the producers of consumption goods, which are confined to those actually sold to consumers; this division thus has no invested capital. For convenience, C_1 indicates the consumption of Division 1; S_1 and S_2 indicate the respective savings of the two divisions; and I indicates the total investment, which will be all in the production goods division. Kalecki's proof goes as follows:

(1) $C_1 = S_2$ [Whatever consumption goods Division 1 consumes must have been produced by, but neither consumed by, nor invested by, Division 2.]

(2) $C_1 + S_1 = S_2 + S_1$ [adding S_1 to both sides]

(3) $C_1 + S_1 = I$ [by definition]

(4) $S_2 + S_1 = S$ [the total savings of both divisions]

(5) $I = S$ [substituting equations (3) and (4) in equation (2)] Q.E.D. See Kalecki, *Essays on Developing Economies*, pp. 41–44. Kalecki gives a more elaborate, but essentially the same, proof in *Selected Essays on the Dynamics of the Capitalist Economy, 1933–1970* pp. 78–92.

It will be noted that Kalecki's proof, like Keynes's, is valid only in "real" terms; that is, neither proof takes account of money or any financial instrument, and thus both are blind to the effects of speculation that we shall encounter in Chapter 14.

As his equations, being written partly in English and partly in mathematical symbols, don't look quite like ordinary equations, so his famous further inference ("Saving, in fact, is a mere residual") is not an ordinary mathematical inference. To the extent that the equations are mathematical, saving and investment are equivalent, and either may be called a residual.

In any case, Keynes quite properly supports his famous inference by referring to the actual world, rather than to his quasi-equations: "A decision to consume or not to consume truly lies within the power of the individual; so does a decision to invest or not to invest. The amounts of aggregate income and of aggregate saving are the *results* of the free choices of individuals whether or not to consume and whether or not to invest; but they are neither of them capable of assuming an independent value resulting from a separate set of decisions taken irrespective of the decisions concerning consumption and investment."[4]

But we are still not so clear as we might be about what is meant by "investment." Keynes unfortunately gives us pretty much of a portmanteau definition: "In popular usage it is common to mean by this [investment] the purchase of an asset, old or new, by an individual or a corporation. Occasionally, the term might be restricted to the purchase of an asset on the Stock Exchange. But we speak just as readily of investing, for example, in a house, or in a machine, or in a stock of finished or unfinished goods. . . ."[5]

We observe at once that this definition is not functional. We observe further that while it may have a sort of validity microeconomically, it is grossly misleading macroeconomically. An individual's income (or at least wealth) may be increased by "investing" indifferently in a share of stock, a house, or a machine, but not all of these

4. Keynes, *General Theory*, p. 65.
5. Keynes, *General Theory*, pp. 74–75.

assets produce goods or services that swell the national income.[6] A house may be a producers' good or a consumers' good, depending on whether it is for sale or for rent or owner occupied. A machine is a producers' good, or it is scrap metal. But what is a share of stock?

A share of stock is a legal asset, a claim on future profits or income, a right (attenuated, to be sure) to participate in control, evidence of partial and restricted ownership. But it is neither a producers' good nor a consumers' good. It is not an economic good at all. The company issuing it may have used the money from the sale to buy a machine. The machine makes things; the share of stock does not (nor does the money used to buy it). To argue otherwise, one would have to point to the things made by the share of stock (or the money), as distinct from those made by the machine.

Nevertheless, trading in shares of stock (and other securities) figures prominently in the "investments" of individuals and of the economy as a whole. It is both a microeconomic and a macroeconomic phenomenon. It absorbs vast amounts of liquid capital. Yet no account is taken of it either in Keynes's quasi-equations or in the more austerely mathematical versions that appear in today's textbooks.

---

6. At this point Keynes was more interested in the macroeconomic equivalence of saving and investment than in his rather offhand definition of investment. In his preface to the French edition of *The General Theory*, he writes, "[T]his relationship between saving and investment, which necessarily holds good for the system as a whole, does not hold good at all for a particular individual. There is no reason whatever why the new investment for which I am responsible should bear any relation whatever to the amount of my own savings." See John Maynard Keynes, *The Collected Writings*, vol. 7, p. xxxii.

My point is the quite different one that while some of Keynes's "investments" yield only personal satisfaction, others are macroeconomically as well as microeconomically effective. Keynes wrote, "Any reasonable definition of the line between consumer-purchases and investor-purchases will serve us equally well, provided that it is consistently applied" (*General Theory*, p. 61). For some purposes this dictum is perhaps acceptable, but it leaves us without a way of explaining, say, the relative success of England and the relative failure of Spain.

INVESTING

Building a factory is investing no matter what school of economics you belong to. In the United States, until a little over a hundred years ago, you would have found it difficult to get your hands on enough money to build that factory. Until 1890, the Supreme Court recognized only the use value of your property; that is, you could, within broad limits, do what you wanted with it. In particular, you could run a business on it; but if a municipal ordinance made it impossible for you to make a profit, you had no recourse. In the Slaughterhouse Cases, the Court held that if you were a butcher in New Orleans, you had to use a municipally run slaughterhouse that charged fees that would bankrupt you. You were not unconstitutionally deprived of your property: you still had your cleavers and saws and hooks and your place of business; no thing had been taken from you. After a twenty-year debate, the Court changed its mind and held that property could also have exchange value (as Adam Smith had recognized a century and a quarter earlier), of which you could not be deprived without due process of law.

Exchange value can be quantified as capitalized future earnings. It is an idea. Once property thus became an idea as well as a datum, the basis on which banks could make responsible loans was radically changed and enlarged. You no longer have to offer physical property—land, a building, a shipload of tea—as collateral for a loan. A well-planned enterprise is (if the bank's loan officer knows his business) much better. In the modern world, investing can generally be financed without curtailing consumption of the good things the economy is able to provide.

There are, however, two provisos: The first is, unhappily, easy to meet: You can't do it if we have full—really, truly full—employment, because if we have full employment, you have to persuade people not to take so many automobile trips (for example) so the road builders will have time to build your factory. As things are in the actual world—and always have been except in wartime—there are plenty of people with time on their hands and eager to help build your factory.

The second proviso is that there must be consumers willing and able to buy whatever it is you intend to make in the factory. Obviously there'd be no point to building the factory otherwise. Equally obviously, if consumers spend money on the product your new factory is going to make, they're going to have that much less to put in their piggy banks. In other words, if people follow conventional advice and cut down on consumption in order to save more, they won't be able to buy your new product; so building a new factory would be wasting, not investing.

"IMPROVING" LAND

What's the first thing you need for that factory? Land, of course. You have to have a place to put the thing. Since saving equals investing, do you have to save the land? If so, how do you do it? Vacant land is vacant because nobody has consumed it. It is there. You don't have to do anything to make it exist. You do, however, have to get the use of it; so you approach the owner and offer to buy or lease it. In neither case do you have to put up any cash—at least nothing beyond a deposit or binder—and when you get going, you make your mortgage or rent payments out of your income. If you buy the land, the seller may take back a mortgage for it; so neither you nor he nor a bank nor anyone else will have to put aside any cash or break any piggy bank to complete the transaction. The seller will have extended credit to you; you will have gone into debt to him.

Now you have the use of the land, but it needs "improvement." You hire a contractor to do the job, and he brings bulldozers and backhoes and earth movers and other big and expensive equipment to make the work go smoothly. Does he make the equipment just for this purpose? Certainly not. He has it in his garage or on his lot, just waiting for jobs like yours, or he rents it from a supplier who has the equipment in his garage or on his lot, just waiting for jobs like your contractor's. Again, no one will have to put aside any cash for the job to go forward, and the same will be true of the contractor who builds your building, and probably of the manufacturer who supplies your machinery.

The steel and bricks and mortar and wiring and plumbing and doors and windows and other stuff needed to build your factory, except for a few fancy details to appease your architect, will not be manufactured especially for you. It is all resting in warehouses, confidently waiting for someone like you to come along, and it will be supplied to you or your contractors on credit.

A couple of hundred years or so ago, when economists first noticed the difference between producers' goods and consumers' goods, the Industrial Revolution had accustomed people to think of producers' goods being used to produce consumers' goods for the market instead of to individual order, or for sale instead of for use. Adam Smith's pin "manufactory" could turn out 48,000 pins a day: Who knew or cared whose hems they would hold in place? What seamstress or tailor knew or cared who had made them? The relationship of seller to buyer became impersonal. The result, as Karl Marx saw it, was "the Fetishism of commodities." A hundred years or so later, Karl Polyani called production for sale "the Great Transformation." We may observe that commodities, like property, are now ideas rather than data.

What we are doing here is extending the ideas, for we are noting that today most producers' goods, like most consumers' goods, are produced for sale rather than for use. Manufacturers, building supply houses, lumber yards, and machine shops carry vast inventories of producers' goods and offer them for sale to whoever is interested. These goods have already been "saved." They have already been withheld from consumption.

SAVING AND WASTING

Relying on the presumed identity of saving and investment, American economists have, for fifty years or more, through Republican administrations and Democratic administrations, steadily advocated what they conceive of as Keynesian policies, intended to encourage saving. There is more than a little irony here, for Keynes held that, except in conditions of full employment, saving "may reduce present investment-demand as well as present consumption-demand."[7]

Since it is plausibly contended that the rich are better able to save than are the poor, the top personal income tax has been cut from 94 percent (subject to a maximum effective rate of 90 percent) in 1945[8] to 39.6 percent today, the severely regressive Social Security tax has been increased, the states have come to rely chiefly on regressive sales taxes, and various schemes, like Individual Retirement Accounts, have been tried. At the same time, the corporate tax rate has been lowered and various inducements to invest have been offered. Despite all this, it is claimed that saving is inadequate in the United States, and our performance is unfavorably compared with that of other nations, particularly, until recently, Japan.

Actually, we save too much and consequently are radically wasteful. Resources can be saved, goods can be saved, all sorts of producers' equipment can be saved. What cannot be saved is labor. (A labor-saving device merely employs labor more efficiently.) Unemployed labor is wasted—worse than that, it does not exist. In this it is not unlike credit, which is meaningless if not used.

Since the cost of labor is somewhere around 60 percent of the cost of the national output, it should be an urgent objective of economic

---

7. Keynes, *General Theory*, p. 210.
8. Pechman, *Federal Tax Policy*, p. 256.

policy to employ it and not waste it. When, as now, several million men and women are unemployed, the problem is one that only the national government is large enough to handle. But it could be handled.

In one way or another, these millions already are provided with something in the way of food, clothing, and shelter. In one way or another, a large proportion of the producers' goods necessary to employ them already exists. Compared with Israel's problem of absorbing the immigrants from Russia and Eastern Europe, the United States' problem of bringing its unemployed and underemployed into the economy is no great thing.

PART III

MODERNIST ECONOMICS AND ITS DISCONTENTS

12

MICRO, MACRO, AND SOCIETY

Though the gross domestic product is a comparatively new idea, and though statistics relating to it have been systematically collected for not much more than fifty years, the term "GDP" has passed into the common vocabulary, where it is frequently invoked as an infallible guide to proper policies. The idea is, however, of severely limited usefulness, and its misuse confuses and misleads public action.

It may be helpful to cite a few examples. A recent budget for the United States space shuttle and related activities was $6.9 billion. The same amount of money could have paid for roughly 100,000 units of public housing, whose construction, incidentally, would probably have employed more workers than the shuttle. It is a matter of judgment whether more communications satellites are more in the public interest than more housing; but the GDP is of no help in making that judgment, because the two programs have closely similar effects on the GDP.

Again: Asbestos products swelled the GDP three ways: first, when the products were manufactured and installed; second, when doctors, nurses, hospitals, pharmaceutical manufacturers, lawyers, judges, and insurance adjusters were employed because of the resulting cancers; and third, when workmen were employed in removing the asbestos installations. Anyone with his eyes solely on the GDP would be delighted with these results, but they were catastrophic for many individuals and wasteful for the society.

Again: Mark Twain dramatized the irrelevance of the GDP in his quip about two women who "earned a precarious living by taking in each other's washing." If a woman renounces home washing and takes a job in a commercial laundry, she thereby increases the GDP. She may also enlarge her life and increase her contribution to society, but whether she does so or not will not be discovered by examining the GDP.

Again: In the 1970s Brazil was widely hailed as a wonder-working economy because of the rapid increase of its GDP. A decade later, however, it was evident that the apparent prosperity had had only adverse effects on the lives of the squatters in the hillside *favelas* behind Rio and the sugar workers in the northeastern provinces. Strict attention to the GDP had misled the world's bankers, who consequently sponsored an economic as well as a social failure.

Again: If you are a manufacturer of a detergent or of anything else for a broad market, you will find the GDP irrelevant or misleading. Your proper concern will be whether there are enough people employed and well enough paid to buy your product. And if you are a purveyor of diamond bracelets, you will base your output on the number of millionaires, not on the GDP.

There is nothing in the foregoing that is not well known, and the examples could be endlessly multiplied. Yet economists and businessmen and public officials maintain their faith in the GDP. Measures that would protect us from pollution of our environment and damage to our health are routinely opposed because they would, it is said, decrease production. (Ironically, those who oppose conservation generally call themselves conservatives.) The habit of thought is pervasive; even so-called liberal economists tend to talk of a trade-off between a healthful environment and production, and Third World public officials protest that they cannot "afford" to be concerned with health or safety.

Such trade-offs are only too obvious in one-company towns where the single factory is a gross polluter of air and water. When threatened with laws requiring it to clean up its operations, the company counterthreatens to shut down the plant altogether and thus destroy the town's excuse for existence. The threat and counterthreat indicate an incompatibility of microeconomics, the economics of the individual or firm, with macroeconomics, the economics of the nation or society.

CONFLICT AND COMMITMENT

Léon Walras, who was no amoralist, distinguished at considerable length between economics as an ethical science (which most of his followers today would not recognize); as an art, which taught how to achieve moral ends; and as pure science, which taught how it worked. Toward the close of the nineteenth century, John Neville Keynes, the father of John Maynard, made a similar tripartite analysis. In our day, Milton Friedman, perhaps indulging a puckish humor, has quoted favorably from the senior Keynes's work.[1]

But there is no such thing as pure economics. Physics can be studied—must be studied—without regard to the willful act of any individual or any group of individuals. (This is not to deny that it takes a willful man or woman to be a physicist.) But there are no sterile events in economics. Walras, whose work was hailed by Joseph A. Schumpeter as "the only work of an economist that will stand comparison with the achievements of theoretical physics,"[2] opened his analysis, af-

1. Walras, *Elements*, p. 64; Keynes, *Political Philosophy*, pp. 32–33; Friedman, *Positive Economics* p. 3.
2. Schumpeter, *Economic Analysis*, p. 827.

ter a long introduction, with the observation "Value in exchange, when left to itself, arises spontaneously in the market as the result of competition." But this pure parthenogenesis is immediately corrupted by willful humanity: "As buyers, traders make their *demands* by *outbidding* each other. As sellers, traders make their *offers* by *underbidding* each other."[3] Walras's emphases underline acts of will.

Without those traders making their demands and offers, there is no economics, pure or applied. With those traders, economics becomes inextricably immersed in questions of ethics. I do not mean merely that trade is impossible unless traders abjure fraud (at least up to a point), although certainly this is true. What I mean is that demands and offers—the fundamental elements of "pure" economics—are not acts of God or events of nature but acts of human beings who necessarily define themselves by what they do, including especially what they do in the marketplace. Perhaps more to the point: Demands and offers can be described and understood only as acts of will. If they are not free and responsible acts, economic discourse collapses into theology or physics.

All exchanges involve ethical questions. In everyday life we cannot live at a constant fever pitch of deliberation. In a famous chapter in his textbook on psychology, William James laid out the importance of habit in allowing us to get on with the business of living without worrying over "which sock, shoe, or trouser-leg [to] put on first."[4] In the same way, social customs and trade practices—what Arthur Okun called the invisible handshake—allow us to go about our work without constantly weighing and agonizing over the ethical implications of our actions.

Nevertheless, all exchanges *ipso facto* involve other people and so by their very nature present ethical questions. A virtuous act enlarges the person, and a vicious act cancels or constricts some possible en-

---

3. Walras, *Elements*, p. 83.
4. James, *Psychology*, chap. 10.

largement. "I could not love thee, dear, so much, loved I not honour more" expresses conflict but not contradiction. A rational exchange looks to the maintenance of both trading partners, and to the continuance of the activities that led to the exchange; but nineteenth-century Social Darwinism and twentieth-century theory of games (among many examples) contemplate the destruction of one partner by the other and hence the destruction of the exchange and the repudiation of its genesis. This is irrational.

Exchanging goods and services is only one of the principal ways of meeting other minds, of being recognized by others, of recognizing oneself, of becoming conscious of one's limits and so of one's powers. We meet one another as buyers and sellers, as teachers and pupils, as patrons and clients, as friends, as lovers, and also as competitors and enemies. Society depends on these relationships. Personality depends on them. Their development is a work of history. They have not always been as they are now. Only a hundred years ago loving was much different from what it is today, as can be seen by comparing Anthony Trollope's *Phineas Redux* with John Updike's *Rabbit Redux*. The differences in ways of economic exchanging are, if anything, greater.

Without noneconomic interests, economic interests cannot be defined or named. A home dishwasher is sold and bought because it is appropriate to a certain way of life; it is not everywhere and always an economic good. Even a mathematical economist like Gerard Debreu was constrained to say, "The fact that the price of a commodity is positive, null, or negative is *not* an intrinsic property of that commodity; it depends on the technology, the tastes, the resources, . . . of the economy."[5]

Different sorts of exchange—and also different possible exchanges of the same sort—may be in conflict with each other. The meaning of a commitment is understood only as it conflicts with another. The conflict

5. Debreu, *Theory of Value*, p. 33.

results not in the obliteration of one by the other, nor in a trade-off that diminishes both, but in a comprehension that modifies and may intensify both. An unconflicted commitment, like that of economic man, is obsession or madness. A resolved conflict is personality; one resolves to be the person one becomes. The controls of economic activity are those that maintain not only the economic modes but the other modes as well—that maintain and rationalize the conflicts among them.

MICRO VS. MACRO

The division between microeconomics and macroeconomics is well established. It was not always thus. The names of the divisions do not appear in the first edition of the *Oxford English Dictionary*, published in 1933, or in the second edition of *Webster's New International Dictionary*, whose last issue was copyright in 1953. Now, however, college courses routinely appear under one rubric or the other. What has been put asunder is not easily joined or rejoined.

Indeed, they cannot be joined so long as economic activity is taken to be the maximization of material gain by the individual, the firm, and the nation. That the material interests of these parties are not always identical or even parallel is too obvious to discuss and consequently is not discussed except in homilies of the sort that everyone recognizes as self-serving. When the boss harangues the workers with the thought that they're all players on the same team, the latter are forewarned of a policy likely to benefit someone else more than it benefits them. When President Eisenhower's secretary of defense "Engine Charlie" Wilson, former head of General Motors, piously proclaimed, "What's good for General Motors is good for America," everyone laughed, and the laughter did not need explanation. When private citizens closet themselves with Form 1040, or corporation financial officers with Form 1120, neither takes seriously the form's inspiring prefatory message from the commissioner of internal revenue.

It is worthwhile to stop a minute and note that the foregoing are all examples of the fallacy of composition, which is so frequently encountered in economics discussions that it may be called the economics fallacy. The error lies in assuming that what is true of every member of a logical class is true of the class itself, or vice versa, that what is true of a class is true of each of its members. Other examples: since every event has a cause, it is illicitly concluded that the universe—that is, all events together—has a cause. Or in economics, since individuals can become rich by hoarding, the nation will be more prosperous if consumption is discouraged.

The division between macroeconomics and microeconomics is more than rhetorical. Standard microeconomics holds that the purpose of business enterprise is profit maximization, and it follows as a principle of successful business management that it's sensible to cut your losses. Any fledgling MBA has a quick eye for seeing how any firm's activities can be divided into semiautonomous "profit centers" and a quick ear for hearing which profit centers are now yielding a desired rate of profit, which ones can be made to do so, and which ones are hopeless. Those in the last category may in fact be profitable; they are just not profitable enough. The minimum acceptable rate of return is the money-market rate. If you can get, say, 5 percent just by lending your money to someone else, why should you go to the bother of running a business that earns less than 5 percent? Or if you do, in the course of your business, borrow money from banks, and if you pay a rate better than that 5 percent, you're obviously not doing very well with a profit center that doesn't earn more than you pay.

So you are advised to sell the weak profit center if possible, otherwise to liquidate it. You will probably have to take a loss, but at the current corporation tax rates, about a third of your loss will be paid for by the government via the reduction of your income and hence of your tax bill. The funds thus freed can then be applied to the promising profit centers, or put into the money market, or used to reduce your corporate debt. However you use the funds, the net profit of your company will be improved.

Consider a profit center that is earning 4 percent on invested capital of a million dollars, while the firm's target is 14 percent. Even if the weak profit center—workers, customers, inventory, plant, and all—were abandoned as a total loss, the after-tax result would be that about a third of a million dollars would be available for use in the centers that earn 14 percent or more. Fourteen percent of a third of a million dollars is $46,667, while 4 percent of a million is only $40,000.

Such vandalism, which is sometimes hailed as "creative destruction,"[6] is bad enough in the arena of microeconomics. The workers and the customers are injured, and the inventory and plant—and the work that went into them—wasted in a world of shrinking resources. The injury and the waste are far greater when macroeconomic problems are approached in the same way. It is said that just as in a firm there are many profit centers, so in the nation there are many firms. On this analogy it is widely thought that national policy should be directed toward encouraging strong firms and weeding out weak ones.

Analogy is a seductive form of argument that at best is only suggestive. In the present instances, there are two crucial differences between the analogues and the actual world. The first is that what is weeded out by the proposed policies are not tares among the wheat but human beings—people, men and women, fellow citizens. The second is that there is no way, in the actual world in which we live, for new industries, no matter how promising, to replace old industries, no matter how unfruitful, in the twinkling of an eye. The replacing can be done in an equation, on paper, in an instant; but in the actual world it takes time. The actual world is a world of human beings who exist in time and only in time. Things done or made take time, and the less primitive they are, the more time they take.

Moreover, the write-off against taxes that provides much of the in-

6. Schumpeter, *Capitalism, Socialism and Democracy*, chap. 7.

centive at the micro level does not work at the macro level. A corporation can shift much of its loss onto the other taxpayers, but the national wealth must suffer the entire loss of any destruction.

It would have been absurd to imagine that the Lockheed or Chrysler plants, both of which teetered on the brink of failure in 1979, could have been immediately—or ever—converted to producing electronic devices or processing information or whatever industries were expected to take their place. Yet ordinarily responsible citizens did in fact allow themselves to brush aside the facts that tens or hundreds of thousands of fellow citizens would have had their livelihoods destroyed, and that millions of dollars' worth of plant would have been laid waste as effectively as if it had been bombed. All this destruction would have been in the supposed interest of some new industry that no one could even name. The proposed destruction might have been acceptable—you can't make an omelet without cracking eggs—if anyone had had in mind how and how quickly the displaced people and plants could be restored to usefulness. But no one has the right to bet other people's lives on the hope that something will turn up for them in the long run.

Nor are such macroeconomic effects valid even in the timeless world of classical economics. If the gross domestic product is the sum of individual productions, then the nation's output is diminished whenever any of the factors of production is withheld or disbarred. The nation's output is greater if people are making automobiles inefficiently than if they are doing nothing. It is greater if they are raking leaves than if they are doing nothing. Something is more than nothing, so every additional thing produced increases the gross domestic product.

Thus profit maximization on the part of a firm may result in diminishing the gross domestic product. This result is quite independent of the harm done to people. Microeconomics can be—and often is—at war with macroeconomics. This apparent paradox is yet another example of the fallacy of composition. What is good for General Motors is not necessarily good for America, and this is no paradox but a well-understood matter of common observation.

CROSS-PURPOSES

It is obvious that whatever I do will have some effect on the firm for which I work, that whatever the firm does will have some effect on the nation's output, that whatever the nation does will have some effect on me and my firm. It is equally obvious that these effects are not all always in the same direction or of comparable strength.

The direction and importance of the effects depend on the purpose pursued. If health is my concern, healthy working conditions and a healthy general environment are in my interest. And in the other direction, since the nation is concerned for the health of the population as a whole, it will be in its interest to control the pollution emitted by factories and to try to eliminate communicable diseases. There is no conflict among these purposes; they all work together. Purposes with a similar unity of effect would include education, efficient communications, safety from violence—welfare in its ordinary sense. Often there are local conflicts that can be compromised; thus, an improved highway may require taking a person's home by eminent domain, and the compensation offered by the state in a given instance may not be reasonable, but there is no difficulty with the principles involved.

With the maximization of material gain, as we have seen, the situation is quite different. Person, firm, and nation may be, and often are, at cross-purposes. Nevertheless, in modern times the maximization of material gain has been thought the proper objective of economic activity. In pursuit of that objective, conservatives have emphasized the creative power of individual energy, and liberals have emphasized the organizing power of the state.

As a practical matter, the conservative-liberal confrontation was considerably papered over during the past hundred years, and especially during the quarter century following World War II. An extraordinary increase in output lent plausibility to the metaphor President John F. Kennedy borrowed from Prime Minister Winston Churchill: "A rising tide raises all boats." Although the relative shares of the national output scarcely changed, the absolute increase in the total—from $209.8 billion in 1946 to $1,077.6 billion in 1971 (even in so-called constant dollars the increase was 135 percent)— allowed almost everyone to benefit dramatically. The subsequent years, however, saw the boats rising unequally, with many sinking.

That some of the widening inequality was deliberately brought about only confirms the judgment that in terms of material gain, microeconomics and macroeconomics are not systematically connected. There was no reason for the 83,384 firms that in 1997 were petitioners in bankruptcy to be cheered by the so-called recovery of that year. There was no reason for the 320,000 new millionaires of the years 1976 through 1980 to be upset by the stagflation of that period.

There is no reason for starving people to be cheered by a rising GDP. For starving people to be reconciled to their fate, they would have to be shown not only that the national prosperity was enhanced by their starvation but also that their sacrifice was the salvation of their fellow citizens and of the nation that nurtured them. Such a showing can be made to a soldier in time of war. But no one pretends that such a showing can be made in economics at any time.

ETHICS AND HISTORY

It should not surprise us to have to conclude that if maximization of material gain is the objective of economic activity, no unification of microeconomics and macroeconomics is possible. Maximization of gain is an undefinable and meaningless concept.

But if economics is a division of ethics and justice is its goal, the two subdisciplines come together readily enough. Indeed, they must come together, because they cannot then maintain themselves separately. Ethics is neither an exclusively private affair nor an exclusively social affair; it involves both individual and society because they define each other. Not only do individual and society define each other, but the mutual definitions are framed in ethical terms. The state requires certain actions and forbids many actions, all in the interest of maintaining just and civil relations among its citizens. The citizens demand that the state do this.

What just and civil relations may be is a historical question. The standards were developed in time and exist in time. More important, they are historical because the future is uncertain and unknowable. The "separate but equal" doctrine of *Plessy* v. *Ferguson* seemed wise and just to most people in 1896; it turned out to have unjust consequences and was overturned in *Brown* v. *Board of Education* in 1954. All individual actions and all social institutions are inexorably subject to similar revision.

POSTSCRIPT: GDP VS. QUALITY OF LIFE

It is claimed that the United States far exceeds all other countries in health-related expenditures. Yet at the beginning of life, the United States ranks twenty-fourth among the nations of the world in a newborn baby's chance of surviving the first four weeks of life. At the end of life, the United States ranks eighth among the industrial nations of the world in the healthy life expectancy of both women and men. In both the beginning and the end (and very likely in between), Canada, Japan, France, Italy, and most of the other members of the OECD provide healthier and longer lives for their citizens.

There is no doubt that the poor showing of the United States is largely due to its absurdly inefficient and expensive health-delivery system, which spends upwards of a quarter of its large share of GDP on contrived competition, fantastic advertising, speculative finance, and golden parachutes for overpaid executives.

13

Money and Bankers

Money is not an ordinary commodity like bread. The practical consequences of this domestic consideration can be quickly shown. If bread is, for whatever reason, overpriced, only the bread bakers languish. We can always eat cake. If, however, money is overpriced—that is, if the interest rate is too high—bankers may prosper rather than repine, for the increase in the rate may offset, or more than offset, a possible fall in the demand for loans. But the rest of the economy will surely suffer. Low interest may lead to a lenders' strike, but high interest leads to a borrowers' strike. The macroeconomic effects are practically identical.

DISINTERMEDIATION

Corporations have cash flows in both directions. A little experience enables corporate financial officers to operate on a day-to-day basis, estimating fairly closely how much they will take in, and planning quite precisely how much they will need to pay out. Whatever cash they accumulate in excess of these diurnal needs represents wasted opportunity unless they immediately put it out at interest.

Obviously, this sort of activity, which is at least moderately nerve-racking, is scarcely worth the bother when interest rates are low. It was not extensively practiced in the early post–World War II years, when the prime rate was 1.50 to 1.75 percent. Corporations then routinely deposited their temporarily unneeded cash in their checking accounts, which drew no interest. Banks liked that and depended on it.

Gradually, however, interest rates rose. This was the doing of the Federal Reserve Board, which was possessed, then as now, of the notion that inflation was an imminent threat, and that a rise in the interest rate was the cure. By the end of the 1950s, the prime rate had gone to 4.48 percent; two decades later it was up to 12.67 percent; in December 1980 and January 1981, it topped out at 21.5 percent. As a result of this surge in rates, there were several tremors in the banking world that went by the name of disintermediation crises. The septusyllabic adjective meant that banks, regulated as they were in the interest rates they could pay, were pushed out of the intermediate position between their biggest depositors and their biggest borrowers, who found ways of getting together more directly to meet their complementary needs. The former depositors thus got a bit more for their money, and the former borrowers had to pay a bit less for theirs. Then in the late 1970s, personal depositors rushed to the new money-market mutual funds. The banks suffered and the thrifts suffered severely.

These crises could obviously have been met in either of two ways. Either the Federal Reserve Board could have pulled interest rates back down, or the regulations (most of which had been prompted by the bank failures of the Great Depression) could have been lifted. Needless to say, the bugaboo of inflation and surviving hatred of the New Deal and aversion to regulation and eagerness for high interest rates made the outcome practically inevitable. The negotiable certificate of deposit, introduced in 1960, allowed banks to compete in the money market on the basis of price. In 1970, interest-rate ceilings were suspended for time deposits of more than $100,000; by 1982, the minimum was down to $2,500, allowing banks to compete freely for all but the smallest depositors, whose business was increasingly handled on a fee-for-service basis. In the meantime, Regulation Q was rescinded, NOW accounts allowed banks to pay interest on checking balances; state usury laws were suspended; FDIC insurance was extended, banks were permitted to sell insured money-market funds; there was a general relaxation of restrictions on branch banks; and by 1999 the New Deal reforms were forgotten.

COMPETITION IN BANKING

Competition is by no means a universal good, and in the case of banking it is almost a universal disaster. Ordinary businesses compete with each other more at the selling end than at the supply end. Their competition at the selling end forces them to exert downward pressure on the prices they pay for their supplies. In the case of banking, the shape of competition is significantly different, because its supply—money—is different. A bank's first problem is to attract deposits, and the most effective solution is to raise the interest it will pay. Raising the rate is especially important to meet competition from money-market funds and Treasury bills. A complementary solution is to open branches where depositors (and perhaps borrowers) are. Today major urban intersections are more likely to have four banks than, as formerly, four filling stations. The same search for funds (together with the delights of not even vestigial regulation) encourages the expansion of international banking.

Having attracted deposits, the banks, now thinking of themselves as businesses like any other, are faced with the other half of the ordinary business problem, namely, how to sell their expensive product at a profit. Some of the solutions are worth glancing at.

Perhaps the most important, at least in the short run, is the encouragement of speculation, whose deleterious effects we shall discuss. New kinds of speculation are constantly invented. In the 1980s, leveraged buyouts absorbed a lot of money at high rates, without in any way increasing production. In the 1990s, more than eighty *trillion* dollars' worth of "derivatives" were circulating. This astronomical sum was the face or "notional" value of the paper, which is always heavily leveraged. The amount of money actually invested is very much less than the face value, but was probably still greater than the total national debt.

Perhaps more important in the long run is the encouragement of agribusiness, resulting directly in heartbreaking bankruptcies in the farm belt and indirectly in possibly permanent damage to the ecosystem—a vital subject beyond the scope of this book.

Unquestionably important in its effect on the state of the world was the frantic competition, following the OPEC oil crises of the 1970s, to see who could press the most money on Third World and Communist bloc nations. As Richard Lombardi has told us, the big banks, bemused by the pointless saying that nations don't go bankrupt, sent vigorous loan officers crisscrossing the world with literally billions of dollars to lend. These loan officers were in effect salesmen; many had quotas like salesmen; they were rewarded on the basis of the amounts of money they contrived to lend; and they were not always careful in investigating the uses to which the money was to be put.[1] The banks competed to offer the Arabs high interest rates for their winnings, which were then "recycled," also at high rates, in loans to the countries that had been hit hard by the OPEC price increases.

In spite of excited stories in the daily press, the trouble with these loans—the trouble from the point of view of the banks, that is—is not that there is scant prospect of their ever being repaid. The trouble is that the interest—generally at rates floating well above domestic

1. Lombardi, *Debt Trap*, chap. 10.

rates—cannot or will not be paid. The banks would be perfectly happy to roll the principal over and over and indeed have done so, if only the interest would keep rolling in forever and ever. If they didn't roll the principal over but somehow collected it, they would have to go to the expense of finding another borrower to press it on.

In all their selling, especially in the foregoing examples, the banks are forced by competition to concentrate their efforts on those situations in which they can hope to enjoy economies of scale. Once you have an organization capable of handling a corporate takeover, you hunt for more and bigger takeovers to support your organization. Likewise, a farmer willing to buy and equip and mortgage thousands of acres is more interesting to you than a lot of people looking for (as a bestseller published in the Great Depression had it) five acres and independence. And, of course, it's easier to persuade a possibly rapacious Third World official to build an expensive state-of-the-art sugar refinery to supply an already glutted market than it would be to find and finance several smaller and more practical projects.

Whenever economies of scale are significant, they become a force for concentration. In the modern banking system, this concentration appears not only as centralized control but also as shared exposure. Only a score or so of the largest banks can afford to play a substantial role in international finance, where interest rates are highest, and where the demand for loans is insatiable. The thousands of smaller banks have been lured—or forced by competition—into a more explicit partnership with the big banks. As the cost of funds has increased for all banks, the smaller ones have had to emulate the big ones by making at least some loans at very high interest rates. This is not merely a search for profits but a struggle for survival. They have managed to survive partly by buying pieces of the foreign loans from the big banks and partly by depositing large sums with the big banks. As a result, the failure of a big bank could bring down not only its commercial depositors but also its small-bank clients, whose larger commercial depositors would in turn be ruined. And the blight would spread. It is for this reason that the threatened failure of any large bank causes so much concern.

Because of the high cost of funds, a bank could be forced into insolvency by refusing to make large loans at high interest.[2] The risk in such loans is ultimately great, but the risk of not making them is immediate. Hundreds of thrifts, of course, were bankrupted by this dilemma. It is probably safe to say that very few loan officers are intentionally sloppy; they are forced to be so by competition. If they aren't sloppy, someone else will be, and they will be out of business.

THE DEFICIT

In recent years, the monetary authorities excused their actions by pointing fingers at the high United States deficit, which would, they claimed, result in increased inflation. It is therefore worth stopping a moment to consider the causes and the effects of the exponential surge of the federal deficit in the 1980s.

According to projections made by the Congressional Budget Office, the tax and spending laws that were in effect on January 1, 1981 (that is, at the end of the Carter administration), would have yielded a *surplus* of $29 billion in 1989.[3] But the austere laws that were in effect nine years later resulted in a 1989 deficit of $206.2 billion. The

---

2. Modern readers will regard wistfully Adam Smith's observation (*Wealth*, pp. 339–40): "If the legal rate of interest [i.e., prime] in Great Britain, for example, was fixed so high as eight or ten per cent, the greater part of the money which was to be lent, would be lent to prodigals and projectors, who alone would be willing to give this high interest. Sober people, who will give for the use of money no more than a part of what they are likely to make by the use of it, would not venture into the competition. A great part of the capital of the country would thus be kept out of the hands which were mostly likely to make a profitable and advantageous use of it, and thrown into those which were most likely to waste and destroy it."
3. Rivlin, ed., *Choices, 1984*, p. 31.

principal causes of this spread were the tremendous increase in military spending, the vast and varied tax cuts of 1981, the "revenue neutral" tax cuts of 1986, and the high interest rate.

Military spending has the virtue that Keynes noted in pyramid building, that there is no end to it.[4] It is also stimulative. In this it is like any government expenditure and, indeed, any increase in aggregate demand. Businesses produce goods if they foresee a demand for them; so public expenditures, being both large and visible, are especially stimulative. Although we could have wished for a better use of our money, the military buildup was, together with the slow reduction of the federal funds rate in the summer of 1982, decisive in the business recovery that started a few months later.

The tax cuts had a different effect. They were intended to stimulate the "supply side," on the theory, whose fallacy we have discussed, that saving leads to investment. Accordingly, the 1981 personal income tax favored all the rich and the 1986 law favored all the rich who had no shelters, the hope being that those who didn't need money would save it.

This hope was disappointed, and for a simple reason. Since the federal budget was already in deficit, the tax cuts necessarily increased that deficit. The increased deficit was funded; that is, bonds to cover it were issued. And to whom were they sold? To those who had money, of course, and these were, in general, those who had benefited from the tax cuts. The upshot was that the rich and prosperous were given money with which to buy government bonds. In effect, they were given the bonds, although of course many used their windfall in other ways. The maneuver accomplished as extraordinary a transfer of wealth—and that to people already wealthy—as America has seen.

This was not all. Since the Federal Reserve Board was keeping the interest rate high, the new bondholders were given a handsome rate

4. Keynes, *General Theory*, p. 131.

of return—14 or 15 percent or more, running thirty years into the future. Before long, the interest payable on the federal debt was greater than the deficit, and the compounding of that interest more than offset savings that might have been made elsewhere in the budget. In consequence, the only way of reducing the deficit, as repeatedly demanded by the Federal Reserve Board in the 1980s, was by raising taxes, which, by reducing aggregate demand, would have had a further depressive effect on the economy—except in the politically unlikely case that the increased taxes had fallen on those who had benefited from the 1981 and 1986 cuts.[5]

This dilemma could have been avoided if the tax cuts had gone to those who would have spent them. It could have been avoided if the Treasury and the Federal Reserve Board had cooperated in holding down the interest rate, as they did during World War II. As it happened, however, both fiscal and monetary policies were misdirected.

FOREIGN INVESTMENT AND THE "STRONG DOLLAR"

The high interest rates resulted in a "strong" dollar. Foreign investors—especially Japanese and German—were attracted to American securities, partly because of the favorable rates, and partly because of America's size and political stability. Bidding for dollars with which to buy these securities, they drove the exchange rate of the dollar steadily upward. From a low of 33.7 in 1979, the multilateral trade-weighted value of the dollar rose to 119.1 in 1998.

"Strong" is, of course, a strong word, and politicians boasted of their prowess in making the dollar stronger. The Federal Reserve Board characteristically approached the question first from the point of view of inflation. A month after his induction as chairman of the Reserve

---

5. Faux, "Reducing the Deficits."

Board, Volcker appeared before the House Committee on the Budget. "Another obvious result of our distressingly poor price performance," he testified, "has been the recurrent weakness of the dollar in foreign exchange markets." The weak dollar, he argued, was itself inflationary, "partly because of the direct effects on costs of imports and partly through the reduced competitive restraints on prices of domestically produced goods."[6]

Volcker's argument was plausible, but its actual consequences were disastrous. The strong dollar strongly compromised America's ability to compete in international trade. Whereas the weak dollar had made our import costs high and our export prices low, the strong dollar did the opposite. Imports, from Mazdas to Madras shirts, became cheap, but we found ourselves priced out of our foreign markets. The Reserve gained what was at best a minor advantage in its perennial wrestle with inflation, but the economy paid for it with major damage to our exporting industries and a stubbornly persisting foreign trade deficit. In the process, upwards of two million Americans lost their jobs.[7]

The Reserve came to put more emphasis on the cause of the strong dollar—the high interest rates that attracted foreign purchasers of American securities. Without them, it was said, the budget deficit could not have been financed, or it could have been financed only by crowding American business out of the money market. Again the argument was plausible, and the actual consequences disastrous. By 1991 the on-budget interest cost was $214.8 billion. And, of course, if historically quite reasonable rates on government bonds (say 2 percent)

---

6. *Federal Reserve Bulletin*, September 1979, pp. 739, 740.

7. Paul Krugman claimed in *Diminished Expectations*, p. 38, that adding two million jobs would cause inflation to "accelerate rapidly." But the point is that two million jobs once existed and then were lost, not that two million would be added. (Actually, 16 million jobs were added in the following decade—and inflation steadily fell.)

had been in effect from 1978 through 1989, the federal debt would have been at least $750 billion less, and there would have been no need even to think of attracting foreign investors to buy Treasury bonds. As we shall see in Chapter 24, the high rates were unnecessary from any point of view.

Since the price of money, or the interest rate, is, both in the price theory we have advanced and in practice, the independent variable, while the supply of money, however defined, and the demand for money are dependent variables, it is clear that the deficit has nothing to do with crowding out. Businesses are certainly deterred from borrowing by high interest rates, but these are not the inexorable consequence of impersonal economic laws but rather the intended result of the deliberate policies of the monetary authorities themselves.

MISTAKEN POLICIES

Even on the Reserve Board's own theory that the money supply (M1 or M2) is the independent variable, the policies have been grievously mistaken. Over the two decades from 1963 to 1983, M1 in relation to GDP fell 39.3 percent, and M2 fell 24.4 percent. (Both have risen since 1982, the rise helping to account for the recovery that started in that year.) The history of those decades was such that a rational monetary authority would have pursued a policy of expansion rather than contraction.

Most important of the reasons for expansion, the labor force increased enormously. First, the post–World War II baby boom was fully operational by the end of the period, adding millions to the national work force. Second, the antidiscrimination measures of Lyndon Johnson's Great Society, together with Supreme Court decisions responding to suits brought by the NAACP Legal Defense Fund and others, made it possible for millions of African Americans, although still handicapped, to enter the nonagricultural labor force. Third, the modern women's movement, launched by Betty Friedan in 1963 with *The Fem-*

inine Mystique, resulted in the self-authorization of the intention of millions of women to escape from what they saw as the stultifying conditions of housewifery. Fourth, the 1970s saw the return to civilian life of close to a million Vietnam veterans and war-industry workers.

There was, of course, some overlapping. It is possible to be an African American, a woman, a war veteran, and a member of the baby-boom generation, all at once. Nevertheless, the civilian labor force as a whole increased from 71.8 million in 1963 to 131 million in 1994.

Finally, this period saw the consolidation of a long revolution in the way business is conducted. Until the time of the New Deal, it was common to see signs in shops reading "In God We Trust. All Others Pay Cash." To be sure, there was money available for speculation, but it was available only to the well-to-do, and only the well-to-do had charge accounts, which they were expected to settle monthly. It was not possible to cash a check except where you were personally known, and not always there. Mortgages were for five years, or often for only one; they were renewed if your standing remained good, but they were not automatically renewable. Credit was tight, but not much was needed to float the economy.

A second way of doing business lasted from the start of the New Deal to, roughly, the Eisenhower administration. At the start of the period, Sears, Roebuck and Montgomery Ward shipped only COD or when payment accompanied order, and Macy's still advertised "6% Less for Cash," but these were merely among the last to give in. The FHA and the VA guaranteed mortgages for twenty years at 4 percent, with only 10 percent down (later such mortgages were available for thirty years, with no down payment). Automobiles and washing machines and radios and furniture were sold on the installment plan. More people had checking accounts, and almost anyone could cash a check almost anywhere locally. Quite a lot more money was needed to float this economy than had been needed for the previous one, but the government kept the interest rates relatively low, and the money was available.

The third way of doing business, characterizing the period we're now in, might be called the credit-card way, although credit cards themselves account for only a small portion of consumer debt. In any case, almost anyone can buy almost anything almost anywhere on credit. This, of course, means that sellers have to wait for their money. And the wholesalers then have to wait, and then the manufacturers, and then the producers of raw materials. Whereas trade a half century ago was largely current, it is now largely afloat. The need for money is enormous.

In addition, it turns out that this way of doing business is explosively dynamic. Just as the New Deal shift from one-year mortgages at 6 percent to twenty-year mortgages at 4 percent resulted in a housing boom, the credit-card shift has brought forth a fantastic expansion of all sorts of consumers' goods and consequently in the whole economy. In the quarter century ending in 1998, consumer credit outstanding increased from $190.0 billion to $1,297.2 billion, and nonfarm home mortgage debt went from $366.5 billion to $4,283.9 billion.

All these factors—the increase in the labor force, the need for capital investment, and the demand for everyday credit (not to mention the vast but uncharted growth of the underground economy)—should, on any theory, have prompted a steady low interest rate.

INTEREST RATE VOLATILITY

Frequent fluctuations of the interest rate introduce an inhibiting and costly uncertainty into business planning and are disruptive of financial markets. In twenty-eight out of fifty years (1950–99) the prime jumped up or down by 10 percent or more. In thirteen of those years the jump was more than 20 percent, and in one it exceeded 50 percent.

Both money and commodities are creations of economic activity.

High activity calls both into being—that is what economic activity is and does—and high activity is at least made possible by low interest rates.

In short, all prices are expressed in terms of money, but the supply of money has no direct and unequivocal or even unidirectional effect on the price of anything.

Monetarists nevertheless contend that there are so many different interest rates that control of "the" interest rate is impossible,[8] while control of the money supply within a narrow range is entirely feasible.[9] The contention, however, is beside the point. Just because it may be easy to control the money supply is no reason for controlling it. It would be easy to control the mining of silver, but it would be idle to do so. The money supply would be the thing to control if it determined the price level either directly or through an effect on the interest rate. Since its actual effects are either negative or indeterminate, its control, which has been a central objective of the Federal Reserve since 1951, is either mischievous or meaningless.

The control of interest, which is an inescapable cost both of living and of doing business, is at the heart of the matter. It is certainly true that there is, at any given moment, a bewildering array of interest rates. But businesspeople are not bewildered; their bankers tell them quite clearly what the applicable rate is. Consumers are not bewildered, for the same reason. Bankers are not bewildered; the various rates are not independent of one another, and their interrelations are mysteries only in the medieval sense that their mastery is essential in the banking profession. Nor need the monetary authorities be bewildered. They, too, can master the interrelations of rates.

In recent years, only about a twelfth of the outstanding nonfinancial indebtedness is new money, that is, debt undertaken in the cur-

---

8. Mayer, *Monetarism*, p. 10.
9. Brunner, "Money Supply," p. 267.

rent year. The rest includes everything from mortgages that some happy few are still paying off at 4 percent to bonds that the federal government will be paying off at 15.75 percent for another decade or more.

Because of the enormous backlog, the average interest rate is comparatively sticky; yet, in accordance with recent monetary policy, the current rate is volatile. Furthermore, the average rate continues to rise, even though the current rate is below the present average, partly because corporate finance has recently tended to rely more on debt (including junk bonds) than previously, and partly because many of the long-term debts now being retired carry interest rates much lower than the new debts replacing or refunding them. This apparent anomaly will, of course, continue until the new bonds and mortgages being issued carry a lower rate than the old bonds and mortgages being retired.

THE INTEREST RATE AND SOVEREIGNTY

Until the 1930s, money was understood to be a commodity, usually gold or silver, and often both. The price of the money-commodity and the fee for its use were both determined as was the price of any commodity. Under modern capitalism, where money is debt, it has no price, but it commands a fee for its use. Setting that fee is one of the necessary and inescapable functions of sovereignty.

This function may be satisfied absentmindedly, as the Federal Reserve Board often satisfies it, but it cannot be passed off on "the market." The money market is as incapable of speaking or writing or otherwise acting as is any market. There are still some whose doctrine requires them to pretend that the Reserve has no control over interest rates, that they are made in the market, if not in heaven, by an invisible hand, and that no mere mortal can do anything about them.

Practically everyone in the United States, however, now agrees that at least short-term rates are indeed set by the Board.

It should be noted that agreement on the malleability of short-term rates is a recent development. Until well into the 1980s, the reports to Congress and other public statements of the Federal Reserve Board invariably took the line that the federal deficit caused inflation, and that inflation caused the soaring interest rates. Nevertheless, the Board certainly acted as though it was setting short-term rates. For example, between September 18, 1979, and February 15, 1980, the Board raised the discount rate three times—from 10.5 percent to 11 percent, from 11 to 12, and from 12 to 13. This was not an idle exercise. The announced and reiterated intention was to inhibit banks' lending, which was expected to slow the growth of the money supply, which in turn was supposed to stop inflation. Despite frequent protestations to the contrary, the Federal Reserve Board was actually and deliberately setting at least the short-term interest rate.

It is now often said that the interest rate is controlled by the international money market, where a trillion dollars or more are envisaged being daily whisked around the world by computer, thus dazzling and overwhelming the few billions the Federal Reserve Board might muster. The fact remains that the money market meekly followed the federal funds rate up the hill in 1987–89, down in 1989–93, up again in 1994–95, and slightly down again in 1998 and up yet again in 1999.

LENDER OF LAST RESORT

The capitalist economy is distinguished from other systems by the method and purpose of borrowing. In other systems, previously accumulated funds are borrowed to meet emergency needs or purposes of aggrandisement or capital gains. Such purposes and methods still exist under capitalism; but the characteristic capitalist purpose is the creation or development of ongoing enterprise, and the typical capitalist borrowing is against future earnings rather than from past savings.

A bank is required by law to maintain a reserve, partly in cash and partly on deposit with the Federal Reserve, adequate for normal needs. It may temporarily deplete the reserve, either to meet an emergency or to exploit an extraordinary opportunity. While hurriedly getting its reserve back in order, it can borrow for a few hours or days from other banks that have excess reserves (paying what is called the federal funds rate for the loan), or from the Federal Reserve itself (paying the discount rate). The Federal Reserve is thus the lender of last resort and is designed to keep the economy solvent.

All banks try to keep their funds fully committed, because they earn no interest on idle money. They know that in the normal course of events they can borrow or lend at the federal funds rate (use of the "discount window" is discouraged but available); consequently, competition among banks forces them all to base the rates they charge on the federal funds rate. By controlling their other expenses, some banks can make loans closer and closer to the federal funds rate. But to go below that rate is to lend at an almost certain loss.

Banks also compete on convenience, services, and "class"; so even vigorously competing banks will seldom offer absolutely identical rates. Nevertheless, by setting the federal funds rate, the Reserve sets the minimum interest rate for borrowing, and, through the workings of active financial markets, all other borrowing rates as well. The bond market is less volatile than other markets, because the future value of a bond becomes more and more certain the closer it comes to maturity.

The Federal Open Market Committee buys and sells long-term bonds in order to target the short-term federal funds rate as well as bank reserves. And traders in today's bond market, like those in the stock market, have a time horizon of twenty-four hours or less, since as much or more money can be won (or lost) in churning the long market as in anticipating the short. With investors (or speculators) in debt instruments, the question is not, What is the interest rate? but,

What will the price be tomorrow or next week? The federal funds rate affects all such questions.

Both borrowers and lenders weigh (among other elements) the relative advantages and disadvantages of long term as opposed to short. Both short-term lenders and long-term lenders must set their rates on a satisfactory rule-of-thumb yield curve, which is a continuum that originates in the federal funds rate and expresses the interrelations of the various interest rates. Given attractive rates, short-term borrowers may shift to long term, and vice versa. All rates and terms are in competition with each other, either directly or through arbitragers. Hence all rates define each other; and when the federal funds rate goes up or down, all market rates follow.

The interdependence of interest rates is enforced by the diurnal problem of capitalist enterprise. Money is constantly needed and ideally is spent as fast as it is accumulated. Cash must flow. Should one borrow long or short? The problem for lenders is of course the mirror image of that for borrowers. In an ongoing economy, few borrowers are systematically or in principle committed to either long or short borrowing. Lenders likewise. Hence long and short rates are forced to depend on each other. If the rates for one get too far out of synch, borrowers will flock to the other. In the same way, ordinary bank rates are tied to the central bank rate. Every bank is restrained in what it can charge by the knowledge that competing banks have access to the same lender of last resort.

Regardless of the Federal Reserve Board's intentions, its actions are responsible for the long-term rate as well as for the short-term rate. A steady and low short-term rate would make possible a steady and low long-term rate. Indeed, any steady short-term rate—low, high, or medium—would lead to a corresponding long-term rate. But a volatile short-term rate, such as we have suffered from for forty years and more, makes control of the long-term rate next to impossible. Moreover, the volatility reasonably leads lenders to demand an increased uncertainty premium and thus pushes the long-term rate even higher.

The same point may be reached from another direction. Keynes deplored the fact that most professional investors and speculators "are concerned, not with what an investment is really worth to a man who buys it 'for keeps,' but with what the market will value it at, under the influence of mass psychology, three months or a year hence."[10] In the years that have passed since Keynes published this judgment, three months or a year has come to seem an unusually long time to hold an investment.

Portfolio managers and professional traders rank all assets according to their relative income, relative potential for growth, relative liquidity, relative safety, and so on. In those rankings it may happen that some long bonds are judged more liquid than some short notes or some common stocks. (After all, common stocks are "longer" than long bonds because they do not promise to return your money ever, let alone in twenty or thirty years.) In all these investments, short or long, the traders' abiding question is, What can they be sold for tomorrow, "under the influence of mass psychology"? not, What will happen over the next quarter of a century?

THE PROPRIETY OF LOW RATES

The foregoing being the case, it follows that the proper policy of any central bank must be to maintain short-term rates steady and low. A low rate will at least make more investment possible, more investment (if it eventuates) will require more employment, more employment will tend to increase average wages, and higher aggregate wages will increase aggregate demand, which will tend to validate the increased investment. If sufficient private investment is not then forthcoming, public investment can surely take up the slack.

---

10. Keynes, *General Theory*, pp. 154–55.

We have the experience of World War II to indicate what is possible. In 1942 the Federal Reserve Board and the Treasury Department established a working agreement to maintain the prices of federal securities issued to finance the war. A "pattern of rates" was maintained, with ninety-day Treasury bills paying 0.375 percent and twenty- or twenty-five-year bonds paying 2.5 percent. The prime inevitably fell into step, staying at 1.5 percent. This pattern remained in force for five years, whereupon the short rate was gradually raised to over 1.5 percent, but the long-bond rate was maintained at 2.5 percent for another four years. The prime went up with the short rate, though only to 2.07 percent.

Never enthusiastic about the agreement, the Reserve Board grew increasingly restive as World War II ended. The Board's objection was that the pattern of rates denied it control of the money supply. Whenever a bond issue was not fully taken up by the public, the member banks of the Federal Reserve System had to step in and buy the balance, thus diminishing their reserves and their ability to make commercial loans.

Since the Board (and the financial community generally) was perpetually worried about inflation, both during the war and after, one might have expected them, good old-line monetarists as they were, to approve of reduced reserves at that time. But they were concerned about the principle of the thing. A slight recession in the winter of 1948–49 gave them an opportunity to stand for a moment on the other side and deplore "the undesirable effect of absorbing reserves from the market at a time when the availability of credit should be increased."[11] Thereafter pressure for abrogation of the agreement intensified, until the onset of the Korean War in June 1950 prompted agitation for the old panacea of high interest rates to control expected wartime inflation.

---

11. Sproul, "The 'Accord,' " p. 229.

In the end, the Reserve won an "accord" with the Treasury in March 1951, dissolving their previous cooperation, with the proviso that the long-bond rate be maintained for a while longer. President Truman later charged the board with bad faith.[12]

Economists often cite their inability to conduct experiments as an excuse when their schemes or prophecies fail. But the wartime "pattern of rates" was in effect an experiment, and a successful one. Steady low interest rates were maintained for five years, and inflationary pressures were better contained than in any other wartime before or since. To be sure, steeply progressive income taxes, price controls, and rationing were also necessary, because extensive investment in production of civilian goods is impossible in time of total war. Indeed, the need for the controls indicates that in peacetime public investment could be very much less than that made by Dr. Win-the-War (although very much greater than that made by Dr. New Deal), and that private investment would be fairly quickly forthcoming.

LENDERS' STRIKES AND CREDIT CRUNCHES

A common objection to low interest rates is that they're supposed to lead to lenders' strikes and credit crunches. Bankers and others with money to lend are loath to make loans unless they are reasonably sure of getting not merely their money but their purchasing power back, plus interest. What is called "money" interest—the interest lenders actually charge and borrowers actually pay—is conventionally divided into two parts: "real" interest, and a premium equal to the rate of inflation. There is some debate about whether past, present, or future inflation should be considered, but whichever rate is settled on, it is, in effect, a cost-of-living adjustment, or a COLA, about which more will be said in Chapter 19.

---

12. Truman, *Memoirs*, vol. 2, pp. 44–45.

Assuming that lenders' claims to a COLA can be contemplated sympathetically, there remains the question of how they are going to manage to get it if the Reserve lowers the interest rate below the assumed rate of inflation. "Real" interest becomes negative. In such a situation many potential lenders don't lend. One is reminded of the slothful servant in the parable of the talents.

Lenders' strikes are scarcely possible in a large country without the cooperation of the monetary authorities. Indeed, when the monetary authorities raise the interest rate, they have the same effect on borrowers, that is, on the economy, as a lenders' strike. And since the "liquidity trap" has proved to be a hobgoblin (to mix the metaphor) of the slothful servant, the strike can be broken by lowering the interest rate.

From the point of view of prospective lenders the major result of a fall in interest rates is a run-up of the stock and bond markets, because a fall in the interest rate increases the capitalized value of every income-earning asset. Prospective lenders who sit on their money during such goings-on will suffer great losses. They may not like the prevailing interest rate, but their choice is between that rate and nothing at all. Convinced though they may be of future inflation, persuaded therefore that the low money interest rate makes the "real" interest rate even negative, they can do nothing with their money unless they accept the money rate. If, like the slothful servant, they bury their money and so preserve it, they will merely forgo all interest, no matter how unreal it seems to them.

Inflation or no inflation, the most successful investing (or speculating) strategy is the one that winds up with the most money. That amount of money may have less purchasing power than what one started with, but it certainly has more purchasing power than a smaller amount of money would have. If you lend $1,000 when the interest rate is 4 percent and the inflation rate is 5 percent, you will have $1,040 at the end of a year, but your purchasing power will have shrunk to $978. On the other hand, if you don't make the loan, your purchasing power will shrink to $950. You will lose more by doing nothing. A negative "real" interest rate, in apparent contradiction of the laws of mathematics, proves to be greater than zero.

In a confrontation with rational and determined monetary authorities, money can run to speculation, consumption, or investment in productive enterprise, but it can't hide. Speculation can be inhibited by sound taxes and banking regulations, and it often carries its own inhibitions in the shape of high carrying costs and unorganized markets. And no one should object to consumption or productive enterprise, for the lower interest rate should have been managed precisely to increase aggregate demand and stimulate investment.

In severe situations, the government has an effective response: debasement. Debasement surely has a bad name. Keynes cited a remark attributed to Lenin to the effect that "the best way to destroy the Capitalist system was to debase the currency."[13] Later in his career, Keynes might have been less unequivocal on the subject. In occupied West Germany after World War II, selective debasement, which did not touch wages, was used to eliminate "liquidity overhang," or hoards that were thought to threaten hyperinflation.[14] And during the Middle Ages, Carlo Cipolla tells us, "the countries which experienced the greatest economic development were also those which experienced the greatest debasement."[15] Debasing the currency both multiplied what was already circulating and forced hoards out of hiding.

The money interest rate is what matters to both lenders and borrowers. The so-called "real" rate, no matter how it may be calculated, does not appear except as a result of the calculation. It is called real, but it has no actual existence. Lenders demand to be paid the money rate, not the "real" rate; and borrowers have to satisfy their debts in current dollars, not in constant dollars. Inflation presents moneylen-

---

13. Keynes, *Economic Consequences*, p. 235.
14. Mayer and Thumann, "Radical Currency Reform," pp. 6–8.
15. Cipolla, *Before the Industrial Revolution*, p. 201.

ders with a serious problem, but they have no more right to be protected from its consequences than do the people who are doing or have done the work of the world. Conservatives are quick to claim that it is inflationary to give cost-of-living adjustments to workers or retirees. It is far more inflationary to encourage moneylenders to tack an inflation adjustment onto the interest rate.

The so-called "real" rate is like the other alleged realities we have encountered: self-interest versus enlightened self-interest, market value versus labor value, current dollars versus constant dollars, money wages versus "real" wages, nominal GDP versus "real" GDP. Economists have wasted much time and confused much thought with their propensity to see the world as a dualism in which, as Charles Peirce said, appearance and reality are like a freight train held together by a feeling of good will between the engineer in the cab and the brakeman in the caboose.

WEAKNESSES OF FEDERAL RESERVE

There are two main weaknesses in the present Federal Reserve System: (1) Not all forms of banking and quasi-banking are under the system's control, and (2) the system itself is not under political control. The independent status of the Federal Reserve makes it almost impossible for the United States to pursue a coherent economic policy. It was, in the first place, unwise in the extreme to place so much power in the hands of an insulated body, and the Reserve has shown itself again and again and yet again unable to use its power except to the grave detriment of the nation and of the world.[16] There have been nine recessions since the end of World War II. The first one, in the winter of 1946–47, was arguably caused by Congress's premature lift-

---

16. See Greider, *Secrets*, esp. p. 752.

ing of price controls, and the sixth, in 1974–75, was arguably caused by President Nixon's imposition of price controls. The other seven were the handiwork of the Federal Reserve—the institution supposed to protect the economy from ignorant and irresponsible politicians.

The Reserve's great power is almost exclusively negative. It can set the discount rate and the federal funds rate very high and thus discourage or inhibit borrowing, but if it sets the rates low, it can't guarantee that the rates will be put to use. It can deplete the banks' reserves and thus constrict the money supply as tightly as it pleases; but even though it should remove the reserve requirement altogether, it can't make people borrow. The Reserve can snub the economy down, bring it to a halt, even force it to back up. But the Reserve's power to reduce the interest rate can only lead the economy to available funds; it cannot make anyone use them.

Congress and the president, on the other hand, have positive as well as negative powers. They can increase the money supply by running a deficit. The deficit is paid for with bonds (or, it may be, by coining or printing money); so the government itself can do the borrowing that expands the money supply even when the private sector is laggard. And Congress and the president can contract the money supply by eliminating the deficit, either by not spending so much or by taxing more. They may, in fact, run a large surplus and make money very scarce indeed.

It might thus appear that Congress and the president have all the necessary power, both positive and negative, and that the Federal Reserve Board is merely a quaint survival from a more innocent day, useful for its clearinghouse operations and, from time to time, as a lender of last resort. Unfortunately, the powers the Reserve does have are fully adequate to cause appalling grief, as is starkly visible in its record, especially in the 1970s and 1980s. Ironically, it has been warmly praised for its actions, thus confirming Keynes's wry observation that in finance it is more praiseworthy to fail conventionally than to succeed unconventionally.

THE RESERVE AND OPEC

Fail the Federal Reserve certainly did. The so-called OPEC inflations of the 1970s were *preceded* by increases in the interest rate. In 1973–74, the Federal Reserve Board apparently thought of itself as strengthening the dollar. The oil countries saw that a stronger dollar would raise the prices they would have to pay for things they wanted to import, and they repeatedly warned that they would retaliate. Neither the oil-importing corporations nor the Federal Reserve Board took them seriously, and after some months of interest rate increases and rising commodity prices, OPEC raised the price of oil. In a characteristically misguided reaction, the Reserve then, and again at the time of the Six Days War of 1979, escalated interest rates on the theory that that would prevent inflation from heating up.

But of course the increased interest costs were necessarily added to the increased oil costs, thus accelerating cost-push inflation. In 1973 net interest was 5.3 percent of the national income; in 1974 it jumped to 6.3 percent. The percentage of the national income that paid for oil jumped from 2.3 percent to 4.3 percent in the same years. In 1979 the net interest cost was 7.7 percent of the GDP, increasing to 9.1 percent in the following year, while the cost of oil went from 5.8 percent to 7.9 percent. In all these years, and in every year on record, net interest has taken a larger share of national income than the cost of oil, and increasing the interest cost has increased, not controlled, the inflationary effect of higher oil prices.

RECESSIONS

Acting with the intention or pretension of controlling the inflation it had instigated, the Board caused a long and deep recession at the start of the 1980s and a less dramatic one at the start of the 1990s, threw millions of men and women out of work, denied employment to millions of others, fastened impossible debt service on Latin America and Africa, destroyed much of our international trade, changed us from the world's largest creditor to the world's largest debtor, and saddled the federal government with astronomical debt service.

Did the Federal Reserve do all that single-handed? Not quite all. It had, throughout, the solemn support of the rest of the banking community, and it could count on the creative policies of the Reagan administration to give it occasions for its actions. But the actions of the Federal Reserve were essential for the disasters I have named.

On the other side of the ledger is the claimed success in throttling inflation. We shall look into that part of the record in another chapter. Here, it is enough to note that the Federal Reserve has been ostentatiously battling inflation for a half century and that, despite all the famous victories, the inflation rate now is higher than it was when the fight started.

It is also claimed that the named disasters would have been worse if the Reserve hadn't kept a tight rein on money. It's hard to see how. Would unemployment have been higher? Would the South American and African and Asian debt service have been harder to handle? Would a weak dollar have weakened our foreign trade? Would our federal debt service have been greater? The answer, in all cases, is surely negative.

Only the naive will fancy that it will be easy to get the banking system under rational control. It can scarcely be expected that today's rogue bankers will go gentle. At the very least, they will make ingenious and determined efforts to find loopholes comparable to those exploited over the past fifty years, and there might even be a surge of high-level loan-sharking. Such efforts could be contained if all branches of government—legislative, executive, judicial, and the citizenry—could disabuse themselves of the notion that banking is a business like any other.

Banking policy must be judged not on the prosperity of the bankers, not on the GDP, not on a low interest rate. A high GDP and a low interest rate are desirable not in themselves but only as contributors to the proper economic objective of free and full employment in a just society.

The interest rate is an index of opportunity. The rate of borrowing is an index of activity. Regardless of the interest rate, there are two sorts of limits to the economy. The first is social or ethical: There are some activities that the society simply will not engage in; moreover, the society will devote only so much time to any economic activity. The other limit to the economy is demographic. Only so many workers are available; consequently, after a certain point, economic activity can be expanded in one direction only by contracting it in some other.

Until the ethical or demographic limit is reached, the interest rate may—should—be reduced until it no longer calls forth entrepreneurial activity. The problem for the monetary authority is not the quantity of money, for in the modern economy money is actualized credit, or debt. The problem is, as far as possible, to universalize entrepreneurial activity.

14

Speculation

If you have saved some money (since you have it, it is saved) and want to use it to get more, you can buy a factory (fixed capital), goods to sell (working capital), shares of stock (claims on future profits), bonds (which will pay fees for the use of your money). You can put your money where your mouth is at Las Vegas or Atlantic City or in any of forty-odd state-run lotteries or racetracks. You can buy gold or a bundle of stocks or a bundle of mortgages or a carload of pork bellies (without having a clear idea of what a pork belly looks like or why anyone would want one). You can buy unimproved land or improved land, rare stamps or toy soldiers, a real Monet or lots of pseudo-Monets.

If you're a red-blooded American, you will expect prices to go up, whereupon you will sell your purchases and reap a capital gain. Or if you are of a more somber turn of mind, you can sell almost anything short and hope to make your gain as prices fall. Alternatively, still expecting prices to fall, you can do nothing with your money, hoarding it (exercising liquidity preference) in anticipation of eventually buying something cheap.

With the possible exception of how you use the first two items in the first paragraph, you will have been speculating or gambling. In ordinary speech, speculation tends to be defined somewhere between gambling and enterprise on a scale of relative riskiness. But betting on dice (which everyone would classify as gambling) is liable to risks that may be closely anticipated, while launching a new product (the quintessential example of productive enterprise) is likely to be very risky indeed. In the publishing business, most new books lose money, though this is not the deliberate intent of either authors or publishers. If no one takes risks of the latter sort, nothing is done; there is no economy to analyze. Riskiness is a tangle, not a continuum.

Instead of relative riskiness, I have proposed the following criteria:[1] Gambling is risking wealth in a zero-sum game. If some players win, some other players must lose the same amount. The winnings and losings (after properly allocating taxes and the house's cut) add up to zero. Speculation differs from gambling in that it is not a zero-sum game. It can happen that all speculators win (though some may win more than others), that all lose, or that some win while others lose; and the sum of the winnings may be quite different from the sum of the losings. Speculation is, nevertheless, like gambling in that it produces nothing but rearranges—often to the great profit of the rearrangers—wealth that already exists. Enterprise is unlike speculation in that it uses wealth to produce new wealth, but it is alike in that it is not a zero-sum game. (If it were, it would be impossible for the economy to grow.) In a healthy economy it is possible for all reasonably astute producers to profit, at least to a degree. Prosperity in one business does not have to be counterbalanced by depression in some other; on the contrary, prosperity tends to spread.

---

1. *The New Leader*, September 7, 1981, pp. 9–10.

THE CONTINUING NEED FOR MONEY

Gambling, speculating, and enterprising all require money on a continuing basis. No sooner does one lottery pay off than its successor begins selling tickets. No sooner does the ball settle in the roulette wheel than the croupier calls for bets on the next spin. First and last, many billions are perpetually tied up in gambling of one sort or another (and we have mentioned here only legal gambling).

The sums invested in speculating are vastly greater. On a quiet day, more than two billion shares will change hands on the different stock exchanges in the United States, to which must be added the option trading on the futures exchanges. All of this must be financed.

Almost all of this trading is of old or "secondhand" securities and has no necessary effect on the enterprises that gave rise to them. It is not denied that there may be indirect effects, as in the way (absurdly exaggerated) in which the existence of a market for old investments may encourage the purchase of truly new issues. But the direct and ordinary effects are nil. It ordinarily makes no difference to an enterprise whether its stockholders are short term or long term, wise or foolish, genteel or riffraff. Nor does an enterprise ordinarily profit or lose from fluctuations in the market price of its securities. Although a price rising faster than the market average may make further financing easier to arrange and may also enhance the prestige and salaries of the firm's executives, the firm itself gets its money from each initial public offering of its securities and is thereafter largely indifferent to what happens to the securities as old investments—except as a takeover or buyout becomes a possibility.

It is safe to say that practically the entire activity of the stock exchanges is devoted to speculation. There seem to be no statistics available on the proportion of exchange activity that concerns truly new enterprise, but even counting all new stock issues (and most of these merely refund old investments), it appears that the proportion is well under 1 percent. This speculative bias is likewise true of what preens itself as investment banking. Taken all together—stock exchanges, commodities markets, and investment banking—this business is very large. It is probably what President Calvin Coolidge had in mind when he said, "The business of America is business."

Exchanges of old investments necessarily cancel out. By definition, no new thing is involved; so whatever old thing someone buys, someone else has to sell. But the economy is not static, and the markets are not static, and something makes the exchanges worth the bother in the actual situation. That something is money.

Although no new thing is involved, the general level of the stock market can rise, because additional money goes into speculation. Since individual investors rush hither and thither like lemmings, Wall Street is one of the few places where the hallowed law of supply and demand works approximately as people suppose it does. Because of the rules of the Exchange, the number of shares admitted to trading is limited. Supply thus becomes effectively an independent variable. Because most of the traders are in search of investment in general rather than in pursuit of a particular investment, demand, too, becomes an independent variable. Consequently, the price of any particular stock is ordinarily dependent mostly on the state of the market as a whole.

The stock market—especially a bull market—swims in a sea of borrowed money. Only a small proportion of that money is in so-called margin accounts, whereby the investor buys, say, a hundred shares of some stock, but pays cash for only half of them. The broker lends money for the other half but the loan is protected by the right to sell if the investor is unable to pay up when the stock falls below a certain level or "margin." In the meantime, the investor pays interest on the loan. The leading brokers make more of their income from lending money than from commissions on buying or selling stock.

The Federal Reserve Board has the authority to regulate margin accounts but has not stiffened the terms for many years because the really big players in the market (from 40 to 50 percent of the sales on the New York Stock Exchange, and from 20 to 25 percent of the sales on NASDAQ are in lots of 10,000 shares or more) are able to borrow otherwise on far better terms. Although the Reserve is worried about the irrational exuberance of the market, it almost condescendingly leaves the margin accounts available to smaller investors (even though they are presumably less able to stand a possible loss). During a bull market the borrowing increases exponentially to keep the prices rising, and the market becomes increasingly fragile.

WHEN THE MARKET CRASHES

Although it is theoretically possible for the general level of the stock market to rise merely because of a reduction in the supply of shares that their owners are willing to sell, a bull market cannot be sustained without a persisting influx of money. Likewise, a panic will greatly increase the supply of available shares and will speed up the trading, so that a crash could theoretically occur without money leaving the market. Nevertheless, when such a panic subsided and the supply was reduced to normal levels, the market would quickly rebound to its prepanic level unless money had actually left it.

Needless to say, there is more to the stock market than the number of shares available. First, there are the "fundamental" values of the corporations that issue the stocks. It is reasonable for increased dividends or increased retained earnings to stimulate demand for a particular stock; but during the bull market from 1982 to 1987, the Standard and Poor's index of 500 industrials rose almost twice as fast as corporate profits after taxes. Second, and in recent years more important, the Federal Reserve Board's shifting maneuvers to try to control the interest rate or the unemployment rate caused reciprocal shifts in the value of every income-earning asset. The resulting volatility encouraged speculation. Neither of these factors is large enough to underwrite a bull market, and neither makes much difference in a crash. For such great movements, the market needs money coming in—or going out.

Ordinarily there is little movement out of the stock market, because ordinarily there are few other suitable places to place one's money. The principal such places are real estate and foreign securities. Strong movement into these markets is an omen of trouble for Wall Street, for it is an indication that less new money may be coming in to the stock market, and that some old money may be leaving or getting ready to leave. If at some point the exodus becomes a panic, the market crashes.

A large part of the money that leaves the market in a crash, as in 1987, simply disappears. The money that had gone into the real estate market lasted a while longer, but much of it, too, disappeared in the recession that followed in 1990. If it had gone into cash, we'd have seen an instant doubling and redoubling of M1. If it had gone into productive investment, we'd have seen a sharp rise in output. If it had gone into the bond or money market, we'd have seen a sharp fall in interest rates. If it had gone into commodities, we'd have seen a sharp rise in these prices. If it had gone into consumption, we'd have seen a sharp rise in retail sales and, presumably, in consumers' prices. If it had gone, in some remarkably balanced way, into all these things, we'd have seen a sharp rise in GDP. But we saw none of these results. The money vanished.

On October 20, 1987, as a free-fall threatened, Chairman Alan Greenspan announced, "The Federal Reserve, consistent with its responsibilities as the Nation's central bank, affirmed today its readiness to serve as a source of liquidity to support the economic and financial system." Thus a full-fledged panic was averted, and evidently the readiness was all. All four money measures fell, on a seasonally adjusted basis, from September to October, while in November M1 fell further, and M2, M3, and L went up only $2.4 billion, $15.0 billion, and $13.9 billion, respectively.[2] (These comparatively small increases can-

---

2. A slightly different picture is given by the fact that "the weekly reporting banks in New York City expanded their loans to brokers and to individuals to purchase or carry securities from $16.7 billion in the week ending October 7 to $24.4 billion in the week ending October 21." See Brimmer, "Distinguished Lecture on Economics in Government: Central Banking and Systemic Risks in Capital Markets," p. 15. It will be noticed that $7.7 billion in new loans amounts to less than 1 percent of the money said to have been lost in the crash.

not, of course, be summed, since the latter of each ordered pair includes the former.) If they were the result of the Federal Reserve Board's offer, they were new money, not money that had somehow safely escaped from the market, and anyhow they represented only a small fraction of the amount lost in the crash.

MACRO EFFECT OF A CRASH

It is not possible to say absolutely how much money disappears in a crash. Estimates of the losses in 1987 seem now to have settled at around a trillion dollars.[3] Whatever it was, a vast sum simply vanished. It fell into a black hole, never to be seen again. Some people and some institutions had it one day; no one had it the next. The market was not a casino; the winnings were a long way from equaling the losings.

Yet the macroeconomic effect seems to have been slight. From this it is reasonable to infer that given the way the producing economy is organized—especially the way its rewards are distributed—it had no use for all those hundreds of billions of dollars. At the very least, we can say that the producing economy did not actually have the use of those hundreds of billions, whether it could have used them or not, and that the so-called recovery or expansion went on its sluggish way as though that money did not exist.

It is also reasonable to infer that the people who lost that money, whether as individuals or as managers of institutions, had no better

3. Ibid, p. 11. I should not be surprised if professional opinion finally accepted a much lower figure for the amount lost. Either way, apologists for the stock market are faced with a dilemma. If the amount lost was large, the exchanges must be brought under tighter control; but if the amount lost was small, no harm will be done to the economy by bringing them under tighter control.

use for it than to put it into the speculating economy.[4] We could, of course, argue about particular cases, but by and large this was true; and it certainly was true that they made no better use of it in fact. Many were no doubt foolish, but many others carefully considered the existing opportunities for productive investment and for consumption and rejected them for the stock market, perhaps as a lesser evil.

The uses to which they could put their money are, after all, limited. It could go into consumption, hoarding (or liquidity preference), new productive enterprise, or existing securities. If money goes into consumption, it causes the producing economy to expand; if it is invested in productive enterprise, it may reduce the rate of interest the producing economy must pay to finance current business or expansion. If, however, it is held liquid or invested in existing securities, it is thereby denied to the producing economy and plays no part in it. Thus, as money flows into the speculating economy, the producing economy loses the increased sales or more manageable financing it might otherwise have enjoyed.

It loses nothing it actually is making use of, and this fact helps explain the producing economy's relative imperviousness to the 1987 crash. The producing economy had not used the money that went into the bull market and so was not affected when the money was lost. What the producing economy lost is merely what might have been. The loss or deprivation came at the very beginning and continued to grow as long as the bull market continued. The bull market climbed on the backs of the deprived.

---

4. The distinction between the producing economy and the speculating economy is essentially the same as that made by Keynes between the "industrial circulation" and the "financial circulation." See Keynes, *A Treatise on Money*, vol. 1, *The Pure Theory of Money*, pp. 41–43. I have chosen to use different terms because speculation today plays a much greater role than it ever has before, with the possible exception of the first quarter of the eighteenth century.

THE COST OF A BULL MARKET

What might have been is lost forever. The jobs that never opened up, the goods that never were made and enjoyed, the services that never were performed—these were forestalled or aborted by the speculating. Their ultimate loss or nullity is what Wall Street cost the nation, and the world. The crash was incidental; the bull market itself had already done the damage.

The immediate sources of the lost money were the double-digit interest rate, which was encouraged to soar on the theory that the way to control inflation is to control employment, and the "supply side" tax cuts of 1981–82, which were mistakenly supposed to stimulate saving and investment. The theories behind the two sources were in conflict, but they share responsibility for the trillion-dollar increase in the national debt (which, as it happens, is roughly equal to the estimated loss in the market crash). These confused policies gave a trillion dollars of American money to people who couldn't use it; these people entrusted it to Wall Street; and Wall Street flushed it down the drain.

Whatever the immediate and intermediate sources of the money that was lost, its original source was the producing economy. Goods were made and sold and services performed, and people were paid for them. The pay took the forms of wages, salaries, interest, rent, profit, and taxes (because government produces goods and services, too). Ideally, those payments should have gone back into the producing economy for more goods and services. But several hundred billions of dollars of the payouts did not.

Some of these billions stayed out because of liquidity preference. As for the rest, it went into the speculating economy for the reasons we've mentioned: The people who had it had no use for it, and the producing economy had no use for it. These reasons are, of course, flip sides of the same coin. The producing economy could have used the money if more people had bought its products, but several million of them didn't have money enough to do so. The tax decreases and the interest rate increases had given too much money to the wrong people. Other people could have spent the money on the products of industry, and industry could have expanded to give many of these people jobs. The industrial expansion could have brought money back from speculation.

The speculating economy exists and grows because the producing economy (including the public sector as well as the private) does not or cannot use all the wealth it produces. The public sector is myopically starved by a doctrinaire bias against public works and services, and there is not enough effective demand in the private sector to encourage investment. When present capacity can produce more than present consumers can afford to buy, producing more is folly. As both cause and consequence, we have a maldistribution of both income and taxation that gives many people more than they know what to do with, leaves vastly more people with less than they need for lives of decency and dignity, and allows the decay of public necessities and amenities.

While a bull market drains money from the producing economy, a crash does nothing to restore it; it merely destroys the money that had been drained away. A bull market serves no purpose whatever. It creates nothing and reproduces nothing. The employment it provides performs no service for the public good. The money it sucks in it wastes. The market's claimed function of financing productive enterprise may be facilitated by liquidity; it is destroyed by volatility.

The misdirected employment of hundreds, if not thousands, of the brightest and best-educated minds of each generation is perhaps speculation's greatest waste. This misdirection is not confined to those who are lured to Wall Street. The most noted executives of American industry are those who prove adept at buyouts and takeovers and mergers. Nor are those who train them immune; in one semester in the early 1990s, every tenured professor of finance of the Columbia University School of Business was on leave consulting or practicing his profession for his own account.

THE WEALTH EFFECT

As the great bull market of the late 1990s wore on, there was much talk of its "wealth effect," which seemed to encourage many of the winners in the market to spend some of their winnings in the way Keynes expected increasingly affluent people to act. While the wealth effect was no doubt important in keeping the expansion alive, it contributed to the polarization of society. The great winners in the market were, ipso facto, rich and spent their winnings as rich people do. The great majority of the rest were delighted to have jobs.

If there actually was a substantial wealth effect in 2000, then the first market crash of the twenty-first century will be noticeably different from the last of the twentieth. When the music stopped in October 1987, there was a brief scramble for the unoccupied chairs. Some speculators were badly hurt; some brokers were slow with their margin calls; a few bankers had to write off a few bad loans. But the Federal Reserve Board's readiness to be lender of last resort forestalled panic. Since there was little or no wealth effect in 1987—at least, no one talked about such a thing then—the crash had little or no effect on the producing economy.

The next crash will be different. The Federal Reserve may still prevent panic, but the wealth effect credited with driving the economy in the last months of the twentieth century will disappear. Instead of looking for ways to spend their money, the new rich will hunt desperately for places to hide it. The real estate market, whose turn-of-the-century boom has been an omen of uneasy money leaving Wall Street, will choke on an upsurge of listings of all sorts of properties—new and old, domestic and commercial, large and small. The building trades will be early sufferers, and so will manufacturers of automobiles and major appliances. The recovery of the Asian Tigers will again be stalled as short-term money looks for the way to go home. In short, the next crash of the stock exchanges may be the first act of a first-rate recession.

SPECULATIVE FRENZY

Why should speculative frenzy get under way in the first place? Society certainly needs markets for old investments so that institutional endowments and pension and insurance funds can at least be suitably liquid. Yet these exchanges are not necessarily frenzied. What makes them become so?

The answer is usually given in psychological terms. Certain people are said to be speculators by nature (Keynes thought this true of Americans), and at times a speculative fever does seem to grip the land. The fever may be related to sunspots or to fear of war or to satisfaction with election returns. Sunspots aside, it will be remembered that the market broke in September 1939, and that it frequently rises after an election, no matter who wins. Such fluctuations are trivial; something more substantial than whim is surely at work in any sustained rise. Extensive speculation follows from, requires, and promotes maldistribution of wealth and income, as E. Ray Canterbery has demonstrated.[5] Tax cuts in recent years have widened the gap between the rich and poor. A 10 percent tax cut across the board gives nothing to a person too poor to pay taxes, gives $250 to one whose taxes are $2500, and gives $10,000 to one whose taxes are $100,000. Regardless of the motive of those who write the law, the gap between rich and poor widens.

And regardless of the intent of those benefitted by the law, an across-the-board tax cut does not substantially increase demand for the products of mass industry; so the rich spend their tax windfalls on luxuries and on existing securities—in other words, speculating in the stock and bond markets and their derivatives. As more money goes in these markets, prices of the securities soar, and the rich become even richer.

---

5. Canterbery, "Casino Effect," p. 169ff.

The more alert (or, perhaps, rapacious) among them see and seize the opportunity to use their securities and other assets as collateral for loans to finance increased speculating. The Federal Reserve, fearing inflation, raises the interest rate to hold down employment and wages. The poor become poorer, as the rich have become richer.

A high rate of interest forces investors—whether individuals or corporations or "institutions"—to hunt for projects that turn around quickly. If the interest rate is 5 percent, the interest costs of a project that matures in six months are 2½ percent or a little less, while those of a project that matures in five years are 27.6 percent. The latter is daunting enough; but when the rate is 10 percent, the five-year interest cost is equal to 55.3 percent of all other costs, or 35.6 percent of all costs, including interest. In contrast, a stock market manipulation that can be accomplished in, say, a week can earn at the rate of 10 percent if it gains as little as 0.2 percent on the money ventured. In the last quarter of 1987, almost half the *daily* shifts of the market were ten times that, or greater than 2 percent.[6]

Such considerations (which include no allowance for entrepreneurial profit) go a long way toward explaining the reluctance of American industry to invest in long-term development. Japanese managers were more farsighted than American managers, not because of differences in education or temperament or diet, but because the Japanese interest rate has been less than half the American. As long as the U.S. prime remains higher than 2 percent, even a crash like that of 1987 does little to modify the systemic bias in favor of speculation.

A volatile interest rate obviously multiplies opportunities for trying to guess which way the rate is likely to jump. Whether the economy is likely to prosper becomes a secondary consideration, as is shown by the regularity with which the market rises on what ordinarily would be thought to be bad news (such as a fall in employment). A volatile rate also opens sudden gaps between the stock and the futures markets, thus sucking in vast sums whose investors hope to profit from the gaps.

---

6. Fedack, "Volatility in the Equity Market," p. 10.

That speculation is relatively short term is certainly of its essence and helps account for its perennial attractiveness. Speculation is a quicker way to make money than is production because it has no production time. Even when one buys land, expecting a town to expand eventually in a certain direction, one can sell out at any time if disappointed by the rate of expansion or if another speculator is willing to pay for a piece of the action. Speculators can make much money fast, and a short-term investment must be concerned with the diurnal vagaries of the market. Today the vagaries are based on various statistics, periodically compiled and released, among them the money supply in its several forms, the budget surplus or deficit, the trade deficit, unemployment, inflation, and corporate plans. Probably less attention is paid to the last than to the others—perhaps because the last can be changed by human beings on their own say-so, while the others seem somehow impersonal. These others, moreover, dictate certain responses to followers of conventional economics—particularly to the governors of the Federal Reserve Board, who can be expected to make conventional adjustments in the interest rate, and hence in the capitalized value of assets. Long-term investment has to be based on both the future of the economy and the future of a particular industry. Although correctly foreseeing great postwar business activity and prosperity, one would have been a fool to invest in a photostatting business with Xeroxing on the horizon.

CAPITAL GAINS

Although it is a perversion of sound public policy to encourage speculation, it is nevertheless true that some sorts of speculation are inevitable and even useful in our world of uncertainty. Being unable to foretell the future, a business firm necessarily guesses when it orders capital goods for future delivery. When the goods come in, they may be worth more—or less—than the contract price, and the firm will accordingly realize what amounts to a speculative profit or loss. To minimize such swings, a firm will sometimes hedge by speculating in stocks, commodities, derivatives, whatever. Thus, if the firm fears the delivered goods may turn out to be less valuable than the current price, it will sell speculations short. Then, if prices do fall, the money gained by the short-selling will offset the money lost on the capital goods. Of course, if inflation is anticipated, the buyer of capital goods is unlikely to hedge against that; but then the seller may hedge by hoping that an increase in the price of the securities he buys will offset increased costs of manufacturing the capital goods he sells.

It should be added that hedging, in spite of its occasional usefulness in helping individual firms to moderate profit swings, has little or no effect on the prices firms charge and consequently little or no effect on the price level. On the other hand, by increasing the amount of money devoted to speculation, hedging participates in the general deleterious effect on the economy. This participation is true also of speculations in foreign currencies and also of collections of art and artifacts, whose prices are supported in large part by the expectation that they can eventually be sold or even given away at a handsome profit underwritten by misguided provisions of the inheritance tax and the charity deduction.[7]

7. There is no doubt that many people plan to make a speculative profit when they buy artifacts ranging from Old Masters to a match-folder collection like the one G. Gordon Liddy sorrowfully shredded to destroy possible Watergate evidence. Such dealing concerns actual commodities, whose sale and purchase function like those of more ordinary commodities in the producing economy. An Old Master may be hung on the living room wall and so be "consumed" as the other furnishings of the room are consumed, and as the room itself is consumed. Or the painting may be held for sale and stored like any other item in the inventory of a profit-making enterprise. It may be consumers' goods one day and producers' the next. In contrast, and regardless of the jargon of brokers, securities are not products and are never either consumers' goods or producers' goods. The principle of opportunity cost puts the prices paid for works of art and "collectibles" on a track parallel to that of the securities markets.

Whenever the monetary authorities raise the interest rate and attempt a contraction of the money supply, speculation will drain money from both production and consumption. Whenever the monetary authorities encourage a volatile interest rate, speculation will be stimulated and enterprise will suffer. Whenever the monetary authorities allow loans to support margin trading on the exchanges, speculation will be encouraged and enterprise will suffer. Whenever the taxing authorities give favored treatment to capital gains, speculation will again be encouraged and enterprise will again suffer.

It would be foolish to try to prevent all kinds of speculation, not because people are psychologically addicted to it, but because the uncertainty of our lives makes it inevitable. At the same time speculation can and should be controlled. The most effective control is to take the profit out of it. Accordingly, gains on assets held less than one year might be taxed at 75 percent, with the rate falling 5 points a year for five years. Since currently tax-exempt "institutions" are responsible for much of the speculating that churns all markets, their capital gains should be taxed the same as everyone else's. Gains certainly should be taxed at the relevant rate when assets change hands by gift or bequest. Principal residences below a certain size and likewise small family farms and businesses might well be exempted from the high rate.

Capital gains are an archaic form of profit. Despite their name, they are characteristic not of the capitalist system but of mercantilism and more primitive economic systems. In the Renaissance, enterprises tended to be one-shot affairs, like the various ventures of Antonio referred to in *The Merchant of Venice*. Gains (or losses) were realized as each investment ended. In contrast, the characteristic capitalist investment continues indefinitely, produces a regular flow of goods, yields regular dividends, offers regular employment, and pays regular taxes.

In addition to the much discussed fairness point, there are sound economic reasons for heavier, not lighter, taxation of capital gains.

15

International Trade

Every American boy or girl who paid even the slightest attention in school knows that mercantilism was a bad idea. It bled the colonies for the benefit of the homeland, and consequently the colonies revolted. Those who listened a little longer also know that the mercantilist striving for a "favorable" balance of trade meant exportation of consumable goods and importation of precious metals, a policy that is ultimately self-defeating because, as Midas found out, gold is not good to eat.

As an example of mercantilist foolishness, Fernand Braudel tells us that in 1703, toward the start of the War of the Spanish Succession, the English were advised to send "grain, manufactured products and other goods" from home to their troops fighting in the Low Countries. They could have bought these supplies easily and presumably more cheaply on the Continent, but the government was "obsessed by the fear of losing its metal reserves."[1] Any follower of Adam Smith or

1. Braudel, *Civilization and Capitalism*, vol. 2, p. 205.

David Ricardo can see that this policy led England to waste real wealth (usable goods) and save nominal wealth (unusable metal).

In the world of theory, the mercantilist passion for a favorable balance of trade seems indefensible. It is surely more sensible to secure what you can use than to squirrel away what is of little or no use in bank vaults. But as Braudel reads the historical record of the actual world, he is forced to recognize that the mercantilist policy was in fact successful. "In any case," he writes, "every time we have to deal with a *comparatively* advanced economy, its trade balance is in surplus as a general rule."[2] Flying in the face of classical economics, the more advanced economies exported usable goods and imported gold and silver.

The classical theory fails here (as elsewhere) because it is both ahistorical and asocial. It describes an instantaneous slice of a world without time, and it concerns things, like the GNP, not people, like you and me. Criticism of the English policy of 1703 silently assumes that purchasing war matériel overseas would have had no effect on English farms and factories. The assumption is that the goods purchased on the Continent would have been added to those produced at home and that the English wealth would have risen accordingly. But in the actual world, English farmers, deprived of part of their market, would have cut back production expenses (which is here another name for employment). And English manufacturers of soldier suits and the like would surely not have continued producing them if the government didn't buy them. Their employment, too, would have fallen. These drops in employment would have meant a decline in the English standard of living. The mercantilist policy preserved that standard of living (such as it was); the classical theory would have reduced it.

In the infrequently noticed catchall Chapter 23 of *The General Theory*, Keynes includes some "Notes on Mercantilism." He observes that

---

2. Ibid., p. 218.

a favorable balance of trade, by bringing in gold and silver, increased a country's money supply, which forced down the interest rate, which stimulated investment.

Investment is not stimulated—not stimulated rationally, that is—for its own sake. From the point of view of the investor, the purpose of investment is to make money by speculating or producing goods that are in demand and can be sold at a profit. From the point of view of the nation, the purpose of investment is to provide employment for its citizens and to produce things that are wanted. Since employed citizens are able to make purchases—create demand—these two purposes can work together, though they do not necessarily do so.

In the early modern world of the mercantilists, the interest rate was, as Keynes said, held down indirectly (and probably unintentionally) by fostering a favorable balance of trade. To have a favorable balance of trade, a country must export more goods than it imports. To export more goods, it must produce more goods. To produce more goods, it must employ more people. The secret of mercantilism's comparative success lies in the increased employment of labor. It must therefore be recognized that mercantilism or anything like it is useful only in cases of severe unemployment, and even in such cases the better policy would be to increase production by, for consumption by, the home "nation" of the unemployed, underemployed, discouraged, and turned off.

The power of labor is very great. Even putting to one side the facts that capital is the result of past labor, and that natural resources can be exploited only by labor, labor power is our ultimate power. The laziest, least competent, least efficiently applied labor can today produce far more than it needs to sustain itself.

Our agriculture and forestry now produce more food than we should or can eat, more than enough natural fibers to clothe us, more than enough lumber to house us with 2 percent of our labor force. Since even at our shabbiest, we allow almost no one to fall through the safety net and actually starve or freeze to death, it is plain that we do not need additional workers to provide for their own subsistence. Therefore, the output of every previously unemployed worker we manage to find work for will raise our standard of living a bit more above subsistence. And we can do this without importing gold or silver to control the interest rate. Since money is not gold or any other commodity, all we need is a monetary authority that has emerged from the age of mercantilism into the modern world.

NATIONS

The first requirement of international trade is that there be nations. If there were no nations, there obviously would be no trade among them. The distinguishing marks of nationhood are sovereignty and citizenship. A neighborhood or a region has boundaries and inhabitants; but it is not a law unto itself. The citizens of a nation have, in the grand old phrase, certain rights, privileges, immunities, and duties that are denied to those who are not citizens. If we who are citizens are not, in this way, distinguished from those who are not citizens, of what meaning is citizenship to us? And if national citizenship is without meaning, of what meaning is the nation?

Perhaps we don't want a nation. Perhaps we shouldn't have one. Perhaps we reserve our loyalty for those who are very near and very dear to us. Perhaps, as D. H. Lawrence put it in *Aaron's Rod*, we "love-whoosh for humanity." But if we have international trade, we have a nation; and if we have a nation, then the well-being of our fellow citizens is vital to us. We can't demand respect for our own well-being unless we, at the same time, to the same extent, and for the same reasons, respect theirs.

In contrast, the theory of free trade is concerned only with commerce. Like classical economics, it has no respect for persons except as consumers. It sees no need for government beyond minimal police protection. As was loudly demonstrated in Seattle in 1999, the World

Trade Organization is not prepared even to consider questions concerning human rights, labor rights, the use of natural resources, or the environment. Even after the financial debacle of southeast Asia, no attempt will be made to rationalize the ebb and flow of money around the globe. In a free trade world, politics stops at the cash register.

Nevertheless, international trade is still trade among nations, and nations actually make a difference in business enterprise. Given these actualities, the task for economics is to discover what special considerations, if any, lead nations to trade with one another and what special principles, if any, govern such trade. It is not enough to show that, in general, international trade expands the market, encourages the division of labor, and permits economies of scale, nor is it enough to show that, in general, international trade is a civilizing activity. Such showings can equally be made regarding interregional or interpersonal trade. Moreover, showing that international trade is advantageous for Belgium or Ghana or Taiwan says little or nothing about its importance for a continental power like the United States or China or Russia.

At the outset, we may name three conditions that set reasonable limits to discussion of international trade:

First, if we are under no obligation to guarantee fellow citizens the right to a particular job in our nation at a particular wage, we are under even less obligation to guarantee foreigners a particular job here or in their homelands.

Second, if no one has a right to a particular job at a particular wage, no one has a right to a particular product at a particular price.

Third, if we have a nation, we have a duty to maintain it.

SINCE SMITH AND RICARDO

Ever since Adam Smith, economists have been practically unanimous in support of free trade. Publishing in the year of American Independence, Smith declared that "Great Britain derives nothing but loss from the dominion which she assumes over her colonies."[3] The loss came not only from the cost of defending and administering the colonies but also from the higher prices that British exporters could charge because of their monopoly. Higher prices in the colonies induced higher prices at home; so all nonexporters suffered.

For Smith, foreign trade was of minor importance, anyhow. It served two main purposes: It enabled countries to exchange surpluses, and it facilitated the division of labor by expanding the market. In furtherance of these ends, he opposed the monopolies and restraints on, or inducements to, trade that were root and branch of the mercantile system.

Over the past two hundred years, the domestic market in any one of a score of countries has become larger than the largest world market Smith could have imagined, and the division of labor has gone far beyond the eighteen operations in the manufacture of pins that he immortalized. More important, the merchant adventurers of his day have been supplanted by today's multinational corporations and international speculative financiers. Nevertheless, his arguments for free trade still circulate and in the United States have inspired a tradition running from John Hay's Open Door in China, through Cordell Hull's Reciprocal Trade Treaties, to the postwar General Agreement on Tariffs and Trade (the World Trade Organization) and the North American Free Trade Agreement.

David Ricardo was of greater importance than Adam Smith to the cause of free trade. In 1817 he advanced his famous Law of Comparative Advantage, which purports to demonstrate that international trade is mutually profitable even when one country is absolutely more productive in terms of every commodity traded.

On the face of it, this proposition seems implausible, but Ricardo explained it this way: Suppose that a certain amount of wine exchanges

---

3. Smith, *Wealth*, p. 581.

for a certain amount of cloth. Suppose that in England it would take a year's labor of 100 men to make the cloth and of 120 men to make the wine, while in Portugal the man-years required are 90 and 80, respectively. In these circumstances, it would be to Portugal's advantage to make only wine and to England's to make only cloth, with the countries then exchanging the surpluses. Portugal would multiply its wine output 2.125 times [(90 + 80)/80] and England its cloth production 2.2 times, and since the cloth and the wine are equal in value, both countries would come out ahead.[4]

Ricardo was quick to concede that his law applied only to international trade. "Such an exchange," he observed, "could not take place between the individuals of the same country. The labour of 100 Englishmen cannot be given for that of 80 Englishmen, but the produce of the labour of 100 Englishmen may be given for the produce of the labour of 80 Portuguese, 60 Russians, or 120 East Indians. The difference in this respect, between a single country and many, is easily accounted for, by considering the difficulty with which capital moves from one country to another, to seek a more profitable employment, and the activity with which it invariably passes from one province to another in the same country."[5]

Ricardo went on to declare that "feelings, which [he] should be sorry to see weakened, induce most men of property to be satisfied with a low rate of profits in their own country, rather than seek a more advantageous employment for their wealth in foreign nations."[6]

What Ricardo could not foresee, and what his modern followers have overlooked, is that the new multinational corporations and speculators fail to share the feelings of patriotism or indeed of prudence that he ascribed (somewhat naively even in the nineteenth century) to the capitalists of his time. Today capital flits freely from here to there,

---

4. Ricardo, *Principles*, p. 82.
5. Ibid, pp. 82–83.
6. Ibid, p. 83.

moving as indifferently from Schenectady to Singapore as it did in Ricardo's day from London to York.

A WORLD WITHOUT TIME

This is not the only weakness of his law as a guide to modern policy. More important is the fact that although the law begins by considering data that would be historical if they were actual (the equivalent values of the wine and the cloth and the numbers of workers engaged in producing them), it ends by assuming that the industrial changes it recommends can be accomplished in an instant and without other consequence—in a word, ahistorically. The British vintners are immediately to become weavers and the Portuguese weavers vintners. The British winepresses are immediately changed into looms, and the Portuguese looms into winepresses. Such transformation was perhaps almost imaginable in the first quarter of the nineteenth century. Even then, if the transformations were not accomplished immediately, in a trice, both parties would have unemployed workers and unutilized factories, as well as shortages of both wine and cloth. The resulting suffering and waste would more than offset the promised 6 or 10 percent increase in output, which could be accomplished in many less traumatic ways.

Like so much of standard economics, the Law of Comparative Advantage is suited to a world without time, where everything happens all at once, or not at all. Also like so much of standard economics, it assumes full employment. If either England or Portugal has substantial numbers of unemployed workers, it would be more advantageous to train them as weavers or vintners, as the case might be, than to keep them on the dole while importing cloth or wine.

What generally happens today, however, is that First World countries like England tend to abandon the production of both cloth and wine and to import both from some country where labor costs are lower. The question then becomes, How will England pay for the imported cloth and wine? By exporting something else, most economists cheerily reply, but they tend to be bashful when asked what that something else might be. If because of their lower wage scales (or for any other reason) other countries can underprice England in the production of every product you can name, and if their unemployment is high, why should they buy anything at England's higher prices?

Well, it may be urged, England, limping into the postindustrial world, can concentrate on service industries; and while some services, like motorcycle maintenance and baby-sitting, are hard to export, financial services are easy. And in fact historians have made much of the importance to the British Empire of "invisibles"—interest, insurance premiums, royalties, profits, and employment for younger sons. Of these, only the last did anything to solve England's unemployment problem, and today it is already happening that financial British (and American) companies are having their computer keyboarding done abroad at low wages.

In any case, the invisibles can only help pay for visible imports. They can't carry the whole load, or even a major share of it. All financial services together, including exploitative profits, seldom amount to more than 40 percent of the cost of a product, and frequently are less than 20 percent, thus leaving from 60 to 80 percent of the cost of imports uncovered. In the glory days of the British Empire, these costs were covered in the usual visible ways of manufacturing and exporting textiles and guns and steam engines and anything else anyone could think of. This is no longer so easy for England to do, nor is it easy for the United States. Japan could to it, but she is not tormented by theories about free trade.

The ultimate consequence of abandoning manufacturing is national stagnation and decline—decline of both power and standard of living. It has happened before. In 1675 a Spanish nobleman, one Alfonso Nuñes de Castro, wrote, "Let London manufacture those fabrics of hers to her heart's content; Holland her chambrays; the Indies their beaver and vicuña; Milan her brocades; Italy and France their linens, so long as our capital can enjoy them; the only thing it proves is that all countries train journeymen for Madrid and that Madrid is the queen of parliaments, for all the world serves her and she serves nobody."[7]

Don Alfonso understated Spain's contributions to the wealth and happiness of mankind. She may have produced little or no cloth, but she provided services—military services, administrative services, ecclesiastical services—to the New World, and also to the Two Sicilies, to the Low Countries, to Burgundy, and to the Holy Roman Empire. These services, valuable though they may have been (there has been doubt on this point), were not enough to support the imperial style in Madrid. When the silver from the Indies ran out, Spain, for lack of trained journeymen, slipped into a slough of despond from which today, three centuries after Don Alfonso, she has yet to escape.

THE RAPID SUCCESS OF FOREIGN COMPETITION

One of the puzzles of recent years, especially for conventional economics, has been the ease with which American industry was penetrated and defeated by foreign competition from the countries we defeated in World War II and from less developed countries of the Pacific rim. Since the United States has a heavy investment in capital plant, both in total and per worker, and since the United States is relatively thinly populated, it has been—and still is—argued that the United States has a comparative advantage in capital-intensive industries and a corresponding disadvantage in labor-intensive industries. On the basis of these supposed advantages and disadvantages, it has been—and still is—argued that the United States should expand its capital-intensive industries and export their surpluses, while shifting out of labor-intensive industries and importing foreign substitutes.

The conventional theory is not only a policy proposal, it is also sup-

7. Cipolla, *Before the Industrial Revolution*, p. 251.

posed to be a description of the actual world, for the advantages and disadvantages should inexorably induce the described result. The trouble is that it does not work out that way. Wassily Leontief made an extensive quantitative analysis that showed "that an average million dollars' worth of our exports embodies considerably less capital and somewhat more labor than would be required to replace from domestic production an equivalent amount of our competitive imports."[8]

Leontief's explanation of his finding has possibly contributed to the talk we've been hearing in recent years about labor productivity. He felt that American workingmen were better educated and more interested than those of other countries; that even though they were generally paid much more and often had somewhat less capital equipment per worker, they were so efficient and ingenious "that in any combination with a given quantity of capital, one man year of American labor is equivalent to, say, three man years of foreign labor."[9] While recognizing that it would take some time for so-called backward countries to catch up, Leontief pointed out that the American position was not unassailable. He wrote, "[T]he factors, whatever they may be, which are responsible for the high relative productivity of American labor might soon become operative in other economies and thus accelerate the elimination of disparity between the effective comparative supply of capital here and in foreign countries."[10]

Leontief was writing in 1953. In less than two decades, Japan had fulfilled his prophecy, to be quickly followed by other countries of the Pacific rim. In the same years, Italy came to dominate the shoe business, Sweden remained prominent in automobiles, and even Yugoslavia tried to make a mark. More recently, American agriculture, which had long tolerated minor wintertime imports from south of the border, has been challenged and sometimes overwhelmed even in its

---

8. Leontief, *Input-Output Economics*, p. 86.
9. Ibid, p. 87.
10. Ibid, p. 96.

home market by produce from Mexico, Chile, Argentina, and Brazil. These are only examples of the great changes that have transformed the United States from an exporter to a net importer.

There are three principal reasons for the changes. In the absence of any one of them, the transformation could not have occurred. The reasons are entrepreneurial, financial, and wage related. They all fulfill themselves in many ways.

ENTREPRENEURIAL STYLE

First, entrepreneurial. Much has been written about the Japanese collegial system. Big government gets together with big banks and big industry (there is no big labor in Japan) and decides what shall be done, and then does it. Sometimes a mistake is made, as when Honda was advised to keep its mind on motorcycles, but until recently the general success of the system has been there for all to see. Also there for all to see is the system's dependence on and exploitation of a hierarchical society. It is not a remarkably pretty system, but no one doubts that it has been a remarkably effective one. It has also been remarkably resilient in meeting competition from neighboring countries. Thus in its planning for recovery after the war, Japan recapitulated the history of the Industrial Revolution by first emphasizing textiles. In this the Japanese were soon challenged by their neighbors, whose labor costs were much too low to be matched. Almost at once Japan gave up the ambition to sell textiles internationally. The home market was protected, but the international market forgone. All effort was, instead, shifted to optics, electronics, automobiles, and, later, computers.

The Pacific rim neighbors' challenge depended not only on cheap labor but also on a new entrepreneurial style—one which has also made inroads in other lines, principally electronics. The new style was, in fact, pioneered by Americans, but it has been developed with enthusiasm, vigor, and excitement, especially in Singapore and Hong Kong.

In the paradigmatic version, an American clothing company sends representatives to the style shows in Paris and Milan, where they buy models they think suitable for marketing in the States. They then take the models to Hong Kong or Singapore, where they work out modifications of the style, partly to appeal to American tastes, and partly to accommodate Asiatic production capabilities. At this point a local entrepreneur takes over and subcontracts with others—to buy cotton, say, in Bangladesh; have it woven into cloth and dyed in Taiwan; cut to pattern in Hong Kong; basted in the People's Republic of China; and finished in Seoul.

Here, again, the path opened by textiles and clothing was soon followed by other industries. Parts for all kinds of electronic devices, from calculators to hearing aids, can similarly be broken down into subparts capable of being turned out by semiskilled workers with relatively inexpensive machines. It is Adam Smith's eighteen steps in the manufacture of pins all over again, but with the steps no longer concentrated under one roof but spread, higgledy-piggledy, over half the globe.

The entrepreneurs who organize these industries are young men—most of them, it would appear, Hong Kong Chinese—of boundless energy and enthusiasm, who make Western "can do" operators seem listless by comparison. Already they are supplying parts for Japanese TVs and cameras, and consider themselves capable of managing the whole thing.

Despite its successes, what we may call the Hong Kong entrepreneurial style is inevitably in a subordinate position. The energetic young Chinese who organize the operations lack an essential ingredient of commercial independence: They have no direct access to the ultimate market. They can quickly cobble together a congeries of small shops to make almost anything you want in almost any quantity at a most attractive price. But they do not themselves decide what to make; and if they did, they'd have no way of selling it. They can go to General Electric and offer to supply parts or even the whole of a hearing aid or whatever, but they do not design the hearing aid, nor do they discover the Western demand for such a thing.

Consequently they are always at the mercy of the Western companies that do control the markets. These may be manufacturers who sell the imports under their brand names, or they may be retailing chains big enough to buy all the sports shirts or kitchen utensils or bicycles the entrepreneurs can supply. Needless to say, the entrepreneurs have some countervailing power. If Sears pushes them too hard, they can go to K-Mart; if Black & Decker seems unreasonable, they can offer their services to Stanley.

To eliminate this pushing and shoving (otherwise known as the competitive system), Western companies become really multinational and open factories abroad under their own names. The multinational style is particularly effective in Africa and South America, where local entrepreneurs are less frenetic, and of course in Europe, where there are markets to supply as well as skilled labor to exploit.

The multinational corporation is a financial institution as well as a manufacturer or retailer. It shows this side of itself first in its decision to expand abroad at all, judging as it does that this is a more profitable way to invest its money than domestic expansion would be. It shows its financial side next as it chooses locations for its operations, being attracted to countries that offer subsidies or tax concessions. It shows its financial side finally and most clearly as it invests in foreign companies.

When General Motors buys 38.6 percent of Isuzu Motors or 50 percent of Daewoo Motors of Korea, it is not engaging in automobile manufacturing. It is investing surplus cash—cash it has earned elsewhere but can't think how to invest or spend elsewhere. Its earnings from Isuzu and Daewoo will show up on its profit-and-loss statement, but not in the top or manufacturing half. By these investments General Motors makes money by helping foreign industry to compete with American industry—even to compete with General Motors itself.

This is not so strange as it may seem. It's only a short step from the Sloan management system whereby Chevrolet competes with Buick and Pontiac as fiercely as it competes with Ford and Chrysler. The theory is that Buick and Chevrolet and Pontiac will meet competition from somewhere anyhow, and that if some of the competition can be internalized, General Motors will win, regardless of the outcome for the subsidiaries. As might be expected, the system acquires a life of its own. The corporation needs a whole new layer or two of staff to supervise the subsidiaries, set their goals, approve their budgets, and pass judgment on their achievements. Looking at what is complacently called the larger picture, the top layers find fulfillment in expanding or downsizing manufacturing divisions and often in buying or selling them. In short, the tendency is toward finance, not industry.

Management neither produces nor sells; its triumphs are financial and legal, especially so its triumphs overseas. Americans are constantly being asked to take pride in this company or that as the largest of its sort in the world, or to be alarmed that, because of some regulation or other, American companies are said to be losing out to foreign competition. If these jingoistic problems are more substantial than totting up Olympic medals as a measure of the success of our society, it is because the gold medals are relatively harmless, while the overseas operations of American multinationals are generally adverse to domestic employment and prosperity.

THE GREAT RECYCLING

Then, the banks. Their self-advertised achievement has been the recycling of the tremendous profits of OPEC's early years into nonperforming loans of American money to the Third World. Had the banks not been available to take this money out of immediate circulation, the OPEC countries would have had to spend it. God knows what they would have bought, but the countries that sold it to them would have become more prosperous and their economies would surely have become more active.

Led by Citicorp, the American banks did not hesitate. If they had, they would have lost out to British and French and German and Italian competitors, thus injuring our national pride. (Asians are concerned about face; we have our pride.) In competition with foreigners and with each other, the major American banks scrambled for their share of the gold mine. The obvious way of attracting the Arabs' attention was to offer high interest rates, a procedure to which bankers are not constitutionally averse. At home they were restrained by Regulation Q from offering prospective depositors more than a toaster or, rarely, a TV. This was nickel-and-dime stuff. Overseas the blue sky was the limit.

Having attracted their share of OPEC's money, the banks now had to complete the cycle. Again they did not hesitate. What with one thing and another, Third World debt went from $7.6 billion in 1960 to over $1,300 billion—that is an increase of more than seventeen thousand percent—thirty years later. The disastrous effects of this indebtedness (not all of it to banks) on the debtors is much commented on.

The effect on the lenders is also disastrous. For to the extent that the borrowings were not squandered on the spot or thriftily sequestered in Swiss numbered accounts belonging to Third World leaders, they were largely spent on enterprises intended to compete with existing enterprises of the banks' home countries. Thus Brazil was lent money to build a steel industry that contributed to the decline of Pittsburgh and Youngstown.

In order to pay off the loans, Brazil has to export more than she imports, thus lowering her standard of living. In order to export, she must underprice American mills, which she can do by cutting pay, thus further lowering her standard of living. This is known, in International Monetary Fund circles, as austerity, and is much admired from a distance.

IMF "REFORM"

The IMF is also a doctrinaire enthusiast for economic "reform," by which is meant radical deregulation and privatization. The announced purpose generally is to reduce payrolls, especially government payrolls. It is seldom or never suggested that debtor countries, as a condition for international assistance, impose equitable taxes on their rich or even make a serious attempt to collect the taxes already on the books. And no one would dream of attempting to stop the flight of money to numbered accounts in Switzerland. Austerity is for the poor and for the middle class, if any.

As Brazil is successful in her austerity, she ruins American mills. Not only does the failure of American mills enforce the austerity of unemployment on American workers, it reduces American exports, thus aggravating the American trade deficit. In order to pay off the deficits Americans must emulate Brazilians and lower their standard of living in the same austere ways.

This, unfortunately, is not all. No one really believes that Brazil and the rest will, in spite of the best austerity in the world, pay off their trillion and a third dollars of indebtedness. There will be defaults. These, too, will impose austerity, for American banks will surely wangle subsidies from a government afraid to let them fail, and the subsidies will require higher taxes from those of us who are not bankers. At the same time the banks' American taxes will fall because of the nonperforming loans, even though, since the loans were made abroad, no American taxes were paid on the profits when the loans were performing.

The great recycling was surely as wondrous as the wheels Ezekiel saw, 'way up there in the middle of the air. It has been our sad fate that the recycling occurred on earth.

WAGE SCALES AND WORKING CONDITIONS

Important though the skills of the entrepreneurs were, improbably feckless though the bankers, the changes foreseen by Leontief could not have come about except through exploitation of Third World workers. It would be more accurate to say that the First World workers are the ones being exploited. Third World workers rush to take jobs at 35 cents an hour, 50 cents, a dollar, or a lordly dollar and a half. These jobs would not be available if First World workers did not perversely resist reducing their wages below the subsistence level, though in recent years they have been relentlessly forced downward.

Even if we accept Leontief's estimate that American workers are three times as efficient as those elsewhere (and it is fashionable now to doubt this), that's not good enough to overcome the wage differential. We see the results at every hand. There is practically nothing that cannot be made more cheaply abroad than in the United States. Even Japan has seen its shipbuilding industry follow its garment trades to Korea, while it imports electronics components from Hong Kong entrepreneurs, just as does the United States.

The fundamentally irresponsible multinational corporation knows no boundaries other than the bottom line. Today capital is perfectly fluid. Aside from a few temporarily secret processes, technology anywhere is quickly available to literate people everywhere. Domestic availability of raw materials has not dictated a country's industry since the Industrial Revolution and certainly does not do so now (nineteenth-century England grew no cotton; twentieth-century Japan pumps no oil). Today the costs of all but one of the factors of production are nearly homogeneous throughout the world.

But the cost of labor is not internationally homogeneous. And since labor is usually the most costly factor, as well as always the original and necessary factor, the heterogeneity of wage scales and working conditions overrides all other considerations. Labor, moreover, is not impersonal. Labor is people, fellow citizens.

NEO-IMPERIALISM

Today, as in the eighteenth and nineteenth centuries, the more developed countries need the less developed countries as sources of raw materials, some of which are not available elsewhere. The multinational corporations also use the LDCs, or some of them, as sources of cheap labor and cheap working conditions. The banks of the First World found the feeble nations of the Third World eager borrowers of money at high interest rates. What was, before independence, imperialism became neo-imperialism.

There has long been a lively debate about whether gunboat imperialism was good for the mother countries. Adam Smith, as we have seen, thought not. Bismarck concurred. "All the advantages claimed for the mother country," he said, "are for the most part illusions." People as various as Cecil Rhodes and Hjalmar Schacht were among those who disagreed.

The Marxian position, scarcely developed by Marx and Engels, was given shape by J. A. Hobson, by Lenin, by Rudolf Hilferding, by Rosa Luxemburg, and finally by Stalin. In the end, the emphasis was on the imperialist wars that were expected to be the last stage of capitalism; but initially and fundamentally it was argued that mature capitalism needed overseas outlets for investments discouraged at home by the alleged law of diminishing returns and overseas markets for goods that couldn't be sold at home, because labor wasn't paid enough.

All sides acknowledged that the colonies were more or less mistreated, perhaps in the course of the white man's civilizing mission, perhaps because of white men's inherent viciousness. Cultivated Brahmans were insulted by half-educated British majors. Belgium kept the subject peoples of the Congo in ignorance. And so on. All this was bad, but it should have ended—and largely did end—with the political liberation of the colonies. Yet neo-imperialism took the place of imperialism.

The vice of neo-imperialism is not so much the social and political domination as the economic extraction. What is extracted is paid for at going world prices, which somehow are almost always low. Farmers everywhere are seldom able to demand good prices, because they are too dispersed for easy organization, their industry is relatively inexpensive to enter, and their products have many substitutes and are perishable and at the mercy of the weather. What is true of farming is also largely true of mining. The farming and mining industries struggle under these difficulties even in the United States, but here they have been able to organize political power to obtain some relief. Nothing like this has proved possible internationally, with the exceptions of OPEC and the diamond cartel.

What is new about neo-imperialism is the influx of the multinational corporations, especially in Asia. There have of course been international business organizations for hundreds of years. The old-line companies were in agriculture, like the United Fruit Company, or mining, like Cerro Chemicals. The new multinationals are engaged in manufacturing, and they are first and foremost international marketing organizations having close connections with retail chains and ready access to big finance. It is no secret why the multinationals have moved into the Third World. They are seldom interested in natural resources. They certainly are not in search of capital or of technology. As everyone knows, the factor of production that attracts them is labor—labor that is cheap, unorganized, and undemanding, willing to work long hours for low wages in substandard conditions.

Thus the distinguishing mark of neo-imperialism is the extraction of labor power. This comes about because the things the multinationals manufacture in the Third World are sold in the First World. Plastic-frame irons General Electric manufactures in Singapore are sold in American discount houses. Steel produced by Brazilian mills is bought in markets formerly served by Pittsburgh. Textbooks printed in Hong Kong are studied in British classrooms. California sports shirts run up in Korea are sold in Florida. In short, the Marxian theory of imperialism doesn't fit what is going on now. The multinationals are not looking for markets in the Third World; they are looking for labor. The markets—most of the time—are still in the First World.

As a result of all this activity, the Third World has things to export, though it seems never enough. The reason why there is never enough is that the exports to the First World are paid for with imports from the First World. It is at this point that the extraction of labor power shows itself, for many times as much labor goes into the exports as into the imports.

The wage differential varies from country to country and from industry to industry, but a very rough idea of comparative wage rates can be gathered from figures on GNP per capita. Today, for a few examples, the figures are $2,800 in the People's Republic of China, $1,380 in Nigeria, $14,200 in South Korea, and $8,300 in Brazil. In the United States the figure is $34,563. On the basis of these figures, we'll not be overstating the case if we say that a dollar commands five times as much labor in the Third World as it does in the First World. This means that when the two worlds exchange goods, the Third World is the net loser of four-fifths of the labor involved. This four-fifths is extracted and gone forever.

It is this extraction of labor power that is the vice of neo-imperialism. It is very likely true that the multinationals, or some of them, are not above diddling their books so that they can declare their profits where taxes are lowest. It is certainly true that the international banks, or some of them, are capable of persuading—or bribing—naive or corrupt Third World officials to borrow money at ultra-usurious rates to build power lines to nowhere and skyscrapers among mud huts. It is also true that the International Monetary Fund then demands austerity (meaning a widening of the wage differential) for the hapless citizens of the countries accepting the loans. There is little in these activities of which the participants can be proud, but their effects are small in comparison with the effect of the extraction of labor power.

THE STRENGTH OF HIGH WAGES

Those advocating the industrialization of the Third World have had before them a working model of how it can be done. The development of the fledgling United States was financed by loans from England and, to a lesser extent, from the Continent. For a century and a quarter, until World War I, the United States was a debtor nation. American canals and railroads, American steel mills and thread factories, American shipyards and coal mines, all relied on foreign capital. Sometimes the foreigners were swindled, as in the Crédit Mobilier, but usually they got their money back with interest. The United States was a good investment for foreigners, and the investments were good for the United States.

But the nineteenth-century United States model does not fit today's Third World. The difference is simple. The industry financed by today's multinationals manufactures goods for export. In contrast, the infrastructure built in the United States with foreign capital was necessarily used in the United States; it could not be exported. Moreover, almost all the goods produced in foreign-financed factories were sold and used in the United States. Britain imported food and raw materials from America, but very little in the way of manufactures.

Ironically, the United States after the Civil War was almost a copybook example of the Marxian theory of imperialism, but it had a diametrically opposite result. Raw materials were extracted; finance charges were exacted; an outlet for excess capital was found and so, too, was a large and eager market. According to the Marxian theory, the United States should have been a disaster, exploited and despoiled by Europe. But it was a success, while the Third World, which does not fit the Marxian theory for failure, is failing.

The United States was able to withstand the pressures of imperialism, and indeed to profit from them, for a reason that may seem surprising: its wage scales were the highest in the world. This used to be a proud and proper boast. Consequently, if there was an extraction of labor power, it was from Europe, not from the United States.

It would be making an irrelevant claim to suggest that the relatively high American wages were, except in a few idiosyncratic cases like that of Henry Ford, the result of deliberate policy. High wages were resisted by the entrepreneurs of the time, but they were in fact inevitable, given the small population in relation to the large country, and given the strong egalitarian tradition of the new nation. Today's Third World nations are not so fortunately situated. In general, their territories are small and their populations overflowing. There is no way in the foreseeable future for their wage scales to approach the highest in the world. They cannot offer the industrialized world much of a market. They present financiers with opportunities to practice usury and speculative skulduggery, rather than investment.

CONSEQUENCES OF NEO-IMPERIALISM

Neo-imperialism is as grave a threat to the industrialized world as to the less developed countries. Before World War II, shelves of American five-and-dime stores were plentifully stocked with imported goods—novelties and notions, mostly: figurines from China or Bavaria, costume jewelry from Mexico or India, Christmas-tree ornaments from Czechoslovakia or Japan. Carriage-trade shops made a snobbish point of offering foreign luxuries of all kinds. American industry necessarily imported certain raw materials and specialties such as German optics and Swiss watch movements.

Taken all together, these imports did not amount to much. Even as late as 1950, imports totaled less than $10 billion, or 4.6 percent of GNP ex services. Furthermore, the imports generally did not displace existing American industry. In most cases the foreign novelties and specialties were long established, and American competition was hardly contemplated.

The situation today is quite different. By 1990, imports were running at a rate of 16.1 percent of GNP ex services, rising to 17.9 percent in 1999. Certain industries were particularly hard hit. Electronics and optics were decimated; textiles were cut in half; steel and automobiles were savaged. There was scarcely an industry that did not feel the effects of foreign competition.

Explanations for what was happening were of two sorts. The one most popular with the Chamber of Commerce, the Business Roundtable, and the National Association of Manufacturers was that American wages were too high and American workingmen too concerned about working conditions to be properly productive. Standard economists also shared this view, since they are oddly disposed to prescribe a drop in wages as the cure for most economic ills.

The other explanation was advanced mainly by investment bankers and a few technologically oriented neoclassical economists. According to this view, there is a natural history of business enterprise. When a corporation or—especially—an industry is launched, it grows very rapidly, partly because its initial base is narrow, but mainly because it is vigorous and innovative. As the industry matures, it becomes increasingly preoccupied with consolidating its gains. Too much has been invested in existing factories for newer and more efficient processes to be adopted. As Schumpeter foresaw, the more creative but disorderly entrepreneurial type is replaced by the more reliable but overly cautious manager. Near-term goals are set; attention is directed to the next quarter's bottom line rather than toward a glorious future. The path to the executive suite, which had lain open to production and marketing geniuses, now is trod mostly by accountants and lawyers. The enterprise, or the whole industry, stagnates. In the currently popular phrase, it has become a sunset industry and should be written off in favor of some industry whose sun is rising.

The wage theory has relied on extensive comparisons of foreign, especially Japanese, industry with American industry. Many of these studies are no doubt casually or deliberately misleading, but there is no need to examine them closely, because they are, in any case, inconclusive. There are always two ways of looking at a comparison. In the present instance, it may be accepted that American wages are higher than Japanese (though lower than Scandinavian, German, and Swiss). From this fact it may be deduced either that American workers are overpaid or that Japanese are underpaid. One conclusion is precisely as logical as the other. In view of the history of labor relations, it would seem probable that the latter conclusion is nearer the truth.

This conclusion is the more certain as one moves from the automobile to the garment industry. The latter is far from a high-wage industry in the United States, but it is being overwhelmed by Asiatic competition. In 1980 in the People's Republic of China, workers in this industry were paid 16 cents an hour; in the Federal Republic of China, the rate was 57 cents an hour; in Hong Kong, it was about a dollar. The rates in Korea and the Philippines were within that range. As a result, imports now account for over half of the United States sales of ladies' and children's apparel, up from only 5 percent forty years ago. The sweatshop has reappeared in America, with illegal immigrants held to virtual peonage in conditions approaching those of the Triangle Shirtwaist fire of 1911.

In short, the argument over wages is irrelevant as it is stated. The question is not whether American workers are better paid than foreign workers, but whether American workers are paid a just wage. Not even the most doctrinaire economist can seriously propose that American workers be paid only 48 cents an hour (the rate in Sri Lanka); yet if free trade made sense, that is the wage that would be arrived at.

Standard economists are not, of course, primarily concerned about wages or the people who earn them. They contend that cheap imports save consumers so much money that the economy gains enormously from them. This argument is plausible enough as long as each industry is considered separately. If a particular American industry cannot meet Asiatic competition, the thing to do might be to scrap it (as Ricardo suggested the Portuguese should give up weaving) and concentrate on something to be sold in Asia. Displaced workers could be relocated or pensioned off. No one can claim a perpetual right to a special job merely because he or she likes it or is experienced in it.

It is, however, an example of the familiar fallacy of composition to transfer this possibly valid argument about a single industry to the economy as a whole.

And the economy as a whole must be considered, because today there is nothing whatever that cannot be manufactured more cheaply in the Third World than in the developed world. On the basis of the Law of Comparative Advantage, all American industry—hi-tech as well as smokestack—should be shipped abroad, and the United States, the industrial giant of the last half of the twentieth century, should return to cultivating its gardens. There is, to be sure, some brave talk about a role in information processing, but with only agriculture and the service industries (including information processing itself) to be informed about, the role at best is not likely to be a large one and at worst would seem to be contemplating one's navel. Since agriculture now engages 1.9 percent of our population (and pays its workers poorly), most Americans would have nothing to do and consequently no earnings with which to buy the cheap imports.

Obviously such a scenario is absurd, but there is nothing in standard economics that contradicts it. Just as Keynes showed that a domestic economy does not automatically operate at full employment, it can be said that the world economy does not automatically employ all the available factors of production.

The absurd conclusion of the scenario is duplicated by the sunset-sunrise explanation of international trade. Indeed, the two views differ mainly in their choice of metaphor. The sunset theorists see that once proud American industries have faltered and been weakened by foreign competition, mainly Asiatic. Following their metaphor, they think the phenomenon natural, inevitable, and irreversible. They therefore recommend abandoning such doomed industries to their fate and mobilizing a massive R & D effort to locate and nurture sunrise industries to take their place. These theorists seem no more impressed than was Ricardo by the waste and suffering consequent on the death of an industry. And it seems not to have occurred to them that what happened once may happen again. There is no reason on earth why our new sunrise industries, whatever they may be, cannot be quickly copied in the Third World and subjected to the same low-wage competition as our sunset industries. Nor is there any reason why our multinationals, having participated in the national R & D program, should not at once open sunrise factories in the Third World, causing our sun to set before it rises. Investment bankers stand ready to finance them, using our money for the purpose, and relying on our government to bail them out if anything goes wrong.

SELF-PROTECTION

The Third World nations will escape from neo-imperialism only as they are able to reduce manufacturing things for the First World and to increase manufacturing things for trading with each other. For many and obvious reasons, this will not be easy, though they will be helped if we help ourselves. That is to say, they may be nudged into trading among themselves if we cut down our labor-extracting trade with them. It is in our interest to protect ourselves from such trade because it hurts our fellow citizens and disrupts our economy.

The way to protect is to protect. First, we decide that a few of our important industries are threatened in our home market by severe competition from foreign industries. Second, we determine whether that threat is made possible by wages or conditions that we would consider exploitative. Third, we refuse entry to goods produced in grossly exploitative conditions.

The proposal is not complicated. It does not cover all industry but only a few industries we declare to be important and threatened in our home market. It does not require elaborate cost accounting (as do the World Trade Organization's provisions against "dumping") but simple, straightforward questions of fact: What are the wage scales? What are the working conditions? Is child labor employed? The proposal does not interfere with foreigners' or multinationals' trade anywhere else in the world. In every respect the proposal is analogous to our present laws refusing entry to contaminated foods or dangerous drugs or unsafe automobiles. Those laws protect Americans as consumers; the proposed law would protect us as workers and, incidentally, as entrepreneurs.

It will be objected that the proposal can't work, because it is impossible to compare foreign wage scales and working conditions with ours. How, if the comparisons can't be made, do the critics of American workers know they are overpaid? What is proposed is merely the reverse of the critics' coin.

Of course, the comparisons can be made, and they will be invidious. The real question is, as the lawyers say, who should have the burden of proof? In the present case, we could reasonably ask those who want access to our markets to prove that their workers are fairly paid and fairly treated by our standards. American unions and American companies would have the right to challenge the proof. No need to make a big fuss about it, any more than a big fuss is now made about determining that certain foreign automobiles don't meet our emissions standards or that certain drugs are inadmissible.

No doubt many will argue against protecting the American standard of living. Two arguments stand out. The first purports to be consumer oriented. Cheap imports, it says, benefit everybody. But they don't benefit those millions whose jobs are taken by the imports, and those other millions who are forced back to the poverty level.

The second argument purports to be producer oriented. Restrictions on international trade, it says, invite retaliation and threaten all our industries, because exports now represent our margin of profit. To this argument there are two answers: (1) Our really threatened industries—automobiles, steel, textiles—have already lost much of their export markets; and (2) we have at home an unexplored market larger than any we might lose.

Our millions of unemployed, plus the millions of working poor, plus their dependents, compose a "nation" of up to fifty million people—bigger than any but a handful of the members of the UN. In spite of our failures—and theirs—these people are better educated than most of the rest of the world, are more familiar with the American work ethic, and are closer to the rest of us in needs and wants. If our national industrial policies were directed to helping these our fellow citizens so that their undeniable wants became effective economic demands, there would be plenty of domestic business to keep U.S. industry fully occupied and highly profitable.

THE HERITAGE OF SMOOT–HAWLEY

The skeleton in the protective closet is the Smoot–Hawley Tariff (technically the Hawley–Smoot Tariff, but easier to make fun of the other way), sponsored by reactionary Republicans in 1930 and ever after blamed by junior-high-school civics textbooks for the Great Depression, the rise of fascism, and innumerable minor irritations. The analysis doesn't rise even to the level of *post hoc, ergo propter hoc*, for the Great Depression was already well under way when Smoot–Hawley was passed, while fascism had been in power in Italy for eight years and was rapidly growing in Germany, and the military was firmly in charge in Japan.

At the time of Smoot–Hawley, international trade, especially American international trade, was relatively unimportant. In the boom year of 1929, United States exports totaled $5 billion and imports $4.1 billion. GNP was $103.1 billion. The net export-import effect in that year was $0.9 billion. By the depression year 1932, exports had fallen to $1.6 billion, imports to $1.3 billion, and GNP to $58.0 billion. Although the net export-import effect had fallen to $0.3 billion, it was still positive, a situation that scarcely obtains today. From 1929 to 1932, GNP fell $45.1 billion and net foreign trade fell $0.6 billion. It is preposterous to claim that the fall in foreign trade caused the Great Depression; whatever causation there was surely ran the other way.

Frank Taussig, author of a leading economics textbook of that day and an organizer of a statement signed by 1,028 economists opposing Smoot–Hawley, later published *The Tariff History of the United States*, in which he wrote, "Regarded as whole, the act of 1930 must be characterized as futile. The new duties on manufactured goods were mostly of a petty sort; most noticeably in such schedules as the cotton, silk, chinaware schedules. This or that article was more heavily taxed, and doubtless some domestic producers got an advantage. On the important branches of these industries the protective system had already been carried so far that no considerable further displacement of imports could be expected."[11]

What was the fuss all about? No one needs to pretend that Smoot–Hawley was a wise law in every respect, or in any respect; at the same time, it is contrary to fact to claim that it made a decisive difference.

A high percentage of foreign trade merely distorts economies everywhere, to the principal benefit of the bankers who finance the transactions. There are certainly many things we want or need to import—oil (because we are too witless to cope with our energy requirements), tungsten, chrome, bauxite, coffee—and there are many things we can, without special government assistance, export to pay for them. But the necessity, or even the desirability, of foreign trade has been grossly oversold.

Much of the concern for foreign trade follows from its place in the calculation of the gross national product. Since imports are a negative factor in such calculations and exports a positive factor, it seems obvious that the way to increase our GNP—and presumably our standard of living—is to increase our exports and decrease our imports. Our future prosperity will depend upon our ability to compete in the new global economy everyone talks about. We must do all in our power to improve our products and lower our prices. We must improve our educational system and retrain our workers—and so on.

Generally overlooked, especially by the IMF and the so-called "Washington concensus," are the facts that not all nations can simultaneously run export surpluses, just as not all the children of Lake

---

11. Taussig, *Tariff History*, p. 519.

Wobegone can truly be above average; that no nation can satisfy most of its needs by forever running large deficits, without slipping into stagnation like Imperial Spain; and that foreign trade is never the most important aspect of the economy of any nation larger than a city-state. Mathematically, of course, when a nation's exports and imports are in perfect balance, its GNP is neither increased nor decreased.

Trade is one of the modes of civilization. Trade also adds to wealth—the wealth of individuals, of nations, of the world. It does this by increasing and rationalizing employment, for wealth is the product of work. When trade expands employment for both partners, the prosperity of both is advanced. Conversely, when trade brings about unemployment for one of the partners, its advantage disappears. Trade will usually result in some unemployment in a competitive situation, and the unemployment will be compounded where the competition is based on gross wage differentials.

Microeconomically—that is, company by company—foreign trade can be attractive. Once a company is successful in its home market—factories built and paid for, experience gained—it takes little extra effort to open an export business, and economies of scale will make that business extraordinarily profitable, especially when stimulated by tax incentives.

When we shift from microeconomics to macroeconomics—from firm to nation—we find the fallacy of composition again. What is good for each firm individually is not necessarily good for the nation. In the circumstances we have been discussing, some (not all) American exports are being paid for by us in the shape of high interest rates that inordinately benefit a few, and we will doubtless bear the further cost of rescuing banks in danger of failing. On the other side, some (not all) American imports are being paid for by individual citizens in the shape of their shattered prospects and hopeless poverty.

These outcomes are not divinely ordained. They are the result of policies deliberately, albeit perhaps blindly, adopted. Rational policies would be in the direction of that millennial day when the world standard of living is uniformly high and trade can be uniformly free.

In the meantime, one would not select extractive industries for protection, because in general our commonwealth will be the stronger the more of our natural resources remain for future use. For similar reasons, it would be prudent to be especially attentive to strategic industries; it would be foolish to allow the steel industry to collapse, regardless of how much cheaper imports might be. Whatever the market may be, it is not a proper judge of national interest.

INTERNATIONAL FINANCE

International trade, of course, requires a system whereby an American merchant, for example, can exchange dollars for yen in order to buy Japanese goods to sell in the United States. Or vice versa. Since 1973 there has been no system: international exchange rates have been afloat. Gold as an international standard failed in the Great Depression because in nation after nation it had failed internally, mainly because there was not enough of it, and because, after all, in a central banking system it was just another, and less convenient, form of fiat money. After World War II, the Bretton Woods Agreement still used gold as the settlement of last resort, and again there was not enough of it.

The United States, which had supported Europe with the Marshall Plan and was continuing to invest in Europe's rehabilitation, found its gold supply—Fort Knox and all—dwindling. Economists argued that the invisible hand would work internationally as well as nationally to provide the most efficient allocation of resources and effort. They have been proved right: laissez faire works as badly internationally as intranationally.

It took more than twenty years for substantial trouble to develop. Exporters and importers gradually found themselves making—or losing—more money on the international money exchange than in selling or buying goods. Speculators increasingly saw that international trade in actual goods was no more necessary to speculating than production and sale of actual goods is necessary to wealth on Wall Street or in Silicon Valley.

In 1967 speculators reaped a billion dollars by betting that the United Kingdom could be forced to devalue the pound. Then in 1997, less than a year after the World Bank had acclaimed the "Southeast Asian Miracle," the Southeast Asian debacle began in Thailand. Crisis followed crisis in Russia, Brazil, Argentina, Chile. "By April 1998, global foreign exchange transactions had reached an estimated $1.5 trillion *per day* (Bank for International Settlements, 1998), enough to finance all the merchandise imports in the world for *three entire months*."[12] In other words, there was at least ninety times as much money churning the international money exchanges as was needed to finance international trade. The tail wagged the dog very roughly.

In the Mexican peso crisis of 1994 it took the United States Treasury several weeks to put together a package to save the peso and the international bondholders. In 1998, the Federal Reserve put together a committee of bankers and brokers and speculators to save a private speculative fund that was on the verge of a failure so massive that it threatened to drag a large part of the American economy, as well as several foreign banks, down with it. And this despite having two directors who had won the Nobel Memorial Prize in Economics for their studies purporting to show how the risks of such funds should be managed.

Since the so-called "Washington consensus" of bankers, brokers, and conventional economists seems to see nothing alarming in these events, we are doubtless fated to experience many more of them before we take action to bring international finance under rational

---

12. Blecker, *Global Finance*, p. 2.

control. The World Trade Organization is now (2001) more likely to allow dolphin-liberating tuna nets than it is to upset the sensibilities of international speculators.

OUR NEED FOR OUR FELLOW CITIZENS

Since we make exceptions to alleged economic laws in order to protect ourselves militarily, it is logically perverse to refuse even to consider other exceptions in order to protect also the morale and well-being of our fellow citizens and of ourselves. Indeed, that is why we have a nation—and why we have international trade.

It is morally wrong for me as an individual or for the citizens of this nation or any nation to pursue private pleasure at the expense of our fellow citizens. I have no need for a state-of-the-art sports car or a state-of-the-style sports shirt, but I do have a moral need for my fellow citizens. They have a right to make a contribution to the common wealth. As we have said, this right is as absolute as the nation's right to hold them to obedience to the laws. Before we pursue policies that deny citizens that right, we have a duty to guarantee that they will have an actual opportunity to make an equivalent contribution in another way. This duty is not satisfied by colorful references to sunset industries or hoped-for results from research and development that someone may be undertaking at some unspecified time. This duty is not satisfied by vague programs, even if well funded (which they never are), to retrain people for new jobs that don't exist. This duty can only be satisfied with alternatives that are specific, actual, and at least equivalent. And time is of the essence. In the long run, we are all dead.

Since such alternatives are exceedingly unlikely—at least no one has ever bothered to name one—we have a duty to protect our fellow citizens by restricting our participation in foreign trade, even if it means forgoing an extra sports shirt or a better sports car.

By exploiting their cheap labor to produce things for export to the developed nations, the developing nations condemn themselves to a neo-colonial status.

By encouraging this sort of exploitation, the developed nations condemn themselves to the stagnation and decay that has been the fate of all imperialisms the world has yet seen.

16

THE "LAW" OF COMPARATIVE ADVANTAGE

The figures Ricardo used in his example of comparative advantage were, of course, merely illustrative suppositions. No one has ever claimed anything more for them, nor, so far as I know, has anyone made even a casual study of the outcomes to be expected from different suppositions. John Stuart Mill credits his father, James, with having noticed as early as 1821 that what I shall call Cases 3 and 4 are not to the advantage of both countries, although he seems not to have seen that they are to the definite disadvantage of one;[1] and many have been aware that Ricardo's theory will not work at all if Portugal is supposed to specialize in cloth instead of wine; but these observations somehow have not aroused curiosity about other possibilities.

In fact, there are eight different possible cases, which are set forth in Table 1. Within each country it may be supposed that productivities are homogeneous (that is, that it takes as many man-years to produce a unit of cloth as to produce a unit of wine), or the produc-

1. Mill, *Principles*, bk. 3, chap. 17, sec. 2.

tivities may be supposed to be heterogeneous. Between the countries, the productivity of each industry may be homogeneous or heterogeneous. Moreover, when productivities are heterogeneous within each country, they may be parallel between the countries, that is, the productivity of the English cloth industry may be to the productivity of the English wine industry the same as the productivity of the Portuguese cloth industry is to the productivity of the Portuguese wine industry. We shall have occasion to doubt the meaning of productivity, but for the moment we can be satisfied that the table will stand, whatever definition (if any) we adopt, and whatever the actual figures may be. Actual figures that fit Case 1 will always be advantageous for both countries and for the world, just as Ricardo said, although, of course, the degrees of the advantages may be larger or smaller. Likewise, figures that fit Case 2 will always be disadvantageous for both countries and for the world, and the degree of disadvantage may be very large or infinitesimally small.

There is one other case—autarky—which is not included in the table, because it is the case of no international trade at all. It may nevertheless serve as the control with which the results of the other cases may be compared. Under autarky, both England and Portugal will produce one unit of cloth and one of wine, or (since the units are of equal value) two units of goods, for an international total of four. Thus any case that yields a total output greater than four units is advantageous for world output. In the same way, any case that yields an output greater than two units for either country is advantageous for that country.

It should be emphasized that all the cases are Ricardian in shape. Neither economies of scale, nor diminishing returns, nor transaction costs, nor tariffs, nor subsidies, nor the wastefulness of abandoning going concerns, nor the expenses and uncertainties of the passage of time, nor the consequences for individuals will be considered. All are assumed away. Furthermore, the table requires none of the more fundamental assumptions of the various schools of theory, such as whether economic agents maximize profits, or money is an illusion, or goods

Table 1

POSSIBLE CASES OF COMPARATIVE ADVANTAGE

Country	*Cloth*	*Wine*	*Speciality*	*Product per man*	*Total men*	*Units of national product*	*Units of total product*
			CASE 1 (*Ricardo's*)				
England	100	120	cloth	1/100	220	2.2	
Portugal	90	80	wool	1/80	170	2.125	4.325
			CASE 2 (*Ricardo Reversed*)				
England	100	120	wool	1/120	220	1.833	
Portugal	90	80	cloth	1/90	170	1.889	3.722
			CASE 3 (*Parallel Productivities*)				
England	100	120	cloth	1/100	220	2.2	
Portugal	90	108	wool	1/108	198	1.833	4.033
			CASE 4 (*Case 3 Reversed*)				
England	100	120	wool	1/120	220	1.833	
Portugal	90	108	cloth	1/90	198	2.2	4.033
			CASE 5 (*Countries Separately Homogeneous*)				
England	100	100	cloth-wool	1/100	200	2	
Portugal	90	90	wool-cloth	1/90	180	2	4.0
			CASE 6 (*Both Homogeneous and Identical*)				
England	100	100	cloth-wool	1/100	200	2	
Portugal	100	100	wool-cloth	1/100	200	2	4.0
			CASE 7 (*One Homogeneous, One Not*)				
England	100	100	cloth	1/100	200	2	
Portugal	90	80	wool	1/80	170	2.125	4.125
			CASE 8 (*Case 7 Reversed*)				
England	100	100	wool	1/100	200	2	
Portugal	90	80	cloth	1/90	170	1.889	3.889

Table 2

CASES CLASSIFIED ACCORDING TO CONTRIBUTION TO WORLD OUTPUT

4 cases advantageous for total (1, 3, 4, 7)
2 cases indifferent for total (5, 6)
2 cases disadvantageous for total (2, 8)

Table 3

CASES CLASSIFIED ACCORDING TO CONTRIBUTION TO NATIONAL OUTPUT

1 case advantageous for both nations (1)
1 case advantageous for one, indifferent for other (7)
2 cases advantageous for one, disadvantageous for other (3, 4)
2 cases indifferent for both (5, 6)
1 case indifferent for one, disadvantageous for other (8)
1 case disadvantageous for both (2)

are grossly substitutable, or commodities are or are not finite in number. What we have may be called the pure theory of comparative advantage.

The results of Table 1 are summarized in Table 2 and Table 3. Ricardo's "law" turns out to consist mostly of exceptions. Of the eight possibilities, only one is as advertised (advantageous for both trading partners), and only four result in a net gain for world output. Perhaps more significant: Only half of the cases are in any respect better than autarky for even one of the partners. Regardless of what we have repeatedly been told, it simply is not true that international trade is invariably desirable for all concerned. It would, in all conscience, be astonishing if it were. After all, intranational trade isn't invariably desirable for all concerned. Why should international trade be exempt from the heartache and the thousand natural shocks that domestic business is heir to?

TESTING RICARDO

What makes Ricardo so important here is that he offered an economic law that seemed to prove it against a nation's interest to interfere with foreign trade. This law (as proposed or as amended) has seemed to Paul Samuelson an example, perhaps the only example, of "a proposition in all the social sciences which is both true and nontrivial."[2]

If this is so, we must be struck by the profession's lack of interest in testing Ricardo's ability to explain empirical data. He published his book in 1817, but it was not until 1951 that a serious attempt was made to find confirmation of his law. The attempt was made by G. D. A. MacDougal of Oxford, who published his results in two issues of *Economic Journal*.

In point of fact, regardless of his intentions, MacDougal did not address the Ricardian theory at all. He set out to study British trade with the United States, but the two countries are not substantial trading partners in the products of the industries MacDougal studied. He therefore decided to compare the trade of these countries with the rest of the world instead of their trade with each other. Consequently what is presented as an empirical test of Ricardo is rather an answer to the question of whether the rest of the world prefers American to British goods when American goods are cheaper.

---

2. Balogh, *The Irrelevance of Conventional Economics*, p. 244.

Not surprisingly, the answer to this question was found to be generally affirmative. MacDougal wrote, "Before the war, American weekly wages in manufacturing were roughly double the British, and we find that, where American output per worker was more than twice the British, the United States had in general the bulk of the export market, while for products where it was less than twice as high, the bulk of the market was held by the British."[3]

This finding is surely plausible, but it is not Ricardian.

Though understood by the profession to be a scientific proposition, Ricardo's law had to wait 134 years for an extensive test. This test was, in fact, a test of a quite different proposition, and in the half century since MacDougal, no one seems to have bothered to redo the test or undertake another as ambitious. This is odd behavior for a discipline that claims to be a science. One can scarcely imagine a proposition in physics being taught as a law for 134 years before anyone seriously tried to test it. Nor can one imagine it still taught as a law when the test was of an only superficially similar proposition. Nor in one's wildest nightmare can one imagine this still untested proposition used to design a structure on which the livelihoods of literally billions of people may depend. An engineer who proposed to build on such a basis would be treated as a madman and locked up as a threat to humanity.

TESTING HECKSCHER–OHLIN

What the textbooks call the Heckscher–Ohlin Theorem is usually described as another modification of Ricardo. The Swedish economist Eli F. Heckscher presented it in a journal article in 1919 as follows: "The prerequisites for initiating international trade may thus be sum-

3. MacDougal, "British and American Exports: A Study Suggested by the theory of Comparative Costs," pp. 697–98.

marized as *different relative scarcity, i.e., different relative prices of the factors of production in the exchanging countries* as well as *different proportions between the factors of production in different commodities*."[4]

In 1933 Heckscher's student Bertil Ohlin developed the theory in a book entitled *Interregional and International Trade*. As his title suggests, he saw the factor-proportion theory as an elaboration of location theory. He wrote, "It is important to note that our interregional analysis applies to domestic as well as to international trade."[5] This being so, their theory is no more an overriding argument for foreign trade than is the law of supply and demand.

And even if it were, it is evidently unreliable, if not false. Heckscher–Ohlin didn't have to wait so long as Ricardo for a test; but when it came, it was devastating. After his painstaking analysis of America's 1947 foreign trade, Wassily Leontief concluded, "The widely held opinion that—as compared with the rest of the world—the United States economy is characterized by a relative surplus of capital and a relative shortage of labor proves to be wrong. As a matter of fact, the opposite is true."[6] From this he made a surprising inference: "In other words, a more rapid rise in our average productive investment per worker would diminish rather than increase the advantage derived by the United States from its foreign trade. . . . This signifies, of course, a reduced incentive to the continued exchange of commodities and services between the United States and the rest of the world."[7]

Psychologists say that the first step in mastering a fear is being able to name it. This the economics profession now did. The inconvenient results of Leontief's work were dubbed Leontief's Paradox—in capital letters. The choice of name was a stroke of genius. Had a more

4. Heckscher, "Foreign Trade," p. 278.
5. Ohlin, *Interregional and International Trade*, p. 159.
6. Leontief, *Input-Output Economics*, p. 86.
7. Ibid., p. 98.

accurate name, such as Leontief's Refutation, been chosen, what has developed into an entire new subprofession would have been stopped ere it began.

WHY RICARDO?

One may surmise that acceptance of Ricardo's theory among scholars has been stimulated by delighted surprise. When one first hears of it, it certainly seems improbable that, in Samuelson's words, "trade is mutually profitable even when one country is absolutely more or less productive in terms of every commodity."[8] How charming to find the implausible made plausible by Ricardo's fortuitous example of Case 1! How congenial to a scholar's passion for hidden truths!

More cynically, one may speculate that men and women of affairs have been attracted to the scheme by the pseudoscientific excuse it provides for a jolly round of labor bashing.

International trade has its uses. Mill put it as well as anyone: "It is hardly possible to overrate the value, in the present low state of human improvement, of placing human beings in contact with persons dissimilar to themselves, and with modes of thought and action unlike those with which they are familiar."[9] One may accept Mill's judgment here and still consider, on their separate and proper merits, proposals to restrict or reorganize international trade.

It is ironical that conventional economics, based as it is on the notion of self-interest, should be so vehement in its insistence that self-protection is invariably reprehensible.

---

8. Balogh, *Irrelevance*, p. 244.
9. Mill, *Principles*, bk. 3, chap. 17, sec. 2.

17

General Equilibrium

A fundamental doctrine of both classical and neoclassical economics is that the economy tends toward an equilibrium, which is described in various ways. Adam Smith's "natural price" is an equilibrium because whenever a quoted price is too high, competing producers will rush to increase the supply and thus force the price down, while whenever the price is too low, suppliers will leave the business, whereupon competing consumers will bid the price up. Similar equilibriums are said to control the interest rate, unemployment, international trade, and indeed every aspect of the economy. A frequently advanced corollary of these propositions is that it is a mistake to interfere with "natural" economic processes.

A somewhat different theory describes equilibrium as an optimum growth path for the economy, which steadily moves upward because saving, investment, production, and consumption are in proper balance. Another, advanced by Frank Hahn and Edmund S. Phelps, makes equilibrium an at least partially psychological state in which the expectations of economic agents are generally satisfied, so that they continue doing what they have been doing.[1]

The long effort to reduce economics to mathematics has understandably reinforced the interest in equilibriums. Since a mathematical equation is itself in equilibrium and achieves its powerful results by continuing in equilibrium, its conclusion will necessarily be in equilibrium.

Philip Mirowski argues that the historical choice of a metaphor for economics has predisposed the neoclassicals to equilibrium. "In pre-entropic physics," Mirowski writes, "all physical phenomena are variegated manifestations of a protean energy which is fully and reversibly transformed from one state to another. When this idea was transported into the context of economic theory, it dictated that all economic goods were fully and reversibly transformed into utility, and thus into all other goods through the intermediacy of the act of trade."[2]

A convenient statement of general equilibrium analysis is *Theory of Value: An Axiomatic Analysis of Economic Equilibrium*, by Gerard Debreu. This little book is now more than forty years old, and a vast

---

1. Hahn, *Equilibrium and Macroeconomics*, p. 24ff; Phelps, *Political Economy*, p. 60ff.

2. Mirowski, *The Reconstruction of Economic Theory*, p. 189. See also Mirowski, *Against Mechanism*, esp. chaps. 1 and 6, and Greg Davidson and Paul Davidson, *Economics for a Civilized Society*, pp. 56–59. For a contrary view, that the "conceptual devices" of economics "embody nothing but habits of the human mind that are as general as ordinary logic," and "may be traced to zoology rather than mechanics," see Schumpeter, *History*, p. 965.

Ecology also has struggled to model itself on classical mechanics. Nature has been assumed to be "naturally" in a state of equilibrium, to which it eventually returns whenever disturbed. A symposium at the 1990 annual meeting of the Ecological Society of America raised doubts about the assumption. Dr. S. T. A. Pickett of the New York Botanical Garden said it "makes nice poetry, but it's not such great science" (*New York Times*, July 31, 1990, p. C1).

Lewis Thomas makes a similar point in *The Lives of a Cell*, p. 145: "To stay alive, you have to be able to hold out against equilibrium, maintain imbalance, bank against entropy, and you can only transact this business with membranes in our kind of world."

amount of work has been done since it was first published.[3] Nevertheless, it remains a canonical book in the field, and its assumptions or axioms are still largely those of its successors, as they were of its predecessors.

"COMMODITY" DEFINED

Debreu begins with the definition of "commodity." He writes, "Summing up, a commodity is a good or service completely specified physically, temporally, and spatially."[4]

To avoid a possible misunderstanding, let it be emphasized that physical, temporal, and spatial specifications will enable us to distinguish one commodity from another. No matter how complete, they do not define "commodity," nor, I think, does Debreu intend them to.

Any thing whatever can be physically described and exists, has existed, or will exist at a time and place. So far, a thing is merely that—a thing. It is not a commodity. A rainy low-pressure area such as now exists in our part of the country is not a commodity, nor is the chipmunk that used to be in our backyard, nor the trash in our cellar, nor the second joint of the third finger on my left hand; yet each of these objects may be physically described and exists or existed at a time and place. As objects so specified, they are in the domain of physics, and the laws that govern them are physical laws, not economic laws, whatever the latter may be.

The specifications, in short, are no part of a definition. For that, Debreu leaves us with a synonym: "a commodity is a good or service." He does not attempt to define either "good" or "service." Instead, he gives us many examples of each, ranging from No. 2 Red Winter Wheat

---

3. See Weintraub, *General Equilibrium Analysis*.
4. Debreu, *Theory of Value*, p. 32.

available in Chicago a year from now to oil fields, and from the labor of a coal miner to transportation facilities. The examples are introduced to show how the goods and services fit into the price system.

Debreu makes the point that "wheat available now and wheat available in a week play entirely different economic roles for a flour mill which is to use them."[5] On similar reasoning, the farmer planting wheat today is economically different from the farmer selling wheat some months later, the mill buying wheat today is economically different from the same mill next week, and the consumer eating bread today is economically different from the same fellow tomorrow. Such fragmentation is easy; but unless commodities, mills, and people can be put back together again, it is impossible to reason about such entirely isolated things and people. How can we call them the same on different dates?

We call them the same because we or they say they are. Agents hold themselves together by acts of will, that is, by doing something. Every doing has consequences and requires further action. The farmers declare that they will grow this kind of wheat instead of something else; the mill proprietors declare that they are in the business of milling certain flour; and the consumers declare that they live, at least to a degree, by bread. It is because of these declarations that No. 2 Red Winter Wheat is defined as it is. Of all the myriad possible physical specifications, only certain ones are relevant, and the relevance is determined by the growers', users', and consumers' acts of will. Without such acts, No. 2 Red Winter Wheat could not be distinguished from other types of wheat, from other vegetables, or even from other things, and it certainly could not be classified as a commodity.

It is, of course, impossible to define all the words that one uses. Schoolchildren learn, from their first introduction to a dictionary, that one word leads to another. Fundamental terms (and, actually, all

---

5. Ibid., p. 29.

terms) are defined as they are used, as they function. They have meaning because they have previously been used and understood and acted upon, and that meaning is progressively clarified (or confused) as they are used.

Nevertheless, it would have been possible to be clearer at the beginning than Debreu has been, for "good" and "service" have been around for a long time and have disclosed some of the difficulties of some of their uses. Thus many schools of economics start with Robinson Crusoe and his old nanny goat; he is said to weigh opportunity costs as he ponders whether to make a coat out of her. If poor Robinson is an economic agent (for my part, I'd deny that he is because he has no trading partners), the possible goods he has to choose among are, for all practical purposes, infinite. The difficulty is not merely that he has to decide whether to lie in the sun or to stroll to the other end of his island in search of a succulent berry. It is not merely that he faces decisions and decisions, that his indifference curves seem beyond number. The difficulty is not that he can't, as a practical matter, complete the counting of possible goods and services, but that he doesn't know where to begin—what to count and especially what not to, and how to avoid overlooking something or counting the same thing several times.[6]

Let me emphasize the point, for it is crucial. For example, how many *things* is the word processor I'm pecking away at? Well, it is one *processor*; it is also several hundred *parts* named or numbered in the manufacturer's parts list; it is several dozens of chemical *elements*, millions of *molecules*, multibillions of *electrons*; it is several *old* things, several *new* things (because it was repaired last week), several *blue* things, several *truly* square things, and it is a thing that stands in certain *relations* to other things in its environs. These classifications obviously overlap; each part appears both in its own right and as a part of many wholes. The same electron might turn out to be counted almost as many times

6. Miller, *Midworld*, pp. 173–75.

as we have classifications. More important, in order to count electrons or molecules or elements or processors at all, we must specify that these specially classified and defined things are to be counted. Pointing to the things to be counted—ostensive definition—will not do, because it's not clear whether one is pointing to a key or to an electron. We might reasonably decide to exclude electrons from our tally. Or we might not. Whatever we decide, we can no longer pretend to be counting *things* as such. We are counting the *sorts* of things we have decided to count; and unless we make some decision, we can't count at all.

"AVAILABLE" DEFINED

At this point, Debreu's explicit assumption, stated immediately after his definition of commodity and reiterated several times throughout his book, looms large: "It is assumed that there is only a finite number *l* of distinguishable commodities." Robinson Crusoe would have found the assumption false. The situation is no different in our teeming cities if goods and services are merely what give utility or pleasure. Even on a city street, one may amuse oneself by taking a soccer kick at a loose stone, as Robinson might have derived pleasure from the most unlikely and nondescript stone if, when he idly kicked it, he recalled some game played in his youth.

The issue obviously must be shifted out of the domain of psychology, and this Debreu does. He writes, "What is made available *to* an economic agent is called an *input* for him; what is made available *by* an economic agent is an *output* for him."[7] Although he is not explicit on this point, I think we may understand that all commodities are inputs or outputs. Thus only goods and services that are available are subject to his equations.

---

7. Debreu, *Theory of Value*, p. 30.

We may, however, wonder precisely what Debreu means by "available." In ordinary usage, all the goods in a mail-order catalog are available to me. If I ask the mail-order company, the reply will be, yes, they are available. And not only to me, but to virtually everyone in the United States or Canada or (the company would like to boast) the whole world. Each item is thus an input to each one of the five or more billion of us, *whether we buy or not*. Even if the company were the only entity that makes things available, the number of inputs and output becomes an absurd and meaningless figure. The meaning of input and output must be limited in some way; otherwise we shall be in the quandary of not knowing what is *not* an input or output and consequently of not being able to determine what *are* inputs or outputs.

A limitation that suggests itself defines inputs and outputs as exchanges that are actually made or contracted for. J. R. Hicks puts it this way: "An input is merely something which is bought for the enterprise; an output something which is sold."[8] At whatever point in time we choose to count them, actual exchanges are clearly finite in number, and so commodities are finite in number. Every actual exchange is a balance of inputs and outputs. Whatever the number of exchanges at a given time, the inputs and outputs are in balance, severally and collectively. They could not be otherwise. What is an input to me must be an output for someone else. Such a balance cannot even be disturbed, because every modification of one side entails an exactly coequal and coincident modification of the other side.

A similar conclusion is reached when we follow Debreu and direct our attention to producers (who produce outputs) and consumers (who consume inputs). He writes that given "the production possibilities of the whole economy"[9] and the price system, a producer "chooses his production . . . so as to maximize his profit. The resulting action is called an equilibrium production of the . . . producer relative to [the

---

8. Hicks, *Value and Capital*, p. 193.
9. Debreu, *Theory of Value*, p. 38.

price system]."[10] We may call Debreu's equilibrium production a micro-equilibrium. Every producer achieves it by definition. This is what producers do. They maximize profits, which means that they can't do any better than they actually do, which means that they have no reason to do anything different from what they do, which means that they are in an equilibrium state, and an optimum equilibrium at that.

This micro-equilibrium is finite. It depends on the producer's selling his products (or his company), because otherwise there are no profits. Like any action, selling is finite. It is done here, not there; now, not then; at this price, not at some other; in this quantity, not more or less. Thus it is the actual selling that achieves equilibrium production, deals in a finite number of commodities, and at least partially satisfies Debreu's assumption.

It is not surprising that the actions of the consumer are a mirror image of those of the producer. Given the price system, the consumer seeks "utility maximization," subject to the constraint imposed by his wealth. "The resulting action is called an equilibrium consumption of the . . . consumer relative to [the price system and wealth distribution]."[11] Regardless of whether his wealth is great or small, a consumer will maximize no utility unless he actually buys something with his wealth. Again we have a micro-equilibrium that is dependent upon finite activity in the marketplace.

EQUILIBRIUM BECOMES INEVITABLE

As a matter of common introspection, everyone—or almost everyone—is aware of occasions when, as Browning said of spiritual aspirations, a man's reach exceeds his grasp. Adam Smith spoke of a

10. Ibid., p. 43.
11. Ibid., p. 62.

distinction between absolute demand and effectual demand. A similar idea appears in Debreu as excess demand, which "describes the excess of the net demand of all agents over the total resources."[12]

It will be easily seen that the problem of defining total resources is merely an extension of the problem of defining commodity. As Debreu says, "The *total resources* of an economy are the *a priori given* quantities of commodities that are made available to (or by) its agents."[13] As we have seen, a finite number of commodities is defined only in the moment of being actually exchanged; and only in the same moment (whatever it is) can the total of resources be calculated.

But if commodities and resources are finite, it is not clear what Debreu means by net demand. Cases of market failure are all too common. Not enough bread was available on the eve of the French Revolution, nor enough gasoline when OPEC had its early success. Here we had what might be called excess microdemand. Excess microsupply is familiar, too. A publisher prints more copies of a novel than it can sell, and it is sadly true that many writers scribble more manuscripts than ever are published. Excess microsupply is the same as deficient microdemand.

We seem now in a position to calculate "the excess of the net demand of all agents." We simply add all the excess microdemands and subtract from their total the deficient microdemands; the result should be net excess (or, possibly, deficient) macrodemand. But what do we have when we subtract deficient demand for a novel from excess demand for gasoline? Plainly, the exercise is nonsense. Excess microdemand and deficient microdemand are incommensurable; they do not net out, nor can even various excess (or deficient) demands be added together. Net macrodemand cannot be determined unless it is understood to be the same as the demand actually satisfied by the exchanges actually made—in which case the modifier "net" is irrelevant.

---

12. Ibid., p. 75.
13. Ibid., p. 74.

There is a much more serious consequence. Debreu's equation for what he calls market equilibrium is as follows: "[T]he net demand must equal the total resources."[14] But this always happens if both net demand and total resources are defined by the exchanges actually made. They are identical by definition. Say's law has been resurrected in a new form: Production and demand have created each other. Since Debreu's proof of the possibility of general equilibrium depends on the equation for market equilibrium,[15] the possibility becomes an inevitability. Since equilibrium is inevitable, all economies are perfectly efficient, and there is nothing to be done about them.

SAMUELSON'S DEAD END

Paul Samuelson reaches a dead end and even more abruptly. He writes, "Within the framework of any system, the relationships between our variables are strictly those of mutual interdependence. It is sterile and misleading to speak of one variable as causing or determining another. Once the conditions of equilibrium are imposed, all variables are simultaneously determined."[16]

"Once the conditions of equilibrium are imposed," all the variables become like the notorious arrow in the paradox of Zeno of Elea, which cannot move because it is where it is and not somewhere else. We begin to solve Zeno's paradox, not by peeking at the "real" world and observing that, as St. Sebastian discovered to his anguish, arrows do move, but by inquiring how the mid-flight arrow, which cannot move, got where it is, and how Samuelson's variables, which have equilibrium imposed on them, got to their pre-equilibrium state.

If causation is ruled out, it is not clear what mutual interdepen-

---

14. Ibid., p. 76.
15. Ibid., p. 76ff.
16. Samuelson, *Foundations*, p. 9.

dence can mean. If one exerts a downward force on one end of a balance beam, one expects the other end to rise. The downward force has caused the upward rise. One may perhaps argue that both ends were passive, although interdependent, and that the force was an exogenous shock. But by definition, an exogenous shock has no place in a general equilibrium. If such an arrangement could be imagined, the exogenous shock would be a vastly more urgent subject of study than the alleged equilibrium, which would seem to be at its mercy.

Moreover, one may wonder how the variables that snap into the equilibrium can be identified and defined in the absence of causal order. Surely not by sense qualities or physical characteristics. Economics is not concerned with objects solely because they are of a certain color or of a certain specific gravity.

Samuelson mentions the demand function as one of his variables. While a function may not be an ordinary thing, it concerns ordinary things. *M.I.T. Dictionary of Modern Economics* tells us that the demand function is "An algebraic expression of the *demand schedule*," which is in turn defined as "A table showing the level of demand for a particular *good* at various levels of price of the good in question," whereupon we learn that goods are "Tangible *commodities* which contribute positively to *economic welfare*." And so on.

All this is perfectly understandable to anyone who has ever used a dictionary. Definition goes on forever. A more pregnant question is, How does it start? Evidently, we must start with ordinary things—things in the ordinary sense. A loaf of bread and a stone are distinguished and defined because one proposes to eat or to build a wall. If one tries to eat the stone, one will discover a causal relationship between the stone and one's teeth. And the bread is defined as edible because there is a causal relationship between it and human physiology. There are many other causal relationships—an infinity of them, in fact—and they are discovered as one actively does something, or tries to.

Definition thus starts with a purpose. The purpose presupposes an attempt at execution. The attempt presupposes the possibility of success. The possibility presupposes an orderly universe, one in which a specific cause has a specific effect, not some other effect. Negation is necessary. If all events had the same effect, action would be meaningless.

If one proposes to bake a certain sort of bread, or at a certain time of year, one uses flour made from No. 2 Red Winter Wheat—*not* some other wheat, *not* rye, *not* sawdust, *not* ground glass—*because* No. 2 Red Winter Wheat is that ingredient that affects and is affected by specified other ingredients in such ways as to achieve the result it is one's purpose to achieve.

It is by one's purpose that one defines and distinguishes No. 2 Red Winter Wheat from other wheats and other things. If flour from any other wheat would serve one's purpose as well as No. 2 Red Winter Wheat, one would not make the distinction, but millers probably would, and farmers certainly would. If one were a manufacturer of fertilizer, one might define No. 2 Red Winter Wheat as a crop that responds properly to one's Brand A fertilizer, but not to Brands B or C. The taxonomic definition, abstract and pure though it is, is also not purposeless. Genera and species are not idly ordered.

Without purpose and the causal order on which it depends, the passive variables of Samuelson's equilibrium can be neither identified nor distinguished. They cannot be described or named. Attempting to describe or name them would be without purpose and without effect. They are by definition without cause and without consequence.[17] The alleged system itself and its alleged equilibrium become an unanalyzable blob of indescribable stuff, perhaps the original of Dr. Seuss's Oobleck, but actually not a thing that ever was.

If we grant Samuelson his equilibrium, everything he says follows. In equilibrium, there is no uncertainty. Aspects of the universe may be unknown, but the universe is complete, finished, and altogether in

---

17. Miller, *Definition of the Thing*, passim. Also, *Paradox of Cause*, pp. 11–18.

balance. Not one jot or tittle may be added or subtracted or changed. Previously unknown details may perhaps be stumbled upon, but this is doubtful, since none is identifiable. In any case, their discovery does not change the system.

In equilibrium there is nothing to explain, because nothing can be explained. Nor can anything be improved or even worsened. Equilibrium theory is laissez faire of economic thought as well as of economic action.

THE DILEMMA OF EQUILIBRIUM ANALYSIS

Debreu says several times, "It is assumed that there is only a finite number l of distinguishable commodities." He discusses his assumption only briefly in a note, where he says that it "has the great mathematical convenience of enabling one to stay within a finite-dimensional commodity space." He recognizes that unnamed "conceptual difficulties" ensue, and he adds that "many of the results of the following chapters can be extended to infinite-dimensional commodity spaces."[18]

Let us test the contrary assumption: that there is an infinite number of commodities. Intuitively this is just as plausible as Debreu's assumption, for everyone knows that the world is wondrous and various. If commodities are infinite in number, resources are infinite also; and no matter how great demand becomes, there are resources left over. Debreu's market equilibrium dissolves into a dew. Furthermore, regardless of how many resources are demanded and utilized, those not demanded are still infinite in number; so there is not even a way of saying that one state of an economy is more nearly in balance than another.

---

18. Debreu, *Theory of Value*, p. 35 n. 2.

Here we have a dilemma of general equilibrium analysis: If there is an infinite number of commodities, general equilibrium cannot even be described. But if there is a finite number of commodities, general equilibrium has at most the sterile consequence that it reasserts itself in some indeterminate way after an upset caused by some exogenous and hence unpredictable force or factor.

Given the price system (whatever it may be), equilibrium occurs at any given moment. But the price system is not given; it is not a datum. It is a *factum*, a deed, something done, something continuously being done, an actuality of our mores, morals, morale. It is our doing and our responsibility.

The most important part of any price system specifies the rewards a society aims at and the way it distributes the rewards among its members. The management of this distribution is the economic problem. There is no economic problem of proving an equilibrium.

EXCLUDED FROM EQUILIBRIUM ANALYSIS

In a note Debreu writes that among the phenomena his analysis does not cover are "increasing returns to scale."[19]

But modern mass production is founded on the rock of economies of scale. Expanding production generally makes possible the utilization of more—not less—efficient machines and processes; and large enterprises, by exploiting opportunities for the division of labor, are able to employ more specialized and more productive laborers. Progressive division of labor makes possible progressive expansion of the market; and as Allyn A. Young showed, the two leapfrog each other.[20]

Vilfredo Pareto, Walras's successor at the University of Lausanne, while discussing the "equilibrium of the producer," wrote, "[T]here

---

19. Debreu, *Theory of Value*, p. 49 n. 2.
20. Young, "Increasing Returns and Economic Progress," pp. 527–42.

are certain goods such that the quantity of B obtained per unit of A increases when the total quantity of A transformed increases. . . ." In these cases, "equilibrium takes place at terminal points." No further movement occurs, because competition is then "complete."[21] In short, enterprises exhibiting economies of scale are in equilibrium only in the moment of their extinction, or when they no longer achieve such economies.

The reason for this outcome was given by Knut Wicksell: "[I]f, in an enterprise which becomes more productive the larger the scale of operations, the labour and the land employed were both paid in accordance with the law of marginal productivity, then the sum of their shares would *exceed* the whole product, so that the entrepreneur would suffer a loss. . . . Under such conditions, equilibrium is impossible."[22]

Thus for Pareto and Wicksell, as for Walras before them and Debreu after them, the ideal or characteristic mode of modern enterprise is beyond the scope of equilibrium analysis.

The search for economies of scale is not the only essential aspect of the modern economy that Debreu excludes from his system. The full text of the note from which I have already quoted reads, "Three phenomena that the present analysis does not cover must be emphasized: (1) *external economies and diseconomies*, i.e., the case where the production set of a producer depends on the productions of other producers (and/or on the consumptions of consumers), (2) increasing returns to scale, (3) the behavior of producers who do not consider prices as given in choosing productions."[23]

In an earlier note he writes, "Two important and difficult questions are not answered by the approach taken here: the integration of money in the theory of value . . . , and the inclusion of invisible commodities."[24] And in another note he writes, "It must be emphasized that

---

21. Pareto, *Manual*, pp. 134–35.
22. Wicksell, *Lectures on Political Economy*, vol. 1, p. 128.
23. Debreu, *Theory of Value*, p. 49 n. 2.
24. Ibid., p. 36 n. 3.

the present analysis does not cover the case where the consumption set of a consumer and/or his preferences depend on the consumptions of the other consumers (and/or on the productions of producers)."[25]

A moment's reflection will reveal that the phenomena Debreu's analysis does not cover are phenomena we encounter every day in the world we live in. Take away these phenomena, and one must wonder what, then, becomes of economics.

ETHICS, HISTORY, AND ECONOMICS

Keynes uses the term "equilibrium" many times (the index of *The General Theory* lists eleven instances). The use that is most similar to current equilibrium theory use describes the actual rate of unemployment as an "intermediate position," below full employment and above starvation. Keynes does not, however, suggest that unemployment continues because of some mathematical or quasi-physical balancing factors in the economy. He is, he concludes, reporting "a fact of observation concerning the world as it is, not a necessary principle that cannot be changed."[26] The persistence of the condition he describes is due to a failure to change it. The failure, which I call a failure of will, is not unlike a failure of Keynesian animal spirits.

Such failure, whatever it may be called, should occasion no surprise. Even monetarists are familiar with a similar failure that may appear in the face of a lowered interest rate. It is well understood that the central bank cannot force borrowers to borrow, no matter how low the rate. A half-century ago it was observed that you can't push on a string, and much earlier than that, everyone knew that you can lead a horse to water but you can't make him drink. Even in the most oblig-

25. Ibid., p. 73 n. 6.
26. Keynes, *General Theory*, p. 254.

ing of times, monetarists expect the bank's maneuvers to require two years to have full effect.

In the same way, unemployed workers, no matter how low their wage demands, cannot force entrepreneurs to employ them. This is, indeed, the point at which unemployment is unquestionably involuntary, and where Keynes saw the classical theory breaking down. It breaks down not only in the failure of the economy to employ available labor, but also in the failure to employ available money and natural resources. The classical theory, which sees economics as a servo-mechanism of supply and demand, cannot explain these failures or even allow that they exist.

In the preface to *The General Theory*, Keynes refers to economics as one of the "moral sciences." Later, in a much-quoted passage, he writes: "If human nature felt no temptation to take a chance, no satisfaction (profit apart) in constructing a factory, a railway, a mine or a farm, there might not be much investment merely as a result of cold calculation."[27] Restating this observation in more clearly ethical terms, we see that an entrepreneur *wills* an enterprise's existence, *wills* its continuance, *wills* its policies and performance. An enterprise is not an act of nature or of God. Its policies are not determined by public law or by economic analysis. Failure to obey the law or to conform to the analysis may forestall the initiation or continuance of an enterprise, but the actual initiation and continuance are willful acts. No one is forced to be an entrepreneur.

Workers, investors, and customers are no less willful than entrepreneurs. No one is required to work, invest, or consume. No one is required to live. In order to live at all, one is required to act, to do something. What one does is what determines the sort of person one is. One determines to do a certain thing and becomes at least the sort of person who does or tries to do that sort of thing.

---

27. Ibid., p. 150.

Needless to say, the things one can do are limited. It is here that history enters ethics and economics. In my daydreams I fancy myself inspiring Congress with an eloquent State of the Union address. Or winning the World Series with an unassisted triple play after putting my team ahead with a grand slam home run in the top of the ninth. Or modestly receiving the adulation of Helen of Troy. But my daydreams are merely dreams. No one has ever suggested that I be even a candidate for a town council. Ring Lardner might have observed that, although I was weak at the plate, I couldn't field either. Helen of Troy was born three millennia too soon. Troilus makes the point to Cresida: "The desire is boundless, and the act a slave to limit."

Our actions are informed by history and limited by history. The past presents the present and its problems to us and makes our action both demanded and possible. We do not and could not start with a tabula rasa. There can be no mind without content, and no universe without unsolved problems and incompleted actions. As Keynes said, "we simply do not know" how these problems will be solved and these actions completed. We do not know, not because of a weakness of intellect, but because our freedom and our responsibility can occur only if the future is constitutionally unknowable. Had not Pandora slammed shut the lid of the casket, our knowledge of the future would have rendered the present—and the past—irrelevant, impossible to distinguish, and effectively nonexistent.

Economics is indeed a moral science. Ethics is historical. History is not the rutted road of path dependency or the lingering charge of hysteresis—notions that slip determinism in under pretense of casting it out. The persistence of the QWERTY keyboard is cited as an example of path dependency, yet the path of the Morse code was once the more deeply rutted. The dissimilar careers of the two systems can be explained, but the depth or length of the ruts has little to do with the case. Every path was once taken for the first time.

The difficulty is not in getting ethics and history into economics but in imagining or crediting an economics that tries to exclude them.

18

Productivity vs. Profitability

Public attention to the idea of productivity is scarcely two decades old. Early in his first term President Reagan appointed two different commissions to study the question. Meetings were held, but otherwise nothing was heard from one of the commissions, while the other published four slim pamphlets urging such frugalities as splitting the envelopes of incoming mail for use as scratch paper.

At the same time, the business press made much of the supposed superior attention to work of German and Japanese workers, their alleged loyalty to their employers, and their passion for saving. In contrast, Sonny Six-Pack was said to be too concerned with his fringe benefits and his working conditions and his plans for the weekend to do his job properly.

None of this, of course, had much to do with productivity as understood by economists, although the academic research program was such that the productivity index became the intellectual support of the fetish of downsizing, which has adversely affected the lives of millions of men and women and the fortunes of hundreds, if not thousands, of enterprises, and is thus one of the most powerful ideas of our time.

THE STRUCTURE OF THE INDEX

Productivity is defined as output per unit of input. The calculation can be made for the economy as a whole, for a particular industry or firm, or for an individual or a division or a special project within a firm.

In the United States, when one speaks of the productivity index, one means a complicated statistical construct whose results are published monthly by the Department of Labor's Bureau of Labor Statistics. In brief, each month the "real" gross domestic product of the business sector of the economy is divided by the hours worked by all persons "engaged" in the period, including the hours of proprietors and unpaid family members.

In the productivity index table, the data for a base period (currently 1992) are stated as 100, and the data for other periods (their index numbers) are given in relation to the base. The productivity figures discussed in the business press are usually the difference between the current year's productivity index number and the previous year's index number. It is important to note that the index number for a single period is meaningless; what matters is the comparison of one period with another or with a series of periods.

Despite all the complications, a productivity index number remains a fraction with output as the numerator and input as the denominator. As we learned in grade school, the value of any fraction can be increased by increasing the numerator (2/3 is greater than 1/3) or by decreasing the denominator (1/2 is also greater than 1/3). This arithmetic truth can obviously result in equivocal inferences from the index. Some will recommend increasing the output, and some will recommend downsizing the workforce ("hours worked"). The productivity index will not help us decide which is the better policy.

EXAMPLES OF "PRODUCTIVITY"

Still concentrating on productivity as a fraction, let's look at a few examples of how it works. First, consider what would happen to our national productivity if we managed to employ the roughly 4 percent of our workforce we currently keep unemployed (forgetting the millions of others not looking for work). Let's pretend that the bad rap on these people is justified, that they're incompetent in all the ways we've heard about, and that on the average they'd be able to add only a third as much to the gross domestic product as the average of those of us who are now employed. Even so, they'd add roughly 1.3 percent to our GDP.

We might think that increasing our domestic product would increase our productivity, but we'd be mistaken. If our present product is x, and our present "hours worked" is y, our present productivity is x/y. After we find jobs for our fellow citizens, our productivity becomes $1.013x/1.04y$ and has thus fallen 2.7 percent. So if the index were truly significant, we couldn't let these people work, which is a pity, because a 1.3 percent increase in GDP would have come to about $100 billion, which, as the late Senator Dirksen would have agreed, is real money. That's how "productivity" works macroeconomically.

Now let's see how "productivity" works microeconomically. Consider what happens to productivity when a journeyman carpenter increases his output 20 percent by taking on an unskilled apprentice gofer. As in the previous example, his original output is x, his "hours worked" is y, and his productivity is x/y. After he takes on the apprentice, their output is up, but their productivity becomes $1.2x/2y$, or $.6x/y$—a decrease of 40 percent.

For sport we may consider a young slugger who lived up to his promise by hitting a grand slam home run his first time at bat in the majors. His next time up, there were only two men on base, so his productivity-minded manager yanked him for a pinch hitter because (aside from drawing a base on balls or being hit by a pitch, neither of which would count as a time at bat) his productivity could only go down.

Then there was the unsung predecessor of Tiger Woods who made a hole in one on the first hole of a club tournament, but retired when his drive on the second hole stopped rolling two feet short of the cup.

"My productivity can only go down," he lamented as he gave his clubs to his caddy and took up water polo to sublimate his aggressions.

The conventional method of calculating productivity is plainly absurd. Are there other ways? Tinkering with the numerator will make no significant difference. It's all the same, whether output is stated in dollars of value added or utils of satisfaction or foot-pounds of work or numbers of doors hung. So long as the denominator is "hours worked," the consequence of hiring the apprentice will be a 40 percent drop in productivity.

Turning to the denominator, we see that "hours worked" is only superficially homogeneous and so is not a satisfactory unit anyhow. Marx thought himself justified in assuming "that the labour of the workman employed by the capitalist is unskilled average labour."[1] If this was a valid assumption in his day (and probably it wasn't), it certainly is not in ours. Our gofer apprentice would not know what to go for (and so could do no work) without supervision by the journeyman. Their skills are, as skills, incommensurable.

The problem is one of relating the different skills—the different kinds of hours worked—to each other and thus devising a truly homogeneous unit. As it happens, Keynes tried to solve the problem, although productivity in the modern sense was not an issue for him. Instead, he felt need for a "labour-unit" in his theory of employment. He wrote that "in so far as different grades and kinds of labour and salaried assistance enjoy a more or less fixed relative remuneration, the quantity of employment can be sufficiently defined for our purpose by taking an hour's employment of ordinary labour as our unit and weighting an hour's employment of special labour in proportion to its remuneration; i.e., an hour of special labour remunerated at double ordinary rates will count as two units."[2] Smith and Ricardo sought to solve similar problems in a similar manner.

---

1. Marx, *Capital*, p. 221.
2. Keynes, *General Theory*, p. 41.

Returning to the productivity problem, we see that if the ordinary money wage is, say, $8 an hour, this may indeed be a truly homogeneous unit, but it is merely a multiple of a homogeneous unit we already had ($1) and tells us nothing new. It does, however, transform the pretended productivity index into a cost ratio. Depending on our choice of factors, it will give us the labor cost per unit of output or per total output, which we may compare with the raw-materials cost or the interest cost or the advertising cost or any other cost that attracts our attention. We may compare our ratios from year to year or between our firm and our competitors.

Cost ratios like these can be valuable tools of business management and control, and we have met them before, in Chapter 3, under the heading of partial analysis. We saw that partial analysis may be valid in treating specific and limited problems, but powerless before a universal problem. And labor (especially when the labor of proprietors and unpaid family members is included) is a necessary factor of production, so large that it is, for all intents and purposes, universal.

Its universality, indeed, goes without saying, as in the currently fashionable argument that economic growth faster than 2.5 percent is unsustainable because our workforce is growing about 1 percent a year, and the productivity index grows, on the average, about 1.5 percent a year. We add them together, it is said, and that's the limit. As it happens, however, our gross domestic product (not "productivity") has grown at a faster rate than that every year for the past forty or more. T. C. Powers, in his fascinating empirical study *Leakage*, shows that in the absence of personal waste and saving, and governmental monetary and fiscal restraint, the growth of the economy since World War II could have been 13 percent per year.[3] In short, "productivity" is a poor guide to public policy.

---

3. Powers, *Leakage*, p. 190. See also Powers's conclusion: "Other than diurnal and seasonal cycles, there seem to be no natural economic cycles. Irregularities of performance are related to maldistribution of income." (p. 28).

PRODUCT VS. "PRODUCTIVITY"

From the point of view of the national economy, the question is, How great is the national product? When we ask this question, we see that every contribution, no matter little, no matter how clumsily produced, will swell the total. The influx of millions of relatively inexperienced women, African Americans, Hispanics, and young people into the labor force in recent decades was said, for a variety of invidious reasons, to have lowered the average competence of our labor force. No doubt the average was lowered. But the total product was raised. Productivity may have been down, but national output was up. As my grandmother used to say, every little bit added to what you've got makes a little bit more. The nation does not become stronger or richer by keeping any potential worker unemployed. The notion of productivity is macroeconomically irrelevant.

Microeconomically, from the point of view of the individual enterprise, the question is, How much does it cost to produce the product? When we ask this question, we see that, again, the notion of productivity is irrelevant. In our carpenter example, a contractor would not hesitate to hire a go-fer to assist the journeyman, provided the go-fer's wages did not exceed the value of the increased output. A sensible contractor would also explore other ways of reducing costs or increasing output. Perhaps the bottom line would be greater if the carpenter were supplied with better tools instead of more assistance. Perhaps the profit would be greater if a cheaper carpenter were found. Whatever the solution, our contractor will be concerned with money costs and money profits. Sales income will be compared with advertising costs, administrative costs, inventory costs, research costs, even postage costs—as well as with labor costs. The number of hours worked it takes to produce the product will be important or interesting only to the extent that it affects costs, and the effects will not always be in the same direction.

The weakness of the productivity idea was underlined by a recent announcement that two Japanese automobile assembly plants in the United States (Nissan and Toyota) had higher productivity ratings than any American manufacturer. But both Japanese plants lost money, while American competitors made money famously. It is obviously more important, at least in the world we live in, to be profitable than to be "productive."

PRODUCTIVITY VS. COST

The other day I spent a happy hour in the local business supply house, stocking up on supplies and the latest gadgets. It happens that the manufacturer of everything I bought was an American company, though the factory was in a foreign land, and the hands were foreign. Were the hands lay engineers or computer experts? Well, we've seen their pictures in the papers and on TV. They were young women with nimble fingers willing to work long hours in uncomfortable and sometimes unsafe conditions for low pay and no fringe benefits. Knowledge of how a computer works was no job requirement for them. And even if a smattering of such knowledge were required of forewomen and foremen (which is most improbable), is it conceivable that the American companies had to go abroad because they could not find a few qualified supervisory personnel among the millions of Americans unemployed? Very likely the American companies had themselves terminated such people as they moved their operations abroad; and those terminated are very likely still where they were dropped, with the lucky ones now exercising their technical skills washing dishes at Wendy's or Taco Bell.

It would be astonishing if the question of productivity, or anything like it, crossed the mind of an American company pondering whether to cross the border. The decisive question surely was cost—low labor cost, low taxes, and convenient lack of regulation. The number of hours necessary to manufacture a pen or computer here or there was irrelevant; it was the unit cost of the goods that mattered.

19

The "Real Interest" Fallacy and the Fed's COLA

In trying to adjust interest rates for inflation, economists of almost every school and almost every persuasion routinely commit what may be called the "real interest" fallacy, which grossly distorts interest rates and has malign effects on central bank policy, particularly in regard to inflation, and hence on the economy of the nation and the world.

The conventional adjustment, dating back to Irving Fisher, is made by subtracting the expected rate of inflation from the actual or "nominal" or "money" interest rate. The result is called the "real" interest rate, as shown by the following mortgage rate data for 1979 and 1980. The data are extreme but not uncharacteristic:

	1979	*1980*
Actual or "nominal" mortgage interest rate	10.79	12.66
less year-to-year change in CPI	11.30	13.50
equals "real" mortgage interest rate	−0.51	−0.84

On the basis of such figures, bankers expect borrowers, whether individuals or corporations or nations, to be grateful for the privilege of borrowing at exorbitant rates.

Rational observers might expect rational bankers to close down their mortgage departments because they would, according to the theory, be contracting to give "real" money away. Actually, mortgages totalling $121.7 billion were written in 1979—more than in any other year between the end of World War II and 1984. At least some of this activity was prompted, not by the negative rate, but by the new variable rate mortgages.

Lest it be imagined that the absurd interest rates were the result of inability to anticipate the future correctly, let it be noted that in these years the rates for 6 months commercial paper (the inflation rates at whose maturity were surely easy for "real interest" theorists to predict) were "really" −0.39 and −1.21 respectively. Furthermore, the federal funds rate, and the rates paid by all Treasury notes and bills and bonds, by AAA corporate bonds, by high grade municipal bonds, and by many Third World nations were also all "negative," while the prime rate was just over the line.

THE FALLACY

Terminology in any discipline can be slippery, especially when using the words "real" and "nominal," both of which have esoteric connotations inherited from medieval philosophy. It is common to speak of "real" dollars when comparing, say, the price level of 2000 with that of 1985. What is meant is merely that the price of a typical market basket of commodities that is y dollars in 2000 was x dollars in 1985.

The interest costs of the relevant years are indeed factors of the prices in those years. But "real" dollars do not compute as earning "real" dollars in interest at "real" interest rates (certainly not negative "real" rates), though of course they should do so if there were a self-consistent "real" universe.

The fallacy of the "real interest" theory is a single misadventure of thought that has had, and continues to have, appalling consequences for the wealth, health, and happiness of the people of the globe. The fallacy is the tacit—and unnoticed—assumption that money that is not lent is not affected by inflation. This strange assumption has as a corollary the equally strange notion that any diminution that occurs in the purchasing power of money that has been lent is due to the act of lending. The wastage of principal because of inflation is erroneously treated as a cost of lending money rather than as a cost of owning or holding money.

Consequently, it is conventionally argued that lenders faced with low or negative "real" interest rates should engage in a lenders' strike and in effect bury their money like the slothful servant in the Parable of the Talents. Those who are clever enough to anticipate inflation are advised to invest in gold or collectibles or natural resources. (Since the whole world has timorously expected inflation for the past fifty years, it's a wonder that any productive enterprise has been able to find financing.)

In our 1979 example, a one-year $1,000 mortgage would have earned 10.79 percent, or $107.90, so that the mortgagee would have had $1,107.90 in 1980. The purchasing power of that sum would have been reduced by 1980's inflation rate of 13.50 percent, or $149.56, and so would have been only $968.34, or less than he had when he started. But if he had not made the loan, the purchasing power of his $1,000 would still have been reduced by the 13.50 percent inflation rate and so would have been only $865. In short, the mortgagee would have lost more than $100 purchasing power by sitting on his hands.

This result, whereby a "negative" interest rate is greater than a zero rate, is of course in flat contradiction of the laws of mathematics. On reflection, it may seem wiser to retain the laws of mathematics, which have served us so well, and abandon the "real interest" theory, which has been misleading and disruptive in its effects on private, national, and (certainly not least) international lending policies and investment decisions. (One can't help wondering whether Fisher's devotion to his "real" theory may not have been at least partially responsible for his celebrated misreading of the stock market in October 1929.)

Although loan officers do much of the talking about the "real" interest rate, it is not fundamentally a banking problem, because banks defy Polonius and are both borrowers and lenders. With the help of secondary markets in bundled mortgages and the like, their monetary assets are substantially matched by their monetary liabilities. (The S&Ls, of course, were unable to maintain a good match.) If there were a "real" interest rate, it would operate on both sides of their balance sheets and so approximately cancel itself out and affect only minimally the spread between their cost and use of funds.

Households, pensions, trust funds, and other unleveraged lenders who, unlike bankers, do not borrow in order to lend, may fuss when the offered "real" rate is low or "negative." But their existential choice is between actually offered interest or none at all, exactly as the worker's choice is between actually offered wages or none at all.

THE FED'S COLA

There are many different definitions of the "real" rate of interest, depending upon which inflation rate—current year-to-year BLS, anticipated, expected, or whatnot—is chosen to distinguish the "real" rate of interest from the actual rate. For convenience, we may call whatever rate is chosen the Fed's Cost of Living Adjustment, or COLA, because, like any other Cost of Living Adjustment, the Fed's COLA is intended to protect its beneficiaries, in this case the lenders, from the ravages of inflation. (Originally I called it the Bankers' COLA. But the Federal Reserve Board, as national lender of last resort, is certainly responsible for it and so should have the honor of the name, while bankers and other lenders enjoy the rewards of the game.)

Every COLA is by definition or intention equal to the inflation rate that afflicts—or is expected to afflict—the economy as a whole. The COLAs in various union agreements—even the COLAs in Social Security—are not uniform in their benefits. No doubt many would like to see such benefits uniform, but in fact they are not. It is fortunate that they are not, for indexing wages to the price level has been at the heart of most hyperinflations of modern times.

Labor and money (either as direct cost or as opportunity cost) are essential to every economic transaction. Unless indexed, wages and salaries are far from uniform. Interest rates, however, being fundamentally set by the Federal Reserve Board (in ways we shall discuss), are substantially uniform for comparable risks from coast to coast, and so are in effect indexed to the price level. In the 1970s, the Reserve, in a manic resolve to "stay the course," raised interest rates to unprecedented heights, and we were well on our way to a hyperinflation caused by escalating interest rates rather than by wage rates. In July 1981, when the federal funds rate reached 19.1 percent, the Reserve began a slow retreat, and the inflation rate followed quickly after.

What inflation is still in the system is largely due to the Fed's COLA, which protects lenders from inflation at an egregiously disproportionate cost to the economy as a whole, including the lenders themselves in their character as members of the polity. Consider some figures for 1998. The gross domestic product for that year was about $8.5 trillion, and the year-to-year CPI change was 1.6 percent. Multiplying the two figures, we get $136.0 billion as the cost of inflation to the economy in that year. (This figure is almost certainly too high, especially if we take the Boskin Commission report at all seriously.)

When we multiply the outstanding debt of the nonfinancial sectors of the economy for that year (about $16.1 trillion) by the same 1.6 percent, we get $257.6 billion as the cost of protecting lenders from inflation. If we include the debt of the financial sectors (about $6.0 trillion), the cost of the Fed's COLA increases to about $353.0 billion. (Both figures are almost certainly too low, because most of the outstanding debt was undertaken in prior years, when the CPI change—and hence the Fed's COLA—was much higher.)

Comparing the results, we see that the amount that lenders engross to protect themselves from inflation is roughly twice as much as inflation costs the entire economy. This relation will be the same, regardless of the number chosen for the Fed's COLA, because the relation is a reflection of the relative sizes of the national nonfinancial indebtedness and the gross domestic product. The former has been greater than the latter at least since the Great Depression, and the relation will not be close to reversing itself in the foreseeable future. Consequently, in the present and prospective economy, elimination of the Fed's COLA will eliminate the subsequent inflation rate. The usual other-things-being-equal proviso of course applies; but the present spread between indebtedness and GDP is so great that the Federal Reserve Board can undertake a correction of its inflation policy with considerable aplomb.

Although there is much chatter about "pre-emptive strikes" against inflation, or about being "ahead of the curve," there should be no doubt about which way the causation runs. Interest rates have to be set before money is borrowed (or budgeted as opportunity cost) to finance the production of any commodity.

Every firm must set its price before it can sell its product (and usually before it manufactures its product); it must know its costs in order to set its price; an important and unavoidable cost is the cost of borrowing, which is fundamentally set by the Federal Reserve Board when it sets the federal funds and discount rates, the lowest rates at which banks can be sure of funds in case of emergency or to capitalize on a sudden opportunity.

In the United States there are seventeen or eighteen million business enterprises of all sizes and shapes, offering for sale or contract all sorts of goods and services. Yesterday these enterprises routinely quoted many millions of prices, changed some, and established thousands of new ones. Scores of millions of customers agreed to the prices, and sales were made; a few haggled for lower prices, and some were successful. All of these actual prices were based in part on what the Federal Reserve did at its last meeting. But there is no way on earth that what the Reserve did at its last meeting could have been based on the prices sellers and buyers agreed to yesterday.

To be sure, there is always a lot of anticipating, or guessing, or expecting going on, on both sides. The Reserve tries to imagine what enterprisers are going to do, and the entrepreneurs try to discount what the Reserve will do. If the Rational Expectations theorists are correct, whatever rational move the Reserve makes will be expected and discounted by rational entrepreneurs. Hence the Reserve is in effect responsible for the result. If, on the other hand, the Reserve's actions are not or cannot be anticipated, then there is no question that whatever prices the entrepreneurs subsequently set will be not only *post hoc* but also *propter hoc*.

The causation indubitably runs from the price of borrowing money set by the Federal Reserve Board to the prices of commodities set by the firms of the economy. It does not and cannot run the other way. Raising the interest rate cannot cure inflation; it causes it.

To be sure, the waters may seem muddied if a large firm raises prices in anticipation of an interest increase, and if the Reserve then raises interest rates to preempt expansion of the perceived inflation. But the Reserve's action merely validates the firm's judgment of the Reserve's probable action. The firm is thus given every reason to maintain its increases, and the rest of the economy is given every reason to follow suit.

While the price level follows the interest rate up, it of course does not do so according to a precise formula. Some entrepreneurs will hold their prices down and be satisfied with a lower profit—or perhaps hope to increase their market and effect economies of scale. Some will cut other costs. Many will downsize their staffs. In all such cases, the increased interest rate has no effect on the price level but does have an unfortunate and pointless effect on profits and on employment—in other words, on the people of the economy.

No matter if the Reserve raises the interest rate with the declared intention of controlling inflation, and no matter if the financial press expects such action at least to damp inflation down, the result of raising the interest rate is an increase in the costs of both production and consumption and hence a decrease in the purchasing power of money—in other words, a surge in inflation.

A DISMAL RECORD

In 1969, despite the first federal budget surplus in nine years (and the last surplus for thirty years to come), the Reserve Board raised interest rates, undoubtedly intending by conventional means to avert the inflation conventionally expected as a result of the guns-and-butter financing of the Vietnam War. The inflation rate increased anyhow, because the increased interest was, of course, an additional cost on top of everything else. This was the start of a fourteen-year run of disastrously misguided central bank policies that, in spite of much insistence on being "serious about inflation," produced a record-breaking 271.4 percent increase in the CPI (equivalent to 18.38 percent compounded annually).

In that period the unemployment rate rose from 3.5 percent to 9.7 percent (respectively the lowest and the highest since the end of World War II). The percentage of families living in poverty increased from 9.7 percent in 1969 to 12.3 percent in 1983 (it had touched 8.8 percent, its lowest to date, in 1973). The capacity utilization rate fell from 86.8 in 1969 to 81.4 in 1983. The index of net business formation hardly changed, but the business failure rate soared from 37.3 in 1969 to 109.7 in 1983. The prime rate topped off at 21.5 percent in December 1980 and January 1981. And there were four recessions in the fourteen years.

Throughout OPEC's decade of triumph, the Reserve's steady increases in the interest rate cost the United States economy more than OPEC's steady increases in the price of oil. When international bankers (not all American-based) then recycled OPEC's winnings to the Third World, necessarily at inflated rates, they laid the basis for today's global crisis. Suffice it to say that Third World debt multiplied a thousandfold in a couple of decades, whereupon the IMF has prescribed austerity for the hapless citizens of the hitherto developing nations—and new contributions by the developed nations to bail out their careless bankers.

All in all, this was a dismal and much misunderstood period in the history of the dismal science in the United States of America and in the world.

THE PRICE LEVEL

The Federal Reserve Board has jurisdiction over many banking costs, but the interest rate is the only general business cost that the Reserve controls directly. The Fed's COLA, like the interest rate of which it is a part, is a pervasive cost of both sides of every economic transaction, both buying and selling. If there were no Fed's COLA, the interest rate would be lower for all, both consumers and producers.

A lower interest rate, leading to lower actual costs and lower opportunity costs of loans, increases the balances available to consumers for purchases, and likewise the balances available to producers for investments. A lower rate increases both the borrowing power (which determines the possible rate of investment) and the purchasing power of money. An increase in the purchasing power of money is, of course, equivalent to a decrease in the price level.

The Fed's COLA is an element in cost-push inflation. In today's developed economies, demand-pull inflation is rare or nonexistent. Practically all commodities are indefinitely replicable, and shortages even of natural resources are localized or of short duration; so demand (including, of course, that generated by suppliers' advertising) is generally satisfied in the normal course of business. More important, the Reserve can control demand only by "taking away the punch bowel," that is, by raising the interest rate, and thus the Reserve itself pushes cost-push inflation toward recession.

To be sure, interest is not the only element in cost-push inflation. Other costs include taxes and rent and labor (which may be broken down into the wages of the working poor, the salaries of the working middle class, and the takings of the working rich). In a happier day, these costs can be controlled by taxation, regulation, and the government as employer of last resort, none of which (apart from some banking regulation) is within the purview of the Federal Reserve Board. The Reserve can control them only in the same way that it can control demand, that is, by so manipulating the interest rate as to cause a recession, affecting all segments of the economy, both consumption and production, both public and private, both wealthy and needy.

It may happen that when the Federal Reserve Board sets the federal funds rate, it has the deliberate intention of thereby controlling the money supply. Whether this is a wise or practical or even possible objective may be disputed. In any case, a figure for the money supply is irrelevant to the practical work of business executives and government officials, who, in order to make use of it, must translate it back to the interest rate, which does concern them, and which the Federal Reserve Board does indeed set.

Reserve Chairman Alan P. Greenspan has referred to "real" interest as "one important guidepost." Given the remarkable spread of the idea since its introduction by Irving Fisher ninety years ago, a search of the records might well reveal similar, and even more transparent, comments by other chairmen and governors over the years. But in the end, it does not matter why the central bank raises interest rates or keeps them up. Any increase, regardless of the intention, increases costs throughout the economy and thus pushes prices up or profits down, or both. Increasing the interest rate does not cure inflation; it causes it.

SQUEEZING INFLATION OUT OF THE ECONOMY

Interest rates are higher today than they were in most of the years since World War II, higher than in most of the years since the establishment of the Federal Reserve in 1913. The virtue of recent Federal Reserve policy is not that the federal funds rate is low (actually it is 62 percent higher than it was only seven years ago). The virtue is that for five or six years it has been fairly steady, especially in comparison with the decades of the 1970s and 1980s, during which period it ranged between a low of 4.4 percent and a high of 19.1 percent. No other factor of production has been so volatile since the Great Depression.

Much more important, is the fact that, from 1994 to 1999 the Reserve resisted the temptation to fight expected inflation by increasing unemployment. To be sure, critics complained that the Reserve's resistance was due, not to distaste for throwing people out of work, but to fear of causing a stock market crash. Whatever the Reserve's reason for its policy, interest rates were not raised until July 1999, and inflation in fact retreated.

The happy work of bringing the interest rate down to squeeze the remainder of inflation out of the economy will take some time. Given the $16 trillion of mortgages, bonds, and other long-term indebtedness now outstanding in the nonfinancial sector, and given the numbers of leases and other long-term contracts with settled prices, five or six years is probably an optimistic estimate, even though most mortgages could be refinanced, and many bonds could be called.

There are too many gaps and lags and cross-currents and arguable assumptions and downright errors in the statistics for the Reserve to proceed with the arrogant abandon it exhibited in the 1970s. Nevertheless, there is some recent experience to rely on. The Reserve brought the federal funds rate down from 9.89 percent in March 1989 to 2.92 percent in December 1992— a drop of over 70 percent in less than four years. Such a drop, starting in 1998, could have brought the federal funds rate to 1.50 percent or thereabouts in 2003 and is evidently feasible. Whether, and to what extent, this is desirable can only be shown by the event. A prudent Reserve will proceed with all deliberate speed.

The recent experience of Japan demonstrates that, as monetarists protest, there are limits to monetary policy. Federal Reserve folklore has an explanation for it: You can't push on a string. Less metaphorically, the Reserve is not responsible for fiscal policy, that is, government spending and government taxing, which are obviously essential. Yet the monetary job is essential, too, and can be done only by the central bank. The Reserve has authority to embark on the operation with a stroke of the pen. A determined bank of last resort can break a lenders' strike, should one threaten, while speculators can hardly expect to score by betting against interest rates that the authorities are in the process of lowering anyhow.

Perhaps we don't want inflation eliminated altogether. As long ago as David Hume, it was noted that a whiff of inflation seems to arouse entrepreneurial appetites. On the other hand, as recently as Dwight D. Eisenhower's whistle-stop election campaign it was understood that even a one-percent inflation, compounded, can cause serious trouble for people who live too long on fixed incomes.

We shall be unable to discuss these questions intelligently until we have abandoned, once and for all, the obfuscating notion of a "real" interest rate.

THE DAMAGE

If the economic models of the Federal Reserve Board had been based on a low actual interest rate that the Board itself had set, there would have been no Fed's COLA; the actual interest rate would not have been kept usuriously high in order to protect an imaginary "real" rate; there would have been little or no inflation; absent the frenzied fear of inflation, there would have been no barbarous practice of a "natural" rate of unemployment; the chasm between the rich and the poor would not be deepening as high rates make lenders and speculators ever richer; the Social Security system and Medicare would not need "fixing"; there need not have been the sad neglect of our resources and infrastructure and our arts and sciences; and there need not have been the financial ruin and economic waste and personal grief of the nine recessions of the last half of the twentieth century.

CONCLUSION

Until recently the only practical use of the "real interest" theory has been as a plausible excuse for the Federal Reserve Board and lenders generally to escalate already outrageous "nominal" rates. A new use has been developed in the current debate over the earnings of the Social Security Trust Fund, which are "shown" by the "real interest" fallacy to be much less than they actually are.

Inflation may indeed be, as has been said, solely a monetary problem, but the money in question is, always and everywhere, not "real," but actual.

POSTSCRIPT: AN "EFFECTIVE" RATE

To determine mathematically the effect of inflation on the interest rate, one multiplies the interest rate by the inflation rate. In the 1979 example, one multiplies the actual interest rate (.1079) by the inflation rate (.1130) to get the effect of inflation on the interest rate. The result is .0122, which, when subtracted from the actual interest rate, gives .0957, or 9.57 percent, which may be called the "effective" rate of interest.

The foregoing calculations may be refined in various ways without substantially altering our observation that the "effective" rate is a long way from the "real" rate of −0.51 percent. More important for a rational and comprehensible universe, the "effective" rate, like the actual or "nominal" rate, is always on the positive side of zero.

The "effective" rate is, moreover, close to the actual rate (and it becomes progressively closer as the inflation rate falls), so that one may be led to conclude that the actual rate will do for most purposes.

20

Inflation and Recession

Inflation is ordinarily thought of as a rise in commodity prices that somehow is not accompanied by a proportionate rise in wages and other income. The cost of living increases, or seems to increase, faster than the ability to pay for it. Commodity prices are, of course, affected by the costs of doing business, which are the prices of the factors of enterprise—wages and salaries, interest rates, rents, entrepreneurial profits, and taxes. There is thus a strong tendency for commodity prices and factor prices to rise or fall together. The exceptions to this rule are numerous, but they are not sufficiently numerous to explain the hold the inflation problem has on society.

If a general price increase should affect all prices, not just those of commodities, but including the conditions of long-term contracts, and if all prices should go up proportionately, in lock-step, everyone would be more or less inconvenienced, but no one would be much hurt, and no one would be much advantaged. If such as event should occur, it would be cause for brief wonder and casual conversation, not for the constant turmoil and agitation we have experienced this past half century. In the other direction, when in 1969 France substituted one new franc for one hundred old ones, thus "deflating" all prices, the exchange went as smoothly as anything does in French politics. It has, moreover, been long recognized that a little price inflation stimulates entrepreneurial juices.

In short, the inflation that has been alternately a curse and a nuisance of our time has been something other than a simple rise of commodity prices or a general price rise. What we have experienced is a pervasive and continuing disruption of the price system, resulting in a massive redistribution of wealth and income.

FOLKLORE OF INFLATION

During the last nine years of his life, Joseph A. Schumpeter worked on the posthumously published *History of Economic Analysis*, a remarkable work of some twelve hundred pages that he almost, but not quite, finished. Schumpeter had studied, practiced, and taught law in Egypt, Austria, and the United States before becoming involved in politics at the end of World War I. He was for a brief time Austrian minister of finance and subsequently president of the Biedermann Bank until it collapsed in 1924. He then taught economics at the University of Bonn before going to Harvard, where he remained from 1932 until his death in 1950.

These biographical details are suggestive in relation to a surprising fact about Schumpeter's monumental work. Although he discusses in great detail the work of all the major economists and almost all those of the second, third, and even fourth and fifth ranks (the index of authors runs to twenty-one double-column pages), there is no entry in the subject index (which runs to thirty double-column pages) for "inflation." Given the cacophony that has oppressed us in recent years, his silence is deafening. Here is a tremendous scholar who, as government official, banker, and teacher, was in the thick of one of the great hyperinflations of all time, and he finds nothing worth noting on the subject in the writings of the great and near-great economists from Aristotle to 1950. He has a great deal to say on monetary theory and on business cycles (he himself wrote a massive book on the subject), but nothing on inflation as such.

The foregoing anecdote strongly suggests that inflation as we know it is a comparatively recent phenomenon, dating roughly from World War II, or the end of the Great Depression. This is the first thing to understand about it. Before the second half of the twentieth century, there were price dislocations aplenty. It was generally believed that business activity was cyclical. Price increases were characteristic of the boom phase of the business cycle, and the bust phase had contrary dislocations. What went up, came down. Whether the cycle was one of forty or fifty years, as Kondratieff thought, or something of shorter duration, it was understood to be a cycle, and inflation was followed by deflation as day the night, whereupon the sequence repeated itself. The Great Depression convinced many that Marx was right, and that the fibrillation of the capitalist system would shake it apart. Much attention was therefore paid to proposals for damping the vibrations down, leading Keynes to remark, "The right remedy for the trade cycle is not to be found in abolishing booms and thus keeping us permanently in a semi-slump; but in abolishing slumps and thus keeping us permanently in a quasi-boom."[1]

Inflation was not a primary concern of Schumpeter's generation, not only because their attention was distracted to the business cycle but also because prices, from the Industrial Revolution to the end of the nineteenth century, had been trending steadily downward.[2] In re-

---

1. Keynes, *General Theory*, p. 322.
2. Commons, in *Legal Foundations of Capitalism*, dates a transformation of the American economy from the Minnesota Rate Case decision of 1890. The growth of the holding company followed, despite the Sherman Antitrust Act of the same year. The prime example was United States Steel, which in 1901 completed the amalgamation of some 228 mills. See Brandeis, *Other People's Money*, p. 104.

cent years, of course, they have been trending steadily upward. We have had nine recessions of varying severity in the past half century, and through them all, prices have kept going up. The business cycle used to be marked by a harrowing deflationary phase. We have suffered none of that. In the recessions there has been some moderating of inflation, but there has been no overt deflation, at least not in the industrialized world. When we congratulate ourselves on licking inflation, we mean merely that we have (we hope) slowed it down.

The second thing to understand about inflation is that hyperinflation is special and different. Its conditions and consequences are special, and there is no reason to believe that it grows out of inflation as we know it. In every case of hyperinflation, the afflicted country is saddled with massive foreign debts denominated in foreign currencies, and usually has wages and prices indexed to each other. This was true of the Weimar Republic, and it is true of much of the Third World today. The Weimar hyperinflation was quite quickly stopped because payment of the war debts was delayed, restructured, and ultimately forgotten. The Third World's hyperinflations will continue until the creditors face the fact that the debts will not be repaid.[3] The United States debt poses no such threat to the nation. It is denominated in dollars. Even if a large portion of it is held abroad, it remains under American control, because it is payable in dollars under American control.

Perhaps the most important thing to understand about inflation is the vacuity of the popular cliché that it is "too much money chasing

---

3. The debts almost certainly will not be fully paid. Whether or not they could be paid is a moot point. Stephen A. Schuker argues convincingly that Germany had the economic capability of paying World War I reparations, and that Latin America is similarly able to pay its debts today. See Schuker, *American "Reparations" to Germany, 1919–33: Implications for the Third World Debt Crisis*, Princeton Studies in International Finance, no. 61 (July 1988). Germany would not pay because the reparations were considered unjust, and Latin America will not pay because the interest rates are considered usurious.

too few goods." Examples abound of insatiable demands arising for particular goods at a particular time and place. The excitement of an auction can lead to extravagant prices. More seriously, when the wheat crop—or the distribution thereof—failed in prerevolutionary France, desperate need bid the price of bread up catastrophically. But there was not "too much money" chasing that bread. On the contrary, people were impoverished as they sold everything they had at distress prices in a frantic effort to raise money for food. In ancient Egypt, Joseph's foresight in the seven fat years enabled him, in the lean years, to squeeze the people and reduce the country's freeholders to sharecroppers. He could scarcely have done this if the pharaoh's subjects had had "too much money."

The modern economy is so large and substitutes are so plentiful that it is difficult for any person or group of people to corner a market as Joseph did; yet the economy is so interdependent that trouble anywhere tends to spread. The gas lines at the beginning of OPEC were only a temporary annoyance, but petroleum enters widely into industry and agriculture, and the rise in its price contributed to rises in all commodities, especially those produced by corporations that value their supplies and inventories on the last-in-first-out basis. Just as there was panic filling of gasoline tanks by motorists and of oil tanks by homeowners, so there was panic stockpiling of all supplies by manufacturers and of all merchandise by retailers. An expected general shortage of commodities resulted in temporary and localized actual shortages. But the general shortage never ensued. In fact, the stores were full of goods, and business was sluggish, because prices jumped faster than people's ability to pay. There was not, at any time in the movement, too much money chasing too few goods. If you can't afford to pay the prices asked, it is silly to claim you have too much money.

Nevertheless this cliché is the explicit or implicit rationale for many doggedly pursued public policies, many of which, as we shall see, are not even well designed to satisfy these fallacious premises.

Obsessed by fear of inflation, and eager for doctrinaire reasons to exercise control of the money supply, the Federal Reserve Board managed to free itself in 1951 from its 1942 agreement with the Treasury to stabilize the prices and yields of government securities, with the incidental effect of holding all interest rates down (the prime in most of those years remained at 1.50 percent). Thereafter the Reserve enthusiastically (and unsuccessfully) attempted to control inflation by inflating the interest rate.

Following the appointment of Paul A. Volcker to the chairmanship in the summer of 1979, the board decided to worry primarily about the money supply, allowing the interest rate to soar erratically. There is no doubt that the policy was designed to do what it ultimately did do: damp down enterprise and throw people out of work. The *New York Times* reported that when Volcker was asked whether tightened monetary policies (which the Board was pursuing) and tightened fiscal policies (which he advocated) would lead to recession, he replied, "Yes, and the sooner the better."[4] A decade later Volcker advised Zdzislaw Sadowski, president of the Polish Economic Society, that "of course" Poland must go through a recession.[5] Standard economics has no cure for inflation other than a recession, and no preventive of inflation other than stagnation. In either case, widespread unemployment is the main ingredient of the regimen.

Not only does speculation survive in conditions that damp down enterprise; it actually thrives in such conditions. Speculation, which usually depends on rising prices, is itself a stimulant to price rises. A rising interest rate requires price rises to pay the bankers' bills. A rising interest rate therefore fuels the inflation it was supposed to dampen. Thus the immediate effect of the 1979 decision to encourage the interest rate to surge was a simultaneous surge of inflation. It

4. Mayer, Duesenberry, and Aliber, *Money, Banking*, p. 466.
5. *New York Times*, May 20, 1990, p. D13.

took four years of depression and all the suffering that that entailed to frighten the Federal Reserve Board into relaxing its interest rate policy and thus allowing inflation to subside to a rate that, being the lowest in ten years, elicited much self-congratulation but was actually substantially higher than the trend of the decades before the Federal Reserve Board began to fight inflation by raising the interest rate.

SAY'S LAW

Mathematically, it is impossible for too much money to be chasing too few goods, provided that the goods that workers produce are at least equal in value to their wages. Since nonfinancial corporate output is currently about 1.7 times wages and salaries, this condition would seem not too difficult to meet. On these premises, perfectly full employment (not 3 percent unemployment or 2 percent unemployment) cannot be inflationary. Indeed, any unemployment whatever will have an inflationary effect because the unemployed will be receiving some sort of relief, thus increasing the money in circulation either directly or indirectly, but will be producing no goods for money to be spent on.

It is safe to say that no one—especially no conservative—accepts the foregoing reasoning; yet it is a logical implication of Say's law, which is widely accepted—especially by supply-side conservatives—as a guide to public policy. Say wrote, "[T]he only way of getting rid of money is in the purchase of some product or other. Thus the mere circumstance of the creation of one product opens a vent for other products."[6] The usual, more aphoristic, formulation of Say's law is "Production creates its own demand." The policy recommendation that follows seems obvious: "It is the aim of good government to stimulate production and of bad government to encourage consumption."[7]

---

6. Say, *Treatise*, pp. 134–35.
7. Say, *Treatise*, p. 139.

If consumption is to be discouraged, one wonders what is to be done with the encouraged (and presumably increased) production. Why should tens and hundreds of thousands of men and women be encouraged to build automobiles that no good citizen is supposed to buy? How will the wage costs and interest costs and supply costs of the automobile manufacturers be met if their output is not to be sold? Or will a new industry of reducing them to scrap be encouraged?

The trouble with Say's law is that empirically it is insupportable. If it were valid, a universal glut (that is, goods no one could afford to buy) would, as he said, be impossible, and inflation would, as we have seen, be next to impossible. But there certainly have been depressions, and there certainly is inflation. Something is wrong with his analysis, and anyone who has ever, as polemicists used to put it, met a payroll knows what it is. It is a distinct possibility that you can't sell all of what you make. Sometimes you can't sell any of it. Mathematically, production creates its own demand; actually, it does not.

What is true of the demand for products is also true of the demand for labor. It may be that my skills are so specialized—or so minimal—that there is no demand for them at any price. It may be that business is so sluggish that a universal glut actually happens, in which case it would be folly for an entrepreneur to hire me to produce more. Keynes's quarrel with classical economists turned on his insistence that involuntary unemployment can and does occur. Millions of citizens in all lands can testify that he was right.[8]

THE MONEY SUPPLY

David Ricardo was insistent on what is known as the wage-fund theory, which holds that a business has a certain fund out of which it pays its costs and its profits; consequently, as Ricardo wrote, "There can be

---

8. Keynes, *General Theory*, chap. 2.

no rise in the value of labour without a fall of profits."[9] This theory continues to be supported by strong gut feelings in many corporate boardrooms, but Schumpeter dismissed it with the observation that "high rates of profit and high wages normally go together."[10]

Yet Ricardo was right—or almost right. His mistake—very common in his day and not uncommon today—was in confusing profits with interest rates. Interest rates and wages are indeed in conflict with each other, because both are costs of doing business. No business can exist without labor, and no business can exist without explicit or implicit interest costs. Both interest and wages are contracted costs agreed to before sales are known, while actual profits, as we have previously noted, are a residual.

Actual profits are a residual, but what I have called planned profits are a determining factor in business estimates and have the interest rate as an opportunity cost. The interest rate thus has a double effect on business plans. In general, a project will not be undertaken unless expected sales are at least equal to the sum of labor costs, materials costs, marketing costs, interest costs, and planned profits. (Whether fixed costs are considered will not affect the point before us.) Since in the actual world prices are set not in an auction but as a result of estimating and planning, labor costs and the double factor of interest costs and planned profits are in the wage-fund relationship

---

9. Ricardo, *Principles*, p. 21. For Marx the wage-fund theory turned the conflict between capital and labor into a zero-sum game that would ultimately be won by the most numerous team. It can, I think, be shown that such a game is a consequence of regarding commodities as finite. Piero Sraffa's curious little book *Production of Commodities by Means of Commodities* thus contends that "to any one level of the rate of profits there can only correspond one wage, whatever the standard in which the wage is expressed" (p. 62). Sraffa, who was editor of Ricardo's works, follows Ricardo in confusing actual profits with planned profits and hence with the interest rate. The rate of profits, he writes, is "susceptible of being determined from outside the system of production, in particular by the level of the money rate of interest" (p. 33).

10. Schumpeter, *History*, p. 655 n. 22.

with each other. If prices are held steady, these rival costs cannot both go up. If either goes up, the other must come down. If one goes up while the other holds steady or if both go up, the selling price must go up or the project must be abandoned.

On the basis of the foregoing, we should expect a positive correlation between high interest rates and inflation, the former being a cause of the latter.[11] It is, however, widely believed that high interest rates stop inflation rather than contribute to it. The belief is so settled that everyone expects as a matter of course that the Federal Reserve Board will—or "must"—raise the interest rate whenever it is imagined that inflation threatens.

Since the Great Depression, there have been two periods of relative stability. In 1952–56, the annual change of the Consumer Price Index ranged between 1.9 percent and minus 0.4 percent, while the prime was between 3.0 and 3.77 percent. And from 1961 through 1965, the change of the CPI inched up from 1.0 percent to 1.7 percent, while the prime was steady at 4.50 percent, except for 1965, when it was 0.04 point higher. Politically speaking, the first period embraced the last year of President Truman's term and the first four years of President Eisenhower's; the second period included the last year of President Eisenhower's presidency, all of President Kennedy's, and the first two years of President Johnson's.

The figures do not support a doctrine that relates high interest to a low CPI. Indeed, they go up and down together. From 1949 to 1967,

---

11. "Whatever their indirect impact, the direct effects of interest rate rises are inflationary. Interest plays a major role in the consumer price index, especially through the housing and consumer credit component. It is a large factor in utility costs. Regulatory agencies allow interest increases to affect rates almost immediately. Movements of interest rates increase the uncertainties and therefore the risks and costs of doing business. Tightening monetary policy has an effect on productivity and efficiency. Investment for the next several years will be less and its costs more because of past interest rate gyrations." Sherman J. Maisel, *Managing the Dollar*, pp. 17–18.

the CPI increased less than 3 points in every year but one, and the prime was under 5 percent in every year but the last two. In the twenty-three years following 1968, the CPI increased more than 3 points in every year except one, while the prime was above 6 percent in every year except two.

Some might be tempted to argue that the Federal Reserve Board was not resolute in restricting the money supply, and that it subsequently was forced, as the sports announcers say, to play catch-up. The record, however, is that M1 as a percentage of GDP fell from 28.2 percent in 1959 to 14.5 percent in 1981. The fall was remarkably steady, with only three upbeat years and only one year in which the fall was more than 3 points. But starting at 15.2 percent in 1982 (the year in which the Reserve is supposed to have got control of inflation) the figure rose to 16.8 percent in 1986, the year of lowest inflation in twenty-two years.

If M1 is the money supply (and it was in fact the quantity that the Federal Reserve claimed to control during these years), it was, as a percentage of GDP, cut almost in half in the years when inflation was growing, but increased with the decline of inflation. The experience with M2 has been different and essentially flat, with a low of 58.8 percent of GDP and a high of 66.4 percent, but its second highest point (66.1 percent) came in the low inflation year of 1986.

In short, the empirical record does not support the theory that a high interest rate controls inflation, and it directly contradicts the theory that inflation is controlled by shrinking the money supply.

INFLATION AND RECESSION

There is every reason to expect a high interest rate to cause a high CPI. First, let us make a minor observation. The inflation rate is not a figure you read off an instrument like a barometer. It is a statistical construct, and one of its factors is the interest rate. This is an arbitrary effect, and one that could be arbitrarily eliminated (though the rate at which homeowners and other consumers can borrow is indubitably an element in their cost of living); but it stands as an actual fact in the actual world.

Second, let us repeat the much more important observation that speculation is vastly stimulated by volatile and rising interest rates. It was said in the 1980s that if high interest rates had not been available to bring in foreign money, federal borrowing as a result of the budget deficits would have crowded producers out of the market. But as we saw in Chapter 14, speculation can always crowd out production, and that is what happens during bull markets, despite foreign money.

There is, third, a much more serious effect than either of these. If you're running a business, and your friendly banker says he wants 10 percent to renew your 5 percent loan, your first defense is to cut the payroll, and your second is to raise your prices. Moreover, the loan isn't the only thing that bothers you, because the opportunity cost of investing in your business rises with the interest rate; so you must raise your planned profit, which increase runs geometrically through the economy, raising prices as it goes.

Of course, it happens, sooner or later, that high prices, high unemployment, and low wages have their adverse effects on business. Sales fall, and payrolls are squeezed further. Unions fear to strike. But since wages have only an arithmetical effect on costs, the net pressure on prices will still be upward as long as interest rates remain high. Even a very severe recession will at best only slow inflation; it will not stop it as long as interest rates remain high.

If the Federal Reserve controlled inflation in the late 1970s and the early 1980s, it did it by so increasing one of the costs of doing business (interest) that a worldwide recession was induced. The claim is made that this had to be done in order to break what was called the wage-price spiral. And what was the vice of the spiral? If it had not been broken, it would, they say, have so increased one of the costs of doing business (labor) that a worldwide recession would have resulted.

One could dispute the relative inefficiency or the relative injustice of the two recession-inducing measures, but on the premises there is no essential difference between them. They both work by escalating the costs of doing business. But that is only theory. No one knows whether a wage-price spiral would actually cause a recession, because such a spiral has never run its course. On the other hand, everyone knows—or should know—what happens when you push up the interest rate. There is a further irony here. The Federal Reserve Board has interfered grossly and grievously with the free market in order to save it. And what was the free market being saved from? It was being saved from a market in which prices moved freely.

THE INTEREST RATE

The most popular theory of inflation (too much money, too few goods) is fallacious in ways we've already discussed. Yet, letting that pass, one wonders how raising the interest rate, or allowing it to rise, could be thought appropriate to the problem. A high interest rate no doubt chills the ardor of borrowers and thus may hold down the amount of money in circulation. Not all borrowers, however, are equally chilled. Speculators, as we have seen, find high rates stimulating.

Consumers are said to try to maintain their accustomed or desired standard of living. They will shoulder heavy debts at usurious rates to do so. Thus their readiness to assume mortgages at more than double the legal maximum interest rate of a few years previously; thus the cavalier expansion of credit-card borrowing; and thus the failure of high interest rates to impede the chase for goods. In fact, since high rates have proved acceptable to consumers, the consumer-loan business has become so attractive to banks that the seemingly paradoxical probability is that high rates have resulted in more money chasing goods, not less.

The famed bottom line, on the other hand, enforces a more circumspect demeanor on businesses, few of which find it profitable to expand when the cost of financing is in the double-digit range. Many find it impossible even to continue. Consequently, high interest rates, which perhaps have only a minor effect on demand, may have a major effect on supply. Whether or not there is more money in the chase, there are fewer goods in the running. Putting it more generally, there are fewer goods than there would have been otherwise.

The interest rate is a special cost of doing business. It is a pervasive, invasive cost. It is an inescapable cost. Even if one does not need to borrow, one does need to weigh the opportunity cost of investing one's money in one's business instead of lending it out. Interest exerts a steady upward pressure on all costs, and hence on prices. Thus interest is *ipso facto* inflationary. It is also necessary; it is the cost of investment. In a noninflationary economy or a healthy business, it is much less than the profitable output that results from investments.

The interest cost is the only cost that has this universal effect. We used to hear much about a wage-price spiral, but a wage increase in the automobile industry (for many years the pundits' whipping boy) works its way only slowly through the economy. Initially it affects only the price of automobiles, and it never brings about a uniform wage scale. Wages of grocery clerks remain low, and all wages in Mississippi remain low. A boost in the federal funds rate, on the other hand, immediately affects the rates charged by every bank in the land; and while it is possible for borrowers to shop around a bit for a loan, they find that rates vary within a very narrow range.

INFLATION: A SPECIFIC PROBLEM

Our half-century-long preoccupation with inflation is evidence of a profound confusion of American will and thought—indeed, the confusion has been practically worldwide. Price inflation is not an evil in itself; some evils may follow in its train, but no particular evil necessarily does. Evils, moreover, are always specific, not general, and are therefore open to specific treatment, while the chosen attacks on price inflation have systematically damaged all aspects of the economy, with the exception of speculation.

In the public discussion of inflation, the evil that used to have most attention was the erosion of the standard of living of retired people and others living on a fixed income. Here is a specific evil that can be assessed and a cure proposed. In fact, this evil was assessed; cures were proposed; and the cures, the first of which has been in effect since 1966, have been remarkably successful. In 1966 Medicare began to protect the aged from one of the most crushing burdens of old age and to provide millions with health care that otherwise would have been denied them; in 1972 and 1973 automatic cost-of-living adjustments were legislated for Social Security payments. Since these COLAs were tied to the CPI, and since the CPI was skewed because of the weight it gave to the mortgage rate, and since the elderly are in general not borrowers anyhow, there is no doubt that many retired persons were better off in 1980 than they had been ten or more years previously. That was, after all, the intention. To be sure, a great hue and cry, led by a committee of investment bankers, persuaded the nation that the elderly had it too good, and managed to raise Social Security taxes and to lower the COLA. That is not the point. The point is that the urgency of doing something about inflation was said to turn on damage done to the elderly. Given the damage, something was done about it. If what was done was considered too much (or too little), that only reinforces the argument that specific cures can be devised for specific ailments. There was no need to adopt monetary policies that ravaged the economy of the nation and of the world to address the problems of a small (though growing) segment of the population. Manipulating the interest rate, which affects all producers and all consumers, is particularly unsuited for correcting a special problem.

The recent attacks on Social Security have traded on the confusion that has existed since the program's New Deal beginnings. From the start, Social Security has been partly an insurance (or endowment) program and partly a welfare program. Social Security taxes are a form of forced premium payments; yet the benefits are not strictly proportional to the premiums. The attacks on the program have concentrated on its insurance aspect. The "bankruptcy" of the program was deceptively foretold. To avoid this alleged bankruptcy, taxes were raised and benefits reduced. This was all very well, but it was flatly subversive of any attempt to solve the problems of those living on a fixed income.

It is sometimes said that the long-term or secular rate of inflation is 3 percent, and excited self-adulation results whenever it is approached. But even at that rate, the consequence in ten years would be a 34.4 percent increase in the cost of living. Policies—of whatever sort—that bring inflation down to this long-term rate may mitigate but cannot solve the problems of people who live on fixed incomes. If solving those problems is a sincere objective of policy, they must be addressed directly, as they were in 1966, 1972, and 1973. Our experience since those years shows that such direct action, emphasizing the general welfare aspect of Social Security, can be successful.[12]

Of course, many have scruples against promoting the general welfare and so want to emphasize the insurance aspect of Social Security. They cannot then honorably use the plight of the elderly as their reason for supporting draconian measures against inflation, because the draconian measures hurt the elderly along with everyone else. They may have other reasons for supporting draconian measures, but the plight of the elderly cannot reasonably be one of them.

To be sure, the elderly are not the only people living on fixed incomes. There are the widows and orphans, over whom many tears were shed in the opposition to New Deal controls of the stock exchanges and the banks. Crocodile tears aside, this problem is admittedly wider than that of Ferdinand Lundberg's sixty American

---

12. Schwarz, *America's Hidden Success*, chap. 2.

families of great wealth. Addressing the wider problem, we might urge that the welfare aspect of Social Security be broadened to cover such of the citizens as are not now covered. Beyond this, it must be acknowledged that people who live on fixed incomes—whether the result of savings or of inheritance—have no greater claim to immunity to the vicissitudes of life than do those who work for a living. As it happened, the programs that were undertaken in the announced intention of controlling inflation in fact caused—and were intended to cause—widespread unemployment. At the same time the soaring interest rate—which was deliberately encouraged to soar—offered opportunities for aggrandizement to banks and to individuals with access to money. In short, the policies actually adopted have favored unearned income over earned income; that is, those whom Keynes, following R. H. Tawney, called functionless investors over those who do and have done the work of the world.

21

The Death of NAIRU

It used to be said that a parrot could pass the orals for a Ph.D. in economics by repeating, "Supply and demand!" Since the late 1960s, the password, certainly more suited to parrots, has been "NAIRU." And now NAIRU is dead.

Even in death, the "non-accelerating-inflation rate of unemployment" demands a chapter for itself, partly because it is the climax of the twentieth century's long struggle with the banshee of inflation, partly because it offers a case study in the development and propagation of an outrageous economic "paradox," and partly because, although falsified by events, and no longer referred to even by its cabalistic pseudonyms, it remains a powerful barbaric force in the universities, the central banks, the legislatures, the newsrooms, the board rooms, the market places, and as the justification of the continuance of the slums and favelas of the world.

NAIRU first attracted general professional attention in 1967 when it was called, perhaps daring listeners to be shocked, the natural rate of unemployment. Later it was given its more descriptive name: the non-accelerating-inflation rate of unemployment. Even this gobbledegook expression was too strong for many economists, who used instead the acronym "NAIRU," which sounds like a languorous South Sea isle, thus hiding their meaning from their readers and perhaps even from themselves.

Journalistic reports of the thoughts of mainstream economists may have led the unwary to imagine that when they talked about 5 or 6 or 7 percent of the workforce being unemployable, they meant that all those millions were too irresponsible, too little educated, too stupid, too malicious, too sick, or too pregnant to participate in the modern economy. What they meant, however, was not exactly that.

Instead, they insisted that there is a rate of unemployment that cannot be reduced without indefinitely accelerating the rate of inflation. Exactly what the effective rate of unemployment was, and how or, indeed, if it might be determined, have turned out to be far from clear.

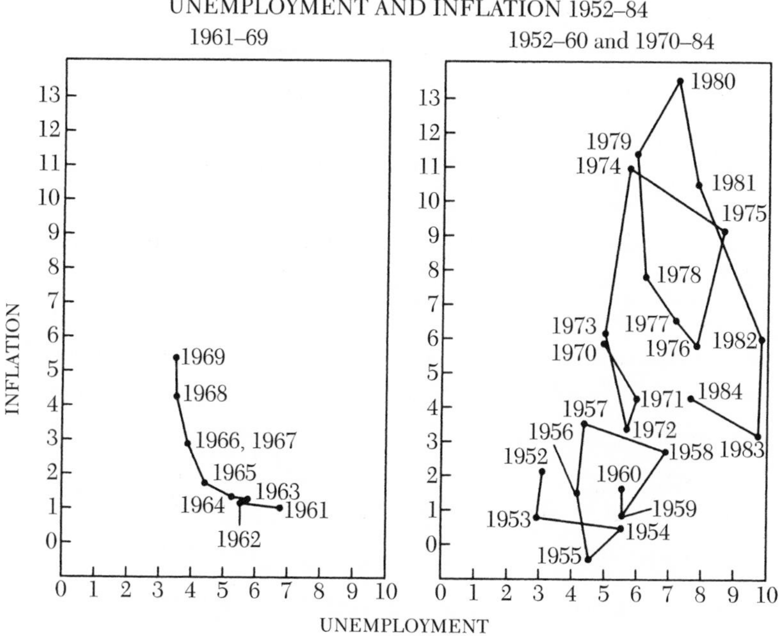

There were almost as many versions of the natural-rate theory as there were theorizers. The Phillips curve, which may be considered at least the godfather of the theory, is now seldom referred to, possibly because it generally proved impossible to replicate. In *Stabilizing an Unstable Economy*, Hyman Minsky[1] juxtaposed the almost perfect United States Phillips curve for 1961–69 with the curves for the preceding and succeeding years, which might have been traced by inebriated moth millers (*See illustration*).

Among other versions of the theory, some were close to Marx's metaphor of the industrial reserve army of the unemployed, whose existence warned those with jobs that they could be replaced if they agitated for higher wages. Some versions amalgamated natural-rate theory with productivity theory (thus compounding fallacies). Some versions turned on an elaborate *pas de quatre* among "real" wages and nominal wages, and "real" prices and nominal prices. Some versions required that inflation be not anticipated, although there surely has not been a time, at least since World War II, when inflation was not anticipated with trepidation by the financial community and especially by the Federal Reserve Board. There was even a far-out version and an international conference, to which even the U.S. Treasury sent delegates, was convened to consider it, that pretended to connect NAIRU with hysteresis, a phenomenon characteristic of ferrous metals in an electromagnetic field. (God, Einstein said, does not play dice, but evidently some economists do.)

The story would be ludicrous were not policies based on this formless theory pursued by central banks all over the world and acquiesced in by bemused legislatures, with the results that tens of millions of men and women were denied employment, and economic growth was deliberately stunted. These millions of men and women might be highly skilled and highly virtuous in every way, but we could not employ them, or disastrous inflation would ensue, and we could no longer be free to

---

1. Minsky, *Stabilizing*, p. 263.

choose among moderately priced commodities. Although sadly many commentators found it easy to slip into complaining about the "underclass," the fault was not in the unemployed. On the contrary, the unemployed were absolutely necessary to the operation of the system. They should have been honored for making it all possible.

All the chatter about ending welfare as we know it, about job training, about workfare instead of welfare, about enterprise zones and the like—all that talk, and there seems to be no end to it, is cruelly deceptive. In many cases, it is deliberately deceptive. As fast as Congress puts welfare recipients to work, the Federal Reserve Board, ruled by whichever version of the natural rate of unemployment is then fashionable, will at best "tilt" toward slowing down the economy sufficiently for an equal number of present jobholders to be fired.

FALLACIES OF NAIRU

The natural rate theory is certainly preposterous, certainly callous, certainly nasty. It is also fallacious.

Those who consider price inflation to be cost-push may take "unemployment" as a crude inverse surrogate for what does have an influence on prices—the cost of labor. And those who consider price inflation to be demand-pull may take "unemployment" as a crude inverse surrogate for aggregate demand. In neither case is the surrogate an improvement over what it stands for. The statistics are not easier to come by or more reliable, the calculations are not simpler or more precise, nor are the conclusions more revelatory.

More important, the cost of labor (or unemployment as its surrogate) radically underspecifies what is involved. In today's American economy, compensation of employees comes to roughly three-fifths of gross domestic product, leaving two-fifths of costs unaccounted for. In addition, "compensation of employees" is hardly homogeneous but includes, together with the salaries and perks of several hundred thousand men and women who severally take home between half a million and half a billion dollars annually, the wages of some ten million men and women who, despite working full time, do not earn enough to lift themselves and their families out of poverty. In between is the famous middle class. These classes have markedly different effects on the price level, and the price level has markedly different effects on them.

Besides labor, the classic factors of economic production are land and capital, to which must be added, in the capitalist system, entrepreneurship and government. The corresponding costs of these factors are rent, interest, profit, and taxes. (Actual profit, to repeat yet again, is a residual that does not affect price because it can be determined only after the product is sold. Planned profit, however, is a factor in price setting.) Foreign trade also affects the price level, but in a different way.

Instead of only two variables in the natural-rate equation (the rate of unemployment and the price level), we now have eight (the aggregate takings of the working rich, the aggregate salaries of the working middle class, the aggregate wages of the working poor, together with aggregate rents, interest, planned profits, taxes—and the price level). The costs that form a floor under the price level thus consist of no fewer than seven factors. Price inflation can, in principle, continue in the face of a decrease in any one—or any six—of these costs.

In the present context, the natural-rate theory will be refuted if price inflation continues in the face of an increase in unemployment. In such a situation it will be evident that something other than the rate of unemployment is responsible for the inflation.

In fact, the Consumer Price Index has retreated only once since 1951, and then minimally, from 26.9 to 26.8. In that year (1955), unemployment fell from 5.4 percent to 4.3 percent—whereas, according to the natural-rate theory, it should have risen. (Also in 1955, interest payments as a percentage of national income fell from 5.2 percent to 4.7 percent—contradicting the conventional notion that the way to stop infection is to raise interest rates.

In the other fifty-odd years in question, while the CPI has continued to climb, the rate of unemployment has had nine peaks and valleys. If the natural-rate theory were valid, the price level should have fallen—perhaps with a lag—as unemployment scaled each of these peaks. The price level did not fall, laggardly or not.

CAUSES OF PRICE INFLATION

There is no denying, however, that something was driving the price inflation of our time. Of the seven factor costs we have mentioned, three can be quickly eliminated—rent (which has fallen as a percentage of GDP since the early 1960s), planned profit (because actual profit, which is at least a guide for planning, has fallen as a percentage of GDP since the late 1960s), and taxes (because the corporate income tax has fallen from 23.4 percent of federal income in 1960 to 9.7 percent in 1990.[2]

Two costs that have fallen less dramatically should also be counted out: the salaries of the working middle class (because the average hourly private-sector cost of wages and benefits, when adjusted for inflation, has fallen more than 10 percent since 1979), and the wages of the working poor (because the minimum wage, despite the 1991 increase, has not kept up with inflation, and the bottom quintile of wage distribution has likewise fallen more than 10 percent since 1979).[3]

Two of our cost factors are left. As we have previously noted, interest as a percentage of national income has increased from 4.6 percent in 1951 to over 20 percent today. Because business executives perservere with their plans and expect to make profits despite this rapid escalation, economists have tended to concentrate on the psy-

---

2. McIntyre, *Inequality and the Deficit*, p. 12.
3. Mishel and Bernstein, *Working America, 1994–95*, pp. 114, 121.

chology of executive expectations. The truly economic effects are there, nevertheless. Explicit interest costs must be paid to satisfy lenders, and implicit interest or opportunity costs must be earned to attract investors of capital. Prices must be high enough to cover these interest costs, or a business fails. The price level is intimately involved and must push upward with the interest rate.

For the takings of the working rich, we have professional sports as handy models of the certainly not mysterious way high salaries and perks are translated into high prices at the ticket window.

In sum, when we specify in reasonable detail the factor costs that underlie the price system, we find that those that have actually pushed prices upward in the present economy are the interest rate and astronomically high salaries. In theory, any of the other factors might have been responsible; in actuality, only these two were.

That only two of seven factor costs account for current price inflation indicates a vast distortion of the price system. These two have been increasing while the other five have been stagnating or falling. The distortion has been magnified and is continuing. In the mid-1990s, it was widely contended that the then-current price inflation of less than 3 percent was insignificant. It would have been insignificant if the inflation had been uniform, but a 3 percent distortion, continuously compounded becomes more than 34 percent in ten years.

THE PERSONS OF INFLATION

So far we have been discussing the factors as though they were impersonal, but economic factors are not impersonal any more than the market is impersonal. Things are owned and traded by persons.

Of first importance is the fact that the recipients of the gains of the "winning" factors were already prosperous. Interest recipients must already have had money to lend and now will have more, while excessively paid executives in all likelihood already had good incomes and now also will have more money than they need for daily living.

Both classes of winners are now in a position to engage in speculation, with consequences for the economy we have seen in Chapter 14. They will be more likely to engage in speculation to the extent that the "losing" factors are being hurt by the disruption of the price system. And the factors where productive investments might have been made are indeed being hurt. Corporate profits, both before and after taxes, are historically weak in relation to the boom stock markets' valuations of the corporate shares. Money has poured into the stock markets, not to invest in production, but in search of capital gains. The same is true of real estate, where speculation has always been endemic.

The hurts of the remaining factors—the salaries of the middle class, the wages of the poor, and taxes—account for much of the sluggishness of the producing economy. These factors are important elements of the demand side, without which the supply side has no purpose.

The distortion of the price system—the inflation of our time—not only has impeded the growth of the economy, but has grossly benefited two comparatively small classes of citizens (rentiers and highly paid executives), and has seriously disadvantaged all the rest.

"SERIOUS ABOUT INFLATION"

There is no doubt that interest is a cost, explicit or implicit, of every business. It is an explicit cost when a firm borrows, and it is an implicit, or opportunity cost when a firm invests its own money in its own operations. In both cases, interest is a cost. It is not income, and it is not neutral. The firm must set its prices high enough to cover this cost. If it does not do so, it goes out of business.

In short, interest is certainly a cause of cost-push inflation. As we have seen, there are other causes, and their relative importance may be debated; but it is beyond debate that interest is always and everywhere one of the cost-push causes.

In the circumstances, one must wonder how this cause—and only this cause—can also be the cure. The conventional solution of this paradox is pseudo-psychological. When the Federal Reserve Board raises the interest rate, it shows that the Reserve is "serious about inflation." It is not, however, clear why any entrepreneur who could increase profits by raising prices should refrain from doing so because the Reserve is as serious as a headmaster. What can the Reserve do for punishment? It can raise the interest rate some more.

Even conventional economics recognizes this outcome to be unsatisfactory. The February 1995 issue of *Economic Trends*, published by the Federal Reserve Bank of Cleveland, made these tortuous observations: "[O]ne of the strongest correlations in economics is the positive relationship between inflation and the fed funds rate. . . . Thus we are left to contend with the paradox that ultimately lower inflation must be associated with *lower*, not higher, interest rates." The anonymous author then invokes Irving Fisher's notion that inflation is caused by expectations, but immediately runs into another paradox: "If higher rates are successful in slowing the rate of inflation, hikes today must eventually be followed by future declines as inflation expectations abate. However, persistently high interest rates may signal to the public that the central bank itself anticipates continuing inflation. This may pose a significant impediment to the Federal Reserve's ability to signal its commitment to price stability." Indeed it may.

THE EFFECTS OF HIGH INTEREST

When we were searching for the cause of inflation, we found it necessary to narrow the specificity of our terms and hence to increase the number of terms. The same tactic will be adopted here as we consider the proposed cure. Instead of being satisfied with the effect of high interest rates on demand in general or on labor as the largest factor of production, let us examine the effects of a rise in interest rates on five classes of prominent actors in the drama, as follows:

If the interest rate rises, the direct effect, other things being equal, on (1) holders of bonds and other income-earning assets is a fall in asset prices; on (2) bankers, speculators, and people with large cash incomes, access to investment bargains; on (3) entrepreneurs, an increased cost of doing business (especially if cognizance is taken of opportunity cost), requiring increased prices, and resulting in lower sales; on (4) workers, rising unemployment and constraints on wage scales; on (5) consumers, higher prices and higher borrowing costs.

The five classes are obviously neither mutually exclusive nor together exhaustive. Almost everyone belongs to the last class and at least one other, and it is not uncommon for some people to be classifiable under all five headings.

The summary analysis shows that an increase in interest rates is not even-handed in its consequences for economic agents. Three points are worth emphasizing. First, while it is common to lump investors in the ongoing economy (the first class) with speculators (the second class), they actually have opposing interests. Second and most important, while current anti-inflation policy is directed primarily at the fourth class of agents, and while it may be said to work there roughly as intended (although not as might be desired), its side effects are disadvantageous for every class except the second, which has generally benefited, and continues to benefit, enormously. Third, the effects on classes three and five include *upward* pressures on the price level.

In short, the price system is not a monolith; and when it is treated monolithically, as it is by current theory, its diversity is accentuated, and its disruptions exaggerated.

Over the past three decades, the Federal Reserve Board's deliberate disruptions of the American economy have increased the polarization of society by transferring wealth and income from the capitalist system's relatively many borrowers to its relatively few lenders, from its workers in the producing economy to bankers, speculators, and rentiers. This transfer is the more malign in that, as we have seen in Chapter 4, borrowers are systematically the more active and creative element in the economy.

That this transfer is not trivial can be shown by an everyday example of the effects of the Reserve Board's increases of the interest rate between June 1999 and July 2000. The payments on a $100,000 mortgage undertaken after the rate increases were about $110 a month greater than if the mortgage had been undertaken before the rate hikes. The mortgagor had done nothing to deserve this considerable loss of wealth (about $1,300 a year, or $39,000 over the life of a thirty-year mortgage), and the mortgagee (presumably a bank) had done nothing to deserve this added income. The transfer was an incidental consequence of the Federal Reserve's misguided assault on inflation as it knew it. Similar transfers occurred with all home mortgages and with all automobiles, appliances, furniture, and vacations bought on time. The cost, especially to the middle class, was of orders of magnitude greater than the benefit expected from the tax cuts periodically talked about, while the tax cuts themselves were rendered more expensive by the increased interest to be paid on government bonds.

Nor was this all. All commercial loans and mortgages were affected in the same way. Borrowers in the producing economy were required to pay vast extra sums to lenders in the speculating economy.

Worst of all, these gratuitous transfers generally aggravated the polarization of society.

ILLICIT USE OF PARTIAL ANALYSIS

It must be recognized that the price system is indeed a system. The natural-rate theorists are correct to this extent: Our shameful rates of unemployment and poverty are of a piece with the prices both of commodities and of the factors of production.

In 1897, reviewing Pareto's attempt to prove the optimality of wages under free competition, Wicksell wrote, "What can be proved is simply that under free competition the worker receives the greatest possible wage *compatible with the current state of rents and interest* (just as the landowners and capitalists obtain the greatest possible yield *compatible with the current wage situation*)."[4]

Sixty years later, Friedman said practically the same thing, naming somewhat more elaborate conditions: "At any moment of time, there is some level of unemployment which has the property that it is consistent with equilibrium in the structure of *real* wage rates. At that level of unemployment, real wages are tending on the average to rise at a 'normal' secular rate, i.e., at a rate that can be indefinitely maintained so long as capital formation, technological improvements, etc., remain on their long-term trends."[5]

Granting Friedman's large and untestable assumption, we see that it can be read in at least two ways. His way undoubtedly requires the rate of unemployment to accomodate itself to the other "long-term trends." But there is nothing in the scenario he presents to us that denies the possibility of a very low rate of unemployment to which the other long-term trends accommodate themselves. And if the interest rate is subsumed under the heading "capital formation," we have a good idea how at least that trend must be shifted.

In the end, the natural rate theory, like Ricardo's wages-fund theory, is an example of the illicit use of partial analysis. As we saw in Chapter 2, partial analysis is a valid and useful tool in solving restricted and specific problems, like "Should our new advertising slogan make fun of Mothers' Day?" It is invalid in the face of a universal problem. In the natural rate theory, it is assumed that all costs other than the cost of labor are fixed. It is also assumed that profits cannot be reduced. It is then concluded that prices must rise unless the cost of la-

---

4. Wicksell, *Selected Papers*, p. 144.
5. Friedman, "Monetary Policy," p. 8.

bor is held constant. But the same form of reasoning would yield the conclusion that profit (or anything else you might name) is the cause of inflation.

America stands for the meaningful enlargement of the life of the common man and woman. In so far as members of what calls itself the mainstream of the American economics profession stood for a theory of a natural rate of unemployment, they stood (or still stand) outside the mainstream of American life.

PART IV

PROSPECT

22

A Few Notes on the "New Economy"

Millions of words have been spoken and written about the "New Economy," but it is still early to say exactly what (if anything) it is. The archetypical company seems to be started by a couple of computer "geeks" fooling around in somebody's garage and coming up with an idea for a product or service based on the Internet, and perhaps not only using the Internet but improving it.

A venture capital fund, probably derived from capital gains won in the stock market and looking for even more profitable ways to invest the money, agrees to take a piece of the action. A company is formed with the "geeks." Stock options are distributed to all hands, including those hired to realize the idea. An initial public offering (IPO) is planned, under the direction of an investment banker. If it is a success—that is, if the founders are instant multimillionaires—production is started in a serious way, and more stock is floated on NASDAQ, the proceeds of which are used to finance mergers and acquisitions of related enterprises, thus starting the formation of a monopoly, the expectation of which attracted the attention of the venture capitalists in the first place.

The foregoing scenario may be a myth, but it is a story with great appeal, especially to members of the baby-boom generation, who are increasingly concerned about their looming retirement in 2010 and thereafter, when their winnings in the "old economy" are likely to prove inadequate to support life on Golden Pond. The blue chip companies of the old economy are paying dividends of about 1.5 percent of their market value, which works out to $15,000 a year on a million dollars—not so much, after all. The dividends paid by the new economy are even thinner; hence the stressful yearning for a killing on the NASDAQ.

A NOTE ON AMAZON.COM

This is not, by any means, a book of investment advice. In discussing, very superficially, one company, our purpose is merely to indicate what, if anything, is "new" about one first-rate example of the New Economy.

The book business was a good choice for a business to serve its customers remotely, without requiring them to go to a store. While it is pleasant to browse a well-run store, it is also pleasant to browse a well-prepared catalog or to search for a well-recommended title. There is always the possibility of being misled by a book's description or being deceived by its cover, but these misfortunes are not altogether avoided by shopping in person. In any case, the seller does not have to tell the customers what a book is or how it can be used. Sellers and customers do not have to meet face to face. So books have long been successfully sold by mail.

But it turns out that the book business is a bad choice for a business organized in such a way that its success depends on achieving monopoly or oligopoly. The first fact to bear in mind about the book business is a number: 60,000. That is, more or less, the number of new books published in English in the United States every year. These 60,000 books were written by every sort of person you can think of, on every sort of subject you can think of, for every sort of reason you can think of. For most of the authors, like the author of this book, it wasn't easy, but they did it. There's a need there—a force—that can't be disregarded.

Now consider the readers. Substantial millions of them read substantial numbers of these books (as well as the half million or more other books in print, not to mention the additional millions in libraries). All sorts of people read these books for all sorts of reasons—there is no such thing as *the* book market—and they read them despite the allurements of TV or jogging or taking a nap. As with the writers, so with the readers: there is a need here—a force—that can't be disregarded.

In between these large and chaotic groups of writers and readers is the book business, which is chaotic, too, and for a surprising reason: copyright.

A copyright is superficially similar to a license or a patent in its purpose and legal form but is quite different in its practical effects. A utility, almost by definition, is something big enough and important enough to need licensing. As for patents, they are almost always interlocking. Someone invents something, and someone else invents an improvement. The improvement is valueless without the basic invention, and the basic invention not only needs the improvement but is usually itself dependent on pre-existing patents for its design or manufacture. There are exceptions; but when you're talking about licenses or patents, you're generally talking about pretty big business.

A copyright is quite different. It applies to this particular book, which depends on other books only in the sense that all aspects of a culture—not just books—are interdependent. Each book actually stands alone. It may be read with only incidental reference to other particular books. As it enters into commerce, it may be bought and sold for itself alone. In contrast, there is no market for a new kind of steering linkage except as part of an automobile, or for a new TV skit except as part of a program.

When one buys a copyright book, one buys a copy of the original. It is, for most purposes, like every other copy. Why should one buy the copy offered by A rather than the copy offered by B?

Amazon.com says one should buy from them because it is convenient, speedy, and a bargain. So far they have been enormously successful in selling millions of books. They have also lost millions of dollars doing so. Obviously their prices are too low for their costs. They feel (probably correctly) that they need to offer the bargain prices to make the sales, but they cannot raise their prices as long as Barnes and Noble, Borders, and others are nipping at their heels. In short, this form of the new economy acts as if it needs monopoly to succeed.

Take away the bargains, and their sales will tumble. Such, indeed, has been the ultimate experience of bargain-based bookselling schemes. The Book-of-the-Month Club, which was innovative in many ways, was so successful by the 1930s that some booksellers subscribed to it as an inexpensive way of stocking their inventory of BOMC selections. At one time it was said that the Book-of-the-Month Club was doing 10 percent of the retail book business in the country. Soon there were scores of rivals, many of them run by the Book Club itself, all competing on quality, convenience, and price.

Ironically, it was quality that reduced the Book Club to its present place far below the salt at the Time-Warner table. In the 1930s the Club was so prominent and commanding that publishers and authors accepted a comparatively low flat fee for a selection. But in the prosperous 1950s, it became usual for the Literary Guild to compete for the most promising titles, so that the two major clubs ultimately were bidding a million or more for books they felt they had to have to stay competitive. The clubs lost their ability to offer dramatic bargains, and bookstores flourished.

The fate of the mail-order business of Sears, Roebuck should be a warning to Amazon's other ambitions.

THE E-BOOKS

The so-called electronic books may succeed as an ancillary to the regular book business, just as talking books and large-type books find comparatively small but profitable extra markets for certain ordinary books, mostly bestsellers or suspense stories. At present, of course, electronic books are clumsy novelties, and it is doubtful that they will ever come close to matching the old-fashioned book in convenience for serious reading and durability. It is easy to riffle through a regular book to reread a passage, and it is easy to mark memorable passages and to argue with the author on the margins. Furthermore, a regular book is not destroyed if tossed on a desk or accidentally dropped on the floor.

In the 1880s or thereabouts, the invention of the coaster brake was expected to make bicycle riding so safe and pleasurable that no one would have time for reading books. Then movies were going to displace books, or the movie business was going to be so powerful that it would dictate what would be published. Then came the radio, closely followed by TV, whose educative powers were thought to be so promising that the major networks rushed to pay record prices for publishers in order to be able to control material for their program divisions.

OTHER RETAIL BUSINESSES

It may prove different with the other retail businesses that Amazon.com has moved into. With most products—say porch furniture—it is rarely possible to produce a design so original and so practical and so desirable that it will sweep the market for porch furniture as every copyright book sweeps the market for that book. Substitution—that "great law," Walras called it—then becomes possible. Competition then is no longer based exclusively or primarily on price (as standard economics teaches it is), and retailers do not need to monopolize a market in order to charge profitable prices.

On the other hand, the Internet offers no particular advantage in most of these other lines. Judging from the basketsful of catalogs a householder receives after a few weeks' absence from home, there are plenty of people willing and able to sell almost anything by mail, and they may be at least as good at it as Internet sellers are. Indeed, there is no reason why Internet, direct mail, shopping malls, discount chains, quality stores, and mom 'n' pop outlets cannot offer their special advantages, as they do now, without cutthroat competition.

One advantage Internet selling will have for several years, because of congressional action, is freedom from local taxation, especially from the sales tax. It would be a well-deserved but unexpected advantage for all if this otherwise incomprehensible action should result in the general abolition of the sales tax, which is not only regressive in its impact on consumers but repressive in its impact on producers.

23

A Few Notes on the "New Finance"

The finance of the New Economy is not particularly connected with the Internet but is, in fact, close to the principles of borrowing and lending emphasized in this book. As we have said more than once, modern capitalism is based on borrowing, and the borrowing is guaranteed by future earnings rather than by past savings. A twenty-year or thirty-year mortgage, now the leading form of personal finance, is obviously oriented toward the future, whereas, before the New Deal, the typical one-year or five-year mortgage enforced rigorous and constant saving. As a result, home ownership, with its consequent advantages, is more widely spread in the economy than ever before.

Business finance, likewise, is more future-directed than formerly. As Hyman Minsky argued, the economy is thereby more fragile; but it is also more open, expansive, and productive. Much of the fragility, furthermore, is due to inappropriate, archaic, and erratic policies of the Federal Reserve Board.

Nevertheless, a modern capitalist corporation is ongoing. It borrows money in order to make ongoing investments in plant and inventory, pays ongoing interest and ongoing wages, produces an ongoing stream of goods and services, earns ongoing profits, pays ongoing taxes. If its management is bright and agile, it is never without plans for the future. It is seldom out of debt.

"NEW" FEDERAL FINANCE

The first thing to understand about the federal budget is that it is only superficially like a personal budget, a corporation budget, a department budget, a municipal budget, a school budget, or a state budget or even the United Nations budget. All these budgets plan for ("budget" is a verb as well as a noun) and subsequently account for the entities' income and expenditures for a period—a week, a month, a year—and show whether income and expenditures balance. If they don't balance (and of course they rarely do), the budget shows a deficit when expenditures exceed income and a surplus when the scales dip the other way.

The federal budget does all these things and one thing more: it can create money. None of the other budgets can create money, but the federal budget can and does. This wondrous capability carries with it responsibilities and powers that are so great that the federal budget is altogether different from the other budgets. Attempts to understand the federal budget by analogy with the more familiar budgets result in confusion and misdirection.

The confusion is compounded by the fact that the national debt is the net total of all the revolutionary and federal budgets from July 4, 1776, to the present. And in all those two hundred twenty-four years, with the exception of a few months in 1836—one hundred sixty-four years ago—the United States of America has been in debt. It is noticeable that the long and deep depression of 1837 started almost immediately after the last creditor was paid off in 1836. Indeed, there have been six other occasions when we made a serious attempt to pay off the national debt, and each attempt led to a serious depression.

The connection between the attempts to pay off the national debt and the subsequent depressions is not accidental. As we have seen, the government's IOUs are money. Reduce the IOUs outstanding, and we reduce the national money. Pay off the IOUs, and we eliminate the national money. Business slows down.

It did not stop altogether, even in 1837, because specie (gold) took care of some interstate business, while local banks issued notes (bank IOUs) that satisfied much local business, although many local bank notes were questionable. (It is safe to say that they did not all suffer from over-strict regulation.)

The federal government would accept only gold to pay tariffs, whiskey taxes, and for purchases of western land. In addition many private contracts required gold. There was not enough gold for these purposes. Depression took over.

Doing business was not easy. If while visiting your cousins in Peoria, you tried to buy a hostess present with notes issued by your bank in Boston, you'd have to wait while the shopkeeper sent a clerk running to her bank to get the latest Peoria quote on the particular Massachusetts issue. Experience would have prepared you for the certainty that your "foreign" currency would be discounted, perhaps heavily, if only to pay for the trouble and risks of cashing it.

Each of the previous attempts to eliminate the national debt resulted in a gold panic. Today, with gold demonetized and the federal government accounting for better than 24 percent of the economy and consequently issuing IOUs for that amount, depression would not come so abruptly if the national debt were to be paid off by 2010 (as some claim it can be). But depression would come. You can't make bricks without straw, and you can't run a modern economy without money.

GENERATION YET UNBORN

Judging from political commercials, speeches, and letters to the editor, the most winning argument for balancing the budget is the folksy one about generations yet unborn. We all know how it goes: "I've worked hard and had a good life. I don't want to leave a big deficit for my grandchildren to pay. It wouldn't be fair."

Well, I don't know about that. I have a $5,000 U.S. Treasury bond that I bought in 1984. My bond will mature in 2014, long after my time, even if I heroically reduce my ingestion of animal fats. The Treasury used my $5,000 to help pay the deficit in 1984. Since then, despite several debt-ceiling squabbles, I've been paid $331.25 interest twice a year, and I thank you all very much.

In 2014 one of my descendants, possibly one yet unborn, who will have inherited this bond, will turn it in to the Treasury, and will get a nice electronic addition to his or her savings for a college education. Please tell me how I, by buying this bond and bequeathing it to my descendant, have shifted a burden from my shoulders onto those of generations yet unborn.

Let's go over the transaction step by step. In 1984 I lent the government $5,000, and the government promised to pay me back in thirty years, plus 13¼ percent annual interest. (The government has an option to pay back slightly more at the end of twenty-five years, but that will be my descendant's affair.) In order to make that payment, the government will have to take $5,000 from the taxes paid in 2014 by the generation that by that time will have come of age. My descendant will be a member of that generation, which is thus both the payer and the recipient of $5,000. In the same way, my generation was both the payer (me) and the beneficiary (all of us living in 1984) of $5,000.

Between the generations, no injustice was or will be done—unless we deprive the mothers of future generations of proper prenatal care, deprive the members of those generations of proper education, and despoil the natural and cultural environments in which we live and in which they will live.

Within the generations, however, there may be injustices. In our confrontational age you may demand to know how I got my hands on $5,000 in the not remarkably prosperous year of 1984. I will confess that I did nothing for it. It was a sort of government handout—a result of the Reagan-Kemp-Roth supply-side tax cuts of 1981–82.

The government gave me money, or let me keep money it knew it needed, thereby increasing its deficit and requiring it to issue additional bonds. I used part of the money given me to buy one of the new bonds. In effect I was given the bond. I was, to be sure, a generally hard-working, law-abiding citizen; but not every generally hard-working, law-abiding citizen was given $5,000. A few were given vastly more, and many were given little or nothing. These many may have a case against me, and I may have a grudge against the few. And similar cases can be imagined against and for my descendant. But these cases are all within the respective generations. The deficit raised no question of intergenerational propriety or justice or affection.

CROWDING OUT

The principal, if not the only, economic reason given for the stern demand that the federal budget must be balanced at any cost is that government borrowing is said to crowd private enterprise out of the money market. The theory holds that the deficit requires the government to borrow, that the increased demand for loans pushes the interest rate up, and that many worthy private enterprises cannot afford the increased interest and thus are crowded out of business.

The trouble with the theory is that it is false. It is, on its face, so plausible that apparently no one has ever thought to test it. The fate of the nation may ultimately hang upon it, and masses of the already impoverished may be utterly ruined by our adherence to it. But this fateful theory has been taken on faith.

Yet it is possible to test the crowding-out theory, not by some esoteric argument, but by the readily available record of what has actually happened. Many government publications give figures for the deficit, the debt, and the prime interest rate (which can be taken as a base to which the mortgage rate and all other rates that individuals and businesses pay are related). If the theory were valid, an increase in the deficit would always cause an increase in the prime, and a decrease in the deficit would always cause a decrease in the prime. In actuality, these expected results do not eventuate even half the time, let alone every time.

Over the past thirty-four years (the length of a generation), from 1966 through 1999, an increase in the deficit has been accompanied by a *decrease* in the prime thirteen times, and a decrease in the deficit has been accompanied by an *increase* in the prime eleven times. In short, the crowding-out theory was, as scientists say, falsified, or proved false, by events in twenty-four years out of thirty-four.

Most strikingly, in 1969, 1998, and 1999, the three years of the thirty-four in which the budget was balanced, the prime was *raised*.

More significantly, the prime moved up or down with the federal funds rate (the principal rate set by the Federal Reserve Board) in every year but two, strongly suggesting that if there was any crowding out in the period (and there was a tragic amount of it, as many can testify), it was caused by the Federal Reserve Board, not by the deficit.

Some may suggest that a lag must be allowed for, between the year in which the deficit changes and the year in which the change has an effect on the prime rate. Such a lag is not likely, since it is usually possible for bankers and other lenders to guess accurately which way the deficit is going to jump months before the budget law takes final shape.

In any event, a lag makes little difference. Allowing for a one-year lag, a rising deficit was associated with a falling prime ten times, and a falling deficit with a rising prime eight times. Even on the most generous assumption, the crowding-out theory proved false eighteen years out of thirty-four.

A test of the crowding-out effect of the national debt obviously has similar results. Just as a wealthy individual can afford a large mortgage, a large nation can afford a large debt; so the debt burden is measured by taking the debt as a percentage of the gross domestic product. Thus it can move up or down with the state of the economy.

Starting in 1977, the debt burden fell steadily, reaching its lowest point of the three decades in 1981. During the years while the debt burden was falling to its low, the prime was rising to its all-time high of 21½ percent in December 1980 and January 1981. It might be argued that Federal Reserve Chairman Paul Volcker crowded President Jimmy Carter out of office, but not that the national debt did it.

The crowding-out argument for balancing the budget is demonstrably false, and there is a better explanation for what it pretends to explain. Follow the money, as Deep Throat said. The Federal Reserve controls the money.

Any theory that fails to fulfill its predictions seventeen or twenty-four times out of thirty-four is surely discreditable and should be discarded as a guide to public policy, especially vital public policy.

One may nevertheless wonder how such a plausible theory can be empirically so clearly wrong. It is an example of the ancient logical fallacy of affirming the consequent, otherwise known as the flat-earth argument (Major premise: If the earth is flat, we won't fall off. Minor premise: We don't fall off. Conclusion: The earth is flat.) In the same way, high interest rates do in fact crowd worthy enterprises out of business, but this fact does not and cannot prove that the deficit causes high interest rates. (High interest rates also increase the costs of doing business, resulting in higher prices, otherwise known as inflation. But that is another story.)

An excuse for the stumble into the crowding-out error is suggested by the definition of "crowding out" in *The MIT Dictionary of Modern Economics*, whose first full sentence reads, "In a fully employed economy a rise in government expenditure will cause an offsetting fall in private investment." There, in the first five words, is the crucial and fallacious assumption of the theory—"In a fully employed economy."

If our economy were in fact fully employed, something like a crowding-out effect would perhaps be observable. What we actually observe is that our economy is not fully employed. Our money is not fully employed, nor are we the people fully employed. Especially not we the people. Why else do we commit so much of our money to gambling in lotteries and derivatives and "aggressive" stock funds? Why else are so many millions of us working part time, and so many millions not working at all?

There is no economic reason whatsoever for the budget-balancing frenzy. Nor is there a historical reason. We have been without a balanced budget sixty-one years in the past seventy, during which time we have risen from the depths of depression to become the wealthiest and most powerful nation in the world.

Yet today we still abjectly cringe before a mythical apparition that bids us to destroy our social and cultural fabric, to permit the decay of our infrastructure and our public amenities, to renege on our human responsibilities to the other peoples of the world, and to acquiesce in the decline or abandonment of artistic, scholarly, and scientific work.

As before in our history, we have nothing to fear but fear itself.

24

Why the Trade Deficit Won't Go Away

Many say we are at the brink of disaster. With the exception of one year (1991) our foreign trade has been out of balance on current account (mainly the exchange of goods and services) since 1982. For a while it could be reasonably expected that if we were out of balance with nations A, B, and C because we imported more from them than we exported to them, we would export more to and import less from nations X, Y, and Z, so that the overall balance would occur in the trade between our creditors and our debtors. It has not worked out that way. Since 1982, our imbalance has grown rapidly in practically every direction, and much to the surprise of many commentators, it is growing more rapidly now that our budget is in surplus.

Our imbalance on current account has been growing since the 1970s. At the end of 1998 it had reached $1,604,543,000,000. If the nations of the world were to grow weary or wary of this sum, and were to try to use it to buy goods and services from us, we'd probably experience an instant inflation, followed by an instant deflation, and there's no knowing who would be near the chairs when the music stopped.

Fortunately, there is practically no possibility of the occurrence of such an event, not because the finance ministers of the world are too clever to let it happen, but because they couldn't pull it off if they wanted to. The catch is that the other nations are holding dollar reserves in excess of $1,358,900,000,000. (The spread between this figure and the figure given for our net accumulated trade deficit may be explained by the capital transfers involved in foreign purchases of American assets and by the "statistical discrepancies" common in this branch of economics.)

If nations should try to deplete their reserves, their currencies would collapse, and there would be no chairs for them to collapse into. Consequently the United States of America, acknowledged to be the richest nation in the history of the world, is ironically in debt to the rest, including the poorest.

These reserves are, of course, not only a convenience for an active foreign trade, but a prudent preparation for a rainy day (or hopeful protection against rogue speculators). It is not, however, obvious why the non-American nations of the world should hold almost three-quarters of their foreign reserves in American dollars. While the United States is the world's largest exporter, for many nations it is not the major trading partner.

As we saw in Chapter 4, the government buys goods and services and pays money for them. It is then in debt to those who have the money. In order to pay the debt, the government levies taxes. Almost all of us need money to pay taxes; so we work to produce goods and services that those who have money will be willing to pay for. We then have money to pay the tax collector. Our debt to the government is paid, the government's debt to the holders of money is validated; and the process is ready to repeat itself. Indeed the process never stops. Regardless of what budget balancers say, a good government is never out of debt, and good citizens are seldom out of money.

Can this domestic process be replicated internationally? The United

Nations can neither coin money nor impose taxes. It is even weaker than the Continental Congress in these respects.

Yet there is one commodity that all nations of the world must have and only a few do have. That commodity is oil. For accidental, but good and sufficient, reasons OPEC has decided to demand dollars in payment for its oil. Consequently the nations of the world that do not produce enough oil for their needs must have dollars. The international need for oil is analogous to worldwide taxation; dollars are the means of satisfying that need; hence dollars are validated for international trade.

To be confident that they will have enough oil as long as anyone else, nations must have large dollar reserves. To build the reserves they must sell goods to the United States and accept dollars in payment. This being the situation, it would be disruptive of world order if the United States should manage to increase its exports or decrease its imports enough to balance its foreign trade on current account.

What has been happening for the past thirty years is not that the United States has failed at exporting but that the rest of the world has needed reserves of a trillion and a half American dollars. American goods, from T-shirts with silly mottoes to Boeing 747s, from wheat to pharmaceuticals, from gangsta rap to Disneyland are admired and desired all over the world. Neither our high prices nor our questionable taste nor the trade barriers that exercise the World Trade Organization account for our inability to balance our foreign trade on current account.

As long as the nations of the world need increasing dollar reserves, they must sell a portion of their goods to us for dollars. For ordinary business needs, the oil-producing nations, too, maintain dollar reserves. All of this, of course, is greatly to our national advantage, provided we do not continue, by misreading its causation, to use it as a handy excuse to keep the interest rate high with the announced intention of attracting foreign capital—which must come to us anyhow—

but with the actual consequence of maintaining a "sustainable" rate of unemployment and thus widening the chasm between the haves and the have-nots of our society.

WHY THE DOLLAR?

It is noticeable that our present concern about our trade deficit appeared as OPEC flexed its muscles in the 1970s, and that our trade deficit grows at roughly the same rate as the world's dollar reserves grow.

The question remains, why did OPEC choose the dollar instead of the yen, the pound sterling, or the euro? There are several possible reasons: The United States is OPEC's largest customer and the world's largest exporter and largest importer; it is therefore easier both for OPEC and for its customers to deal with the United States than with anyone else. Perhaps even more important, the United States is the largest producer of goods the OPEC nations need, namely agricultural products and military material.

Most important, despite the best efforts of the supply-side Reagan revolution and the general equilibrium theory of the Washington consensus, the United States is still a demand-side economy. We remain a nation of consumers eager to exchange our dollars for goods and services in any market open to us. Consequently, dollars are about in the world in sufficient quantities to form the backbone of the foreign reserves of the oil-needing nations.

In contrast, the United Kingdom still carries the baggage of a mercantilist empire, while Japan displays the ultimate weakness of a supply-side economy. Both the United Kingdom and Japan have extensive investments in the United States. When these are successful, their earnings are not in pounds or yen, but in dollars, which must be spent in the United States or held in dollar reserves, in both cases strengthening the dollar in international markets, and in both cases subject to American policy and law.

Japan was enormously successful in building its export industries and capturing world markets, but its overemphasis on saving stunted its domestic market and left it with no use for its great foreign balances except more of the same, followed by frenetic speculation and gaudily bursting bubbles on its real estate and securities markets, followed, in turn, by a lingering depression.

THREE FALSE PROPOSITIONS

Our position, however, is not foolproof. No doubt angered by our role in the World Trade Organization's banana war, France is showing a willingness to break the embargo of Iraq, which is, for its part, showing a willingness to sell oil for euros (which, of course, did not exist at the time of the first oil crises). It is not impossible that something not unlike bimetallism may develop, making every day a field day for speculators.

In the meantime, we shall do well to recognize that three propositions, all of which were commonly held by economists in the 1980s and early 1990s, have all been falsified (as hard scientists would say) by events of the turn of the twenty-first century.

First, and most obvious: A trade deficit and a budget deficit were said to be positively related. The current record shows that we can, and do, have one without the other.

Second, and most important for policy and history: It used to be said, especially during the 1980s, that we saved so little that we needed high interest rates to induce foreigners to invest in our public debt. Since most of the rest of the world needs dollar reserves and needs them in safe and liquid form, there is not now, and never has been, a better place to put them than in U.S. Treasury bonds.

Third, and most important for fundamental economic theory: A trade deficit used to be considered an invariably negative constituent of a nation's prosperity, not because the availability of consumers' goods is thereby reduced (of course it isn't), but because portions of the nation's productive capacity are rendered unnecessary (or never develop), with the result that domestic labor and capital are both underemployed.

Our experience of the past decade suggests that a trade deficit can become a positive constituent of our prosperity if and when monetary (and fiscal) policies allow the unemployment rate to approach zero.

25

On Being Fully Human

There is a fatality about economics that in the end chokes any society that makes too great a distinction between the rewards of the favored and of the disfavored. It is a commonplace of legal theory that a law must not only be just but must also be seen to be just. It is the other way around with economics, where it is more important for a policy to be fair than to be accepted as fair. This is particularly true when it comes to policies determining the distribution of society's rewards.

Gross inequality of economic rewards is certainly nothing new. It has been with us from the beginning of time. It may actually be less now than in previous centuries. Slavery has been largely abolished, and some sort of egalitarianism is at least a widely endorsed ideal. Nevertheless, the gap between the rich and the poor is enormous, unconscionable, and growing again, not only in the United States but in the rest of the world, especially in the Third World.

What has changed, and continues to change at an accelerating rate, is what the rich do with their money. Before the middle of the nineteenth century there was little question what they did with it. They invested in land and in improvements thereon: châteaus and stately homes and protoscientific agriculture. Of course, there were always commissions and sinecures to buy, and colonial adventures for younger sons, and gambles to take a flier on; but land was everlasting. Money that was made by craft methods on the land was invested in craft improvements on the land.

In the eighteenth century, maldistribution showed its effects at the top as well as at the bottom of the income scale. Prospective lenders on the Continent were frequently unable to find willing borrowers at 4 percent or less. The situation was somewhat different in Britain, partly because she was notoriously a nation of shopkeepers. Even so, Braudel tells us, England "did not summon up all her reserves to finance her industrial revolution."[1] The South Sea Bubble in Britain and the Mississippi Bubble in France, both of which burst in 1720, were only the most dramatic instances of the speculation that developed in place of productive investment.

The economics of the rational greedy economic man sees no connection between such "bubbles" and the wastes and the horrors and the griefs of early industrialization. But the money that blew away as bubble after bubble burst had been accumulated at the expense of appalling labor and suffering of underpaid men, women, and children in mines and in milltowns, on ships and on industrialized farms—at the expense, too, of wanton destruction of the natural environment.

THE INDUSTRIAL REVOLUTION

The Industrial Revolution was not, of course, a single event that turned the world upside down on a certain date. It was a series of events of many kinds and many magnitudes that, although concentrated in the

---

1. Braudel, *Civilization and Capitalism*, vol. 2, pp. 395–400.

hundred years following 1775, stretched over many years, starting perhaps with the invention of printing from movable type in the fifteenth century and coming down to the latest computer chip of only yesterday.

Adam Smith, writing at the start of the "revolution" proper, opens *The Wealth of Nations* with these words: "The greatest improvement in the productive powers of labour, and the greater part of the skill, dexterity, and judgment with which it is any where directed, or applied, seem to have been the effects of the division of labour."[2] Smith is properly impressed by this productiveness and notes that workmen who specialize in a relatively narrow aspect of a trade are soon able to suggest improvements in the tools. This, which might be called the bright side of the division of labor, is what interests Smith at the beginning.

The dark side appears in Book V of *The Wealth of Nations*: "The uniformity of [the labourer's] stationary life naturally . . . corrupts even the activity of his body, and renders him incapable of exerting his strength with vigour and perserverance, in any other employment than that to which he has been bred. His dexterity at his own particular trade seems, in this manner, to be acquired at the expense of his intellectual, social, and martial virtues. But in every improved and civilized society, this is the state into which the labouring poor, that is, the great body of the people, must necessarily fall, unless government takes some pains to prevent it."[3]

The dark side became darker as the "revolution" proceeded. Thirty years after Smith, William Blake was writing of the "dark, satanic mills." Another thirty years, and Thomas Carlyle dubbed economics "the dismal science." A few years more, and Charles Dickens was describing "Coketown" in *Hard Times*, and Karl Marx was writing the work posthumously published as *Economic and Philosophic Manuscripts of 1844*, in which he advanced his theory of the alienation of the worker from his work, from his fellow workers and, in the end,

2. Smith, *Wealth*, p. 3.
3. Smith, *Wealth*, pp. 734–35.

from himself. So far, the story is merely another retelling of a very old tale, familiar in tribal divisions of hunters and gatherers, in caste systems, and in the myriad class divisions that have appeared in history.

Ordinarily the Industrial Revolution is presented as a series of engineering triumphs—Thomas Watt's redesign of the steam engine, James Hargreaves's spinning jenny, Richard Cartwright's power loom—that extended and improved the division of labor. Such works of the Enlightenment all gave us greater control over the natural world and our lives in it.

The inventions we have mentioned and countless others like them were essentially or mainly what may be called social goods. Social goods enriched not merely their owners, but society as a whole. They contributed to the macroeconomy. They were improvements of capital goods, and hence, improvements in the production of consumption goods.

In contrast is Emerson's claim that if a man could make a better mousetrap than his neighbor, the world would beat a path to his door. This was not exactly in conflict with the Industrial Revolution, but it did miss a point. A truly revolutionary invention would have been a machine to mass produce serviceable mousetraps. Then the world would have been flooded with traps after only a few entrepreneurs had trampled the inventor's lawn.

FACTORIES AND FORTUNES

Changes that had started in the Commercial Revolution came very rapidly in the Industrial Revolution. Immense fortunes could be made in the new factories, which quickly overwhelmed their craft-based predecessors, first in textiles and then in all sorts of industry, especially iron and steel. Two conditions impeded industrialization: illiquidity and exposure, both of which made it imperative for prudent gentlemen to become actively concerned in the enterprises they invested in. This was something that few gentlemen were inclined or qualified to do. Fortuitously, the development of relatively efficient stock markets took care of one impediment, and the invention of the limited liability company took care of the other. And then, as we saw in Chapter 8, another momentous change took place; property—the bundle of rights the law would protect—was enlarged from use value to include exchange value.

The opportunities for what came to be called the functionless investor seemed almost limitless. Industrial capacity was now theoretically very great. The practical problem was to find a market worthy of it. Technological advances in agriculture had released a large population desperate for factory work at low wages. The low wages made low prices possible but at the same time restricted the size of the effective market.

At this point the inequities of economic rewards became a decisive restraint on production. Since the Great Depression, the restraint has been appreciably relaxed by the expenditures of big government; but we still have 5 or 6 million people we cannot think how to employ at all and millions more people we count as employed but cannot think how to employ full-time. This costs us, and may finally destroy us; yet it would seem that substantial majorities of American voters, although worried about the future, have been satisfied with the intent of recent policies. The policies are seen to be fair, but their actual unfairness may be our undoing.

THE MASS ECONOMY

Industry today is built on mass production. Karl Polyani's "great transformation" to a market economy has become a giant transformation to a mass economy. The economy, however, cannot sell all that it might produce. The wealthy do not spend their incomes on the products of mass industry, because it would be not merely vulgar, nor merely irrational, but flatly impossible to do so.

The value of the product of mass industry is equal to the mass-industry earnings of the nonwealthy plus the mass-industry earnings of the wealthy, not all of which, of course, are in the form of wages. To the extent that the wealthy withdraw their earnings, to that extent demand for the product of mass industry must fall short. The nonwealthy may be willing enough to enjoy what mass industry could produce, but their incomes are not enough to pay the bills. According to standard theory, the wealthy, after providing for their security and comfort, will return their surplus earnings to the economy in the form of investments, which will create more and better jobs. In actuality, however, they largely turn to speculation, for reasons and with results that we have seen.

In a brilliant empirical study, the late Treval C. Powers demonstrated that this leakage (as he called it), together with losses in bankruptcies and constrictions in the economy caused by actions of the Federal Reserve Board, has kept the economy operating far below its potential growth, which Powers shows to be a quasi-constant of about 11.4 percent per capita, per annum (in contrast with the Federal Reserve Board's present target of 2.5 percent).

"When the demand for consumer goods and services is reduced," Powers wrote, "so also is the demand for capital expenditures. They are not independent variables, and any macroeconomic theory that treats them as such is bound to be false. . . . Leakage during the postwar period has amounted to about one-fifth of the whole amount of capital income. That fifth is undoubtedly in the hands of a few of the wealthiest recipients of capital income, or has been lost in bad investments."[4]

We have no right to sit in judgment of our forebears, but we do have an obligation to understand what they did and a duty to judge ourselves. We have our burgeoning "institutions"—and we have the

---

4. Powers, *Leakage*, pp. 342–43.

devastated lives lived in our inner cities and decaying towns. We have our international financial empires—and we have the *favelas* of Rio and the slums of Cairo and Lagos and Bombay and Tokyo. We could afford to throw away a trillion dollars in 1987 and other large sums in 1989 and 2000—yet we do not summon up the will to afford fair jobs and decent living conditions for millions of our fellow citizens.

The bull market that started in 1982 took five years to absorb a trillion dollars. The bull market that started in 1988 absorbed a trillion dollars in less than four years and is well on its way to six trillion more. The words "seven trillion dollars" can be spoken trippingly on the tongue, but the devastation, disorder, and despair resulting from the extraction of $7,000,000,000,000 from the producing economy in less than twelve years challenge our capacity to understand. "Challenge our capacity to understand" likewise can be spoken trippingly on the tongue. I do not know how to be emphatic enough. We are talking of tragedies compounded.

The economics of the rational greedy economic man failed our forebears. It is failing us. We fail ourselves if we refuse to understand that failure.

EVILS OF POLARIZATION

Economic polarization has malign consequences all across the distribution scale. The poor are unable to buy the products that giant industry could produce; industry consequently has fewer opportunities for further expansion; the rich consequently have fewer opportunities for investment; workers consequently have fewer job opportunities. If the rich are then frustrated in their attempts to consume their incomes, they turn to speculation. The amount of money that flows into speculative markets—preeminently the securities markets—is increased; so prices in these markets escalate. Escalating security prices mean escalating opportunity costs; corporations of the producing economy must increase their planned profit in order to attract the capital necessary just to continue in business. Interest rates tend to fall as security prices rise, but the fall and the rise are seldom if ever proportionate, the interest rate being in general stickier than security prices. During a bull market, moreover, the speculating economy competes strongly with the producing economy for funds, thus slowing or reversing any fall in the costs of financing productive enterprise. Planned profit—not, it will be remembered, actual profit—is in conflict with wages; so wages must be further restrained or payrolls downsized or "rationalized," thus increasing polarization and reducing the market for industry's products—a consequence Robert Averitt calls the Paradox of Cost Reduction.

An essentially unrelated factor has a vast and unexpected effect in the same direction. Prudent individuals save for their old age and insure against risks of various kinds, particularly torts, accidents, illness, and unemployment. What is here prudent in an individual, however, is foolish in a society, where its pursuit is a fallacy of composition. A society cannot insure itself, because insurance merely spreads the risk through the society. In an economy as large as that of the United States, the actuarial problem is easily managed. The risks are as level as can be. The number of people to reach old age in any given period can be nearly foretold, and the number to suffer injury or illness can be foretold within reasonably narrow limits. Catastrophes, whether natural or manmade, must be specially met anyhow. This being the case, it would be sensible to treat the costs of all these risks as a current expense. Instead, we are funding them.

It happens that all public and many if not most private funds are set up as costs of employment, as burdens on jobs. Social Security taxes are paid only by people who work and people who employ them. Corporate fringe benefits are paid for in roughly the same way. Medical malpractice insurance is an expense of doctoring. In these cases, the cost always inhibits and sometimes prohibits work.

Even if these bad designs were corrected, the funds are now so enormous that they will continue to have such consequences on Wall Street as we have recently observed. For by far the largest part of the trading now being done on the securities exchanges is being done by "institutions," that is, by pension plans and insurance companies, by colleges and churches and foundations of all sorts, and also by mutual funds.

Most of the institutions, it will be seen, are owned by or are for the primary benefit of the middle class. There is surely little harm in that, for in a certain sense the middle class is the society, the superrich feeling themselves exclusive and the infrapoor being excluded. Yet these institutions, by their means of existence, soak up purchasing power and weaken aggregate demand. By their speculating, they deprive the producing economy of efficient financing. The consequent constriction of the producing economy increases unemployment, exacerbates the polarization of society, advances the erosion of the middle class the institutions were created to shelter, and intensifies speculation itself.

The Federal Reserve Board and all mainstream economists continue to be amazed that the United States economy continues to plod ahead, increasing at a rate of 4.6 percent or better, or twice what their "models" tell them is possible or sustainable. Yet there were three years in a row in which the economy grew at a steady rate almost three times the present rate, with little inflation.

Of course, there was a war on. On the one hand, there were wage and price controls and shortages and rationing. On the other hand, more than half the national product was useless in peacetime, while more than a quarter of the labor force was engaged in disagreeable make-work at the risk of their lives. In addition, the Federal Reserve was patriotically engaged with the Treasury in maintaining a "pattern of rates" that resulted in a steady prime rate of 1.5 percent.

The economy grew at a rate of 13.2 percent a year from mid-1940 to the beginning of 1944, and the unemployment rate fell to 1.2 percent. Can we learn from the experience? We haven't done so yet.

MALDISTRIBUTION

The rich can turn to hoarding or speculation, but the poor can turn only to the state, which may fail them. It will certainly fail them if all it offers is some form of the dole, and that is all it will offer unless we can somehow be aroused from our long bemusement with the self-interested economic man. I dare not predict when this will occur or if it will occur. Massive and sudden shifts are surely possible. The Great Society was derailed by the Vietnam War. The "me generation" of quintessential economic men and women may yet become appalled at its own greediness.

In 1929, on the eve of the Great Depression, income distribution in the United States was so skewed that the total incomes of the top one-tenth of 1 percent of American families equaled the total incomes of the bottom 42 percent, and some 60 percent of all families were living below the poverty level (then about $2,000).[5] These figures are for what is still thought of as a time of unexampled prosperity. Four years later, with almost a quarter of the civilian population unemployed (not counting most women as even prospective workers), things were exponentially worse.

It took four harrowing years to shock the nation into making a start on reform, and it took the industrial mobilization of World War II to show how reform was possible.

It is an open question whether our morale may not be so corrupt, our power of empathy so feeble, and our ability even to be interested in economics so meager that it would take another depression to make resumed reform possible. If so, the prospect is dark—ironically dark, because big government has made a full-fledged depression unlikely.[6]

The gravamen of the charge is unjust treatment of our fellow human beings. In the light of that charge, it is barely worth considering that gross maldistribution of income and wealth, although evidently effective in the rise of our civilization, is now leading us to its decline. The maldistribution may, as many argue, be the consequence of cycli-

5. Leven et al., *America's Capacity to Consume*, pp. 55–56.
6. Minsky, *Can "It" Happen Again?*, pp. xxiii–xxiv, 3–13.

cal swings in the economy. It may, as others say, be the result of technological change. For centuries, it was thought necessary to goad economic man to work. The explanation of the maldistribution will influence our corrective measures, not the necessity for correction.

In the meantime, as long as we refuse to make fundamental reforms,[7] we can expect further difficulties, which may come about as a result of Third World debt, or a crisis in the insurance business, or bankruptcy of the FDIC, or collapse of the Pension Benefit Guaranty Corporation, or resurgence of OPEC, or another market crash, or (ironically) misuse of the surplus, or something quite unforeseen; and each time unemployment and inflation will inch upward. We may nevertheless avoid an old-fashioned depression—unless doctrinaire bias simultaneously prevents big government from taking up the slack.

The slow deterioration of a society can go on for a very long time. The Pharaonic World, the Roman World, the Medieval World, the Mandarin World, all stagnated for centuries. The Modern World (it will be our successors who name it) can do the same.[8] And it will do

---

7. The most equitable and effective measure to correct the current maldistribution of wealth would be a confiscatory or near-confiscatory death duty. It would not deny achievers the enjoyment of their achievement and so would not, as the saying goes, sap their incentive. Nor would it deny the offspring of achievers the satisfaction of earning their own living. Economists as far apart otherwise as Hayek and Keynes are in favor of it. I leave to the reader the listing of reasons why it's not an immediate possibility.

A progressive income tax would still be necessary. See Joseph A. Pechman's posthumous presidential address to the American Economic Association: "The Future of the Income Tax," pp. 1–20.

8. It is perhaps worth distinguishing this dismal prognosis from two that are superficially similar. Marx expected the polarization of society to lead to revolution rather than to stagnation. And in the 1940s Alvin Hansen expected stagnation to be the consequence of four factors then apparent: (1) the growth of personal and corporate saving, (2) the declining rate of population growth, (3) the disappearance of geographic frontiers, and (4) the tendency for inventions to be capital saving rather than capital absorbing. See Benjamin Higgins in *Income, Employment and Public Policy*, p. 90. In contrast, the present analysis emphasizes polarization and speculative profits as the opportunity cost of productive investment.

the same as long as we the people continue to believe that the economy and government and society and we ourselves are merely natural phenomena determined as are the phenomena of mechanics or zoology. Keynes was right about the power of ideas; but he may have underestimated the staying power of old ideas.[9] As long as we think intuitively in mechanistic metaphors, we shall pursue policies suitable for the operation of machines, not for the guidance of free men and women.

If there is a dead hand lying upon contemporary economic thought, it is the invisible hand discovered by Adam Smith. Two hundred years ago, this was a liberating hand, which participated in freeing us from arbitrary rulers. But it did so at the cost of conceiving of us as greedy servomechanisms.

THINGS OF SMALL URGENCY

Galbraith posed the most pregnant economic question of our time: "Why should life be made intolerable to make things of small urgency?"[10] Because modern industry is so wildly productive, its goods cannot be distributed without intensive and expensive selling effort. Even for the ancient necessities—food, clothing, and shelter—demand must be created. The world may beat a path to an inventor's door, but only after it has been told how to get there, what will be found at the journey's end, and why it wants it. The same applies to books and all the other carriers of culture, and to all the amenities and frivolities of civilization. (The vices can depend on the media and on television evangelists to advertise their arcane attractions.) Even unique events, such as concerts and special museum exhibitions, have to be heavily

9. Keynes, *General Theory*, pp. 383–84.
10. *Affluent Society*, p. 288.

merchandised in order to be noticed amid the clamor of information. And the information highway is broadening every day.

Thus there is justice in Galbraith's conclusion that the necessity, or merely the prevalence, of advertising proves that the particular commodities advertised are "of small urgency." We must not, of course, push the point to a fallacy of composition. What is true of each particular commodity is not true of commodities as a class. Another laundry soap, more or less, makes little difference, but *some* detergent (and a washing machine to go with it) is a vast improvement over beating clothes on a rock in a polluted river.

Moreover, there is no way back, at least no royal way. There are too many clothes to be washed, and too many other things worth doing. There are too many of us for all to be fed from kitchen gardens or clothed in homespun or sheltered in thatch-roofed hovels. It would take centuries of unlikely population control for us to be able to renounce mass production and mass-market distribution. Luddism is two centuries dead, and not to be revived in the lifetime of anyone now living.

Must life, then, be made intolerable? As long as economics is a "hard" science, the price system is as impervious to criticism as is the solar system; there is no escape. As long as the law of supply and demand is held in its traditional form, all prices are the result of an invisible hand, known in our crasser metaphor as "market forces," and no one is responsible. There is no use pretending that the market is capable of reforming itself, of doing good or evil. It has no way of making work tolerable or of making commodities urgent. It has no way of making things worse. It is systematically feckless.

But if the primal economic act is an exchange between a price maker and a price taker, then whatever is done, whether of good repute or bad, is a free act of free men and women. Neither intolerable work nor nonurgent commodities just happen. Likewise a decent work place and excellent commodities don't just happen. Somebody is responsible, if only infinitesimally. The world is a better place, and some man or woman is a better person. And of course free men and women can make the world a worse place, and diminish themselves accordingly. We are all members one of another, as St. Paul said; and as Lillian Smith showed, what we do unto others, we do to ourselves.[11]

The cynic of Oscar Wilde's witticism—he who knows the price of everything and the value of nothing—is today balanced by the dogmatist who knows the value of everything and the price of nothing. A task of any future economics will be to bring price and value together, to establish their economic identity; and this will be done in part by proscribing certain economic acts—particularly certain low (or high) wage rates and interest rates—just as certain acts are proscribed in love and even war. Economic activity—like all human activity, from love to war—will be understood as a mode of self-definition, and so will no longer be beyond ethical judgment. Finally, economics will have a clearer and more obvious relevance to our daily lives in our mundane world.

Since it is not in our stars that we are underlings; since we are the captains of our souls; since, as we may say more prosaically, we are autonomous, then we all, severally and collectively, have the opportunity—the right and the duty—to participate in shaping an open and confident and generous economy that allows and even challenges all its members to be fully human. This is the task of any future economics.

11. Smith, *Killers of the Dream*, p. 39.

EPILOGUE

We Are All Ends in Ourselves

In 1939, there were economists who pronounced that Germany would win or lose the war quickly for lack of sufficient gold reserves.

The fundamental problems of employment and welfare and national defense are not solved—do not even exist—on so-called economic grounds.

Although one could scarcely imagine it from the way we talk or the way we write in our newspapers and textbooks, justice is actually more important to us than is efficiency or cost-effectiveness or market discipline. Why else should we have abolished (to take the most obvious examples) slavery and child labor?

To be sure, we had to fight a Civil War to abolish slavery, and it wasn't until 1938—eight years into the Great Depression—that we were able to get a child labor law through the Congress and past the Supreme Court. But we managed to accomplish both reforms, and neither reform depended on considerations of efficiency or cost-effectiveness or market discipline.

Many of us are apparently ashamed of what we did. Some say that slavery had become unprofitable, and that it would have died out anyway, sooner rather than later. Some also argue that most slaves were reasonably well cared for, because they were worth good money, and that slave labor was really more expensive than free labor. The quasi-Marxian conclusion of these claims is that the "real" force behind abolition was the profit motive, not the brotherhood of man. It is not explained why it was necessary to abolish by law, let alone by force of arms, what was economically unprofitable or indifferent.

The child labor problem was not altogether dissimilar. Although few have defended requiring half-naked children, and their mothers, to scramble on all fours like stunted donkeys, dragging wagons of coal through constricted mine drifts, it was not market discipline that eliminated such cost-effective atrocities. Even today we are told that we must support child labor because of globalization.

As we said at the beginning, so we insist at the conclusion, human beings are not means to an end; we are all ends in ourselves. We prove ourselves human by the way we treat, and treat with, each other. Economics is the study of one of the ways and means by which we become worthy of our humanity.

REFERENCES

The following is neither a recommended reading list nor a list of works consulted but gives bibliographical information on works quoted or cited in the text. These works are identified in the textual footnotes by the author's last name, a short title of the work, and the page numbers of the passage quoted (e.g., "Smith, *Wealth*, pp. 339–40.")

Fuller bibliographical information is given below. In all cases the information given concerns the edition cited. Emphases in the passages quoted in the text are those of the original author.

Areeda, Phillip, *Antitrust Analysis*, 2d ed. (Boston: Little, Brown, 1974).

Aristotle, *Politics*, 1258a.

———*Nicomachean Ethics*, 1133a.

Arrow, Kenneth J., and F. H. Hahn, *General Competitive Analysis* (San Francisco: Holden-Day, 1971).

Balogh, Thomas, *The Irrelevance of Conventional Economics* (New York: Liveright, 1982).

Berle, A. A., and Gardiner C. Means, *The Modern Corporation and Private Property* (New York: Macmillan, 1933).

Blecker, Robert A., *Taming Global Finance* (Washington: Economic Policy Institute, 1999).

Block, Fred, "Bad Debts Drive Out Good: The Decline of Personal Savings Revisited," *Journal of Post Keynesian Economics* 13 (Fall 1990).

Brandeis, Louis D., *Other People's Money* (Washington, DC: National Home Library, 1933).

Braudel, Ferdinand, *Civilization and Capitalism*, vol. 2 (New York: Harper & Row, 1985).

Brimmer, Andrew F., "Central Banking and Systemic Risks in Capital Markets," *Journal of Economic Perspectives* 3, no. 2 (Spring 1989).

Brunner, Karl, "Money Supply" in John Eatwell et al., eds., *The New Palgrave: Money* (New York: W. W. Norton, 1989).

Canterbery, E. Ray, *The Making of Economics*, 3rd ed. (Belmont, CA: Wadsworth, 1987).

——— "Reaganomics, Saving, and the Casino Effect," in James H. Gapinski, ed., *The Economics of Saving* (Boston: Kluwer Academic, 1993).

——— *Wall Street Capitalism: The Theory of the Bondholding Class* (Singapore: World Scientific, 2000).

Chamberlin, Edward H., *The Theory of Monopolistic Competition*, 9th ed. (Cambridge: Harvard University Press).

Cipolla, Carlo, *Before the Industrial Revolution*, 2d. ed. (New York: W. W. Norton, 1980).

Coase, R. H., "The Problem of Social Cost," *Journal of Law and Economics* 3 (October 1960).

Colander, David C., *Economics*, 4th ed. (Homewood, Il.: Irwin, 1998).

Commons, John R., *Legal Foundations of Capitalism* (New York: Kelley, 1974).

Cournot, Augustin, *Researches into the Mathematical Principles of the Theory of Wealth* (New York: Kelley, 1960).

Crystal, Graef S., *In Search of Excess: The Overcompensation of American Executives* (New York: W. W. Norton, 1991).

Darby, Michael R., "Three-and-a-Half Million U. S. Employees Have Been Mislaid," *Journal of Political Economy* 84, no. 1 (1976).

Darwin, Charles, *The Origin of Species*, chap. 14.

Davidson, Greg, and Paul Davidson, *Economics for a Civilized Society* (New York: W. W. Norton, 1988).

Davidson, Paul, *Money and the Real World*, 2d ed. (London: Macmillan, 1978).

——— *Post Keynesian Economic Theory* (Brookfield, VT: Edward Elgar, 1994).

de Roover, Raymond, *The Rise and Fall of the Medical Bank, 1391–1494* (New York: W. W. Norton, 1961).

Djilas, Milovan, *The New Class* (New York: Praeger, 1957).

Douglas, Mary, and Baron Isherwood, *The World of Goods* (New York, W. W. Norton, 1979).

Ebersole, J. F., "The influence of Interest Rates upon Entrepreneurial Decisions in Business." *Harvard Business Review* 17 (Jan.–Feb. 1934).

Erikson, Erik H., *Childhood and Society* (New York, W. W. Norton, 1951).

Faux, Jeff, "Reducing the Deficit: Send the Bill to Those Who Went to the Party," *Briefing Paper* (Washington, DC: Economic Policy Institute, November 1987).

Fedack, Marilyn G., "Volatility in the Equity Market," *Investing* (Fall 1989).

Federal Reserve Bank of Cleveland, *Economic Trends* (February 1995).

Federal Reserve Bulletin (September 1979).

Fisher, Irving, *The Purchasing Power of Money*, 2d ed. (Fairfield, NJ: Kelley, 1985).

——— *The Theory of Interest* (Philadelphia: Porcupine Press, 1977).

Forstater, Mathew, "Working Backward: Instrumental Analysis as a Policy Discovery Procedure," *Review of Political Economy*, vol. 11, no. 1, 1999.

Friedman, Milton, *Essays in Positive Economics* (Chicago: University of Chicago Press, 1953).

——— "Quantitative Theory of Money," in Eatwell et al., eds., *The New Palgrave: Money* (New York: W. W. Norton, 1976).

——— "A Response to Burns," in Martin N. Bailey and Arthur M. Okun, eds., *The Battle against Unemployment and Inflation* (New York: W. W. Norton, 1982).

——— "The Role of Monetary Policy," *American Economic Review* 78 (March 1968).

Galbraith, John Kenneth, *The Affluent Society* (Boston: Houghton Mifflin, 1958).

——— *American Capitalism* (Armonk, NY: Sharpe, 1980).

——— *Economics and the Public Purpose* (Boston: Houghton Mifflin, 1973).

Galilei, Galileo, *Dialogues Concerning Two New Sciences* (New York: McGraw-Hill, 1963).

Greider, William, *Secrets of the Temple* (New York: Simon & Schuster, 1987).

Hahn, Frank, *Equilibrium and Macroeconomics* (Cambridge: MIT Press, 1984).

Hayek, Friedrich, *Individualism and Economic Order* (London: Routledge and Kegan Paul, 1949).

——— *The Road to Serfdom* (Chicago, University of Chicago Press, 1944).

Heckscher, Eli, "Foreign Trade and Distribution of Income," in Howard S. Ellis and Lloyd A. Metzler, eds., *Readings in the Theory of International Trade* (Philadelphia: Blakiston, 1949).

Heilbroner, Robert, *The Nature and Logic of Capitalism* (New York: W. W. Norton, 1985).

——— *The Worldly Philosophers*, 5th ed. (New York: Simon & Schuster, 1980).

Hicks, J. R., *Value and Capital*, 2d ed. (Oxford: Oxford University Press, 1946).

Higgins, Benjamin, in *Income, Employment, and Public Policy: Essays in Honor of Alvin H. Hansen* (New York: W. W. Norton, 1948).

Hobbes, Thomas, *The Leviathan* (Harmondsworth: Penguin, 1968).

Hume, David, "Of Money," in *Political Discourses*.

James, William, *Psychology*.

Jevons, W. Stanley, *The Theory of Political Economy*, 5th ed. (New York: Kelley, 1965).

Kaldor, Nicholas, *Economics without Equilibrium* (Armonk, NY: Sharpe, 1985).

Kalecki, Michal, *Essays on Developing Economies* (Hassocks, Essex: Harvester, 1976).

——— *Selected Essays on the Dynamics of the Capitalist Economy, 1933–1970* (Cambridge: Cambridge University Press, 1971).

Keynes, John Maynard, *Collected Writings*, vols. 7 and 14 (London: Macmillan, 1973).

——— *Economic Consequences of the Peace* (New York: Harcourt, Brace, 1920).

——— *Essays in Persuasion* (New York: W. W. Norton, 1963).

——— *The General Theory of Employment, Interest and Money* (New York: Harcourt, Brace, 1936).

——— *A Treatise on Money*, vol. 1, *The Pure Theory of Money* (London: Macmillan, 1930).

Keynes, John Neville, *The Scope and Method of Political Economy* (New York: Kelley, 1965).

Knight, Frank H., *The Ethics of Competition and Other Essays* (New York: Harper & Row, 1935).

——— *Risk, Uncertainty and Profit* (Boston: Houghton Mifflin, 1921).

Krugman, Paul, *The Age of Diminished Expectations* (Cambridge: MIT Press, 1990).

Landes, Ruth, in Margaret Mead, ed., *Cooperation and Competition among Primitive Peoples* (New York: McGraw-Hill, 1937).

Larson, Eric D., et al., "Beyond the Age of Materials," *Scientific American*, (June 1986).

Leven, Maurice, Harold C. Moulton, and Clark Warburton, *America's Capacity to Consume* (New York: McGraw-Hill, 1934).

Levins, Richard, *Evolution in Changing Environments* (Princeton: Princeton University Press, 1968).

Leontief, Wassily, *Input-Output Economics* (New York: Oxford University Press, 1966).

Locke, John, *Second Treatise of Government*.

Lombardi, Richard, *Debt Trap* (New York: Praeger, 1983).

MacDougal, G. D. A., "British and American Exports: A Study Suggested by the Theory of Competitive Costs," *Economic Journal* 61 (December 1951).

Machlup, Fritz, "Marginal Analysis and Empirical Research," *American Economic Review* 36 (September 1946).

Maisel, Sherman J., *Managing the Dollar* (New York: W. W. Norton, 1973).

Marshall, Alfred, *Principles of Economics*, 8th ed. (London: Macmillan, 1989).

Marx, Karl, *Capital* (New York: Modern Library, n.d.).

——— *Critique of the Gotha Program*, in Robert C. Tucker, ed., *The Marx-Engels Reader*, 2d ed. (New York: W. W. Norton, 1978).

——— *Estranged Labor*, in Tucker, *Reader*.

——— *The German Ideology*, in Tucker, *Reader*.

——— *The Holy Family*, in Tucker, *Reader*.

Mayer, Thomas, (of IMF) and Gunther Thumann. "Radical Currency Reform: Germany 1948," *Finance & Development* (March 1990).

Mayer, Thomas, (of University of California, Davis), *The Structure of Monetarism* (New York: W. W. Norton, 1978).

———, James S. Duesenberry, and Robert Z. Aliber, *Money, Banking, and the Economy* (New York: W. W. Norton, 1984).

McIntyre, Robert S., *Inequality and the Federal Budget Deficit* (Washington, DC: Citizens for Tax Justice, 1991).

Mead, Margaret, *Cooperation and Competition among Primitive Peoples* (New York: McGraw-Hill, 1937).

Menger, Carl, *Principles of Economics* (New York: New York University Press, 1976).

Mishel, Lawrence, and David Frankel, *The State of Working America 1990–91* (Armonk, NY: Sharpe for Economic Policy Institute, 1991).

Mishel, Lawrence, and Jared Bernstein, *The State of Working America 1994–95* (Armonk, NY: Sharpe for Economic Policy Institute, 1995).

Mill, J. S., *Principles of Political Economy*.

Miller, John William, *The Midworld of Symbols and Functioning Objects* (New York: W. W. Norton, 1982).

——— *The Definition of the Thing* (New York: W. W. Norton, 1980).

——— *The Paradox of Cause* (New York: W. W. Norton, 1976).

Minsky, Hyman P., *Can "It" Happen Again?* (Armonk, NY: Sharpe, 1982).

———, *Stabilizing an Unstable Economy* (New Haven: Yale University Press, 1986).

Mirowski, Philip, *Against Mechanism* (Totowa, NJ: Roman & Littlefield, 1988).

——— *The Reconstruction of Economic Theory* (Boston: Kluwer-Nijhoff, 1986).

Mitchell, Wesley Clair, "Quantitative Analysis in Economic Theory," *American Economic Review* 15 (March 1925).

Moore, Basil J., "Money Supply Exogeneity: 'Reserve Price Setting' or 'Reserve Quantity Setting'?" *Journal of Post Keynesian Economics* 13 (Spring 1991).

Muth, John F., "Rational Expectations and the Theory of Price Movements," *Economica* 29 (July 1961).

Myrdal, Gunnar, *Monetary Equilibrium* (London: William Hodge, 1939).

Ohlin, Bertil, *Interregional and International Trade*, rev. ed. (Cambridge: Harvard University Press, 1967).

Pareto, Vilfredo, *Manual of Political Economy* (New York: Kelley, 1971).

Pechman, Joseph A., *Federal Tax Policy*, rev. ed. (New York: W. W. Norton, 1971).

——— "The Future of the Income Tax" *American Economic Review* 80 (March 1990).

Petty, William, *Economic Writings*, vol. 1 (New York: Kelley, 1962).

Phelps, Edmund S., *Political Economy* (New York: W. W. Norton, 1985).

Phillips, W. A., "The Relation between Unemployment and the Rate of Change of Money Wage Rates in the United Kingdom, 1861–1957," *Economica* 25, (November 1958): 283–99.

Planck, Max, *The Philosophy of Physics* (New York: W. W. Norton, 1936).

Plato, *Republic*, 2.

Pigou, A. C., *The Economics of Welfare*, 4th ed. (London: Macmillan, 1982).

Powers, Treval C., *Leakage: The Bleeding of the American Economy* (New Canaan, CT: Benchmark Publications, 1996).

Raymond, Fred I., *The Limitist* (New York: W. W. Norton, 1947).

Ricardo, David, *The Principles of Political Economy and Taxation* (New York: Everyman's, n.d.).

Rivlin, Alice M., ed., *Economic Choices, 1984* (Washington DC: Brookings Institution, 1984).

Robinson, Joan, *The Economics of Imperfect Competition* (London: Macmillan, 1933).

———, *An Essay on Marxian Economics*, 2d ed. (London: Macmillan, 1966).

Royce, Josiah, *The Philosophy of Loyalty* (New York: Macmillan, 1908).

Russell, Bertrand, *Our Knowledge of the External World* (New York: New American Library, 1956).

St. Thomas Aquinas, "Of Cheating, Which Is Committed in Buying and Selling," *Summa Theologica.*

——— "Whether It Is a Sin To Take Usury for Money Lent," *Summa Theologica.*

Samuelson, Paul, *Foundations of Economic Analysis* (Cambridge: Harvard University Press, 1947).

Say, Jean-Baptiste, *A Treatise on Political Economics* (New York: Kelley, 1971).

Schumpeter, Joseph A., *Capitalism, Socialism and Democracy* (New York: Harper & Row, 1950).

——— *A History of Economic Analysis* (New York: Oxford University Press, 1954).

Schwarz, John E., *America's Hidden Success* (New York: W. W. Norton, 1983).

Sen, Amartya, *On Ethics and Economics* (Oxford: Blackwell, 1987).

Senior, Nassau, *Industrial Efficiency and Social Economy*, vol. 1 (New York: Arno, 1972).

Shackle, G. L. S., *Business, Time and Thought* (New York: New York University Press, 1988).

Schuker, Stephen A., "American 'Reparations' in Germany, 1919–1933. Implications for the Third World Debt Crisis." *Princeton Studies in International Finance* No. 61 (July 1988).

Simon, Herbert A., *Models of Bounded Rationality*, vol. 1 (Cambridge: MIT Press, 1982).

Smith, Adam, *The Theory of Moral Sentiments* (Oxford: Oxford University Press, 1976).

——— *The Wealth of Nations* (New York: Modern Library, n.d.).

Smith, Lillian, *Killers of the Dream*, rev. ed. (New York: W. W. Norton, 1961).

Sproul, Allen, "The 'Accord'—a Landmark in the First Fifty Years of the Federal Reserve System," *Federal Reserve Bank of New York Monthly Review* (November 1964).

Sraffa, Piero, "The Laws of Returns under Competitive Conditions." *Economic Journal* December 1926, vol. XXXVI. no. 144, pp. 535–50.

———, *Production of Commodities by Means of Commodities* (Cambridge: Cambridge University Press, 1960).

Steuart, James A., "An Inquiry into the Principles of Political Economy," in Philip C. Newman, Arthur D. Gayer, and Milton M. Spence, eds., *Source Readings in Economic Thought* (New York: W. W. Norton, 1954).

Stigler, George L., *The Economist as Preacher* (Chicago: Chicago University Press, 1982).

Taussig, Frank, *The Tariff History of the United States*, 8th ed. (New York: Johnson Reprint, 1966).

Tawney, R. H., *The Acquisitive Society* (London: Collins, 1961).

——— *Religion and the Rise of Capitalism* (New York: Harcourt, Brace, 1952).

Thomas, Lewis, *The Lives of a Cell* (New York: Viking, 1974).

Thurow, Lester, *New York Times*, op. ed. page, October 11, 1984.

Tobin, James, *Essays in Economics*, vol. 1, *Microeconomics* (Cambridge: MIT Press, 1981).

Truman, Harry S., *Memoirs*, vol. 2, *Years of Trial and Hope* (New York: Doubleday, 1956).

Turgot, Anne-Robert-Jacques, *On the Formation and Distribution of Riches* (New York: Kelley, 1971).

Tyler, Gus, "Those New Deal Years," *The New Leader* LXIV, no. 24.

Veblen, Thorstein, *The Theory of the Leisure Class* (New York: Modern Library, 1934).

Vickrey, William, "Fifteen Fatal Fallacies of Financial Fundamentalism," Working Paper No. 1, January 2000, University of Missouri-Kansas City.

von Raumer, Hans, quoted in Stewart B. Clough et al., eds., *Economic History of Europe: Twentieth Century* (New York: Harper & Row, 1968).

von Weiser, Friedrich, *Social Economics* (New York: Kelley, 1967).

Walras, Léon, *Elements of Pure Economics* (Philadelphia: Orion Editions, 1984).

——— "Geometrical Theory of the Determination of Prices," *Annals of the American Academy of Social Sciences* (July 1892).

Weintraub, E. Roy, *General Equilibrium Analysis* (Cambridge: Cambridge University Press, 1985).

Wicksell, Knut, *Selected Papers on Economic Theory* (New York: Kelley, 1969).

Wicksteed, Philip H., *The Alphabet of Economic Science* (New York: Kelley, 1970).

Wray, L. Randall, *Understanding Modern Money: The Key to Full Employment and Price Stability* (Northampton, MA: Edward Elgar, 1998).

Young, Alan A., "Increasing Returns and Economic Progress." *Economic Journal* 38 (December 1928).

Zimmern, Alfred, *The Greek Commonwealth* (New York: Oxford University Press, 1961).

APPENDIX

Some Propositions Old and New

THE OLD DISPENSATION	ANY FUTURE ECONOMICS
1. The motive of economics is greed.	1. The control of economics is justice.
2. Money is a special sort of thing.	2. Money is a special sort of credit.
3. Prices are set by the market, which reconciles schedules of supply and demand.	3. Prices are set by buyers and sellers, who announce what they *will* buy or sell.
4. Property, which is made by labor, is a thing to have and to enjoy.	4. Property, which is earned by labor, is a bundle of rights that may be exercised.
5. Interest, wages, and rent are all rewards for abstinence or for doing something disagreeable.	5. Interest, wages, and rent are all contracts for future performance and payment.
6. There shall be no law impairing the obligation of private contracts.	6. Rights and contracts are defined and enforced by the free state.

INDEX